MW01006102

AN ILLUSTRATED ENCYCLOPEDIA OF
THE UNIFORMS OF THE
ROMAN WORLD

AN ILLUSTRATED ENCYCLOPEDIA OF
THE UNIFORMS OF THE ROMAN WORLD

A detailed study of the armies of Rome and their enemies, including the Etruscans, Samnites, Carthaginians, Celts, Macedonians, Gauls, Huns, Sassanids, Persians and Turks

KEVIN F. KILEY
CONSULTANT: JEREMY BLACK MBE

LORENZ BOOKS

To my lovely wife, Daisy, who has been with me 'through the fire' on every occasion, and to my beloved son, Michael, the namesake of a warrior, who, hopefully, will never have to hear the 'muttering of the guns' in anger.

This edition is published by Lorenz Books, an imprint of Anness Publishing Ltd, Blaby Road, Wigston, Leicestershire LE18 4SE; info@anness.com www.lorenzbooks.com; www.annesspublishing.com

If you like the images in this book and would like to investigate using them for publishing, promotions or advertising, please visit our website www.practicalpictures.com for more information.

Publisher: Joanna Lorenz
Editorial Director: Helen Sudell
Executive Editor: Joanne Rippin, Copy Editor: Jonathan North
Illustrations: Tom Croft, Simon Smith and Matthew Vince.
Designer: Nigel Partridge
Production Controller: Pirong Wang

© Anness Publishing Ltd 2012
All rights reserved. No part of this publication may be reproduced, stored in a retrieval system, or transmitted in any way or by any means, electronic, mechanical, photocopying, recording or otherwise, without the prior written permission of the copyright holder.
A CIP catalogue record for this book is available from the British Library.

PUBLISHER'S NOTE
Although the information in this book are believed to be accurate and true at the time of going to press, neither the authors nor the publisher can accept any legal responsibility or liability for any errors or omissions that may have been made.

Page 2: Leader of the Gauls, Vercingetorix, surrenders to Julius Caesar after the Siege of Alesia in 52BC.

The Publishers would like to thank the following agencies for permission to reproduce their images: The Bridgeman Art Library: pp7t, 9, 10b, 11 all, 12 all, 13tl, 14bl, 17 all, 19 all, 22, 23, 26tr&tl, 27t, 28 all, 30b, 32, 33 tl&tr, 34 br, 35tr&b, 38br, 41t, 43t, 44br&bl, 45b, 47tr, 48b, 51t, 52, 54br, 57b, 59b, 79t, 97b, 99t, 124t, 126t, 136, 138b, 139b, 140br, 142 all, 173t, 178, 180t, 182bl, 183t, 224 all, 225bl, 242t, 248br, 250t. The Picture Desk: pp6, 20, 24, 26b, 38t, 39b, 42b, 50b, 55, 56, 58t, 61tl, 86b, 97tl&tr, 101, 140t, 141t, 182t&br, 183b, 222, 225t, 246t. Corbis: pp2, 6b, 8, 13tr, 14br, 15 all, 16, 18 all, 22t, 27b, 29t&bl, 30t, 34t&bl, 36, 37tl, 41b, 46 all, 47b, 48t, 50t, 51b, 57t, 94, 96bl, 181 all, 194tr, 233br. Istock: 10t, 31t&bl, 37b, 40t, 44t, 49b, 59b, 96t, 143b, 180b. Alamy: pp13b, 29br, 31bl, 33b, 35tl, 37tr, 38bl, 39t, 68bm, 123tl, 125tr, 138t, 140bl, 141b, 157tr, 245br. Photo12: 42t, 43b, 45t, 47tl, 49t, 143t. Mary Evans: p119.

CONTENTS

INTRODUCTION

Rome, whether the republic or the empire, left an indelible mark on European civilization. Rome developed from small settlements along the Tiber River in central Italy and, in its struggle to survive among hostile neighbours, gained eventual supremacy over them through an innate toughness, a will to survive and conquer, and a belief in eventual triumph no matter what the situation or what disaster was being currently endured. The Romans did not always win, but they survived for over two millennia.

When looking at or studying the Romans, the usual period covered is from Rome's founding in the 8th century BC to 476AD when Rome fell in the West and the last Roman emperor was overthrown. However, Rome, or more properly, the Roman Empire was continued by the eastern half of the empire, and lasted another thousand years until finally falling to an overwhelming onslaught by the Ottoman Turks in 1453. During those two millennia, the civilization of Rome, whether of the eastern or

▼ *Roman military triumphs were awarded to generals who had accomplished great feats.*

▲ *Roman architecture is still evident today in Europe, the Middle East and North Africa. This is Vindabona, today's Vienna, and how it might have looked during the Roman Empire.*

western kind, left a legacy to world culture, art, law and government, and a military organization unmatched for centuries. It is on the military aspect that this book concentrates.

Rome's Way of War

The ancient era was a brutal age, and this was reflected in Roman warfare. Prisoners, if taken at all, or defeated foes, were not treated well. Captives of all kinds, whether soldiers, warriors, or civilians, important personages or common people, were treated the same, and were either sold into slavery or executed, the most brutal form of which was crucifixion.

In the taking of cities, either by storm or by siege, looting and pillage were not only expected, but were normal practices of the times. The Romans were methodical about sacking cities. Areas of the city were allotted to the different Roman units before it was taken, and the troops allowed to pillage their portion. After a time limit specified by the commander, all pillaging would be stopped, and the Roman soldiers would then restore order for the survivors.

The Legion

Rome's famous legion, made up of steady, well-trained, and well-disciplined Roman infantrymen, was the main instrument of Roman conquest. The legion itself went through an evolutionary process from its earliest employment in the early republic to its apogee at the height of Roman imperial power, and its gradual decline into obsolescence before the fall of the west. No matter how it was organized, however, the heart of the legion was the legionary, the sword- and shield-bearing armoured infantryman commanded by the stalwart centurion of legend, the solid backbone of every Roman legion.

Roman Enemies

The Romans fought a myriad of enemies in conquering and then defending their empire. Beginning with the indigenous peoples of Italy, the Romans fought Celts, Gauls, Britons

▲ *This relief depicts Romans building the roads that unified the empire, and allowed for swift troop movements when necessary.*

and the various Germanic tribes of northwestern and central Europe. The Carthaginians, Greeks and Macedonians, and the eastern peoples such as the Parthians, Sarmatians, Syrians and Jews, were all conquered, and reconquered if they rebelled. Sometimes, the Roman legions suffered defeat, sometimes disastrously, as in the Teutoborg Forest in 9AD, or in the east where the Romans encountered formidable armies who relied on their cavalry, consisting of horse archers and armoured heavy cavalry, that were alien to the Roman way of war. Finally, nomadic barbarian enemies were encountered during the great migrations, such as the Goths, Vandals and Huns, whose repeated onslaughts finally brought down Rome in the west.

Eastern Romans

The Roman Empire in the east, centred on the city of Constantinople, survived the barbarian onslaughts and learned lessons from the fall of the west. They created a different army from the old legions, based on the emergent battlefield power, the cavalryman. The eastern Romans still fielded excellent heavy infantry, but the main striking power of an eastern Roman army would be the heavy cavalryman, the cataphract, combined with the hitting power of the horse archer. This new Roman army would be effective and impressive for centuries, maintaining

much of the eastern empire until disaster struck in 1071, leading to a slow decline until the empire disappeared in 1453. Until then, however, the eastern Roman Empire provided a shield for the developing nations of western Europe who began a new existence with the fall of the west. Largely ignored and underrated by the west, it was the eastern Roman Empire that allowed the new nations of Europe to grow and flourish while holding a plethora of enemies at bay in the east. They fought the Avars, Russians, Bulgars and Slavs, and were also pitted against the emerging and deadly enemy that would be created by the rise and flourishing of Islam in the 7th century.

Roman Hegemony

While Rome, both east and west, flourished, a lasting culture and influence would be brought to the successor nations after Rome's final fall. Both western Roman law and the Code of Justinian I in the east would have a lasting impact in the development of law across the three continents where the writ of the Roman empire ran (Europe, western Asia and North Africa). Roman art and architecture would later be adopted in various parts of the world, and would be noticeable in both Napoleonic France and the new United States in the late 18th and early 19th centuries. And, finally, the tradition and structure

of the disciplined Roman armies, whether infantry or cavalry based, would influence military thought through the Renaissance and into modern European history.

Roman Arms, Armour and Equipment

Uniforms, in the modern sense, were not worn or used by any Roman army, western or eastern. That concept was still in the future. However, there was a definite uniformity in both the legions of the west and the tagmata of the east. Armour was similar among the troops, as were the weapons wielded in the ranks and by the officers. Units were distinguished by assigned numbers and titles, and were often identified by coloured helmet crests, plumes, and flags or standards. Tunics would be the same colour for each unit, and, when drawn up in line of battle, Roman armies presented themselves as a uniformed, well-trained force ready to do battle with any and all enemies. Moreover, it was a force confident of victory – Roma Victor!

▼ *These three Roman soldiers span the republic, the imperial, and the eastern empire eras. On the left is an excellent example of the legionary of the late Republic, after Marius' reforms. The central figure is the quintessential depiction of the imperial Roman legionary. The figure on the right is an eastern Roman heavy cavalryman, from the height of the eastern empire.*

THE GLORY THAT WAS ROME

Rome. The name conjures up images of towering architecture; straight roads, marching legions; the immense Colosseum and the dust, blood, and sweat of gladiatorial combat. This peak of empire, however, developed gradually from a settlement on the River Tiber in Italy, in the middle of the 8th century BC. At this time the Romans were just another Latin tribe trying to survive in the midst of potential enemies, but what was coming was a juggernaut of epic proportions that would impose its own brand of civilization first to Italy, then to the Mediterranean world and beyond. The rise of the Roman Empire was built on a foundation of military expertise, crafted in early wars and honed to a level of brilliance that allowed the Romanization of great swathes of the known world. Its collapse in the 5th century AD was apocalyptic and left western Europe in what would become known as the Dark Ages.

▲ *Even in its earliest form, as a citizen's army rather than a professional force during the Roman republic, the soldiers of Rome were formidable opponents.*

◀ *Roman architecture was heavily influenced by the classical Greek model, but the Romans developed their own style as the empire grew. The arch of Septimus Severus on the right, and Trajan's column, still intact today, can be seen in this 18th-century depiction of Rome.*

THE FOUNDING OF ROME

There are two legends of Rome's founding, the first tells that survivors from the fall of Troy, under Aeneas, drifted across the Mediterranean and finally settled on the seven hills along the River Tiber. The second has more to do with religious mythology. Greek and Roman myths often tell of their gods' ability to take human form, come to earth, and influence the life of mortals. So it is that the legend of Romulus and Remus begins.

Mars, the god of war, descended and found Rhea Silvia, a beautiful princess whose father had recently been deposed from his kingdom, Alba, by his treacherous brother. When the princess rebuffed Mars' advances, he raped her and left her pregnant with twins. The babies were named Romulus and Remus when born. Their uncle, afraid that they might grow up and seek vengeance for what he had done to their father and their inheritance, took them from their mother and abandoned them on the shores of the River Tiber. A she-wolf found them, suckled them, and cared for them until a kindly shepherd found

▼ Romulus and Remus being suckled by their adoptive wolf-mother. This legendary image is a centrepiece of Rome's founding mythology.

and took them as his own. Eventually finding out who they were and what had happened to their father, they did seek revenge on their uncle, deposed him from his usurped throne and reinstated their grandfather.

Leaving Alba to set up their own kingdom, the legend then tells that on the banks of the River Tiber the two brothers had an argument over where to begin building their new kingdom, each brother preferring a different hill. In the dispute that followed, Romulus killed his brother, and began work on a settlement that he named Rome.

The Sabine Women

Romulus soon realized that his growing settlement was short of women, and he launched a clever offensive against the Sabines, a tribe that occupied an area of land close to Rome. Using guile instead of strength, a feast was arranged for the Sabines at which the followers of Romulus plied the Sabine men with drink. When they were overcome with alcohol, Romulus and his men made off with the Sabine women. After the initial shock of being forcefully taken, the Sabine women are said to have agreed to stay, later arranging a peace between the remaining Sabines.

▲ The famous and dramatic sculpture 'Rape of the Sabine Women' by Giambologna, 1582AD, depicts the legend of how early Romans increased the female population of their city.

Romulus' eventual end has two versions. One has Romulus being murdered by disgusted followers after his ego grew too large, the other that he disappeared in a storm en route to a meeting with the gods. Later Romans elevated Romulus to divine status under the name Quirinus.

Historical Foundations

Legend apart, we know that there were basically two ethnic groups that inhabited the Italian peninsula, the Latins, which included the Romans, and the Italics. One of the other important tribes at this time were the Etruscans, who lived in the region of Italy later known as Tuscany. A Latin tribe chose to settle in the area of the seven hills along the Tiber, with close access to the sea, and the place began to thrive and grow as a settlement and then as a city. They were not the first Latin people to establish a settlement in central Italy, nor were they initially

▲ *A romantic rendition of Romulus returning from the conquest of Acron bringing with him the loot and spoils of battle. The clothing, armour, and weapons are of a much later period rather than 8th century* BC.

the most powerful, for example in the early years the Etruscans dominated, at one point actually ruling Rome, but the Romans were industrious and eager to trade and expand. They were an aggressive people from the start, willing to expend resources and blood if necessary, to ensure their survival.

▼ *An engraving of an artist's impression of how Rome may have looked at the beginning of the reign of Romulus.*

The Etruscan Kings

In the beginning, Rome was not a republic but a type of monarchy. What would become the 'dynasty' of Etruscan rulers of Rome probably began around 650BC and lasted until *c*.509BC when the last of the legendary seven Etruscan kings, Tarquinius Superbus, is said to have been overthrown by his Roman subjects. This period in Roman history gave rise to a great distrust of absolute monarchs and led directly to the development of a republic and the rule by the 'Senate and the people of Rome'.

With the demise of the Etruscan ruling elite, the Romans either made allies of the other Latins and Italics, or

conquered them, and very early on established a national character. Early defeats and humiliations made the Romans adopt a 'conquer or die' attitude that would set the tone of future Roman warfare and was as unforgiving as it was useful in the spread of the Roman civilization. From the start, the practice of taking prisoners back to Rome as slaves, and publicly humiliating and executing their leaders, was established, and triumphant Roman commanders were feted and praised.

▼ *This sewer, developed in early Rome by the Etruscans, was the Cloaca Maxima, one of the first sewage systems in ancient Italy.*

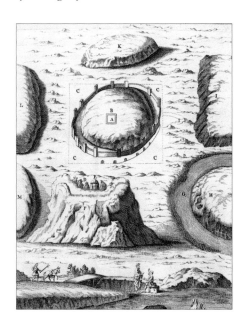

THE BIRTH OF THE REPUBLIC

With the expulsion of Tarquinus, Etruscan rule was gradually replaced by elected Roman officials, who instigated an impressive level of conscious civic organization into Roman society.

The Etruscan Legacy

Historically, little is known about the Etruscans. They were most established to the north of Rome in Tuscany; from the Roman word for Etruscan, 'Etrusci', sometimes shortened to 'Tusci'. Early Roman military tradition and religious practices were certainly learned from the Etruscans, and Romans were sent as young boys to Etruscan schools to be taught the Etrusca Disciplina – their moral code. The seven Etruscan kings of Rome, listed in legend, may not have actually existed, but it is certain that the sophisticated and powerful Etruscan society did much to mould and influence the Roman one that eventually overcame it.

Political and Social Structure

The famous governing body of the Roman Senate began as a select group of 100 men, initially perhaps advisors to the king. Once the kings were overthrown, the Senate grew both in size and influence, eventually becoming a legislative body that would survive the numerous, and frequently vicious, attempts later to suppress it. The Senate, and the officials that made up its body, both became symbols of the republic and were generally respected throughout Roman society.

Romans were divided into two classes, the patricians – or nobles – and the plebeians – everyone else – and the social division between the

▲ The Etruscans sent their musicians into the field with their armies. These musicians are depicted on a 5th century BC Etruscan fresco.

two was profound and distinct. The Senate was drawn only from the patrician class and eventually was enlarged to 300 members, supposedly as a reflection of the growing number

▼ People gather for an Etruscan religious festival, held in the open air.

▲ *This beautiful Etruscan statue of Apollo was completed in the 6th century BC, and was part of the Temple of Veio in Portonaccio.*

of Italian tribes being absorbed by Rome. Eventually it was enlarged further, this time as an indication and counterbalance to the beginnings of corruption by various politicians vying for personal power and prestige.

The Senate's administrative functions were to supervise the state religions and their ceremonies, to prepare legislation, decide foreign policy, and oversee financial affairs. The Senate would eventually also appoint public officials to take charge in time of war and appoint those who would lead the army in wartime, whether qualified to do so or not, the important attribute being that they were politically well-connected and had the proper family background.

▶ *Roman bridges were built to last. The Pons Fabricus, begun in 62BC, crosses the River Tiber in Rome. One of the oldest bridges in the world, its arches are geometrically perfect.*

Religion

Roman religion was a blend of various traditions of pagan polytheism. Etruscan religious practices were probably adopted by the new Roman state, but it also added and adapted ancient Greek gods and ceremonies; the venerable Greek gods' names being Romanized in the process. This tendency to absorb foreign beliefs lasted throughout Roman history, gods' names being changed to Latin, and other pagan sects sometimes adopted as Rome expanded.

As the city of Rome itself began to enlarge it became dotted with scattered temples dedicated to one deity or another. Temples became the locations where sacrifices or libations would take place, and where the cult statue of whatever deity the temple belonged to would be kept. Public religious ceremonies continued in the Etruscan tradition of being conducted outside.

Building and Engineering

The Romans would become exceptional engineers, but they were hardly original in their designs of buildings, whether public and private. Much of what they designed and built was based on Greek architecture, especially the use of different styles of columns. However, what would distinguish Roman engineering as the republic grew and the territory governed by Rome expanded, was the

▲ *Roads criss-crossed the city of Rome and the empire. The Via Sacra, which crosses the Forum, is the oldest street in Rome. According to another legend, on this road Romulus and Titus, the Sabine king, signed a peace treaty.*

system of well-built roads connecting Roman cities and territory, and the brilliant design of aqueducts that would bring water to urban areas. Roman bridge building also developed to a high degree. Roman roads, bridges and aqueducts have survived the ages and can be seen throughout Europe to this day. Many Roman bridges in various parts of Europe, notably in Spain and in Germany, are also still in use – a fitting tribute to the planning and construction capabilities of the Roman engineers.

ROMAN REPUBLIC TIMELINE
753–132BC

753 Founding of Rome.

650 The era of the Etruscan kings ruling in Rome begins.

578–35 The first Roman assembly is formed during the reign of Servius Tullius. This assembly is named the comitia centuriata.

534–09 The last Etruscan king of Rome, Tarquinius Superbus, is thrown out of Rome. The era of kings comes to an end. The Roman republic is formed and Roman officials are now elected. At some point in this period the first treaty with Carthage is signed.

496 The Romans defeat the Latins at the Battle of Lake Regullus. A treaty with the Latins follows the victory.

450 The first written laws of the Roman republic, the Twelve Tables of the Law, are published.

440 A law, the Lex Cannuleia, is passed which establishes equality before the law between patricians and plebeians.

425 The Romans take the town of Fidanae from the Etruscan city of Veii.

▼ *A stela – a commemorative marker – depicts an Etruscan warrior c.420-300BC, carrying a circular shield. Stelas were used as funeral markers or headstones.*

405–396 The Romans lay siege to Veii and capture it after a prolonged siege.

400–390 The Celts raid into northern and central Italy from Gaul and overrun much of the country. In 390 they invade and sack Rome.

378 The Servian Wall is built around Rome to prevent the city from being captured and sacked a second time. This is the first fortification that the Romans build around their home city.

343–1 Rome wins the 1st Samnite War.

338 Rome defeats the Latin League and dissolves the confederation. Roman power and influence are extended further into Italy.

329 The Romans establish a colony at Terracina.

326 The 2nd Samnite War begins.

321 The Samnites defeat the Romans at the Battle of Caudine Forks, humiliating the Romans they capture. The Romans seek vengeance against the Samnites.

312 The Romans start to build the first of their roads which will eventually link their empire. This is the Appian Way which runs from Rome to Capua. Concurrently, the first Roman aqueduct, the Aqua Appia, is also built to bring fresh water into Rome.

298–90 The 3rd Samnite War.

295 The Romans defeat the Samnites at the Battle of Sentinum, avenging the humiliation of the Caudine Forks.

287 Plebiscites, a yes or no vote of the people, become the law of Rome. This is the Lex Hortensia.

283 Rome establishes the province of Cisalpine Gaul in northern Italy.

280–75 The Romans go to war with King Pyrrhus of Epirus. The term 'pyrrhic victory' is named after the costly way of waging war by Pyrrhus, who is finally defeated in 275.

272 The Greek colony of Tarentum surrenders to Rome and the rest of the Greek colonies submit to Roman rule in Italy.

264–41 The 1st Punic War with economic rival Carthage.

260 The birth of the Roman navy. The Romans build their first fleet to fight the seaborne power of Carthage.

259 The Romans are victorious against Carthage in the naval battle of Mylae.

256–5 Regulus launches an invasion of Africa but is defeated by the Carthaginians.

249 The Carthaginians again defeat the Romans at the Battle of Drapana.

241 The Romans defeat the Carthaginians at the sea battle of the Aigates Islands. The Romans take Sicily, which becomes a Roman colony.

238 The islands of Corsica and Sardinia are annexed by Rome.

223 The Romans establish colonies in Cisalpine Gaul after a successful military campaign.

219 Hannibal of Carthage campaigns in Spain, taking the city of Saguntum.

218–01 The 2nd Punic War with Carthage begins.

218–17 Hannibal invades northern Italy after crossing the Alps with his

▼ *A view of the Appian Way, which connected Rome to Capua. It was used for both civilian and military traffic and is probably the most famous of the Roman roads.*

▲ *The painting 'The Continence of Scipio' by Poussin. A modern rendition of the story of Scipio Africanus refusing the favours of a captured Carthaginian princess lest he be corrupted by the spoils of war.*

army. He defeats the Romans at the Trebbia and at Lake Trasimene. His army threatens Rome and the Romans raise new forces to face the Carthaginian threat.

216 Hannibal annihilates an entire Roman army at the Battle of Cannae. Carthage makes an alliance with King Phillip V of Macedonia, who goes to war with Rome. Some of Rome's Italian allies join Hannibal and support him against Rome.

214 The Roman's Siege of Syracuse is defeated with the help of siege engines designed by Archimedes.

214–05 The 1st Macedonian War. Rome fights a war on two fronts against both Macedonia and Carthage.

213–11 The Siege of Syracuse in Sicily.

211–06 In Spain the Roman general Scipio campaigns against the Carthaginians.

209 Scipio, successful in Spain, captures the city of Cartagena.

203 Scipio, soon to be named Scipio Africanus, invades North Africa, ignoring Hannibal in Italy. Scipio marches on Carthage and defeats them at the Battle of the Great Plains.

202 Hannibal is recalled from Italy and faces Scipio at the Battle of Zama outside Carthage. Hannibal is badly defeated and the war ends.

200–196 The 2nd Macedonian War resulting in the defeat of Philip V of Macedon who is forced to abandon all his possessions in Greece.

197–79 Gracchus successfully ends the wars in Spain and two colonies are formed from the territory taken. Philip of Macedon is again defeated.

195 Laconian War against Sparta.

▼ *The ruins of the city of Carthage in North Africa. Rome completely destroyed the Carthaginian capital after the Third Punic War, but later rebuilt a city on the site.*

194 The Romans evacuate Greece.

192 The Syrian War, fought against the Seleucid Empire under Antiochus the Great, ending in 188.

191 Northern Italy (Cisalpine Gaul) is finally conquered by Rome.

181 The 1st Celtic-Iberian war fought with the tribes of Hispania Citerior.

179 The Amelian Bridge, Rome's first stone bridge, is built over the Tiber.

168 The Macedonians, under Perseus, are finally defeated at the Battle of Pydna. Macedonia is not made a colony, but instead is transformed into a Roman dependency.

167 The Romans take and sack Epirus, enslaving over 100,000 Greeks. The Senate abolishes direct taxation of Roman citizens.

154 The 1st Numantine war and 2nd Celtic-Iberian war.

149–6 The 3rd Punic War. Carthage is besieged, taken, sacked, and destroyed and her population, those that survived the long siege, are sold into slavery. Achaea and Macedonia become Roman provinces in 146.

143 The 2nd Numantine and 3rd Celtic-Iberian war.

135–2 The 1st Sicilian Slave War.

133 With the death of Attalus III of Pergamum, who willed his kingdom to Rome, the Mediterranean Sea becomes a Roman lake and is called by them our sea, 'Mare Nostrum'.

CAMPAIGNS OF THE REPUBLIC

The Romans were an aggressive people, gifted in exploiting success and at learning from failure. They quickly developed a military to suit their expansionist outlook. The army they would build was to be the most effective, organized, and disciplined in the ancient world. It was also the most resilient, able to sustain disastrous defeats with very heavy losses in manpower and equipment and then come back the next time to fight again, and usually win. The success of the Roman military system was based on its rigorous discipline, on and off the battle field, its ability to endure

▼ *The blind Roman politician, Appio Claudio Cieco, appealing to the Senate not to accept the peace terms offered by Pyrrhus of Epirus.*

hardship and adapt to different situations, climates and enemies.

While the Roman army was successful, and succeeded far beyond what Alexander the Great and his Macedonian army accomplished, it was not an undefeated army nor was it unbeatable. During its long history and development, the Roman army experienced crushing defeats, where sometimes the army in the field was annihilated in battles against what appeared to be weaker foes.

Pyrrhus of Epirus

In 295BC the Romans finally defeated an army of Samnites, Gauls and Umbrians at the Battle of Sentinum. This undoubtedly led to the unification of Italy under Roman

domination, but the Greek settlements in southern Italy were to resist Roman encroachment. This led to the intervention in Italy of a Greek king, Pyrrhus, who ruled the region of Epirus, upon the invitation of the Tarentines who were already in conflict with Rome. Pyrrhus was a competent king and commander, but his campaigns in southern Italy and Sicily were ultimately a failure, and these territories came under Roman rule.

The Punic Wars (264–146BC)

The three wars between Rome and Carthage span more than a century and are known as Punic because the Carthaginians were Phoenician in origin ('punicus' in Latin). The cause was a clash of interest between the two expanding empires, and a struggle for influence over neighbouring territories.

The long 2nd Punic War, in the 3rd century BC, saw Roman armies suffer three great defeats at the hands of the very capable Carthaginian general – Hannibal Barca. Hannibal's most famous victory over the Romans, at Cannae in 216BC, was a true battle of annihilation, with the Roman army surrounded and cut down nearly to the man. Prior to that, Hannibal had fought and defeated the Roman legions and their allies at the Trebbia river and Lake Trasimene.

Hannibal was an excellent tactician and strategist who had brought his army from Spain over the Alps and into Italy in order to bring the war to the Romans on their own territory. He was the most skilful general that the Romans would face, and the grimmest threat to Rome until the Barbarian invasions that finally brought about their downfall.

What Hannibal could not defeat, however, no matter how many tactical victories he won and how many losses he inflicted on the Romans, was the Roman ability to raise new legions and armies to defend itself. Legion after legion would be raised to replace their losses and sent against the isolated Carthaginians, who were far from home and with diminishing support from those they had left behind.

Reliance on native soldiery, and not depending on mercenaries as the Carthaginians did, was one of the main reasons the Romans were able to raise armies repeatedly during the war. Hannibal spent 15 years in Italy without achieving final victory over the Roman state, and finally had to withdraw back to North Africa when Rome sent an army across the Mediterranean to threaten the Carthaginian homeland. The general commanding that Roman expedition was Scipio, later to win the title 'Africanus' for defeating Hannibal at the Battle of Zama in 202BC.

The Conquest of the Iberian Peninsula (154–33BC)

Carthage had colonies on the coast of Iberia (now Spain), and after defeating the Carthaginians in the Punic wars, Rome dispatched forces to conquer and occupy the Iberian peninsula and establish its rule over the peoples of Spain. The Numantines defeated a Roman army under Mancinus and forced their surrender in 137BC.

▼ *The Battle of Zama in 202BC, the decisive action of the 2nd Punic War, where the Roman general Scipio defeated Hannibal.*

▲ *Carthage was a thriving commercial port, protected by a strong navy. Some of the fortifications of the city are pictured here, including the huge naval harbour.*

However, the most important action in Iberia was the siege of Numantia commanded by Scipio Aemilianus. Numantia had impressive fortifications and was located on the River Duoro (Durius) which enabled the defenders to be resupplied by water.

Scipio not only established effective siege lines around Numantia, but he effectively blockaded the river at both ends of the city in order to stop supplies from reaching the city. Roman artillery was effectively employed during the siege of eight months after which the starving garrison and population finally surrendered in 133BC. During the siege, supplies were so completely cut off from the city that

the population was said to have resorted to cannibalism. Surrender was unconditional, and the surviving 4,000 defenders and inhabitants marched out into Roman captivity.

Jugurtha of Numidia (112–06BC)

The North African ruler Jugurtha of Numidia was the grandson of the former Roman ally, Masinissa. Masinissa was a friend to Scipio, nevertheless Rome became wary of Numidian power in North Africa after the victory at the Battle of Zama. Upon Masinissa's death, Rome ensured that Numidian power was curtailed by having the African kingdom divided into three parts, one to each of Masinissa's sons. However, Jugurtha on his own succeeded in reuniting Numidia and either talked or bribed his way out of the first Roman threat of invasion.

Jugurtha travelled to Rome under safe conduct in order to present his case, and convinced the Roman political leadership of his claims through energetic bribing of key Roman officials. Jugurtha returned to Numidia and defeated the next Roman army sent against him. Finally, Roman general Lucius Cornelius Sulla 'arranged' for the capture of Jugurtha, who was betrayed to the Romans by his ally Bocchus, king of Mauretania. In the negotiations with the Romans Bocchus had the opportunity to betray Sulla to Jugurtha, but wisely chose the other course; Roman vengeance against allies who let them down could be vicious. After being paraded in a triumph, Jugurtha died in prison.

▲ *The Roman general and dictator Sulla forces his way into Rome with his army in c.88BC in one of Rome's internal struggles.*

The Macedonian Wars (214–167BC)

While Rome was in a death struggle with Carthage in three separate wars, there was continued trouble with Macedonia and the Greeks. This distraction had to be dealt with on a separate front and with troops that could have been used to better effect against Carthage. That Rome was able to conduct these wars demonstrates a military robustness that was uncommon in any age. In addition, that these wars were eventually successful speaks volumes for Roman military proficiency and staying power.

The Macedonian Wars actually took place between 214–05BC, from 200–196BC, and finally from 172–67BC. The first conflict was caused by Macedonia's king, Philip V, allying himself with Carthage, and was probably a war that Rome did not want and could not afford. The war, though long, ended indecisively. The 2nd Macedonian War, however, was begun by Rome as they believed that Philip was becoming too powerful in the east and his aims were in direct conflict with Rome's. Philip was decisively defeated by 196BC. Finally, the Macedonians under Perseus were

defeated in the 3rd, and last, conflict with Macedonia at the Battle of Pydna in 168BC. Roman hegemony was now beginning to spread into the eastern Mediterranean.

The Germanic Threat (131–01BC)

Trouble with tribes migrating south out of Jutland in northern Europe began a long conflict with various Germanic peoples in Gaul and Germania that would last until Rome finally succumbed to a series of barbarian invasions in the 5th century AD. Troubles and conflict with three main Germanic tribes, the Teutones, Ambrones and the Cimbri, would lead to a severe Roman defeat at Noricum (now southern Austria).

Not being able or willing to cross the Alps into Italy, the Germans opted to move into Gaul. Trying to stop them in 105BC, the Romans were badly defeated at Arausio, where their army was nearly wiped out. Command in Gaul was given to Marius, one of the most competent Roman generals of the period, and he eventually defeated the Germanic tribes, eliminating first the threat of the Teutones, then moving north to defeat the Cimbri.

The Roman Civil Wars (88–31BC)

Rome is sometimes seen as a stable, political monolith through the lens of history. However, being a republic,

with no permanent head of state, led to some political instability when men from different powerful patrician families vied for power. The most familiar is that between Julius Caesar and Gnaeus Pompey, sometimes referred to as 'the Great'. Prior to this titanic internal struggle, however, was the struggle between Lucius Cornelius Sulla and Gaius Marius, which both Caesar and Pompey witnessed and lived through as young men.

The struggles of Sulla and Marius with the Senate and each other took place after the Social War (91–88BC), which was the last great resurgence of independence from Rome's Italian allies. Sulla actually led his army in a march on Rome in 88BC, took control of the city, imposed his will on the Senate and was declared to be dictator; a title and position that was only used in times of crisis to the state.

This struggle took place during a war with Mithridates of Pontus, which was not concluded until 66BC. Marius died in 86BC, but not before the civil war had taken its toll on Rome, and it remained unsettled until Sulla's death in 78BC. The conflict was marked by vicious massacres of the supporters of

▼ *A bust of Pompey the Great, one of the ruling triumvirate of Rome, with Julius Caesar and Marcus Licinius Crassus.*

▲ *A view of the Roman Senate in session in the 'curia' or meeting house. There were several such buildings in Rome's history.*

both men and their families, which were undertaken to settle old scores. What was to come later would dwarf this bloody upheaval and lead to the fall of the Roman republic.

In 59BC Caesar and Pompey formed a ruling triumvirate in Rome with Marcus Licinius Crassus, who had put down the Spartacus slave revolt. In 53BC Crassus was defeated and killed by the Parthians at the Battle of Carrhae, and by 49BC Rome was dominated by Caesar and Pompey and their political factions (called the Populares and the Optinates, respectively).

The political struggle transformed into open warfare when Caesar crossed the Rubicon river, a move forbidden to any general by the Senate. Civil war erupted and lasted until 45BC after Caesar finally defeated Pompey at the Battle of Pharsalus in 48BC. Pompey fled to Egypt, followed by Caesar, who upon landing was famously presented with Pompey's head in a sack, an act

that disgusted him. Caesar ruled as dictator for the next four years but was then plotted against in his turn, and assassinated by his fellow senators in 44BC. In 43BC a new triumvirate was formed by Octavian (Julius Caesar's nephew), Mark Antony (Caesar's loyal lieutenant), and Marcus Lepidus. This alliance degenerated into civil war

between Mark Antony and Octavian, with the latter being victorious and becoming the first emperor of Rome under the name of Augustus. The old Roman republic was dead.

▼ *The goddess Roma, signifying Rome itself, appearing to Caesar on the River Rubicon beckons him to make his fateful crossing.*

THE ROMAN MILITARY SYSTEM

Roman military development can be roughly broken down into a number of key stages: the early Roman armed bands; the citizen militias that gradually formed from the armed bands; and the organization of the legion, which took two forms, the first being the manipular legion followed by the cohort legion. So it was that, gradually, the Roman army was transformed from a citizen militia into a standing professional army.

Lastly, in response to the repeated threats of the 'barbarian hordes' and the transformation of the empire into western and eastern divisions, the Roman army changed dramatically from an infantry force into a mounted one, the cavalry in the east becoming the main striking arm of the eastern Roman army and the infantry, still well-trained and formidable, being the supporting arm. This was a complete change in emphasis on the primary means of fighting for the Romans and reflects adaptation from the enemies the Romans had to face.

Armed Bands

The war band was the earliest form of military organization that the Romans established. Chiefs would organize the male members of the clan, doubling as warriors and farmers to either raid their neighbours, or rally them to defend their own land against the raids of outsiders. Conflicts would be settled usually by one clash or battle with the 'enemy' and settled until the next dispute or plunder raid occurred.

Leadership was provided by a warrior experienced in battle, usually chosen by those he would lead. Weapons and armour were expensive, and the warriors in the war band would not be armed and armoured alike; some would not be armoured at all. If the war band was successful against the enemy war band, arms and armour would be taken from the dead on the field, and further incursions

against the enemy might occur, raiding into their territory and either capturing or destroying them in their villages and towns, taking women and children as hostages or slaves, or taking them to assimilate them as Romans. It was an inefficient way of making war and haphazard at best. The war band was composed of warriors not soldiers; warriors fight on their own, not as an integral and trained unit, while a soldier is uniformly trained and possibly equipped and armed, who fights as part of a unit. Warriors in war bands would not be as cohesive in a fight, especially a prolonged one. Leadership, especially in combat, would make a significant difference to both warriors and soldiers; an army can survive and even win with mediocre leadership, whereas a band of warriors usually could not.

Greek Influence

Combat organization was gradually influenced by Greek fighting methods, particularly the phalanx, and Greek-style arms and armour were in evidence with the early Romans, as

▲ A mosaic of a Roman garrison outside Italy, c.80BC. From the shape of the shields, the white tunics, plumes, and muscle cuirasses these are likely to be military tribunes.

well as with the other Latins in the Italian peninsula. Both the Etruscans and the Romans were greatly influenced by the Greeks who had a presence in Italy along the coasts where they had established cities for trade and colonization. Apparently, the Romans adopted the phalanx from the Etruscans and not directly from the Greeks. In clothing and weaponry, the early Roman fighting man undoubtedly appeared much as the early Greeks did in the field.

For a phalanx to function properly on the battlefield, extensive training was essential. The phalanx had to maintain a rigid front for it to be effective and this solid frontage of shields and long spears, nearly unbeatable if maintained, could quite literally sweep the field. Discipline was strict, and losses were replaced by the men in the rear ranks stepping up to take the places of the fallen.

The Phalanx, Maniple and Cohort Formations

The structure of one of the principal subunits of the phalanx, further subdivided into four smaller units.

The line of the phalanx, in fighting order. The phalanx was divided into six or more subunits depending on the situation.

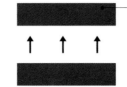

The phalanx in motion. The arrows show the direction of movement of the phalanx moving 'in line.' The phalanx could also manoeuvre in column formation, which made keeping order much easier.

Phalanx: The Roman use of the phalanx developed from the Greek influence in southern Italy and Sicily. The strength of the phalanx was its rigid front of heavy spear-armed infantry from a minimum of 4 deep up to 32 men deep, depending on the terrain and the opponent. For special missions, Greek phalanxes were known to be 50 men deep, but this was unusual. The normal depth of a phalanx was the file of eight men, and the phalanx would be at least four times as wide. When fighting the Samnites in central Italy *c*. 4th century

▲ *A Greek or Roman phalanx battle array. The hoplites are in line facing the enemy.*

BC, the Romans found that the phalanx was at a disadvantage and could be outmanoeuvred and flanked by an enemy used to fighting in hilly terrain.

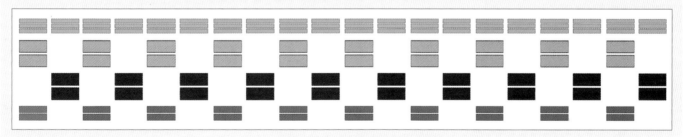

Manipular Legion: After their experiences fighting the Samnites, the Romans reorganized their army into legions of about 6,000 men, based on three types of heavy infantry: the hastati, principes and triarii. The first two were young men in their prime armed and equipped as heavy infantry, the triarii being older veterans. Lightly armed velites were used as skirmishers, supporting the main body. The maniple was made up of two centuries of 60 men each, although the triarii maniples were half the strength of the hastati and principes maniples. There were 10 maniples of each type of heavy infantry

▲ *The manipular legion in line of battle. The three lines of heavy infantry in yellow, red, and blue would be supported by skirmishers, or velites, here depicted in green, at the front of the formation.*

who on the battlefield were arranged in three lines, in a chessboard formation.

Cohort Legion: While the manipular legion was vastly superior to the phalanx, the individual maniples of the legion were not strong enough for independent missions. In the 1st century BC, when Marius was instituting his army-wide reforms, the legion itself was reorganized. While the maniples remained at least in theory, the three types of legion infantry were reduced to only one type, the legionary, and the strength of the legion was established at 5,000 heavy infantry plus auxiliaries. The strength of the century was

increased to 80 men. The number of maniples and centuries remained the same, but the centuries were now organized into significant units called cohorts, each of six centuries. The 1st cohort was doubled in size, the other nine

▲ *The cohort legion in line of battle. At the right of the line is the first cohort, twice as strong as any of the other nine cohorts.*

cohorts were all of the same strength and organization.

▲ *Horatius's heroic defence of the Sublican Bridge over the Tiber, against the Etruscans.*

The large rectangle of determined troops coming directly forwards had to be terrifying. The first two ranks would have spears levelled at any approaching enemy and the ranks to the rear would have their spears raised to stay out of the way of the front ranks. This was a virtually impenetrable formation from the front, and they would either attack raising a cheer as they moved forward, intending to unnerve their opponents, or might come on in complete silence, which was even worse as the only thing being heard would be the nearly uniform tramping of the feet of those in the phalanx behind the terrible hedge of sharpened spear points aimed directly at the attacker. All that could be done was to prepare for the inevitable crunch of an almost overwhelming impact.

On an open and level plain, the phalanx was terribly efficient. But as the Romans found out to their chagrin, in broken country or in hills, the phalanx had trouble maintaining the formation and its front. Fighting in the hill country or in the foothills of the Apennines that ran almost the length of the Italian boot, the phalanx was not the ideal formation to fight in. It was a formation best suited to the plain and if an enemy elected to fight in broken terrain, then the phalanx formation could prove fatal. It required

coordination and discipline, and was not about individual glory.

Ironically, then, it was during this period the legend of Horatius and his courageous stand against the Etruscan army trying to take Rome developed. Whether or not Horatius was an actual person, there apparently was a defence of the bridge over the Tiber, fought as a delaying action against the invading Etruscans. Horatius is said to have finally fought off the Etruscans single-handed, denying them the crossing point until he finally broke away to escape into Rome with an epic poem later written to 'record' his valiant stand alone on the bridge.

As an aside, the exploits of Horatius are also said to include taking part in a three-on-three fight between champions of the warring factions. As the fight progressed, Horatius' two companions were slain by the enemy and Horatius was faced with a one-against-three disadvantage. However, two of his enemies had been wounded by his now-dead comrades-in-arms, and after hard fighting, Horatius emerged victorious.

▼ *A marble relief, c.100BC, from Rome showing legionaries of the late Republic. The almost rectangular Roman scutum (shields) are represented here very accurately, as are the plumed helmets, arms and chain mail.*

Citizen Militia

Rome's citizen army probably dates from the reign of Servius Tullius, who reigned from 579–34BC. These 'Servian' reforms obliged all male citizens to respond to a census and to arm themselves according to which class he belonged to, of which there were five based on the relative wealth of each citizen. These classes were further divided into 'centuries', a basic organization of what would become the Roman legion that would last until the death throes of the western empire.

In each of the five classes, half of the centuries were composed of men aged 47–60, the seniors, who were usually employed as garrison troops and did not take the field with the main army. The other half of the centuries were made up of men from 17–46, considered the prime age for campaigning and fighting in line of battle. The classes themselves did not contain the same number of centuries because the wealthier men would be able to better provide themselves with arms and armour. So, Class I was made up of 80 centuries, Class II–IV of 20 centuries each, and Class V of 30 centuries. There were also 18 centuries of the most wealthy Romans, who made up the cavalry, and these 'aristocrats' took precedence over the infantry in status.

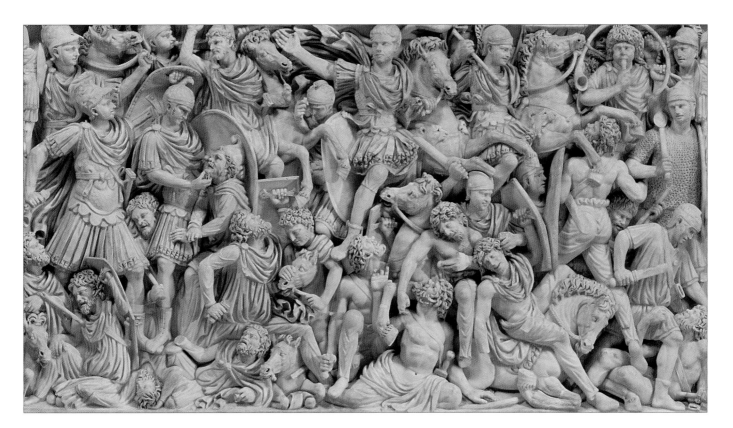

▲ *Romans decorated their burial chambers with scenes of military conquest. This portion of the Ludovisi sarcophagus shows legionaries in generally accurate arms and armour fighting against barbarians, c.250–80AD.*

The Manipular Legion

Rome's organization of its army into legions took two forms, the manipular and the cohort. The manipular was the first reorganization of the legion since its Greek phalanx roots. Fighting in the hills and rugged country of Italy against enemies that were comfortable fighting there, the Romans abandoned the phalanx, and divided the legion into maniples of two centuries each. Here, the maniple, and not the century, was the basic fighting unit of the legion. The term maniple, or in Latin manipulus, means a 'handful' and reportedly was taken from the 'handful' of straw that was originally used as a standard in the early days of Rome, the straw being attached to a staff. There were 30 maniples in the legion, each composed of heavy infantry of three types: the hastati, principes and triarii.

The hastati were in the first line of the legion. They were the youngest and least experienced in the legion, and they were organized in centuries of 60 men each. Twenty velites (lightly armoured infantry armed with javelins) would be administratively attached to their century but they didn't fight with it, being deployed instead as skirmishers along the front of the legion in combat.

The principes made up the second line of the legion. They were organized in the same manner as the hastati and had the same battle strength. They were more experienced in combat than the hastati and backed up the hastati line to be committed to action on command. The triarii were in the legion's third line, and were usually less numerous than either the hastati or the principes. They were veteran infantry; instead of 120 men in the maniples of the other heavy infantry, there were only 60.

There were also two other elements of the manipular legion: the velites and the equites – the cavalry element. The velites would be massed along the legion's front in combat and would be the first troops to engage. When they were withdrawn the first line of maniples, the hastati, would be engaged, first with pilum (the plural is pila), then with sword and shield.

Centuries were commanded by centurions, the officers of the legion. There were two per century – the centurion who commanded the century and the second-in-command, the optio, whose place in battle was in the rear of the century. There were also two standard bearers per century, as well as a trumpeter. Their names in Latin were the signifier and cornicen, respectively. Each legion had only one standard bearer, so the allocation of two per century was probably in case of casualties.

Centurions could be either appointed by their superior officers, or elected, but they had to be experienced soldiers in order to command the respect of their subordinates. The senior centurion of the legion was the primus pilus who commanded the first maniple of the triarii. He outranked the other centurions of the legion and his position carried prestige and respect.

The equites, the cavalrymen of the legion, numbered roughly 300 horse per legion. These 300 troopers were organized in 10 turmae of 30 men each. Each turma had three decurions to command them, with an optio as his second in command.

◄ A Roman tomb relief depicting a Roman prefect and two legionaries, 1st century BC. The armour of the prefect is more elaborate but all three are well armed and armoured.

Decurions were distinguished in the same manner as a centurion, wearing a crossways horsehair crest on their helmets.

The legion during this period learned to make an entrenched camp, and that became standard practice on campaign at the end of each day's march. The camp, surrounded by a wall and ditch, was suitable for defence and was properly outposted and guards set so that the legion would not be surprised at night.

The Cohort Legion

The manipular legion was changed into the cohort legion when the maniples were abolished during the reforms of Marius, and the cohort of six centuries each became the manoeuvre or tactical element of the legion. This led to a simpler organization for the Roman army and was probably more flexible on the battlefield than the more stratified manipular legion. It also gave the legion a stronger internal organization, which was capable of more independent action in either small operations, or on the battlefield where legion 'task forces' of a cohort with supporting troops could be assigned a mission that would support the overall orders of the legion. Eventually in this organization the distinctions between hastati, principes and triarii were

abolished and all legionaries became indistinguishable from one another in function, position, armour, equipment and weapons. Prior to that reorganization, however, the triarii of the third line of the manipular legion were brought up to the strength of the hastati and principes.

Legion Auxiliaries

While the original cavalry of the legion was made up of native Roman citizens, later cavalry units, or alae, were recruited from native horsemen such as Celts (especially Celts from the Iberian peninsula) Thracians, assorted Germans, and Gauls. These tribes were thought to make the most efficient cavalrymen because the general impression of them to the Romans was that they were born in the saddle.

Auxiliary troops of almost every type were incorporated into the Roman army. Skilled archers and slingers were used to support the legionaries in the field and though the main strength of the army remained the legion, the auxiliary troops were well-trained and led, and were cared for in the same way. They added greatly to the fighting power of the Roman army. However, when the Roman army began to be made up of more foreign auxiliary units than native soldiery, the Roman army began to fail repeatedly in its ability to defend their huge empire.

'Bring Another'

Often, when studying the armies of the ancients – especially that of Rome and perhaps of the eastern Romans, those armies – and the men who served in them, are generally treated as a monolith. The faces, actions, and motivations are the same for all of them; a legion is a legion, and all are the same and alike, no matter their service, place of recruitment, their accomplishments or their eventual fate. It is very rare that stories come down about the men in the ranks, and the centurions who led them. It is interesting, therefore, to find out that certain men from a particular legion were present at an act familiar to most of us, the crucifixion of Christ around 35AD. It is recorded that there were legionaries present, and probably a centurion. Those legionaries and that centurion almost certainly belonged to the famous 10th Legion, Julius Caesar's finest and most faithful, as it was one of two legions stationed in Palestine at the time.

Then there is the story of the centurion, 'Bring Another'. The vine stick was the symbol of rank and authority of the centurion, of whom there were about 60 per legion, the senior centurion being the primus pilus, or the 'spear point'. 'Bring Another', nicknamed such by his men, had the habit when annoyed of breaking his vine stick over one of his legionaries, immediately telling another soldier to 'bring another' for his immediate use. Undoubtedly a legionary would hurry to bring his centurion another vine stick.

This particular centurion, despite his no doubt painful way of getting the attention of a recalcitrant legionary, was perhaps not always popular with his troops but he must have been respected, and it is highly doubtful that any would fail to 'bring another' when the centurion was in need of a replacement.

ROME'S ENEMIES

The enemies of Rome were many and varied. They ranged from the organized armies of Greeks and Carthaginians that significantly tested the Romans in combat and inflicted stinging defeats on the Roman legions, to desert tribesmen, and Celtic and Germanic enemies to the north.

Initially, the Romans faced other Italian and Latin tribes. These tribes were eventually absorbed into the expanding territory of Rome, and their warriors came with them. New fighting techniques of their neighbours were learned, and influenced the development of the Roman army.

▼ *At the end of the republic, Rome straddled Europe and North Africa, but further territorial gains were to come as the empire spread north into Britain, and east into Asia.*

The Etruscans, Samnites and Greeks all were formidable foes as the Romans expanded. The Etruscans ruled Rome for a significant period, and Roman and Etruscan culture, civilization, and armies began to resemble each other. The Greeks held significant portions of Italy as well as Sicily, and Greek fighting techniques, as well as arms and armour, were an influence in what became the Roman way of waging war.

Celts and Gauls

The Celts were present in many places in Europe, especially in the early period, and the Romans would fight Celtic armies and raiders until they withdrew from Britain in the later empire period. The Celts were vicious and individualistic warriors, rather than soldiers, and generally fought in

an undisciplined manner. Great commanders, such as Hannibal, could harness that warrior spirit of the Celts and make them an efficient and deadly part of his mercenary army, but commanders of the calibre of Hannibal are few in military history. Celtic arms and armour were adopted by the Romans from time to time.

The ancient Gauls were another fierce breed of warrior that fought Rome for long and bitter periods, and Julius Caesar's famous *Commentaries* recount the long campaigns he fought against the Gauls before his political ambitions tore Rome apart with civil war. Caesar's Siege of Alesia, the stronghold of the Gauls in modern France, is a classic example of how to conduct a siege as well as defeating a hostile relief army.

At the death of Caesar, 44BC

At the death of Augustus, 14AD

At the death of Marcus Aurelius, 180AD

▲ *In the midst of a desperate battle with the Volscians, a Roman commander throws the legion standard towards the enemy line. By doing this, the legionaries would renew the attack in order to retrieve the unit's standard, as losing it brought disgrace to the legion.*

Carthaginians

Carthage was probably founded in what is now Tunisia in the 9th century BC as a colony of the Phoenicians, a seafaring people whose ships roamed the Mediterranean in search of trade and wealth. The Romans called the Carthaginians the Poeni, mutated into 'Puni'. The name Punic Wars comes from this Latin. When Tyre, possibly the home city of the Carthaginians, was destroyed by the Babylonians under Nebuchadnezzar in the 6th century BC, Carthage became the most mighty seapower in the Mediterranean.

The Carthaginians were expansionist and sought to dominate the Mediterranean, adding Iberia (Spain) Sicily, Sardinia and the Balearic islands to their possessions as well as founding colonies along the west coast of Africa by sailing through the straits of Gibraltar and along the west African coast. Carthaginian settlements have been discovered in the Canary Islands,

▲ *This relief from the republican period, clearly shows the Roman muscled cuirass, the short sword, or gladius, and the distinctive Roman helmet, now with cheek pieces attached to protect the face of the wearer.*

Morocco, Mauritania, Guinea, Senegal and Madeira.

Inevitably, this growing empire quickly collided with a similarly minded Rome after the Romans had conquered most of the Italian peninsula. The 1st Punic War erupted in 264BC over who would occupy and control the large island of Sicily. This war would last until 241BC. The war saw Roman success in Sicily, at sea and in North Africa and the Carthaginians sued for peace. The Romans insisted on very harsh terms, which the Carthaginians refused and the war continued with mixed success for both sides until the Romans defeated the Carthaginian fleet at the naval battle of the Aegates Islands. This ended the 1st Punic War in 241BC. Carthage sued for peace and ceded Sicily to Rome.

The 2nd Punic War (218–202BC) saw Hannibal besiege the Greek city of Saguntum in Spain, an ally of the Romans, taking it after an eight-month siege in 218BC. The next year he

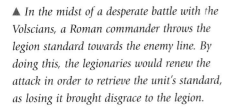

◀ *Two Samnite infantrymen depicted on a well-preserved funerary frescoe from the 4th century BC. The warlike Samnites are accurately depicted here with their very short tunics, round shields, and distinctive helmets with unusual crests.*

▲ *A painting depicting the Roman consul and general Marcus Atilius Regulus urging the Romans to refuse Carthaginian peace overtures in the 1st Punic War. Regulus was a successful Roman general and naval commander until his defeat at Tunis, where he was taken prisoner by the Carthaginians.*

famously invaded Italy with an army that included war elephants, which inflicted defeats on the Romans at the Battle of Ticinus and at the Battle of the Trebbia. In 217BC Hannibal worked his way down the Italian peninsula, crushing an entire Roman army at Lake Trasimene and then, in August 216BC, at Cannae, he annihilated the Roman army sent to meet him.

The aftermath was an anticlimax. Hannibal ranged the length and breadth of Italy, winning some of Rome's former Italian allies as allies for the Carthaginians, but Rome kept raising army after army to fight the invaders. Continuous losses and defeats led Rome to appoint Quintus Fabius its general in Italy. Fabius refused to fight Hannibal's veterans with raw troops, and settled on a strategy of delay and harassment. For this successful strategy, which allowed time for new troops to be recruited and trained, Fabius was given the title 'Cunctator' or 'Delayer'. Hannibal failed to defeat the Romans in Italy, and when the Romans went on the strategic offensive and landed in North Africa, he was recalled to Carthage only to be decisively defeated on the plains

of Zama, effectively ending the war in Rome's favour when Carthage again sued for peace.

The 3rd, and last, Punic War erupted in 149BC but did not last long. Two years later the Romans, who had again invaded North Africa, successfully blockaded and besieged Carthage by land and sea and the city surrendered the next year. Ninety per cent of the population had either been killed in the fighting, or had died of disease or starvation. The Romans razed Carthage and the survivors were sold as slaves. The Carthaginian empire was no more.

Barbarians

From Rome's point of view, if you were not Roman, you were inevitably a barbarian. Rome saw itself not only as a conqueror of barbarian peoples, but the harbinger of civilization, bringing it to barbarian peoples whether they wanted it or not. Rome did spread western civilization across the known world, but often used the most brutal of means.

The barbarians that the Romans faced were many and varied. Germans of various sorts and types came from north of the Danube and across the Rhine frontier. Britons and Celts were faced by Caesar and his successors as Britain was invaded twice and finally brought under Roman rule. Picts, Scots and others north of the Antonine Wall in Scotland were never really brought under Roman rule, but they certainly had a part in shrinking Roman Britain

through continuous fighting as well as raids and incursions.

Large, established empires were fought by Rome, Carthage being the most remembered. However, there were Persian and Sassanian empires in the east as well as the remnants of Alexander the Great's conquests, including his homeland of Macedonia. Some of Rome's most humiliating defeats took place in the east, in what is now Palestine, Iraq and Iran.

▼ *This portion of the Arch of Constantine in Rome depicts the surrender of a barbarian chieftain to the Romans. Structures such as this give us primary source documentation of the arms, armour, and dress of the Romans.*

EARLY ROMAN EMPIRE TIMELINE
107BC–79AD

BC

107–100 Marius institutes long-reaching reforms in the Roman army. The Roman army is now a professional fighting force that will be maintained as a standing army.

106 The Consul Marius leads a Roman army against the Numidians and defeats their king, Jugurtha.

105 A Roman army is defeated at the Battle of Arausio by the Cimbri and the Teutones.

104–100 The 2nd Sicilian Slave War.

102 Marius defeats the Teutones at the Battle of Aquae Sextaie.

101 Marius defeats the Cimbri at the Battle of Vercelli.

91 Rome expels all non-Roman citizens with the exception of slaves.

91 The Social War begins.

90 Full Roman citizenship is granted to all Italians under the Lex Julia.

89–5 The first war against Mithradates.

87 Marius, popular with both the army and the people, takes power in Rome without the authority of the Senate.

86 Sulla, another successful Roman political general, takes and sacks Athens. Marius dies.

82 The 2nd Mithradatic War. Sulla

▲ *Depicted here, in a much later painting, is one of Caesar's triumphs after his return to Rome from conquests in the east.*

marches on Rome, seizes power, and becomes dictator.

80 Sulla resigns as Roman dictator.

73–1 The Spartacus slave revolt.

70 Pompey, soon to be Pompey the Great, and Crassus, the victor over Spartacus, become consuls.

67 Pompey hunts down and is victorious over the pirate menace in the Mediterranean.

66 Pompey is assigned the eastern

army command by the Senate.

60 The first ruling triumvirate of Pompey, Caesar and Crassus is formed.

59 Julius Caesar is designated a Roman consul for the first time.

58–1 Caesar establishes his military reputation as a successful general in his Gallic campaigns.

55–4 Caesar attempts to invade Britain. He is initially successful, but there is not a lasting Roman presence established by the operation.

53 Crassus is killed in action at the Battle of Carrhae.

49 Caesar, bidding for ultimate power in Rome, crosses the River Rubicon with his legion, knowing this act will cause civil war in Rome and war with his longtime rival, Pompey.

48 Pompey defeats Caesar at Dyrrachium but later Caesar decisively defeats Pompey at the Battle of Pharsalus in Greece.

47 Pompey flees to Egypt where he is murdered and beheaded.

47–6 Caesar continues his conquests

▼ *The assassination of Julius Caesar by his fellow senators, conspirators who were afraid of Caesar's assumption of absolute power.*

▲ *The naval Battle of Actium took place in 31BC between the forces of Octavian and Mark Antony. Octavian's victory brought him sole power and was the harbinger of the establishment of the Roman Empire.*

in the east and in North Africa.

44 Caesar is assassinated in the Senate in Rome by conspirators who believe he will keep and hold absolute power.

43 A second ruling triumvirate of Lepidus, Mark Antony and Octavian is formed in the wake of Caesar's murder and the power vacuum that results. Mark Antony is defeated at Forum Gallorum as well as at Mutina.

42 Sextus Pompey intercepts the

▼ *A bust of Octavian, who took the name Augustus and became the first emperor of Rome, ruling wisely and justly.*

triumvirate fleet, with reinforcements in transports, in the Adriatic and destroys or captures most of the fleet. Mark Antony is victorious over the republicans at the Battle of Philippi. The Roman Empire is divided into ruling spheres of influence.

36 Sextus Pompey takes the field against Octavian and is defeated.

31 Octavian defeats Mark Antony at the naval Battle of Actium. Octavian is now sole ruler of Rome.

30 Octavian annexes Egypt after invading it and in the wake of Mark Antony's suicide and eventually becomes Caesar. The Roman Empire is once again united after the civil war.

29–7 Roman conquests expand to the Danube in Macedonia by Crassus, grandson of the triumvirate member.

27 Octavian becomes emperor in

Rome and assumes the title Augustus.

27–19 North-west Spain is conquered.

25–2 Military expeditions to Arabia are conducted. The attempt to take Aden fails. Galatia is added to the empire by annexation.

20 Legion standards captured by the Parthians from both Crassus and Mark Antony are returned to Rome.

17–9 Gaul is invaded by the Sugambri tribe. Tiberius annexes the Alpine and Balkan territories for Rome after a successful campaign. Roman power and influence in Europe reach the Elbe in Germany.

▼ *The Battle of the Teutoburg Forest in Germany in 9AD was a disaster for the Roman Army. The Roman legions were destroyed by Germanic tribesmen under Arminius, supposedly a Roman ally.*

▲ The death of the virtuous Germanicus, destined to be emperor, was a sad day for both his family and the empire.

AD

4 Herod the Great dies in Judea. General unrest in the Jewish population under Roman rule will eventually lead to a bloody revolt.

6 The Great Pannonian revolt breaks out and lasts for three years. Judea becomes a Roman province.

9 The Roman frontier is withdrawn to the River Rhine after Varus is defeated and killed in the disaster of the Teutoburg Forest by Germanic tribes under Arminius. Three legions, the 17th, 18th and 19th are destroyed and virtually wiped out by the Germans.

14–16 The emperor Augustus (Octavian) dies and is succeeded by Tiberius. The Rhine legions mutiny but are successfully suppressed by Germanicus who then hunts the Germans who had defeated Varus across the Rhine.

17 Cappadocia (now in Turkey) is successfully annexed to the empire.

18–28 There are revolts in Africa and Gaul, and by the Frisians.

19 Germanicus, Tiberius's adopted son, heir apparent as emperor and popular with the army, dies in Syria.

25 Agrippa begins building work on the Pantheon in Rome.

37 Tiberius dies in mysterious circumstances, leaving Caligula to be made emperor.

39 Caligula campaigns in both Gaul and Germany.

41 Caligula is assassinated by the Praetorian Guard, who proclaim Claudius emperor.

43 Britain is again invaded, this time successfully. The southern part of the country is Romanized and the native Britons gradually become Romano-Celts. Throughout the empire, the Roman (imperial) civil service is beginning to be taken over by literate freedmen, sometimes former slaves.

45 Thrace, in northern Greece, becomes a Roman province.

50 The city of Londinium (London) is founded in Britain.

54 Claudius adopts Nero as his heir. In the same year Mauretania (present day Algeria and Morocco) is subdued by Paulinus and is successfully converted into a Roman province. There is a revolt in Dalmatia, but Thrace becomes a Roman province. The eastern Pontus (now in Turkey) is also annexed and the Frisians are defeated. Claudius is poisoned in yet another palace plot and Nero becomes emperor.

60–1 Boudicca's revolt in Britain.

64 The Great Fire destroys a good portion of Rome.

66–72 The 1st Jewish War.

68 Nero commits suicide and is replaced by Galba.

68–9 The year of the Four Emperors – Galba, Otho, Vitellius and Vespasian.

70 Jerusalem is besieged and captured by Vespasian's son Titus.

79 Vespasian dies, Titus succeeds him.

84 Britons defeated in Scotland at the Battle of Mons Grapius; the battle is fought by Roman auxiliary cohorts supported by legionaries.

▼ This detail of the Arch of Titus depicts the loot taken from the temple during the sack of Jerusalem in 70AD. Roman reaction to revolt was never benign. Again, details from a Roman triumphal arch supply excellent references for the Roman army of the period.

DEFENDING THE EMPIRE TIMELINE
80–212AD

80 Work on Rome's Colosseum, with seating for 50,000, is completed.

81 Titus dies and his brother Domitian becomes emperor.

85–92 Domitian's campaign against the Dacians ends in failure and the Romans are forced to pay tribute.

96 Domitian is assassinated. His successor, Nerva, is proclaimed emperor by the senate in Rome.

98 Human sacrifice is outlawed in the Roman Empire.

98 Nerva dies and is succeeded by Trajan who campaigns successfully against the Dacians from 101–6, creating a new province for Rome.

106 Arabia Petraea (modern Jordan) is annexed.

111–14 Trajan's column, depicting his military victories, is built in Rome.

113–17 Rome conducts campaigns against the Parthians, and conquers Assyria, Mesopotamia and Armenia.

115–17 The Jews in Cyprus, Egypt, and Cyrene revolt against Roman rule.

121–2 Emperor Hadrian travels to Britain and construction on what will be known as Hadrian's Wall begins.

▼ *A portion of Trajan's column depicting his military victories. It has stood the test of time and still stands in Rome.*

▲ *The rising sun illuminates a section of Housesteads, one of the Roman forts of Hadrian's Wall, built during 122AD, in what is now Northumberland, northern England.*

131–5 Another Jewish revolt in Palestine breaks out under the leadership of Bar Kochba.

138 Hadrian dies and is succeeded by Antoninus Pius. North of Hadrian's Wall the Antonine Wall is built across what is now Scotland.

142 Hadrian's Wall is abandoned by the Romans.

150–163 There is a revolt against Rome in northern Britain and the Antonine Wall is also abandoned.

161 Antoninus Pius dies and Marcus Aurelius and Lucius Verus become co-rulers of Rome.

162–6 The Parthian War

167 Germanic tribes, the Quadi and the Marcomanni, cross the Danube to raid Roman settlements. Some raids reach northern Italy.

167–80 Marcus Aurelius successfully conducts his wars in Germany.

180 Marcus Aurelius, the 'philosopher emperor', dies before his work is finished, and is succeeded by his son.

192 Commodus is assassinated and Pertinax is proclaimed emperor in Rome. A civil war begins.

193 Pertinax is murdered, his successor, Didus Julinus, is killed, and Septimius Severus becomes emperor.

193–211 In addition to campaigning against the Parthians, Mesopotamia is added to the empire.

211 Septimius Severus dies in York in Britain. The empire is divided between his two sons, Caracalla and Geta. Caracalla murders Geta the same year.

212 Rome grants citizenship to all free men in the empire, no matter where they were born or live. This is the Antonine Constitution.

▼ *Marcus Aurelius, the philosopher emperor, was more at home with his books and his writing than he was on campaign.*

ANARCHY AND DISINTEGRATION

The story of the emperors of Rome is a combination of extraordinary national leaders, and complete incompetents who eventually led the western Roman Empire to ruin.

Highs and Lows

Emperor Vespasian (70–9AD), who assumed the purple at the end of the year of the Four Emperors, was not only a skilled and popular general, but a wise and competent emperor. His son Titus (79–81AD), who followed him, was also a competent commander and emperor. Trajan, who ruled from 98–117AD was the last of the Roman conquerors, and his campaigns against the Dacians were successful. Marcus Aurelius (161–80 AD), the philosopher emperor was also an effective administrator and ruler, but after his death, the empire started on a slow decline that would also, fortunately, have a few shining stars left in the pantheon of outstanding Roman emperors. Constantine I, also known as 'the Great' (306–37AD) had to fight a civil war to win his throne, and he also set the stage for Roman survival with the establishment, in the east, of Constantinople. Unfortunately, these men were exceptions, and not the rule.

Within the space of a single century, 27 military officers proclaimed themselves emperors and reigned over parts of the empire for months or days, all but two meeting with a violent end. The time was characterised by a Roman army that was as likely to be fighting itself as fighting an outside invader. This in-fighting reached a low point around 258AD. Ironically, while it was these usurpations that led to the break up of the empire during the crisis, it was the strength of several frontier generals that helped reunite the empire, at least partially, through force of arms. Interestingly, the political capital of the western empire was not always Rome; it moved first to Milan, and finally to Ravenna, though the city of Rome would always be the cultural heart of the western empire.

The Crisis of the 3rd Century

The 3rd century was a dark time for the Roman Empire. Emperors were assassinated in a string of attacks from within, and every emperor that assumed the throne must have felt how shaky the crown was on his head. During this time, encroachments along the empire's borders increased, and a state of anarchy became the norm in Rome. Emperors changed thrones as one would change daily clothing and at least 30 men, competent or not (and most of them did not have a chance to demonstrate competence as their reign was so short), wore the purple during this period.

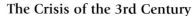

◀ *After his military successes in Palestine, Titus, the son of the emperor Vespasian, was given a 'triumph' in Rome, parading the spoils he had taken from Jerusalem. He would succeed his father as emperor.*

▲ *A Roman gold coin, the solidus, with the image of Emperor Julian the Apostate. Julian apparently wears a cuirass and military cloak.*

▲ *A Sassanian relief of the surrender and debasing of the Emperor Valerian in 260AD by Sassanid King Shapur I. Valerian was the only Roman emperor to be captured in action.*

The Struggle with the Sassanid Empire (226–372AD)

The Parthian monarchy was defeated and overthrown by the Sassanian Persians in 226AD. The Sassanians (or Sassanids) were a formidable power in the east until 649AD and were never conquered by the Romans. The Sassanians captured the emperor Valerian in 260AD, but the Romans campaigned successfully in the east and recaptured the Mesopotamian provinces in 297AD. This would be followed by Emperor Julian being killed in the east, which prompted the transfer of Roman units eastwards in an attempt to reinforce those units already in position.

As various barbarian peoples invaded the western empire during the 4th century the Roman northern frontier was overrun by 410AD, and the problem of the Persians passed to the eastern empire. They remained as Rome's enemies until 649AD when they were defeated by Islamic forces.

The Collapse of the Western Empire (402–76AD)

The western Roman Empire collapsed under the repeated blows from barbarian tribes and armies that were migrating from the east. Successive groups of Germanic peoples, searching both for land on which to live, and to escape nomadic tribes pushing them westwards, first sought shelter in the lands of the empire, and provided troops to the Roman army.

At this point, the Roman army was no longer the strong, well-trained and disciplined infantry legions of the height of the empire. Legions were still in existence, but they were only about 1,000 strong, whereas the old legions had been of 5,000 well-armed and equipped infantry. Old habits were sometimes there, as well as titles and ranks, but the traditional Roman infantry army no longer existed, especially after the Battle of Adrianople in 378AD, and the defeat of the Roman infantry by the Gothic cavalry.

The Goths (who eventually divided into the Visigoths and Ostrogoths), Vandals, Huns, Lombards and others gradually won territories in the western empire. They were, however, turned back from the eastern empire, whose leaders understood what was happening and were determined to survive intact. Barbarian chieftains were carving out their own kingdoms from the wreck of the western empire, and would turn to fight each other, or ally themselves with capable Roman commanders who would fight for the empire and sometimes win, as Aetius did against Attila the Hun. However, when Odoacer overthrew the last Roman emperor, Romulus Augustus, and sat on the throne of the Caesars, the western empire was finished.

▼ *The last Roman emperor in the west, Romulus Augustus, abdicating to Odoacer after the fall of Rome in 476AD. Romulus spent the rest of his life in retirement.*

THE FALL OF THE WESTERN EMPIRE
TIMELINE 217–476AD

217–38 After a string of imperial assassinations, there is anarchy in Rome and the empire for about 50 years. During this time, there are at least 30 emperors in Rome.

230 Mesopotamia is invaded by the Sassanid Persians, but they are then defeated in 233 by Alexander Severus.

235 Soldiers loyal to Julius Maximus assassinate Emperor Alexander, starting a 50-year long civil war.

244 The new king of Persia, Shapur, begins a war with Rome in the east. Roman emperor, Gordian, is assassinated by his own troops on campaign against the Persians.

249 Decius rebels against Emperor Philip the Arab, who is killed in action, Decius becomes emperor.

251 Emperor Decius is killed in action against the Goths, the first Roman emperor to be killed in action.

260 The administrative capital of the empire is moved north to Milan. The Emperor Valerian is captured and humiliated by the Persians.

261 Odenathus, king of Palmyra, attacks and defeats Sassanians as

▼ Diocletian was one of the few fortunate Roman emperors who was able to abdicate and plan his retirement. He built a huge palace and fortress for himself in what is now Split, Croatia, parts of which still stands.

▲ The spectacular ruined city of Palmyra, Syria. The city was at its height in the 3rd century AD but fell into decline when the Romans captured its queen, Zenobia, after she declared independence from Rome in 271.

Rome's ally. He then annexes Anatolia, Arabia and Armenia for Palmyra.

266 Odenathus is assassinated, Zenobia, his queen, succeeds as ruler of Palmyra.

269 Zenobia attacks and conquers Egypt and expells the Roman governor.

270 Emperor Claudius II dies of plague. The Roman army nominates Aurelian as his successor. Aurelian begins to rebuild the walls of Rome.

271–4 Campaigning energetically, Aurelian attacks and defeats the invading Germans. He then campaigns against Zenobia in Syria, taking and

destroying Palmyra. He brings Zenobia to Rome, quelling the eastern rebellion and reuniting the empire. Turning against the rampaging Gauls, Aurelian defeats them and supervises new fortifications for Rome. Unfortunately, he is murdered by his officers.

276–84 Probus defeats the Alamanni and the Franks in his campaigns in Gaul as well as the Burgundians and the Vandals. He also campaigns in both Asia and North Africa, defeating various bands of nomads and bandits, but in his turn is murdered by the praetorian prefect Carus. Carus is struck by lightning on campaign in Persia and his son Carinus is probably murdered as the Romans retreat. The commander of the bodyguard, Diocles, is proclaimed emperor by the army and takes the name Diocletian.

285 Diocletian becomes emperor and begins a co-rulership with Maximian.

286 The empire is divided between east and west in Diocletian's reforms.

293 A 'tetrarchy' (rule of four) is established, with Constantius I and Galerius being appointed 'Caesars'.

▼ Constantine became emperor after his victory at the Milvian Bridge outside Rome. He claimed that he saw a divine vision that foretold his coming victory, and eventually made Christianity the state religion.

▲ *Ravenna became the capital of the western empire, relegating Rome to second city status. The mosaics here, from the 4th and 5th centuries, depict Galla Placidia, daughter of Theodosius I and mother of Valentinian.*

297–8 Another war erupts in Persia, and Rome makes gains in the east.
305 Both Diocletian and Maximian retire from ruling the empire.
306 Constantine I becomes emperor after the death of his father Constantius. Civil War follows and Maxentius claims to be sole emperor.
312 Constantine defeats Maxentius at the Battle of the Milvian Bridge.
313 Religious tolerance is granted by Constantine with his Edict of Milan.
324 Constantinople is founded by Constantine and becomes the capital of the eastern empire. Constantine is now sole ruler of the Roman empire.
337 Constantine dies and divides the empire among his sons; Constantine II, Constantius and Constans, who for a while ruled jointly.
364 Valens and Valentinian I are proclaimed co-emperors in east and west.
375 Valentinian I dies of a stroke.
378 Valens is defeated and killed at Adrianople by the Goths.
379 Theodosius I becomes sole emperor of the Romans and is the last emperor to rule both east and west.
394 Theodosius 'the Great' defeats both of his rivals for the throne, Eugenius and Arbogast, at the Frigidus

▲ *A depiction of an incident during the Hunnish incursions into Roman territory: Pope Leo I courageously going out unarmed to face Attila the Hun and persuading him to leave Italy.*

River, on the eastern border of Italy.
395 Theodosius dies and the empire is divided between his sons, Arcadius and Honourius.
404 The western capital of the empire is moved to the city of Ravenna.
406 Trier, the capital of Roman Gaul, is sacked by Germans raiding across the Rhine.
410 Rome orders the last troops stationed in Britain to return home. Alaric leads his Visigoth raiders into Italy and Rome is taken and sacked.
421 Constantine III is now the ruler of the western empire.

425 Valentinian III becomes the western emperor.
434 Attila becomes 'King of the Huns'.
439 Vandals, moving into North Africa, raid and capture Carthage.
446 The Romano-Celts appeal to Rome for help against the barbarians. No support is sent, the Romano-Celts are on their own.
451 The Roman general Aetius meets and defeat Attila at Chalons.
452 Attila invades Italy but his invasion is halted by the Pope, Leo I.
476 The western empire falls. The last emperor, Romulus Augustus, is deposed by Odoacer.

▼ *Roman general Aetius, who defeated Attila at the Battle of Chalons in 451AD, is shown here forcing Clovis 'the long-haired', King of the Franks, into a retreat across a river.*

THE EASTERN ROMAN EMPIRE

While either Byzantium or the Byzantine Empire are common terms in modern historical usage for the eastern empire that outlasted the western Roman Empire for one thousand years, the rulers, soldiers, and citizens of that empire did not use those terms to define themselves. They were the direct inheritors of the Roman civilization and empire, and they thought of themselves as Romans and considered their empire as the eastern Roman empire. In this study the term that shall be used is the eastern Romans, for that is what they called themselves. They even referred to their empire sometimes as 'Romania'. The term 'Byzantine' did not come into common usage until the 16th century, and then only in the west. It was a product of historical misunderstanding of who the eastern Romans were.

Capital of the East

The beginnings of the Eastern Roman Empire can be traced to the founding and establishment of the city of Constantinople by Constantine the Great in the 4th century AD. The spot chosen by Constantine was a strategic position near the Black Sea at a choke point where the Black Sea empties into the Mediterranean Sea. A tiny village, Byzantia, was nearby (and quite probably this is where the terms Byzantine and Byzantium come from), but Constantine chose to name the new city after himself.

Initially, the eastern part of the empire was administered from Rome, but as the city of Constantinople grew in importance, the decision was made to govern the eastern half of the empire from that city. What grew from that decision was in fact two distinct empires under the title of 'Roman'.

The eastern Romans were serious about the study of warfare and they waged a deadly version of it, for every time they took the field the empire was in jeopardy. Constantinople was often besieged during the empire's life and – safe behind its walls with solid troops to defend it – it defeated most attempts to take the city. There were two exceptions. The European armies of the 4th Crusade turned on their Christian fellows and assaulted and

▲ *This modern view of the position of the city of Constantinople (now Istanbul, Turkey) shows the Golden Horn, an inlet of the Bosphorus and the world's largest harbour, which enhanced the city's defensive capacity.*

took the city in 1204, establishing a Latin kingdom that lasted a mere 60 years, the eastern Romans re-establishing what was left of their empire after throwing the invaders out. The second time Constantinople fell was the last, in 1453, when the ancient walls that had defended the city for so long were at last breached by the cannon of the Ottomans.

Eastern Dynastic Rule

Like their western counterparts, the eastern Roman emperors were not from one continuous ruling family from the late 4th century until 1453, but from many. At least 15 different families, or dynasties, produced emperors for the eastern empire, three of them before Rome fell in 476AD (Constantinian 306–63AD, Valentinian 364–79AD and Theodosian 379–457AD). During the fall the

▲ *Remnants of the Colossus of Constantine I, thought to have been created in the emperor's lifetime, show an element of portraiture, with a hooked nose, deep jaw and prominent chin, all thought to be his facial characteristics.*

Eastern Dynasties

The eastern Roman dynasties after the fall of the west were:
Justinian (518–602)
Heraclian (610–711)
Isaurian (717–802)
Nikephoros (802–13)
Amorian (820–67)
Macedonian (867–1056)
Comnenian (1057–9)
Doukid (1059–81)
Comnenian (1081–1185)
Angelid (1185–1204)
Paleologus (1261–1453)

▶ *The magnificent Theodosian walls of Constantinople are currently being restored to their former magnificence in certain areas. Certainly some of the most beautiful fortifications ever built, they were also famous for their strength.*

Leonid dynasty was in power, (457–518AD), and from then onwards 11 different dynastic families ruled. There were five non-dynastic periods (363–4, 602–10, 711–17, 813–20, and 1056–7). One dynasty, the Latin emperors (1204–61), was western and ruled for the short period after the 4th Crusade took Constantinople.

Emperor Justinian

There were several outstanding eastern Roman emperors, the best of the early emperors being Justinian I (527–65), who surely deserves the title 'the Great', though it has not been given to him by history. Under his just and generally wise rule, an outstanding code of laws was written and promulgated, and large amounts of territory belonging to the western empire were reconquered by his two famous generals, Belisarius and Narses.

Belisarius, born to Thracian peasant stock, and Narses, a eunuch from the emperor's household, apparently the eastern Roman equivalent of a grand chamberlain, and, it would seem without prior military experience, proved themselves to be capable generals and superior to those they faced. Belisarius, though virtually unknown and not often studied in western military history, is one of the most successful generals in history.

▲ *The interior of the ancient Roman water reservoir in Constantinople. Built by Constantine, it was a valuable water source for the city, especially during the numerous sieges the population endured.*

It is noteworthy that from Justinian's assumption of the throne in Constantinople in 527 until the apocalyptic defeat at Manzikert in 1071, eastern Roman generals were almost uniformly successful against a string of enemies. Additionally, this period was one of almost constant

warfare, sometimes against more than one opponent at a time. The eastern Roman Empire, though largely ignored in western historiography is eminently worthy of study. The empire's navy virtually ruled the Mediterranean, the organization and employment of the empire's army was decidedly modern, and many, if not most, of that army's successes and victories were gained despite being outnumbered.

Emperors Maurice and Heraclius

Maurice (582–602) is famous for his military treatise, *Strategikon*, and was another forward-looking and just emperor, as well as an excellent soldier. Heraclius (610–41) was another soldier-emperor who campaigned successfully in the eastern lands of the empire. Under his rule the theme system, a way of organizing manpower

structured on the empire's provinces, or themes, was expanded and firmly established. This gave the eastern Roman army the redoubtable, native-born soldiery from Asia Minor that defended the empire until it was mostly destroyed by careless emperors, inward-looking bureaucrats, and the inept commanders at Manzikert.

Basil the Bulgar-slayer

Another formidable eastern emperor, Basil II (963–1025) led an eastern Roman military resurgence that held the borders, gained back lost ground, and virtually ended the Bulgarian

▼ *Basil II (963–1025) was the last of the great Eastern Roman emperors, pictured here in full or parade armour. Effective, ruthless, and an excellent general, the Roman army under his control was at its peak of efficiency.*

▲ *The figure with the halo in this mosaic is the emperor Justinian I, one of the greatest of eastern Roman emperors. He is pictured here in court dress, as is his able general, Belisarius, standing to the emperor's right.*

▼ *Alexis I Comnenus brought order out of chaos, ending ten years of civil war after the defeat at Manzikert in 1071. A competent general and an excellent emperor, he gained back for the empire much of what had been lost by his immediate predecessors.*

threat from the north. Basil became known as the 'Bulgar-slayer' for his contemptuous treatment of captured Bulgarian prisoners, but he was known as a wise and just ruler, as well as ruthless general.

The Comnenus Dynasty

Alexis I Comnenus (1081–1118) founded the last dynasty that ruled over the last eastern Roman resurgence. Emperor during the 1st Crusade from the west, he used that opportunity to gain back territory lost to the Turks.

Lastly, though he ruled for only five years, and was the last of the eastern emperors, Constantine XI Paleologus, deserves mention. The empire he inherited was an empire in name only, its lands shrunken because of foreign encroachment and conquest, yet he died fighting, sword in hand, either on the walls or in the last breach in the walls made by the Ottoman artillery. Fittingly, he was also a Constantine, a name which connected him to the great founder of his capital.

As for the myriad other emperors, some were competent, some were not, and in their ranks were scholars, scoundrels, usurpers, murderers and saints. Together they make a fascinating study, ruling as they did over an empire that allowed the chaos in the west after the fall of Rome to dissipate, and granted time for the nations of western Europe to form.

Eastern Legacy

It can be argued that perhaps the most enduring legacy of the eastern Roman Empire was that, not by design or long term strategy, they succeeded in keeping the Muslim or Turkish enemies in the east out of central and western Europe until those regions could properly defend themselves. Ultimately the Byzantine emperors acted as the bulwark against an aggressive Islam that was bent on ever-expanding western conquest. By the time the Ottomans finally took Constantinople, however, and ended the eastern Roman Empire in fire and rubble, the nations of the west were ready to take on the Muslim onslaught.

▲ *The entrance of the Ottoman Mehmet II into Constantinople on 29 May 1453 after his troops had stormed and taken the city. He ordered that Emperor Constantine XI be brought to him, but the body of the last eastern Roman emperor was never found, and was probably buried in a mass grave.*

▼ *Michael III, sometimes referred to as 'the Drunkard' was the last of the Amorian or Phrygian dynasty to rule the eastern Roman Empire. He is shown in this illustration with Basil of Macedonia, who later had Michael assassinated and took the purple for himself, beginning the Macedonian dynasty.*

THE EASTERN ROMAN ARMY

After the defeat at Adrianople, the eastern Roman army developed along different lines from the old Roman army, although initially it inherited the training standards, discipline, and organizational traditions of the western Roman armies. Eventually, the organization of the eastern Roman army was superior to its many enemies and that was one of the reasons for its many successes on the battlefield. The main striking arm of the eastern Roman army was to be the cavalry, and not the infantry. The army still contained well-trained, disciplined and well equipped infantry, but the eastern Roman cavalry, especially after the introduction of the stirrup, was the key offensive arm of the army.

▼ *This illustrates the building blocks of the thema, the Eastern Roman equivalent of the modern division. There were ten kentoubernia in each kentarchiai, two kentarchia in each bandon, two bandon in each droungai, six droungai in each tourma, and four tourma in each thema, the thema making up the imperial tagmata. It was a very flexible unit, which gave the eastern Romans an organizational advantage over its enemies.*

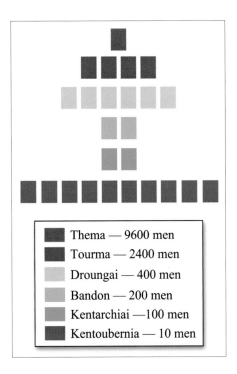

| Thema — 9600 men |
| Tourma — 2400 men |
| Droungai — 400 men |
| Bandon — 200 men |
| Kentarchiai —100 men |
| Kentoubernia — 10 men |

▲ *Belisarius in battle against the Goths in Italy (535–40). Belisarius was always loyal, but Justinian was suspicious of any general who was highly popular with his troops.*

Themes

At its height the eastern Roman Empire was organized in themes, especially in Asia Minor, the empire's best recruiting ground. The themes were organized so as to be both administrative entities and territories to be defended from outside incursions. The themes were in essence military provinces and in 950AD, for example, there were 17 themes in Asia Minor, mainly Anatolia, but also in Armenia, Cappadocia, Isauria and in Thrace.

The strength of the themes were based on the needs of the empire or province, and were not uniform, with the outlying or border themes being the strongest, perhaps having as many as 8,000–12,000 troops. The interior themes might field half as many.

Cavalry

Recognizing that cavalry would be the decisive arm and adapting themselves to the peoples and armies that they would undoubtedly have to fight, the eastern Romans developed a cavalry arm, based on the heavily armoured and armed cataphract and the deadly horse archer, so effectively used by eastern peoples.

The basic unit of eastern Roman cavalry was called the banner. Its strength could vary between 50 and 400 troopers. Three banners would make up a drounga, and three droungai, each of 150 or more cavalrymen, made up a tourma of 450 troopers or greater (depending on the initial strength of the banner). Three tourmai made up a tagma of at least 1,350 horsemen. Three or more tourmai made up the stratos, or army. Logically based on units of three from the banner upwards, the tourma and stratos were tactically very flexible. One eastern Roman commander is supposedly have stated that 5,000 cavalrymen and the help of God was all an eastern Roman general needed to be successful in combat.

Individual units were identified by their flags, which would be close to the modern guidon, but with at least three coloured tails, not merely two as in the modern equivalent. The unit emblems in the solid portion of the flag next to the staff would sometimes, if not always, be composed of geometric figures in a specific design, and both the design and colours would represent which unit was present. Supposedly, the troopers in the units might wear coloured horsehair plumes from the top of their helmets in the same colour as that of their banners for identification purposes.

▲ The eastern Roman navy was unchallenged at sea for most of its existence. Here, in 678AD, they use their much feared Greek fire to attack and destroy a Muslim fleet.

The Navy

Eastern Romans were very aware of the potential of naval power and through the 10th and 11th centuries their navy was dominant in the Mediterranean. Their well-designed and capably crewed galleys, the dromons, were armed with the dangerous and lethal Greek fire, which was pumped from inside the galley to a tube on the bow and used as a flame-thrower to project burning fuel on to enemy warships. A highly volatile mix, it could not be extinguished with water and some accounts hint that sea water might have fed the flames on target.

The navy also gave eastern Roman field commanders great strategic mobility, enabling the swift movement and concentration of eastern Roman armies to either reconquer former territory in Italy, Spain and North Africa, or to project eastern Roman power where needed.

Strategy and Tactics

Eastern Roman generals studied warfare and their foes: 'know your enemy' was a truism for them. This study would dictate both eastern Roman strategy and the tactics of the field armies when they encountered their opponents. Asian horsemen from the steppes would be attacked during the winter months as their horses would be ill-fed from a hard winter and were in no shape to fight the tourmai. Other tribesmen, who relied on ambush and fighting in bogs and swamps that they knew intimately, could also be effectively handled in the winter when those obstacles would be frozen. Those enemies who hailed from hot regions and desert locales could be attacked successfully in inclement weather, which desert dwellers were not accustomed to.

The eastern Roman armies were professional, well-trained, and struck with a ruthlessness that would sometimes cow their enemies into either retreat or a treaty advantageous to Constantinople. Many of their successful generals later became emperor and waged war with a seriousness not seen again until Napoleon. Where force failed to earn a favourable outcome, the eastern Romans might either bribe an enemy to leave their territory or sign a truce until a more favourable outcome was possible. The navy would work in concert with the army against their enemies. If the army was faced with defeat and retreat, the eastern Roman navy might raid the enemy's coast unexpectedly, which could force their army to suddenly retreat and return home. Roman strategy was not always to achieve complete defeat of an enemy, but to preserve the empire and as much of its territory as possible. Their strategy was not always defensive, and aggressive wars of conquest were also waged. And knowingly or not, the eastern Romans served as a bulwark, preventing a European Islamic conquest that would have changed the course of history.

▼ Eastern Roman heavy cavalry (cataphracts) pursue their Muslim enemies in a scene taken from the Greek Scylitzes (or Skylitzes) Chronicle, of the 11th century.

CAMPAIGNS OF THE EASTERN EMPIRE

Of the many enemies the eastern Romans faced through the centuries (Bulgars, Avars, Slavs, Russians, Magyars, Normans and Lombards) none were more deadly than the resurgent Arabs after their conversion to Islam in the 6th and 7th centuries AD. They were called to holy war (jihad) to convert the uninitiated to their new religion, whether people wished to convert or not. The eastern Romans met this new threat with all the skill and professionalism that they met any enemy, but gradually the empire was shrinking from the Muslim conquests, It may be, however, that a schism that developed in the religion between Sunni and Shi'a put at least a temporary halt to the continuous invasions and raids, and gave the eastern Romans a breathing spell.

A more deadly Muslim enemy, the Ottomans, were bent on European conquest and above all on taking the city of Constantinople. This they eventually did in 1453, destroying an empire that stretched back for over

▼ *A medieval depiction of the 1453 siege of Constantinople by the Ottomans. The view of the city is stylized, but the strength of the city's defences is not underestimated.*

2,000 years. Fittingly, the last eastern Roman emperor, Constantine XI, died on the walls of Constantinople defending his city, sword and shield in hand, fighting to his last breath. Whatever his worth to the greatly shrunken empire, at the end he proved himself to be as worthy as Basil the Bulgar-Slayer, Heraclius, and even perhaps Belisarius.

Persian Wars (502–628AD)

The Persian Empire that the Romans initially faced before the fall of the west was a succession of different peoples and dynasties (Scythians, Parthians, Sassanians) that generally either ruled or held sway where the Persians and allied or subject peoples

▲ *A depiction of the Battle of Bulgarophygon in 896AD, which resulted in a resounding victory for the Bulgars, and left the eastern Roman army completely destroyed.*

had always been located. Their armies were usually composed of horse archers and heavy cavalry (cataphracts) and the western Romans never conquered them.

The Persian wars of the eastern Romans were fought with a new Roman army that was adapted to fight against the mounted armies of the east. The eastern Roman cavalry became much more proficient with the introduction of the stirrup in the 6th century. Both empires were equally strong during the height of their almost continuous struggles for supremacy in the east, but the Persians were so weakened by this constant warfare with the eastern Romans that with the rise of the Muslim threat they finally succumbed to that onslaught.

The series of wars with Persia was exhausting for both empires. The two opposing forces were evenly matched on land, and territory changed hands repeatedly. Despite numerous ceasefires and peace treaties, the empires continually clashed over territory, weakening them both, the Persian Empire especially. With the unexpectedly fierce onslaught of the Arab Muslim threat, the Persian Empire went under, and finally became part of the greater Muslim territories.

Meanwhile, the eastern Romans held on, sometimes gaining and sometimes losing to first the Arabs and then the Turks.

The Wars against the Muslims (780–1180AD)

The rise of Mohammed, soldier and self-proclaimed prophet of a new and warlike religion, was the greatest danger ever faced by the eastern Romans. Religious fervour and a united, warlike Arab juggernaut swept through the Middle East, North Africa and across the Pillars of Hercules and into Spain. The invasion was stopped in France by Charles Martel at Tours in 732AD, which marked the extent of their western Europe conquests.

After losing territory to the Muslim onslaught, the eastern Romans rallied and made inroads into the Muslim conquests. And, while the Muslim Arabs were trumped in some of the areas under conflict, they were soon to be replaced or overcome by another, more deadly Muslim threat, the Turks.

Victory over the Bulgars (971–1018)

The kingdom of the Bulgars was a belligerent neighbour to the north of the empire. Continuous confrontations and wars with this aggressive Slavic

▲ *The taking and sack of Constantinople by the western Europeans of the 4th Crusade is one of the worst examples of treachery in the history of warfare.*

neighbour finally resulted in the devastating campaign by Emperor Basil which ended the Bulgarian threat.

The 4th Crusade (1198–1204AD)

This western European effort, supposedly aimed at the Holy Land and the Turks or Saracens, ended up as a campaign to take Constantinople. The eastern Roman Empire being

nothing like what it was before fell to the crusaders' assault, supported by the Venetians. The westerners established a short-lived Latin empire that lasted but 60 years and fell to resurgent eastern Romans who re-established what they could of the once-powerful empire.

The Fall of Constantinople, 1453

The Turkish Ottomans were a resurgent Muslim-inspired people whose predecessors had defeated the eastern Romans in the disastrous Battle of Manzikert in 1071, virtually destroying the old eastern Roman army.

They continuously attacked the empire and besieged Constantinople four times. After failing to breach the walls and defences and failing three consecutive times, the Ottomans under Mehmet II were successful in the final, overwhelming attempt in 1453. The Ottomans finally found the weapon to breach Constantinople's famous defences; gunpowder artillery. Constantinople finally went under fighting hard. It would not be until 1571, at the naval battle of Lepanto, that the Ottomans would finally be checked. Their last attempt to take Vienna was defeated in 1683 by a coalition of Christian powers.

▼ *Mehmet II's successful Siege of Constantinople in 1453 was masterly and determined, and his skilful use of artillery helped to bring about the city's fall.*

EASTERN ROMAN EMPIRE TIMELINE
324–1453

324 Founding of Constantinople by Constantine I (the Great).

325 New defensive walls are built.

378 The Battle of Adrianople is fought between Valens' eastern Roman army and the Goths.

423 The Theodosian walls, larger and stronger, are completed around the city of Constantinople.

474 Emperor Zeno recognizes the legitimacy of Vandal rule in North Africa.

488 Zeno orders the king of the Goths, Theodoric, to reconquer Italy.

502 War with the Persians.

506 Truce signed with the Persians for seven years.

507 Byzantine navy raids Italy. The Byzantine fleet goes largely unchallenged at sea.

525 War breaks out again with the Persians, who invade Spain and occupy a large part of the peninsula.

527 Justinian I becomes eastern Roman Emperor.

533 Belisarius, Juntinian's finest general, reconquers North Africa from the Vandals. Eastern Romans and the Persians sign the 'Endless Peace'.

▼ *This mosaic is an inaccurate portrayal of Constantine as there is no evidence that he ever wore a beard.*

535 Justinian invades Italy with armies commanded by Belisarius and Mundus. Sicily is taken and Illyricum is also occupied.

536 Belisarius defeats a rebellion in North Africa. He takes his army to Italy and captures Naples.

537–8 Siege and battle for Rome.

540 The Goths try to bribe Belisarius by offering him the title King of the Goths and of Italy. Belisarius refuses, defeats the Goths and leaves Italy.

542 The eastern Romans are defeated at the Battle of the Mugello. Belisarius takes the war to the Persians who retreat to Persia.

544 Belisarius is sent back to Italy to deal with the Goths.

549 The eastern Romans are again at war with Persia.

551–5 Narses is given the Italian command and defeats the Goths at the Battle of Taginae. Spain is again invaded by the eastern Romans. The Goths surrender in Italy and Cartagena is taken in Spain.

561 The eastern Romans and the Persians sign a peace treaty. The conquest of Italy is completed.

565 The death of Belisarius, followed by his emperor eight months later.

602 Maurice writes the *Strategikon*, one of the military treatises of the eastern Roman Empire. Eastern territory in Asia Minor is attacked by the Sassanians.

▲ *The fortifications of Constantinople after a modern restoration. The layered construction of the fortification was a mighty obstacle for any army to face and attempt to overcome.*

610 Heraclius I becomes emperor by overthrowing the usurper Phocas.

614 Jerusalem is captured by the Sassanians.

619 Egypt is overrun and conquered by the Sassanians.

621 Eastern Roman territory in Spain is conquered by the resurgent Visigoths.

624–9 The Persians and Avars lay siege

▼ *Belisarius and Justinian's relationship was not always this cordial, especially under the influence of Theodora, who detested Belisarius.*

to Constantinople. The siege fails.
626 Sassanians besiege Constantinople.
627 Heraclius takes the strategic offensive and defeats Sassanian king, Khusrau II, at the Battle of Nineveh.
628 Syria is reconquered from the Sassanians by the eastern Romans.
633–50 Eastern Roman possessions in Syria and Egypt are lost to the Arabs.
636 Inspired by their newly adopted faith, Arab armies invade and conquer Syria and Palestine.
639 The Muslim offensive moves into the eastern empire's southern themes.
668–77 Arab siege of Constantinople begins. The siege is unsuccessful.
680 Constantine IV's campaign against the Bulgars ends in defeat, forcing the empire to recognize the establishment of Bulgaria in Moesia.
688–9 The Balkan campaign of Justinian II secures the coastline between Thrace and Macedonia.
697 Carthage falls to the Muslims.
714 The second unsuccessful siege of Constantinople by the Arabs begins.
718 The Muslims besiege Constantinople but Leo III holds it.
741–52 Constantine V takes advantage of Muslim disunity and civil war and recovers Cyprus and Armenia.
8⌐3–17 The Bulgars capture of Sofia begins the Bulgar Wars. After suffering

▲ *The Emperor Theophilus orders the Eparch of Constantinople to execute the accomplices of Michael III. Poisoning, blinding, castration, and exile was the fate of many in the ruling circle of a former emperor.*

▼ *An excellent depiction of an eastern Roman soldier in the 13th century. The helmet with aventail (armoured veil covering the back of the neck) is particularly accurate.*

defeats at Pliska (811) and Versinikia, as well as major Bulgar raids into eastern Thrace, Leo V the Armenian (who became emperor in 813) defeats the Bulgars at Mesembria, securing a 30-year peace.
813 Leo V adds an outer wall to the defences of Constantinople. Krum the Bulgar besieges the city and fails.
860 The Russians lay siege to Constantinople. It fails.
867 Basil I becomes emperor, founding the Macedonian dynasty.
879 Cappadocia is reconquered from the Muslims by Basil I.
894–6 War with the Bulgars erupts again over trade rights. Bulgars under Tsar Simeon win an overwhelming victory at the battle of Bulgaroyphon. The eastern Romans agree to pay tribute and restore the market for Bulgarian goods to Constantinople.
895 Emperor Leo VI writes his famous *Tactica*, another of the eastern Roman military treatises.
963–69 *The Composition on Warfare* is written while Nikeforos Phocas and Basil II are co-rulers.
968 Syria is retaken by Nicephorus II and the Muslim threat recedes.
976–1025 Basil II, nicknamed the Bulgar-Slayer, humiliatingly defeats the army of the Bulgar king at the Battle of Kleidion in 1014.
1018 Bulgaria is defeated and annexed by Basil II, under whose rule the eastern empire reaches its zenith.
1071 The Battle of Manzikert results in the destruction of the old eastern Roman army.
1081–1118 The reign of Alexis I.

1122–6 War with Venice.
1143–80 Military expeditions against the Seljuk Turks result in a treaty favourable to Constantinople. War with Venice ends with no clear victory.
1204 The 4th Crusade takes Constantinople. The Latin Kingdom is established.
1261 The Latin Kingdom is destroyed and the eastern Roman Empire is restored.
1263 Eastern Romans are defeated by the Achaeans at the Battle of Prinitza but the Bulgarian Black Sea ports of Mesembria (Nessebur), Anchialus (Pomorie), Sozopol and Develtus (Bourgas) are won by the Romans.
1281–5 War with Venice.
1329 Eastern Romans lose Anatolia to the Ottoman Turks because of defeats at Pelekanon and Philokrene.
1345–51 Extensive repairs to the walls of Constantinople, including the sea walls.
1373–85 Civil war in the empire based on dynastic problems.
1396 Constantinople is besieged by Bayzeid the Thunderbolt. He fails.
1402 and **1422** Ottoman sieges of Constantinople. Both fail.
1430 Ottomans retake Thessalonika.
1444 Battle of Varna.
1453 Ottomans under Mehmet II besiege, and finally breach, the great walls, and take Constantinople.

WESTERN ROMAN EMPERORS

▲ *Augustus was a firm and just ruler who set a fine example for his successors on how to rule, which sadly most failed to follow.*

31BC–14AD Augustus became the first emperor with the agreement of the Senate; at his death he was rumoured to have been poisoned.

14–37 Tiberius, died of natural causes.

37–41 Caligula, murdered.

41–54 Claudius, poisoned.

54–68 Nero, committed suicide.

68–9 Galba, murdered by the Praetorian Guard.

69 Otho, committed suicide.

69 Vitellius, murdered by Vespasian's troops.

69–79 Vespasian, made emperor by the

▼ *Hadrian was a conscientious emperor who travelled the length and breadth of his empire.*

army, ruled well and justly, died of natural causes.

79–81 Titus, son of Vespasian, unfortunately died of malaria just two years into his reign.

81–96 Domitian, assassinated.

96–8 Nerva, the first of the 'five good emperors'. He died of natural causes.

98–117 Trajan, conqueror of Dacia. He died of a stroke.

117–138 Hadrian, travelled the empire and built the famous wall across the north of Britain. Died of disease.

138–161 Antoninus Pius, his reign was the most peaceful of the principate. He died of natural causes.

161–180 Marcus Aurelius* successfully campaigned against the Germans. Died from natural causes.

161–9 Lucius Verus*, co-emperor with Marcus Aurelius. Died a victim of the plague.

180–92 Commodus*, strangled.

193 Pertinax, murdered by the Praetorian Guard.

193 Didius Julianus, murdered by order of the Senate.

193 Pescennius Niger, captured and executed.

193–7 Clodius Albinus, committed suicide.

193–211 Septimius Severus, seized power with the support of the army, died of natural causes.

211–17 Caracalla*, murdered.

211–12 Geta*, murdered by Caracalla.

217–18 Macrinus*, murdered.

217–18 Diadumenian*, executed.

218–22 Elagabalus, murdered.

222–35 Severus Alexander, murdered by the army.

235–8 Maximinus Thrax, assassinated.

238 Gordian I*, committed suicide.

238 Gordian II*, killed in action.

238 Balbinus*, murdered by Praetorians.

238 Pupienus*, ruled with Balbinus for just three months, murdered by Praetorians.

238–44 Gordian III, suspected to have ben murdered.

▲ *The equestrian statue of Marcus Aurelius definitively demonstrates to posterity the regal nature of the philosopher emperor.*

244–9 Philip I (also known as 'the Arab')* killed in action.

247–9 Philip II*.

249–51 Trajan Decius* killed in action.

251–3 Trebonianus* murdered by his own troops.

251 Hostilian* victim of the plague.

251–3 Volusian, murdered.

253 Aemilian, assassinated.

253–60 Valerian* died in captivity.

253–68 Gallienus* murdered.

259–68 Postumus** murdered by troops.

268 Laelianus**, murdered by Postumus.

268–9 Marius**, murdered by soldiers.

269–70 Victorinus**, assassinated by one of his officers.

270–3 Tetricus**, died of natural causes.

268–70 Claudius II***, died of the plague.

270 Quintillus, brother of Claudius II, murdered or committed suicide.

270–5 Aurelian***, murdered by Praetorians in a court plot.

275–6 Tacitus***, assassinated.

276 Florianus***, murdered by his soldiers.

276–82 Probus***, murdered.

282–3 Carus***, struck by lightning.

283–4 Numerian* ***, defeated by Diocletian and assassinated.

▲ *Theodosius I came into conflict with the formidable Bishop of Milan, Ambrose, over a massacre of 7,000 people in Thessalonica.*

283–5 Carinus* ***, killed in action.
284–305 Diocletian, a rare emperor who lived long enough to plan and enjoy his retirement.
286–305/8 Maximian**, abdicated.
293–305 Constantius Chlorus**, founder of the Constantinian Dynasty, died of natural causes.
3C´–06 Constantius I**, died of natural causes.
305–06 Severus**, committed suicide.
306–07 Severus II**, forced suicide or murder.
293–305 Galerius***, issued the Edict of Toleration for the Christians and was a successful campaigner against the Germans and Sassanians. Died of natural causes.
305–10 Galerius***, natural causes.
310–13 Maximinus Daia***, suicide.
309–13 Maximinus II***.
307–12 Maxentius***, killed in action at Milivian Bridge.
307–37 Constantine I (the Great)**, established Constantinople as the new capital, died of natural causes.
306–12 Maxentius** killed in action.
309–13 Maximinus II** (Daia).
308–24 Licinius I*** executed by order of Constantine I.
316–17 Valerius Valens, executed.
337–40 Constantine II** killed in action.

337–50 Constans**, assassinated.
337–61 Constantius II***, succeeded to the throne after the deaths of his brothers. Killed in action.
350 Vetranio, briefly proclaimed emperor in struggle between Constans and Magentius, abdicated in favour of Constantius and retired.
350–3 Magnentius**.
355–61 Julian the Apostate**.
361–3 Julian II** mortally wounded in action.
363–4 Jovian** suffocated by fumes.
364–75 Valentinian I**, elected by the army, died of natural causes.
364–78 Valens*** killed in action at Adrianople.
367–83 Gratian** murdered by mutinous army units.
375–92 Valentinian II** murdered or committed suicide.
379–95 Theodosius I (the Great)***, the last emperor to rule over both halves of the Roman Empire as a united entity. Died of natural causes.
383–8 Magnus Maximus**.
393–4 Eugenius**.
383–408 Arcadius *** eldest son of Theodosius, a weak ruler dominated by his wife and powerful ministers.
395–423 Honourius**, younger son of Theodosius, like his brother a weak emperor in time of great troubles, dependent on his general Falvius Stilicho, died of dropsy (edema).
408–50 Theodosius II***, son of Arcadius, also known as Theodosius the Younger, supported and influenced by his elder sister Pulcheria, built the walls of Constantinople. Died in a riding accident.
409–11 Maximus**.
421 Constantius III**, a prominent general and politician, he ruled for only 7 months, died of natural causes.
421–5 Joannes**, usurped the throne in power vacuum after the death of Honorius. Deposed and decapitated.
425–55 Valentinian III**, assassinated.
455 Petronius Maximus**, instrumental in assassination of Valentinian III and Flavius Aetius. Killed in Vandal sack of Rome.
450–7 Marcian, considered a good ruler, stopped tribute to Attila, died of disease, perhaps gangrene.

▲ *Gold coins in the empire usually bore the image of the current emperor. Constantine II here is depicted in armour.*

455–7 Avitus**, deposed and murdered.
457–61 Majorian**, died in mysterious circumstances.
461–5 Libius Severus III**, assassinated.
467–72 Anthemius**, executed.
472 Olybrius**, ruled for seven months, a puppet of general Ricimer, Died of natural causes.
473–4 Glycerius**, deposed, became bishop of the Church.
474–5 Julius Nepos**, assassinated.
475–6 Romulus Augustus** retired after being deposed by Odoacer.
* Co-rulers
** western emperors after 259AD
*** eastern emperors after 259AD

▼ *A votive platter, commemorating the 10th anniversary of Theodosius's reign. The soldiers have a Germanic look, consistent with the Roman army of the 4th century, when round shields and spears were common.*

EASTERN ROMAN EMPERORS

395–408 Arcadius, eldest son of Theodosius I. Died of natural causes.
408–50 Theodosius II, builder of the walls of Constantinople, died in a riding accident.
450–7 Marcian, died of natural causes.
457–74 Leo I*, died of dysentery.
473–4 Leo II*, assassinated.
474–91 Zeno*, died of natural causes, possibly dysentery or epilepsy.
475–6 Basiliscus, executed.
491–518 Anastasius I was an excellent administrator, he married Zeno's widow Ariadne, died of natural causes.
518–27 Justin I, founder of the Justinian dynasty, he rose through the ranks of the army to become emperor at 70. Died of natural causes.
527–65 Justinian I (the Great), lawgiver with the Justinian Code, oversaw eastern Roman reconquest. Died of natural causes.
565–78 Justin II, went insane.
578–82 Tiberius II (Constantine), poisoned.
582–602 Maurice, executed.
602–10 Phocas, executed.
610–41 Heraclius, conqueror of the Persian Empire, died of natural causes.
641–2 Heraclius Constantine and Heracleonas, poisoned/died in exile/deposed.

▲ *A period depiction, from Jean Skylitzes's Byzantine Chronicles of Emperor, of Basil I's marriage to Eudocia Ingerina.*

▼ *A copy of the great gold medal of Emperor Justinian I, found in Cappadocia at Caesarea, c534AD, on which a mounted Justinian is preceeded by winged Victory.*

642–68 Constans II, assassinated.
668–85 Constantine IV, died of dysentery.
685–95 Justinian II, deposed in popular uprising.
695–7 Leontius, executed.
697–705 Tiberius III (Apsimarus), executed.
705–11 Justinian II**, reinstated, but despotic 2nd rule led to army deposing and murdering him.
711–13 Philippicus Bardanes, deposed.
713–15 Anastasius II Artemius, deposed, killed attempting to regain the throne.
715–17 Theodosius III, abdicated and retired to a monastery.
717–40 Leo III (the Isaurian), noted for civil reforms and for successfully defending the empire from the Muslim threat. Probably died of natural causes.
740–75 Constantine V Copronymus, an able soldier and administrator he died on campaign against the Bulgars, probably of natural causes.
742–3 Artabasdos, deposed and blinded.
775–9 Leo IV, died on campaign against the Bulgars, but suspicions remain that he was murdered.
779–97 Constantine VI, deposed, blinded and died from his wounds. Succeeded by his mother, Irene.

797–802 Irene of Athens, deposed, died of natural causes in exile.
802–11 Nicephorus I, killed in action.
811 Stauracius, badly wounded in action and paralysed, died in a monastery.
811–13 Michael I Rhangabe, abdicated and died in a monastery.
813–20 Leo V (the Armenian), murdered.
820–9 Michael II (the Amorian), a competent administrator and statesman. Was imprisoned by his predecessor, but on Leo's death was freed and proclaimed emperor.
829–42 Theophilus, well-educated and an able soldier and emperor, he fought the Muslims for 11 years.
842–67 Michael III, murdered. (Theodora was regent 842–855)
867–86 Basil I (the Macedonian), died as a result of a hunting accident.
886–912 Leo VI (the Wise), finished the Basilika, the Greek translation of the Justinian Law Code; also the author of the military treatise *Taktika*. Probably died of natural causes.
912–58 Constantine VII Porphyrogenitus, probably died of natural causes.
912–13 Alexander III.
919–45 Romanus I Lecapenus, probably died of natural causes.
958–63 Romanus II, a pleasure-loving sovereign, he may have been poisoned by his wife.
963–1025 Basil II, conqueror of the

Bulgars, led the empire to its greatest height since Justinian I.

963–9 Nicephorus II Phocas, and able ruler and soldier. Assassinated.

969–76 John I/Zimisces (co-regents), probably died of natural causes, but John may have been poisoned.

1025–8 Constantine VIII, may have died of natural causes, but rumoured to have been poisoned.

1028–34 Romanus III Argyrus, ineffective, probably either poisoned or drowned in his bath by his wife, Zoe.

1028–50 Zoe, daughter of Constantine VIII and wife of three emperors; Romanus III, Michael I and Michael V, was co-ruler between 1042 and 1050 with her sister Theodora.

1034–42 Michael IV (the Paphlagonian), victim of both epilepsy and dropsy. He probably died of natural causes.

1042 Michael V, reigned for only four months, was deposed by Zoe, blinded and castrated.

1042–55 Constantine IX Monomachus, died of natural causes.

1055–7 Theodora, last of the Macedonian line, she died of an intestinal disorder.

1056–7 Michael VI Stratioticus, abdicated and retired to a monastery.

▼ *The Comnenian dynasty restored order to the empire after ten years of disastrous civil war. John II, the son of Alexis I, was a gifted ruler and statesman and continued his father's work in his reign from 1118 to 1143.*

1057–9 Isaac I Comnenus, probably died of natural causes.

1059–67 Constantine X Ducas, probably died of natural causes.

1067–78 Michael VII Ducas, probably died of natural causes.

1067–71 Romanus IV Diogenes (co-regent), deposed, blinded and exiled.

1078–81 Nicephorus III Botaniates, overthrown.

1081–1118 Alexis I Comnenus, re-established the empire as a concern after ten years of civil war, probably died of natural causes.

1118–43 John II Comnenus, died from a hunting accident with a poisoned arrow.

1143–80 Manuel I Comnenus, died from a fever.

1180–3 Alexis II Comnenus, deposed and murdered.

1183–5 Andronicus Comnenus, overthrown and murdered.

1185–95 Isaac II Angelus, overthrown, blinded and imprisoned.

1195–1203 Alexis III Angelus, died in captivity.

1203–4 Isaac II Angelus**, reinstated by 4th Crusade, but died soon after.

1203–4 Alexis IV, son of Isaac II, strangled by Alexis Ducas.

1204 Alexis V Ducas, blinded, captured, and executed.

1204–05 Baldwin I***, first emperor of the 'Latin Empire' begun by the French crusaders after they stormed Constantinople.

1205–16 Henry***, probably died of natural causes.

1217–19 Peter***, probably died of natural causes.

1219–28 Robert***, probably died of natural causes.

1228–61 Baldwin III***, probably died of natural causes.

1204–22 Theodore I Lascaris, had skill as a commander and helped keep the new Latin Empire contained around Constantinople.

1222–54 John III Ducas, died during an epileptic fit.

1254–9 Theodore II Ducas, died of epilepsy.

1259–60 John IV Ducas, deposed.

1260–82 Michael VIII, founder of the Palaiologon Dynasty, the last to rule in

▲ *Gold scyphate depicting future emperor Michael VII standing between his brothers, Andronicus and Constantine. c.1067–71.*

Constantinople. He reinstituted the eastern Roman Empire after the Latin kingdom collapsed.

1282–1328 Andronicus II Paleologus, abdicated and became a monk.

1328–41 Andronicus III Paleologus, enjoyed hunting and engaging in warfare, reorganized the navy, but could not stop the progress of the Ottomans. His death led to a seven-year civil war.

1341–91 John V Paleologus, died of humiliation. He had recognized the suzerainty of the Ottomans over the eastern Romans.

1347–54 John VI Cantacuzenus (co-regent), died of natural causes.

1390 John VII, emperor for 5 months.

1391–1425 Manuel II, spent much time searching for European allies against the Ottomans and withstood two sieges of Constantinople by the Ottomans during his reign.

1425–48 John VIII, a type of quasi-emperor in Constantinople, he took advantage of a civil war in the Ottoman empire to gain back some of the coastline in Asia Minor.

1448–53 Constantine XI, brother of John VIII, killed in action.

* Emperor in the east when the western Roman Empire finally fell to the barbarian onslaughts.

** Restored emperors.

*** western, or Latin, emperors who ruled in Constantinople after the western Europeans of the 4th Crusade stormed and took Constantinople.

MILITARY LEGACY OF THE EMPIRE

▲ *A Roman commander along the northern frontier 'reviews' Germanic prisoners taken after a victorious campaign. The massed standards of the legion can be seen on the left.*

The image of stolid, steady and virtually unbeatable Roman legions advancing rank after rank against their enemies is an enduring depiction that has been passed down to us over the course of time.

That image has a basis in historical reality. The Roman legions were for hundreds of years literally unbeatable, and that makes for an enduring legacy even though, ultimately, they failed.

Uniformity

That powerful sense of success against all-comers is not the only concept that the legions left to posterity. Armed with a gladius (sword) and pugio (dagger), curved scutum (shield) and javelins, armoured in either flexible metal plates or chain mail, and wearing the distinctive Roman-style helmet, the Roman legionary is easily recognizable to even the casual observer today. Uniformity of dress, armour and weapons was a hallmark of the western and the eastern Roman armies. That careful ruling on how soldiers should dress was something new, but it has been a distinction of disciplined armies ever since. Coloured

▼ *A section of Trajan's column in Rome depicting victorious Roman legionaries and their defeated enemies, the Dacians.*

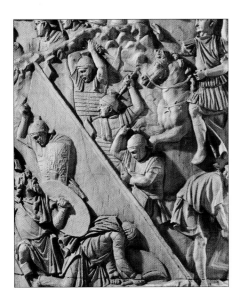

plumes on helmets, as well as coloured lance pennons and flags, marked the units on the battlefield and served as rallying points after a charge. The organization and uniformity of the eastern Roman army would surpass that of even its western Roman forebears.

Order and Discipline

The solidity of the legions, the idea of a disciplined, well-trained and competently led Roman heavy infantry that conquered from Britain to the Near East, has remained almost as tangible as the ruins of great buildings, aqueducts, the still-usable roads and solid, well-designed bridges. The idea of a centrally organized professional army, as well as the legion structure itself, has come down through the ages as models for other armies, as does the primary idea of the professional soldier trumping the warrior. The

soldier is one who fights as part of an organization, and submits to the rules and discipline of the force, while the warrior can only fight as an individual.

In a sense it is the organizational heritage that has proved most rigid, perhaps best exemplified in language. We speak not only of arms as weapons, but also of arms of service, and of an army, the military, or a legion. These have all evolved from the Latin terms, and have Roman origins. Most importantly, so too does the word soldier, derived from the term for one who receives pay, specifically one who receives the solidus, a Roman coin which gained currency under Constantine. That word entered English in the Middle Ages when military pay, rather than feudal service, once again became established.

Leadership

The great Roman commanders, such as Julius Caesar, Pompey the Great, Marius, Aetius and countless others gave examples of how to organize and lead armies that spread Roman civilization across Europe and around the Mediterranean. Their legions followed them to the ends of the known world, and Caesar's 10th Legion became a byword for loyalty and military efficiency, to be quoted by that most loyal of Napoleon's marshals, Louis Nicholas Davout, whose famous III Corps was cast in the mould of the 10th Legion.

Eastern Legacy

When Rome fell in the west, the empire of the eastern Romans remained, and they developed their own military system based on the heavily armoured cavalryman and the horse archer who also remained virtually unbeatable for hundreds of years. That image is less well-defined in western military history, unfortunately, and this is partly because it happened on the edge of Europe and Asia. For many in the west that history remains hidden except for those who have made it a point of study. And the eastern Roman army with its heavily armoured cataphracts, lightly armed horse archers, and all the inherited skill of the western Romans in engineering and sieges, deserves greater scrutiny and merit.

The new eastern Roman legions were not called legions any longer, but they still functioned in the same way as their military ancestors. And they fought a plethora of enemies just as varied as did the old Roman legions. Eastern Roman heavy cavalry and horse

▲ *After the capital moved to Milan then Ravenna, and the population of Rome fell, its public buildings were no longer maintained and fell into gradual ruin, although the great Pantheon, on the left, still stands today.*

archers, and the solid infantry base of the army that was a true descendant of the old legions, would fight outnumbered and win on countless unnamed battlefields under commanders that were at least as skilled as those of the western empire.

Belisarius, who served a sometimes ungrateful Emperor Justinian; Heraclius; and Basil II 'the Bulgar-Slayer' – the latter two both being competent heads of state as well as excellent field commanders – all left a legacy of generalship to be emulated and examined, with many parallels in their operations that are as valid today as they were when they defended Roman civilization against their countless enemies.

Yet both of these military systems were Roman in both thought and action and they left an enduring military legacy that is important and in

◄ *Roman commanders were brilliant in their use of engineering, building either trestle or pontoon bridges, as shown here. Their crossing of the Rhine on wooden bridges is one of the great engineering feats of the ancient world.*

many cases suitable for emulation. For over two thousand years the legions of the west and the tagmata of the east established a military and combat reputation second to none and while they both would eventually go down in defeat, and the empires that they protected would fall, the memories of what these armies accomplished, and their military prowess, would endure and later be copied by armies on at least two continents. Their military influence is still felt by modern armies, and the ruins of their presence from Britain in the west to Babylon in the east, reminds all who see them of the days when Roman armies marched and conquered under the watchful eyes of their centurions. No one who has seen an ancient Roman structure, complete or not, and touched it can doubt of the greatness that was once Rome and Constantinople.

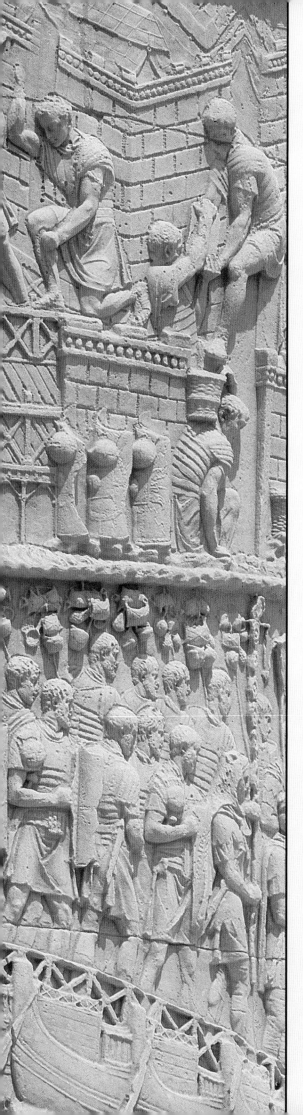

THE ROMAN REPUBLIC 753–146BC

The Roman army developed from the war clans that defended the embryonic settlements in and around the seven hills. They were armed and armoured in a similar fashion to their neighbours and they fought in generally the same way. They were influenced by the Greeks, the invading Celtic tribes, and by the sometimes hostile neighbours that surrounded their first settlement. From those beginnings the Romans developed a military system that would in turn create an almost unbeatable army based on the Roman infantryman, armed with pilum, gladius, and shield, armoured in either chain mail or plate armour and wearing an iron or steel helmet. They would also build a political and military system that set a precedent in the peninsula and one which was destined to allow Rome to overawe local enemies and export conquest to the shores of the Mediterranean and beyond.

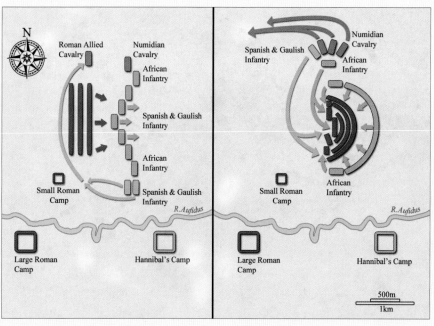

▲ *The Battle of Cannae in 216BC between Hannibal and the Roman commanders, the consuls Varro and Paullus. This overwhelming Carthaginian victory was a virtual battle of annihilation with up to 50,000 Roman dead left on the field.*

◀ *A Roman army crossing the River Danube on Trajan's column, a depiction of the considerable engineering skill of a Roman army on campaign, this time against the Dacians. It shows a pontoon bridge, a particular skill of the Roman military engineers.*

THE SETTLEMENT OF ROME AND ITS NEIGHBOURS

The 'strategic' situation Rome faced upon her founding was precarious, surrounded by potential enemies in the centre of Italy – who undoubtedly coveted her prime position – in particular the strong and dominant Etruscans to Rome's north. The tentative 'alliance' of Romans and Etruscans evolved into a monarchy of the Etruscan kings.

By the time the rule of kings had ended, Rome itself was a bustling small city or large town surrounded by a defensive wall that had been built by one of the kings, Servius Tullius; this 'Servian Wall' served Rome well for years. Roman foreign policy became quite simple: either her neighbours would be subjugated or they would be persuaded to become Roman allies under the Roman sphere of influence.

The Ligurians

To the north of the Etruscans were the Ligurians, whom Plutarch referred to as the Ambrones. Not much is known about these people, but they may have existed in the Iberian peninsula before migrating to northern Italy. Their influence may have been felt as far as the Rhone Valley in modern France, as well as the large islands of the western Mediterranean; Sicily, Sardinia and Corsica. Over 40 different Ligurian tribes have been named or mentioned by the historians of the ancient world.

Ligurian mercenaries may have been recruited by the Carthaginians under their general Hamilcar in the early 5th century BC. After opposing Rome, and Roman expansion for decades, if not centuries, the Ligurians in northern Italy were finally brought under Roman control and influence during the 2nd century BC.

The Samnites

Samnium, home of the Samnites, was located in southern Italy. Originally landlocked, the Samnites for a short time extended their territory to both the east and west to reach the sea. The Samnites probably included four tribes: the Caracini, the Hirpini (meaning 'wolf' in the Oscan language), the Frentani and the Pentri. The Samnites came into direct conflict with Rome because both peoples wanted to extend their influence and rule on the Italian peninsula.

A treaty with the Samnites in 354BC was deliberately broken by Rome in 343BC, but the two antagonists came to an understanding and fighting between them ceased. This did not last long and they were at war again by 326BC. Rome was winning convincingly, until the humiliating defeat at the Caudine Forks in 321BC. The Samnites set up a clever and deadly ambush for the Roman army, catching them and defeating them decisively, and the Romans were forced to surrender. The victorious Samnites then deliberately humiliated the captured Romans by forcing them to 'pass under the yoke'.

The situation finally came to a head in the 3rd Samnite War, which culminated in two great Roman victories, the Battle of Sentinum, supposedly the largest battle that ever took place in Italy (with very heavy losses), although that has not been proven, and the Battle of Samnium. These two defeats forced the Samnites to surrender to Rome in 290BC.

▼ *Ancient Italy, c.400BC, showing the Samnite, Etruscan, Celtic, and Greek peoples, all of which had a significant impact on the development of the Roman republic.*

▼ *According to the legend of the founding of Marseille, the daughter of a Ligurian chief is said to have married a Greek sailor from Phocaea and together they founded the city.*

However, the Samnites would ally themselves with the Carthaginians in the 2nd Punic War, then again in the Social War (91–88BC), and paid dearly; their lands and towns were destroyed by the Roman general Lucius Cornelius Sulla, and the people scattered for ever.

The Latin League

Inhabitants of central Italy formed what is referred to today as the Latin League, which was not a contemporary term. At first, the Latin League was formed to oppose Roman encroachment, but later Rome assumed leadership of the League and eventually the 30 or so members of the League were absorbed by Rome.

The original leader of the League was apparently the city of Alba Longa. The members of the League, according to Cato the Elder, were Ardea, Aricia, Cora, Lanivinium, Lanuvinium, Pometia, Tibur and Tusculum. The first war between the Latins and Rome occurred as early as the 7th century BC. Apparently, several Latin towns were taken and demolished, the surviving citizens introduced to and absorbed into Roman society. In the 6th century BC the Latins again were at war with Rome and the eventual result was Roman leadership of the Latin League. Latin and Roman troops were merged into combined units and were successful against later wars with the Aequi and Volsci who attacked from the Apennines.

The League eventually dissolved in to the Latin War (343–38BC), the original Latins being dissatisfied with Roman leadership. Roman victory of this war absorbed the peoples of the Latin League into Roman society, and they officially became 'Roman colonists' and part of Rome.

The Celts

Celts inhabited large areas of Europe from the 9th century BC onwards. By migration or conquest, tribes of Celtic peoples eventually inhabited Gaul, Iberia, northern Italy, the British Isles, the Balkans, and much of central Europe. Celts then declined, either conquered by the Romans or pushed

▲ *A Samnite cavalryman depicted in a fresco of the 4th century BC from Campania. He wears a short tunic, and a bronze cuirass held on with belt and shoulder straps.*

westwards by the great barbarian migrations from the east. Celtic influence and culture became largely restricted to western France, in areas such as Brittany and the Vendée, western Spain and the British Isles.

The Celtic 'heartland' is thought to have been Gaul by some ancient scholars, but the Romans referred to the Celts as Gauls, making no differentiation between locations in which the tribes lived. An opposing modern view believes that the Celts originated in Germany, east of the Rhine. Some believe that the Celts originated specifically in southern Germany, but the Romans divided the Celts and Germans as different peoples, with the conclusion that they had separate origins as peoples, with the Gauls being related to the Celtic tribes in Britain.

The Celts were accomplished ironworkers, and their weapons were excellent. So was their jewellery; distinctive torques – neck rings made from strands of metal twisted together – brooches used to fasten their cloaks, and well-designed and worked armlets were all prized and widely worn.

Celts also wove clothing in a tartan pattern, the men frequently wearing trousers of this type. Tunics with long sleeves were also worn, and clothing was made of either linen or wool. Silk clothing may have been worn by the

wealthier members of a tribe. Cloaks were also worn, usually in the winter. A warlike people, Celts were fierce in battle and aggressive as a people. There was considerable conflict between the various tribes, and they were notorious for taking the heads of their enemies, and displaying them as trophies.

Contemporary descriptions of the Celts of Gaul portray men as tall and muscular with blonde hair. Apparently those who were not blonde, bleached their hair in 'limewater'. Some were clean-shaven and some not, although most had at least a moustache, which was long and drooping. Their hair was worn long and pulled back to the nape of the neck to secure it.

Celtic women were also active in warfare, and there is evidence that they not only fought alongside their men, but sometimes commanded them in battle. The British Celtic queen of the Iceni, Boudicca, who organized and led a revolt against the Romans which was for a time successful before being finally defeated, was not unique. There is a story that has come down from Cassius Dio relating a remark from a Celtic woman 'the wife of Argentocoxus, a Caledonian' to the Empress Julia Augusta regarding the sexual habits of Celtic women: 'We fulfil the demands of nature in a much better way than do you Roman women; for we consort openly with the best men, whereas you let yourselves be debauched in secret by the vilest'.

Julius Caesar in his famous *Commentaries* notes that the descendants of the original Celts in Gaul also lived in what is now Switzerland, the Netherlands, Belgium and northern Italy. Their tribal culture matured to a level where they organized, constructed, and lived in towns, with an internal social structure that was quite advanced and would have been recognizable to a contemporary Roman. Further, they coined money and had a written language. Culturally, then, the Celts that faced the Roman expansion were an advanced civilization, though still tribal and not organized at a 'national' level as the Romans were.

THE ARMY OF THE ROMAN REPUBLIC

The Roman army was initially a citizen's army. It could be considered a militia, since the army was not professional in recruitment and every able-bodied citizen was bound to serve in times of emergency. Troops were not expected to serve for a lifetime, armies raised in times of war and national emergency were largely disbanded when the war was over, and the men went back either to harvest their crops or to their pre-war professions if they were artisans.

The Roman Soldier

From the outset of the Roman civil state, military service was required and expected from the Roman landowners. These civilians were expected to clothe, arm, and equip themselves for war when called by the state to serve. Some sources have stated that these troops were similar to militia in later history, as they were not regulars or professionals, but one reliable source better defines them as conscripts, as they had no choice in their service to the state.

The basic arms and equipment of the Roman legionary consisted of helmet and shield, sword, spear or javelin, and dagger, helmet and body armour of some type. As the army became more uniform in appearance, so did the armour and other accoutrements. The tunics worn by the legionaries were usually white (which at that time was the easiest colour to keep in a uniform colour) and were made of undyed wool or linen (depending on the season) although red and blue tunics might also be worn. Cloaks were almost a 'regulation' piece of clothing for that is what the Roman soldier lived in on campaign as it was shelter, overcoat and worn in bad weather to keep out the elements.

Training took place as needed, and when called up and formed for war, the legions would have to be trained

▲ *Ranks of Greek warriors, all carrying their hoplon, or round shield, from which the term hoplite was derived. An early Roman phalanx formation would have looked similar to this.*

on the march or in camp. The men might or might not have formed a cohesive unit before combat.

The Command System

At any time during the existence of the Roman state, the heart of the legion was the centurion. An officer of proven merit and combat worthiness, the centurion commanded a century of either 60 or 80 men, depending on the period. They were similarly armed to the men they led and fought in the ranks with. Centurions were distinguished by the decoration on their helmets and by carrying a vine stick, which was both their symbol of rank and a quick means of corporal punishment to any offending legionary. It was carried in the manner of the modern 'swagger stick' used in some armies.

Senior officers, tribunes, of which there were usually six per legion, were political appointees or the sons of

well-to-do Roman citizens or senators. They were assigned to the legions to gain experience and as a prelude to a political career, during which they might rise to the rank of army commander. The commander of a legion, at least in the later period of the empire, was the legate. Politician or soldier, the legate could also be the army commander, an army usually, in its basic form, being composed of two legions plus auxiliary units.

The Evolution of the Legion

Over time the Roman legion evolved from the original Roman war bands. There were three particular periods of organization for the Roman army. First, learning from the Greeks, the Romans formed and fought in the phalanx. From that solid beginning, the Romans developed the maniple and finally the cohort organization of the legion.

The phalanx was a solid infantry formation composed of ranks of armoured spearmen (sometimes the term 'heavy infantry' was used) arranged in a rectangular formation, shoulder to shoulder. The name is from the Greek 'phalanga' (phalanxes or phalanges in plural, the latter term being used by the Macedonian army under Alexander the Great). The term itself means 'finger'. The Romans probably adopted the phalanx from their encounters with the Etruscans.

The phalanx would fight and manoeuvre as one solid mass and while there was no 'regulation' number of infantrymen forming the phalanx, a usual depth to the formation was eight, or more, spearmen deep for the Greeks and from 16 up to 32 spearmen deep for the Macedonians. The depth of the formation would vary according to terrain and other considerations, but the phalanx was always wider than it was deep. The phalanx was abandoned as a formation and tactical system by the Romans after their humiliating defeat at the Caudine Forks (321BC), where a Roman legion surrendered to the Samnites without offering any resistance.

The maniple was an organization of two centuries adopted from the Samnites during the Samnite Wars of 343–290BC. It replaced the rigid phalanx around c.315BC in order to suit the terrain and the environment.

The term 'legion' comes from the Latin word 'legio' meaning 'levy' or 'military levy'. Before the Marian reforms of the late 2nd century BC, legions were organized and fielded as they were needed. They were not permanent units, but were raised for national emergencies only. Long service might make the legions steady and battle-worthy, but there was no permanence to the Roman army before Marius. The legion had an authorized strength of between 5,000 and 6,000, reinforced with auxiliaries.

The Reforms of Marius

During the reforms of the Consul Marius in c.107BC the maniple system gave way to the cohort system, which will be covered in more depth later. Each cohort was formed of six centuries of 80 men, each for a total of 480 legionaries. This was a much more robust formation, which was capable of independent missions.

Marius opened the legion to all Roman citizens, not merely landowners. The poor were recruited and the Roman army was converted to a permanent force with troops who were now professionals. Legions were assigned permanent numbers in the Roman order of battle and it was Marius who gave the legions their famous eagle standard, first in silver, and later in gold. The legion had changed, just as the old Roman republic was bound to change from a republic to an empire.

▼ *A depiction of moment when a soldier, dispatched to kill Marius after he was sentenced to death by Sulla, is overpowered by Marius's rank and force of personality.*

▲ *Gaius Marius, the famous reformer of the Roman army, is depicted here in the full panoply of a Roman general.*

The Wars of Rome 509–146BC

509BC The last Etruscan king is ejected from Rome. Rome becomes a republic.

390BC The city of Rome is taken and sacked by the Gauls raiding from northern Italy.

295BC Romans defeat the Samnites, Gauls and Umbrians at the Battle of Sentinum.

280–75BC War with King Pyrrhus of Epirus; coining of the phrase 'pyrrhic victory'.

264–41BC The 1st Punic War with Carthage.

225BC The Battle of Telamon where the Romans defeat another Gallic army raiding in Italy.

218–01BC The 2nd, and decisive, Punic War with Carthage.

214–05BC The 1st Macedonian War.

200–196BC The 2nd Macedonian War.

192–89BC The 1st Syrian War.

172–68BC The 3rd Macedonian War.

154–38BC Lusitanian War.

154–1BC 2nd Celtic-Iberian War.

149–6BC The 3rd, and final, Punic War. Carthage is completely destroyed and the surviving population is sold into slavery.

THE CARTHAGINIANS

Carthage was a regional power and a rival which threatened to challenge dominance of the Mediterranean. With a formidable navy, and an army built around a core of mercenaries and reliable regional allies, it was to prove a capable foe and one which would test republican Rome to the limits.

The Empire of Carthage

As Rome developed as the dominant land power in central Italy, the dominant sea power of the period was developing in North Africa, centred on the city of Carthage. First founded by Phoenician traders in 814BC, Carthage developed into a maritime power that dominated the Mediterranean and sailed where they pleased. Referred to by the Romans as the Punic Empire (Punic being a form of the word Phoenician) Carthage was also an aggressive empire and it was inevitable

▲ *A good depiction of the 'corvus', the ramp used by the Roman navy to transfer infantry to the decks of Carthaginian warships.*

▼ *The Carthaginian Empire, showing the various stages of its territorial holdings before the triple disasters of the Punic wars.*

that Rome and Carthage would eventually clash for dominance in the waters of the Mediterranean.

The Carthaginian navy dominated Mediterranean trade, protecting merchantmen from pirates and any other naval threat and becoming wealthy through this trading system. Not only did Carthage maintain a large and excellent navy, they built and maintained the infrastructure to support it. The city had two harbours strategically located within it – one for trade and one, the inner harbour, for the navy. Construction and dockyard facilities were excellent and along the circumference of the circular naval harbour were shelters for the ships that would be beached when not at sea.

Unlike Rome, Carthage relied on mercenaries rather than native soldiers to defend the homeland and these soldiers came from a variety of sources. Troops were recruited from Numidia in Africa, Spain and from various groups of Celts, but they could be moulded into effective fighting forces through solid leadership, which the Carthaginians certainly provided.

The Punic Wars

Rome and Carthage fought three long wars against each other. The outcome of the 1st Punic war (264–41BC) was not decisive, but the 2nd (218–01BC)

GERMANIA

GAUL

IBERIA

HELVETII

R.Rhone

R.Po

ITALY

CORSICA

Rome

R.Tiber

Adriatic Sea

ILLYRIA

N

BALAERIC ISLANDS

SARDINIA

Carthage

SICILY

Mediterranean Sea

	Carthaginian possessions, 265BC, beginning of 1st Punic War
	Carthaginian losses by 238BC
	Carthaginian conquests by 218BC, beginning of 2nd Punic War
	Carthage, 201BC, end of 2nd Punic war

200 miles
200 km

▲ *Hannibal's army rampaged through Italy during the 2nd Punic War, taking allied cities and threatening Rome's very survival.*

nearly brought Rome to her knees with Hannibal's invasion of Italy from Iberia and his army making an epic march into northern Italy across the Alps. Hannibal won overwhelming victories against the republican legions at the Trebbia (218BC), Lake Trasimene (217BC) and Cannae (216BC), the last being forever after in military history a synonym for complete and total victory, which generations of generals of many nations strove to repeat.

Rome being a land power and Carthage generally being a sea power, the strategic problem for both antagonists was how to get at each other. Carthage did not use its sea power to land on the Italian mainland. Troops were gathered in Iberia and put under Hannibal's command. This polyglot army was well-trained and disciplined and was commanded by arguably the best general of the period. Hannibal led his troops over the Pyrenees into Gaul, then tackled the massive undertaking of crossing the Alps. Many of the troops survived this epic journey but most of the elephants did not, dying of exposure and the difficulties of the conditions. The Carthaginians embarked them in large

rafts to cross the rivers and while crossing the River Rhone the animals panicked, wrecking the rafts and dumping themselves and their handlers into the river. The elephants reportedly swam across the river with their trunks sticking above the surface of the river, but most of their handlers were drowned.

The Carthaginian army emerged from the Alpine passes into the strategic rear of the Romans and caught them by surprise. This impressive achievement was accomplished by an ancient army with no modern machinery or assistance from any outside source. It stands in military

history as a great achievement by a great captain who had the confidence of his army. Without that, Hannibal would not have succeeded.

Hannibal failed to push home this stunning victory, however. Roman legion after legion may have been defeated or destroyed, but Rome raised more men to send into the field to face the Carthaginian threat.

After Cannae, one Roman general stood out against Hannibal. Fabius Cunctator waged a cautious campaign against Hannibal, wearing him down and avoiding another decisive battle. Frontinus in *Strategems* described Fabius as not taking any 'dangerous risks'. What Fabius did was season his raw legionaries into a cohesive fighting force capable of meeting the Carthaginians in combat, and giving time for Scipio to invade North Africa and defeat Hannibal at Zama in 202BC.

The Carthaginians, after being defeated in their homeland, were forced into a humiliating peace by Rome, who now became the dominant power in the Mediterranean.

The 3rd Punic War (149-6BC) was almost an anticlimax, albeit a bloody one. Carthage was taken by siege and completely destroyed by the Romans, ending up as a Roman colony.

▼ *Rome eventually built on the ruins of their once-powerful enemy, and the ruins of the baths of the emperor Antoninus Pius at Carthage are Roman and not Carthaginian.*

EARLY ITALIANS: THE ETRUSCANS

The early Italian war bands, including those of the Romans, were armed and equipped in the same manner and generally fought as something akin to armed mobs. Wars were quick and deadly, and the defeated force would usually go home, lick its wounds, and try again later.

Italian Military Development

Weapons and armour were varied and were influenced by different cultures, but that of the Greeks became predominant because of the Greek influence in

Italy. Leather and bronze cuirasses became the norm, the latter sometimes being of the 'muscled' type, looking like an idealized male torso.

Leather or cloth cuirasses, which were articulated and coloured, covered the chest and back of the wearer, and were joined by strips at the shoulder. This type of armour was in fact metal plates covered in either leather or cloth and was probably much more popular than the bronze muscle cuirass because it was articulated and could move as the wearer moved. All-leather cuirasses were not unknown and would later be employed by the Roman army after it developed into legions.

Shields were constructed of wood, moulded and fashioned in a bowl shape, with a leather lining and an outward portion coated in bronze. Helmets were of the Hellenic type, probably the most common being the Corinthian helmet, which could be lowered to cover the face, although this must have narrowed the wearer's vision on the battlefield, which could be deadly. The helmet was probably uncomfortable and it became common practice for the Greeks to wear it pushed back on the head, even in combat. Horsehair crests of different colours were common and this gave the impression of greater height for the wearer. One later development adopted by the Romans was the Greek

◄ **ETRUSCAN WARRIOR, 6TH CENTURY BC** *Etruscan infantry were armed and equipped in the Greek style with greaves and a round hoplite-type shield, but with a flexible cuirass.*

▶ **ETRUSCAN CHIEFTAIN, 6TH CENTURY BC** *This Etruscan officer shows the heavy Greek influence on military clothing on the Italian peninsula due to the Greek settlements in southern Italy and Sicily. The Greek classical helmet is prominent, as is the muscled body armour.*

Phrygian helmet of bronze, which no longer had a face plate that covered the infantryman's face, but had hinged cheek pieces that were attached to the helmet.

The infantryman was armed with sword and spear, the spear becoming the main weapon as the Romans developed phalanx tactics, the sword being a weapon of self-defence at close quarters. The spear might have a hand grip for better handling in combat and it was not used as a missile weapon as the later pilum would be.

▲ *A detail of a painting, showing the battle of the Amazons, on an Etruscan sarcophagus of the 4th century BC. The arms and armour depicted are Etruscan of the period.*

▶ ETRUSCAN WARRIOR, 6TH CENTURY BC
This infantryman is equipped with the native Italian-style pot helmet and with chest armour that, while still referred to as a cuirass, afforded less protection than the Greek type.

Tunics could be a mixture of colours, the three known base colours being white, red and a medium blue. Helmet crests could be of a solid colour or multi-coloured and they were shaped in the Greek fashion, front to back, though there were also coloured horsehair crests that were worn crossways, parallel to the wearer's shoulders, very much like the crests later worn by centurions.

Finally, the Greeks had developed greaves worn on the leg to protect the infantryman's calves. They developed to an extent where they would follow the contours of the wearer's legs, but must have been heavy, uncomfortable and restrictive. The Romans would eventually abandon this piece of armour, though centurions would continue to wear them for years, if only for ceremonial occasions as a symbol of rank.

Dress and Weapons

Etruscan armour consisted of muscled cuirasses, both full and of the three-disc variety. They also wore colourful leather or cloth armour with metal plates sewn inside the cuirass, another borrowing from the Greeks. Helmets were of the late Greek variety with movable cheek plates and not covering the entire face. Shields were round, as they were with most early Italian troops, and there were designs on the shields of both humans and animals.

▶ ETRUSCAN FLUTIST, 6TH CENTURY BC
Music has followed soldiers all through recorded history and undoubtedly before that. This man is a musician and not a warrior or soldier and would definitely not be engaged in combat. He would probably move to the rear once an engagement was imminent.

Swords were either curved, broad bladed at the end, or were straight. They were worn from a baldric across the body and were probably worn on the left side of the bearer. Spears in the Greek manner were carried as the primary infantry weapon. Etruscans usually employed flute or lute players to precede their troops on the march and in combat, something they may have adopted from the Greeks. These men and boys were musicians and their job was not to fight. They may have been employed for morale purposes.

EARLY ITALIANS: THE VILLANOVANS

The earliest Romans, as well as the other inhabitants of the Italian peninsula, were warriors not soldiers. The difference being that warriors fought alone on the battlefield and not as a trained unit, as soldiers did. Their arms and armour were typical of the period from *c*.700BC through the 'hoplite' period and up to the development of the Roman army into legions after the phalanx was deemed not to be the best way to fight in the hilly Italian terrain.

The earliest forms of battle dress in Italy probably consisted of pot-shaped helmets, tunics and sparse armour, which consisted of a metal plate covering a portion of the upper torso, held on by leather straps across the shoulders and back, and around or just above the waist. Alternatively, pot-shaped helmets topped with a spike or rounded ball ornament would be worn. Shields – either round or oval, usually undecorated, and with a prominent boss in the centre – would be carried.

Tunics were probably white, as this was the easiest colour to keep clean with no risk of the dye running out and the material fading, and were either plain or had coloured bands around the base of the tunic as well as around the 'skirt'.

A leather belt around the waist would support a sword and a dagger, and spears were also carried. These warriors may or may not have worn shoes of any type.

Hoplites

A hoplite was a heavy infantryman in the Greek style, who would march and fight in the phalanx. He was named after his round shield, the hoplon, and the name carried over to Italy and the Romans and other Italian groups who adopted this form of armour and weaponry. These people followed the

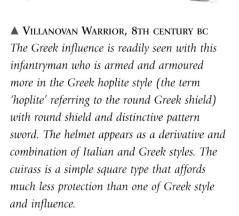

◀ VILLANOVAN WARRIOR, 8TH CENTURY BC *Villanovan warriors were equipped more in the central Italian style wearing a distinctive helmet and crest that no one else seems to have copied. Note the scutum (shield), which is starting to become more rectangular in shape, and is also curved slightly. The Greek hoplite influence is not evident here.*

▲ VILLANOVAN WARRIOR, 8TH CENTURY BC *The Greek influence is readily seen with this infantryman who is armed and armoured more in the Greek hoplite style (the term 'hoplite' referring to the round Greek shield) with round shield and distinctive pattern sword. The helmet appears as a derivative and combination of Italian and Greek styles. The cuirass is a simple square type that affords much less protection than one of Greek style and influence.*

Greek hoplite tradition until it became obsolete and the phalanx disappeared from Italy as a tactical formation.

Hoplite shields might have had different designs, such as mythological figures, horses, boars or human head designs on them, as the Greeks did. It was during this period that the story of Horatius at the bridge evolved, depicting Romans pitted against superior numbers of Etruscan hoplites, and the legend was told and retold as a tribute to Roman valour against overwhelming odds. It was also during the Roman hoplite period that the Celts invaded Italy in large raids, and even sacked Rome, which raised havoc with the Romans. The Romans learned their lesson and their city was fortified after this disaster.

Villanovans

The ancient Villanovans were occupants of central and northern Italy, especially in the Po River valley. By the 7th century BC the Villanovans had become greatly influenced by the imported Greek culture that was taking root in southern Italy, notably in Sicily. Greek influence could be seen outwardly in arms and armour, as well as in jewellery, and demonstrated the adoption of the Greek hoplite's equipment into Italy.

The Villanovans initially cremated their dead, which appears to be a normal practice in early antiquity, though cemeteries have also been discovered. They used or developed what has been called 'hut urns' for the

ashes of the dead. The urns were shaped like small houses, and the same hut shape was used in the manufacture of their warriors' helmets. Inverted, the helmet could be used as an urn to bury the warrior's ashes. It is likely that this sophistication in

▶ **VILLANOVAN CAVALRYMAN, 8TH CENTURY BC**
Villanovan cavalrymen were armed as infantry and also wore the Villanovan-style helmet with the distinctive metal crest. Villanovan cavalry may have used the horse only for transportation and then dismounted to fight on foot.

design and technology indicates that it was the Villanovans who introduced iron-working to the Italian peninsula, they were certainly one of the earliest iron age cultures in the Mediterranean.

Villanovan Warriors

Infantry and cavalry wore short white or red tunics, the same length as those of the Samnites, and they wore the relatively small, square breastplate attached to the body by leather straps. Helmets were based on the pot-shaped so common in this period and either had a centrally located falling plume at the top centre of the helmet or a curious metal comb that sat in the middle of the helmet and ran from front to back.

Shields were round or oblong and do not seem to have had any particular design on the front. A sword, again hanging from a baldric on the left side of the body, and a spear of a least five feet in length completed the panoply of war. The Villanovans might also have carried a round embossed shield, but this may have been a ceremonial shield and not one for use in combat.

Villanovan arms and armour were made of bronze, their shields in particular being made entirely of bronze. The metal fittings for their horse harness were also made of bronze. As shown in the mounted figure on the left, Villanovan horsemen wore their heavy shields on their backs when not in use. It would seem that the size of the shield was not suited to mounted combat, being too large to be handled deftly together with spear or sword. Held to the warrior's back while mounted by a leather strap, it could be brought quickly into action on the ground.

EARLY ROMAN TROOPS

At Rome's beginning, citizens fought when need be, acting as warriors in a war band. There was little or no formal organization to the war band, and its leader would have been either the cleverest, or the bravest Roman, or both, able to lead his fellow warriors into battle. There was also not any standardization of arms, armour, or equipment, and whatever the warrior owned or could find would be what he took into battle.

Being victorious in the battle or raid, the Roman warrior would attempt to enrich himself and his family at the expense of the enemy. Plundered equipment and weapons were highly prized and would then be used to equip the victor in readiness for the next foray into enemy territory or to answer the next emergency.

The appearance of the war band would illustrate this variety of arms and equipment from the many enemies the war band had fought and defeated in earlier encounters. At this time there was no Roman legion and the phalanx had yet to be introduced. What did happen is that Roman military abilities were being affected by their neighbours and enemies (often the same thing) and out of the chaos, the war band would develop.

The Roman Hoplite

Greek influence upon the Romans, as well as the Etruscans, was strong not only in arms, armour, and equipment, but in organization and tactics. Greek hoplite armour, either in bronze or in leather, was introduced to the Romans on a wide scale, and greaves became a staple part of the panoply of the Roman warrior, now evolving into a soldier trained to fight as one part of a unit.

The round Greek shield was introduced during this period, as was the spear and sword, but the most single important part of the Roman army of this period was the adoption of the Greek fighting

◀ ROMAN SOLDIER, C.700BC This early Roman infantry wears typical crude, yet quite effective, armour common in central Italy in the 8th century BC. The pot helmet has a stiff horsehair crest, and the cuirass covers almost the entire torso above the waist. The helmet is of Villanovan origin, probably common in central Italy.

▶ ROMAN SOLDIER, C.700BC The cuirass worn by this figure is almost the same as that shown on the left, but more 'form fitting' on the sides. The pot helmet is simple, but effective. The clothing has become shorter and easier to manage in combat. Sword, spear, and shield are becoming common 'issue' with the Romans and will remain so for some time.

formation, the phalanx. This formation would be put to good use by the Roman army until factors of terrain and enemy tactics would force the formation's obsolescence.

Opposing armies both using the phalanx would fight a bloody battle, quite literally a 'meeting' engagement. As the phalanxes would approach each other, speed undoubtedly increased for the expected crash of shield against shield, and the opposing lines of spearmen to cross. It is not wholly out of the realm of possibility that after that initial clash the entire front ranks of both opposing forces would go down dead or wounded, impaled on their opponents' spears.

The strength of the phalanx was in its rigidity, depth, and the deadly hedge of spear points that projected from the front ranks. The hoplites would 'lock shields', forming what for all intents and purposes was a shield wall that had to be maintained in order to gain victory.

Hoplites who were killed, badly wounded or fell out of formation were replaced as quickly as possible by the men in the next rank. If that failed, the phalanx could be broken, which would lead to a melee and a slaughter of one side or the other, whichever was broken first. When this happened, the light troops of either side would come into their own and assist in the slaughter of the enemy.

Against an opposing force that was not as well-armoured or disciplined, the phalanx would be very effective, as shown by the Spartans at Thermopylae in 480BC against the Persians. The phalanx worked best on flat, level ground. On uneven ground it was difficult to maintain the tactical rigidity necessary and the phalanx could be at a disadvantage. Much later, in the later Middle Ages, it is documented that Swiss pikemen stood in the ancient phalanx formation, and crossed pikes with their

◀ ROMAN HOPLITE, 6TH CENTURY BC *The Romans, like the Etruscans, were definitely influenced in their arms and armour by the Greek presence in Italy and Sicily. This early Roman infantryman's appearance is influenced by the Greek style; with muscled cuirass, round shield, and greaves. His simple but effective helmet is noteworthy and might be a definite predecessor to the classical Roman helmet of the later legions. While wearing greaves, he has no shoes or boots.*

▲ ROMAN HOPLITE, 6TH CENTURY BC *This Roman infantryman is similar in attire and armour to the figure on the left. Though his helmet has a short horsehair crest, it is again a harbinger of later Roman helmets. The innovative device on the shield would become a traditional one, the Romans being fond of using the boar, wolf, horse and bull.*

German counterparts, the Landsknechts. It is said that when the front ranks fell, succeeding ranks would step up and over their fallen comrades. This could continue until one side or the other would give up.

Etrusco-Romano Troops

The Etruscans were an ancient Italian civilization that has always been closely associated with the Romans. The legendary kings of early Rome, until they were thrown out and the Roman republic founded, were

▼ ETRUSCO-ROMAN MEDIUM SPEARMAN, *C.*550BC *Etrusco-Roman infantrymen of this period were classed in four separate groups based on arms and armour (or the lack thereof). This is a Class II, or medium infantryman, armoured with only a helmet and scutum. He is armed with both sword and spear, but his scutum is now becoming rectangular instead of round in the Greek style.*

Etruscans and at Rome's beginnings the Etruscans bordered Roman territory. The Romans called them the Tusci or the Etrusci. The area that the Etruscans occupied is modern-day Tuscany, and quite possibly Etruria.

An ancient civilization, which may have been related to the Villanovans at one point, the Etruscans endured as a separate people until they were finally absorbed by the Roman republic during the 1st century BC. The Etruscans originally formed a league or confederation centred around the eastern Alps and the Po Valley. Rome was the junior partner in the Etruscan-Roman

'alliance' but the Romans eventually became the dominant presence and the separate Etruscan civilization vanished into the Roman cultural labyrinth.

Infantry Class System

The Etruscan period in the history of the Roman army clearly demonstrates Greek influence in arms and armour,

▼ ETRUSCO-ROMAN HOPLITE, *C.*550BC *For all intents and purposes, this is a Greek hoplite in arms and armour. The Etruscan overlords reorganized their army and established four classes of infantrymen. This figure is of class I, a heavy infantryman in full armour who would have fought in the phalanx formation.*

but it also shows the development of the legion into what would later become the manipular legion, with the four types of troops manning the four vertical lines of the Roman battle array.

It was during this period that the four types of infantry in the battle array were designated as Class I, II, III and IV, with slingers classed as V. There were 40 centuries in the Roman battle array of infantry with an additional 15 centuries of light troops armed with the sling for skirmishing. Class I was composed of 10 centuries of heavily armed spearmen and they were very similar to the Greek hoplite. A muscle cuirass was worn, as was the usual Greek-pattern full helmet with a round shield, the front of which was decorated in the Greek manner. A sword was worn on a baldric on the warrior's left side and the helmet had a Greek-style horsehair crest, sometimes multi-coloured and sometimes of a single colour. Greaves were worn.

▼ **ETRUSCO-ROMAN LIGHT SPEARMAN,** *c.550BC While this Class III infantryman is a light spearman, in armour and appearance he is very similar to a Class II medium infantryman. The rectangular shield, however, may have been smaller than the Class II men. All classes wore the caliga, the shoe studded with hobnails and worn by the ordinary roman soldier.*

▲ **ETRUSCO-ROMAN LIGHT INFANTRYMAN,** *c.550BC Etrusco-Roman light infantrymen, whose job it was to skirmish in front of the phalanx, had no armour but used a shield. They were also armed with both a spear and javelins, which were missile weapons. Note that the scutum is not only quite rectangular, but is beginning to be curved.*

Class II troops were without body armour, though they wore a pot helmet with a coloured falling plume in the centre of the top of the helmet. The shield was rectangular and greaves were worn on the calves.

Class III troops were armed as the Class II men. A Volsci-style helmet was worn. Class IV troops were probably light troops, though armed very differently from the Class V slingers. They were armed with shield and javelins and wore no helmet.

THE SAMNITES

Early Rome was merely one 'tribe' among many in early Italy. While in the pursuit of a united Italy, which meant Italy under Roman rule, the Romans had to contend with the Etruscans, Samnites, Villanovans, Campanians, Acqui and Senones among others. Some were Latins like the Romans themselves, and others were Italians, the differences being mainly cultural and linguistic.

The Samnites were a powerful group in Italy, with great influence in the development of Roman armour and arms. The four Samnite tribes, the Pentri, Caraceni, Harpini, and Cardini, usually banded together during wartime. Livy, the early Roman historian, states that they fought in a phalanx-type formation, but it was probably a square, instead of the rectangle formation of the Greek and Roman phalanx. Apparently the Samnite phalanx was tactically flexible enough to suit the hilly terrain in which the Samnites preferred to fight. They fought three wars with Rome.

Samnite Warriors

The Samnite tunic was very short, probably the length of a long

◀ **SAMNITE LIGHT INFANTRYMAN, 4TH CENTURY BC** *A lightly accoutred Samnite infantryman, armed and equipped for the fighting that would take place in the highlands of central Italy. His pot helmet is equipped with cheek pieces, and, as depicted in Samnite artefacts, he is wearing neither shoes nor boots.*

▶ **SAMNITE SPEARMAN, 4TH CENTURY BC** *Samnite heavy infantryman were lavishly equipped compared to the light and medium infantry. This figure has an elaborate helmet with crest, along with a cuirass, and has a greave on one leg, which would become common with Roman legionaries at a later period. His scutum is comparable and quite similar to the developing Roman one, not being round but quite rectangular.*

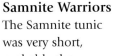

▲ *A bronze Samnite triple-disk cuirass, 4th century BC. Three identical breast and back plates formed the armour.*

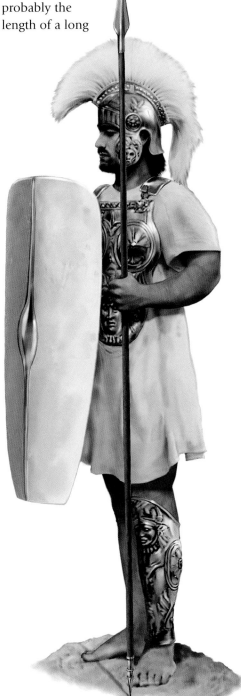

coloured patterns and designs used to decorate their shields. It appears that shield shape had something to do with the bearer's assignment to infantry, light infantry, and cavalry. Both spears and javelins were used.

Samnites had both infantry and cavalry, sometimes they were armoured and sometimes not. Apparently their light infantry would wear crested helmets with the crest alternating in various colours, red, white and black being common. They would also carry javelins for use in the skirmish line. While cavalry seemed to be armoured, sometimes with muscle cuirasses, mounted standard bearers and senior officers might not be. It appears that all Samnite warriors wore some type of helmet, without decoration or topped with feathers or horsehair crests. Cheek pieces were movable.

Samnite Armour

Livy notes that the Samnites wore two 'types' of armour in their battle array, half were in silver and the other half in gold-coloured armour. Helmets, greaves and cuirasses all

matched with the warriors of one side or the other. It was also noted that their Roman opponents did not 'shine' as brightly as the Samnites in formation and the Romans were told not to worry, but to be brave with sword and shield.

This Samnite armour would later be worn by gladiators in the arena where three types of gladiators were employed: Samnite, Thracian, and Gauls. Gladiators armed and accoutured 'in the Samnite manner' were popular until the games went out of fashion, long after the Samnites had disappeared from history.

◀ SAMNITE INFANTRYMAN, 4TH CENTURY BC *There was considerable 'cross-fertilization' of arms, armour, and equipment of the different 'armies' in Italy during Rome's formative period. This infantryman could be classed as a Samnite 'medium' infantryman; he wears no body armour except for his elaborate helmet, but he is equipped with a shield.*

▶ SAMNITE SPEARMAN, 4TH CENTURY BC *This Samnite heavy infantryman is well-equipped and armoured with a muscled cuirass and a pot helmet with upright feathers attached in a line. His shield, while not round in the Greek style, is not yet the rectangular shape that other Italian troops were developing.*

modern shirt and came down to the upper thigh. Body armour was still of the small cuirass type, which only covered part of the torso. Helmets were smaller than the Greek and at a distance have taken on the appearance of what Roman helmets would look like during the republic. They were decorated with either crests as the Greeks used, falling plumes from a central knob in the helmet, or by coloured feathers arranged crossways across the helmet. Shields were no longer always round, but were taking on the shape later adopted by the Romans for their scuta, and there were

THE CAMPANIANS, VOLSCI AND SENONES

Not all of Rome's Italian enemies fought in the same way. Those who lived in the plains and lowlands fought in a manner similar to the Romans. Those who did not and lived in the highlands or hilly countryside of the foothills of the Apennines fought differently, their tactics being dictated by terrain. It was there, against the peoples who lived in the hills, that the Romans found that the phalanx was not flexible enough a formation for different terrains; they needed a new formation, and the manipular legion was developed.

Rome's Italian enemies were armed and armoured in a similar fashion to the Romans, and most of these trends had been borrowed from the Greeks and whatever outside influences came across the Alps into Italy.

The Campanians

Probably originating in the Apennine Mountains that run down the middle of the Italian peninsula, the Campanians had migrated down to the lowlands by the 1st millennium BC and occupied the area of Italy known today as Campania. They came into direct conflict with the Greeks who had settled in southern Italy, initially to no avail, but finally driving them from Campania in the middle

▶ CAMPANIAN CAVALRYMAN, 4TH CENTURY BC *The Campanians fielded quite well-equipped cavalrymen who might also carry a round shield and quite possibly would fight on foot and not mounted. The elaborate helmet is noteworthy and quite distinctive.*

of the 5th century BC. When the Samnites began encroaching into Campania, the Campanians allied themselves with Rome in 343BC to resist the Samnite aggression. The Campanians were given that name by the Romans

themselves and remained allied to Rome as long as it was beneficial for them to do so.

The Volsci and Acqui

Known to the Romans when they first settled on the Palatine Hill in 753BC, the Volsci were a hill people, violent and aggressive, with an established presence in the Pomentine Plain, near to Roman territory. Frequently allied with the neighbouring Acqui, the Volsci proved to be a dangerous neighbour, frequently fighting the Romans for control over land and for prestige and influence. While there was long conflict between the two states, the Volsci also could be friendly towards Rome when she was threatened with an outside aggressor, and they could be relied upon to sell grain to Rome

and the Acqui was in 458BC at Mons Algidus. At first the action seemed to be shaping up into an Acqui victory, but the situation was reversed by the Roman commander, Lucius Quinctius Cincinnatus. This was not the end of Rome's problems with the Acqui, however, and they were only finally defeated after the 2nd Samnite War.

The Volsci and the Acqui, were generally armed and armoured in like manner to the Villanovans. White tunics seem to have been preferred and their helmets were of the pot type, with a metal comb down the centre, topped with a horsehair crest, red and white being known to have been used. The entire helmet had a rim or brim around the base of the helmet.

The Senones

Senones were a Celtic tribe that lived in either northern Italy or along the Adriatic coast. Aggressive and warlike as the other Celtic peoples were, the Senones fought Rome for over 100 years. They were finally defeated by Rome in 283BC and were expelled from Italy over the Alps. From there they moved eastward joining other groups of Gauls migrating to eastern Europe. Later, during Caesar's Gallic campaigns, the legions would again encounter

Celts called Senones, but these were not the same people that had been expelled earlier from Italy.

Senones appear to have worn a type of trousers without shirts in combat, some of the warriors fighting naked. They carried a long, broad sword, a long rectangular shield and were also armed with a long spear. Helmets were worn, the pot type with movable cheek pieces and sometimes with an elaborate decoration on the top that appears to have been somewhat unwieldy for use in combat, but must have added an impressive height.

▲ ACQUI OR VOLSCI INFANTRYMAN, 4TH CENTURY BC *The central highlands of Italy produced excellent warriors who were generally well-armoured, armed, and equipped. The disc cuirass, and pot helmet with elaborate horsehair crest, are typical of the Volsci and the Acqui tribes.*

in order for the Romans to withstand a siege from other hostile peoples. Eventually, the Volsci would be absorbed, as other peoples had been, into the expanding Roman state and in later years many prominent Romans, including Marius, the great reformer of the Roman army, and the Emperor Caesar Augustus, would be born in the former territory of the Volsci.

The Acqui were an Italian people whose civilization predated Rome. They fought against Rome, many times allied with the Volsci, in order to maintain their independence. The most important battle between Rome

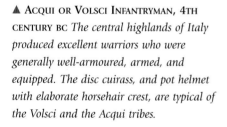

► CHIEFTAIN OF THE SESONES C.300BC *The Senones were Celts, and it was these hardy warriors that sacked Rome in the 4th century BC. The plaid garments are typical of Celtic attire and the well-developed helmet would later be copied and developed further by the Romans. Celtic weapons greatly influenced weapons development in Rome. The helmet 'crest' is unusual and quite distinctive. This warrior is a chieftain and is therefore well-equipped. The men he led would not be so well-armed and equipped and might actually fight naked.*

FROM PHALANX TO LEGION

As the Roman army developed from phalanx to legion, arms and armour became somewhat standardized, even though there were five different 'types' of soldiers in the legion. These were the hastati, the principes, and the triarii, which were all heavy infantry, the velites, which were light infantry, and the eques, the cavalry.

Arms and Equipment

All troops except for the velites, wore armour, usually mail by this time, worn over the usual tunic, which was most often white. This tended to be the favourite colour worn by Roman troops, although sometimes red was used. The tunic had slits for the arms, although sleeved tunics were also known. They were made to extend below the knees but were often shortened by the wearer for comfort and mobility.

Roman spears were usually of uniform length and construction, with a solid head or point.

The pole arm that became the most widely used and issued was the javelin, with a wooden shaft and elongated point and a metal shaft made of cast lead, which would bend after hitting its target. Rather than being considered a pole arm, the Roman javelin was actually a missile.

The Romans had conquered Italy using a sword that showed strong influence from the Greek colonies in Southern Italy. It was longer than the gladius, which would only come to be used later, and closely resembled the pointed xiphos of the Greeks. The blade and hilt were of one piece, with additional protection riveted to the squared guard, and with handles made of wood, bone, or, more rarely, iron. It was not especially long, used for thrusting, and it had wide currency throughout the Mediterranean world.

The heavy infantry and cavalry all wore a helmet, and there is evidence that velites might have also worn a helmet of sorts, if not one actually like that of the heavy infantry.

◀ ROMAN TRIARIUS, 4TH CENTURY BC *The third and final line of the early republican legion was formed of triarii, an early Roman legionary who formed the final line in battle and were composed of the oldest soldiers in the legion. They were armoured and armed quite differently from the other legionaries and might not be committed to combat except in an emergency. This figure is 'taking the knee', an official resting position for troops.*

▲ EARLY ROMAN WARRIOR, 6TH CENTURY BC *The earliest Roman warriors, not yet developed into soldiers, wore what they wore in civilian life. This was a kind of toga-like garment, secured by folds and tucks, which must have been fairly restrictive to physical activity. To this was added different types of cuirasses and weapons of choice, depending on what was available. Round shields were in use by almost all of the Italians and Latins, and pot helmets were universal.*

Manipular Tactics

The Romans of this period, in what would later become known as the manipular legion, fought in four lines. The velites, or skirmishers, would open the action and when it became time for the more heavily armed infantry to be committed to the fray, the velites would retire between the maniples and reform behind the maniple to which they were assigned.

Upon the retirement of the velites, the first line of heavy infantry, the hastati would move forward in formation behind their shields. When they came into range for throwing their pila (about 13–18m/15–20 yards), they would let fly on command with a volley of pila and probably a second volley too. Drawing their swords, the primary weapon of the Roman infantryman or legionary, they would press their attack and engage the enemy with sword and shield.

It should be remembered that the Roman legionary used his scutum, or shield, as a weapon both offensively and defensively. In that drill he was deadly, and infantry who could not manoeuvre or fight as a unit could be literally 'torn up' in the close-quarter fighting Romans trained for.

The remaining two lines of Roman heavy infantry stood in ranks waiting to be committed. If the enemy was defeated by the actions of the velites and the hastati, then these troops would either not be committed or would be used to clean up the battlefield of any enemy stragglers or to chase away any enemy troops that still had fight left in them. Roman commanders would keep their princeps and triarii fresh by having them rest on the battlefield, still in their disciplined ranks, by 'taking a knee' that is they would put their right knee on the ground, place their shields in front of them for protection, and hold their spears at a 45 degree angle, resting but ready.

▼ **ROMAN PRINCEPS, 4TH CENTURY BC** *The principes were men who formed the second line of the legion and were in the prime of life. They were also well-armed and equipped and were usually armoured in a mail cuirass as shown. Shields were now being painted with different symbols on them, often legion-specific.*

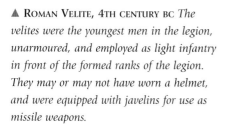

▲ **ROMAN VELITE, 4TH CENTURY BC** *The velites were the youngest men in the legion, unarmoured, and employed as light infantry in front of the formed ranks of the legion. They may or may not have worn a helmet, and were equipped with javelins for use as missile weapons.*

The helmets could have been all of one style, but that probably was not the usual case. Shields were used by all five types of troops, though the cavalry shield was lighter and modified for mounted movement and combat. Sandals of some type would be worn, though at this period they probably were not the universal issue of the caliga of a later period.

THE ROMAN ARMY OF THE PUNIC WARS

The manipular legion with which the Roman army fought the series of wars with Carthage was still organized with four different types of infantry: hastati, principes, triarii and velites. The hastati were the first-line men, the youngest of the infantry with the exception of the velites. At this point, the Roman army of the 3rd century BC was still not a professional fighting force, it was rather a conscript army based on land

▶ ROMAN LEGIONARY, 220BC *Well-equipped heavy infantrymen were the mainstay and heart of the Roman legion. This stalwart could be a princeps or one of the triarii, or in the transitional phase of the legion where all of the heavy infantry would be armed and equipped in the same manner.*

ownership. However, as the wars were growing longer, and the legions began serving outside Italy, a certain level of professionalism was growing and being recognized inside the army.

The Republican Legion

Soldiers of the republican legion were probably armoured with the small cuirass that only partially protected the torso, but they did wear the same helmet as the older two groups of heavy infantry. This would be decorated with feathers, sometimes from a central point on the top of the helmet, or straight across the middle of the helmet. It was a pot-type helmet but with cheek guards on each side that gave good protection to the face and jaw without hampering the wearer's visibility.

Heavy Infantry

The legionaries, whether centurions or enlisted men, were armed with pilum (javelin) and scutum

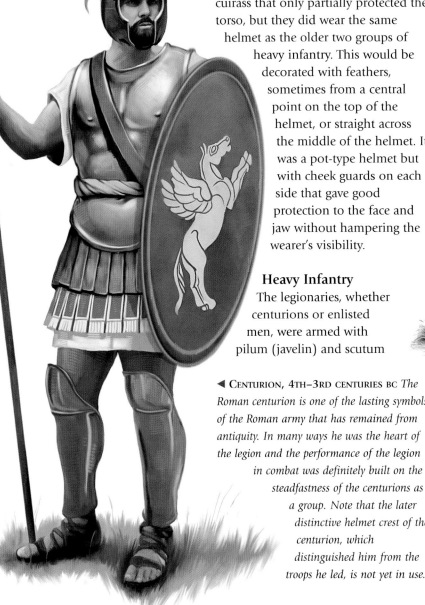

◀ CENTURION, 4TH–3RD CENTURIES BC *The Roman centurion is one of the lasting symbols of the Roman army that has remained from antiquity. In many ways he was the heart of the legion and the performance of the legion in combat was definitely built on the steadfastness of the centurions as a group. Note that the later distinctive helmet crest of the centurion, which distinguished him from the troops he led, is not yet in use.*

(shield), the scutum beginning to take on the longer shape it would have later in the republic and empire. Their swords were still relatively long, with a two-edged, leaf-shaped blade. It was short enough to allow the Romans to adopt the tactic of thrusting from behind their shields, but was not yet the famous gladius.

The principes and triarii were now better armoured, wearing either a well-made mail shirt that came down almost to the bottom of the tunic or a muscle cuirass, though mail was now becoming the preferred armour of the legionary. It was easier to wear, was articulated, and gave adequate protection against sword and missile

▼ TRIBUNE, 3RD CENTURY BC *Tribunes, of which there were as many as six per legion, were armed and equipped as officers befitting their social rank. They may or may not have been efficient officers, and they were not in the same league as the centurions. They were expected, however, to lead from the front as Roman officers and take their chances along with everyone else in the legion.*

weapons. While these troops might still be armed with a spear, the pilum was becoming the pole arm of choice because of its advantage in being used as an effective missile weapon.

The shield was becoming more defined and at this stage probably came up to the legionary's waist when he rested it on the ground. The shield was not merely defensive, it was used as a weapon along with the sword. The legionary became skilled in its use as such and the combination was deadly in close, no-quarter fighting. The shields of all the infantry of the legion would usually have the same design on them so that they could be identified in combat, and it also represented the legion to which they belonged.

Light Infantry

The velites were lightly armed light infantry. They were the youngest and poorest soldiers in the legion and their name, velite, means 'cloak men'. They wore the same tunic as the heavy infantry but completely without any body armour. Animal skin headdresses were worn and the gladius was also carried on a leather belt around the waist. They carried a small round shield and short javelins, as well as the gladius, and their mission in combat was to skirmish in loose order and impede an enemy's advance, tiring them as much as possible and reducing their ranks as well as attempting to put the enemy's formation into disorder. This was done before the heavy infantry of the legion was committed or, if on defensive, before they met the enemy's attack. In the pursuit phase of the battle,

▲ ROMAN LIGHT INFANTRYMAN, 220BC *Another view of a velite, or veles, which clearly shows how lightly armed and equipped they might be, with no protective equipment or armour. With the transition of the legion from a manipular to a cohort organization, the velites would disappear and not be employed again.*

or if formed combat degenerated into a melee, the light infantry, which had reorganized behind the heavy infantry after withdrawal, would join in the combat as relatively fresh troops.

Senior Officers: The Legate

The senior officers of the legion, the legate and the tribunes, were armed and armoured in a more expensive fashion, as befitted their station in society and the army, and their dress could be adapted to suit personal tastes. Muscle cuirasses, some heavily and expensively engraved, would be

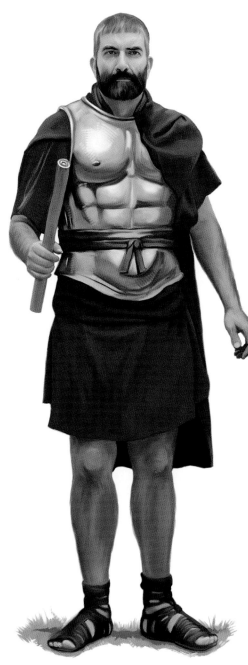

worn, as would helmets of their own purchase and sometimes design. In the field senior officers could be easily picked out by friend and foe alike and would make a rich prize if captured or killed by the enemy. Coloured sashes would be worn around the cuirass above the waist to designate their rank, and the plumes of their helmets would be either white or red. The plumes were usually of two types, the falling plume that was attached in the centre of the helmet or the rigid horse hair plume worn in the Greek style. Tunics were red, or white with red stripes, and the red military cloak would also be worn. They were armed with the gladius and perhaps a dagger, and some carried ceremonial spears as a symbol of rank.

Centurions

The centurion was the backbone of the legion. Centurions commanded the centuries, and apparently they also commanded the maniples, though some sources dispute this. If they did not, however, there would have been no effective chain of command in the legion. The intermediate level would have to be commanded by someone, and the tribunes and legates, the de facto senior officers of the legion, would have had to have given orders directly to the centuries; awkward at best and disastrous at worst.

The centurion was dressed and equipped differently from the legionaries under his command. He might wear a muscle cuirass as did the senior officers of the legion, but he might also wear mail as did the men under his command. At this period the centurions probably wore greaves,

while the legionaries would not, and his shield might be of a different shape than that of the men and might also be of a different size and design. Centurions wore a baldric across their body to carry their gladius and at this period the helmet was of the same design as the troops.

Signifer and Standard Bearers

The standard bearers and musicians wore animal skins of different types (bears, lions, etc.) in order to distinguish themselves from the ordinary legionary. They were armed and equipped exactly the same, except that their shields were smaller and round so they would not

▲ LEGATE, 3RD CENTURY BC *A legate was generally the commander of the legion and was a high-ranking officer. The muscled cuirass was usually the norm for a legion commander, though leather, flexible cuirasses were also worn. Generally speaking, a legate could arm and equip himself as he wished. He had to be visible to his troops however.*

▶ SIGNIFER, 3RD CENTURY BC *Roman standard bearers were armed for self-defence rather than attack, hence his small shield. The distinctive 'uniform' of the standard bearers became the lion and bearskins they wore over their armour. Standards usually had an iron tip at the base of the pole in order to ram it into the ground. The piece of fabric on top here was probably a unit affectation.*

interfere with the carrying of their standards. Maniple standard bearers were different in that depending on their designation, they did not always wear armour. The legion standards were composed of a staff with various attachments, often with a plinth at the top which carried the legion's number and on top of the plinth the legion's symbol, usually of an animal such as a bull, boar, horse, or perhaps a she-wolf suckling Romulus and Remus.

The Cavalry

Roman cavalry was becoming an integral part of the legion. As the stirrup had not yet been developed riding was an acquired skill, and the Roman saddle was designed to keep the cavalryman mounted firmly on his horse. Roman cavalry, until the rise of the eastern Roman Empire after the fall of Rome itself, were auxiliary troops, used for scouting, skirmishing, and to combat enemy cavalry. They were never the main striking force of a legion or a Roman army in the field.

Initially unarmoured, the cavalryman had a helmet and shield, the shield initially being the round type used by the velites, w`h the usual decorations for the unit.

Helmets could be the same as the heavy infantry, but also of a modified Greek type with a small horsehair crest along the top from front to rear. The cavalry were armed with a long sword, the spatha, developed or copied from Roman enemies, probably the Celts, as well as a spear. The unusual cavalry helmet was undoubtedly of Roman design and was intended to protect both the head and neck of the horseman. The Roman cavalryman was intended for mounted combat and did

not dismount to fight on foot unless absolutely necessary. Roman cavalrymen of this period or shortly thereafter began to wear a helmet of the same design as the infantry, though without the cheek pieces.

▼ ROMAN CAVALRYMAN, 3RD CENTURY BC
The Roman army was primarily an infantry army, and the cavalry were an ancilliary arm. The Roman cavalry was necessarily a small unit, it was, however, recruited from the equestrian class, and was well-equipped and armed. The distinctive, oddly shaped helmet here is reminiscent of the helmets worn by Alexander the Great's companions.

THE CARTHAGINIAN ARMY
264–146BC

Carthage recruited armies from among its own diverse population, but also made use of mercenaries and auxiliaries from regional allies. Under a capable commander, this made for a formidable and flexible force.

Native Carthaginians

Portions of Carthage's armies of the period were composed of native Carthaginians, and they were armed and armoured to the

▶ **HANNIBAL BARCA, 216BC** *Hannibal of Carthage was one of the most – if not the most – formidable enemy commander the Romans ever faced. He is dressed here as a senior Carthaginian commander and needed to be conspicuous on the field of battle in order to be recognized by his troops.*

same high standard as the best of the Romans. The army was composed of both infantry and cavalry units. The cavalry might wear plate armour covered with leather or cloth as in the Greek manner, and the infantry probably wore a mail shirt over their tunics. Both carried round shields, had a metal helmet with cheek pieces, sometimes with a coloured plume flowing from the top of the helmet. Swords and spears were carried by infantry and cavalry, and both types of soldiers wore greaves. The cavalryman's horse might wear an early form of armour across the chest.

Elephants

As has already been mentioned, the Carthaginians also used elephants in combat. Fighting or encountering such large animals, with soldiers placed on top of them either shooting arrows or throwing spears from above, could be a frightening prospect. The Romans learned not only to defeat armies equipped with elephants (which was done by ham-stringing the animals to bring them and their human cargo down, where the enemy troops could be dispatched before they got up, if they survived the fall) but

◀ **CARTHAGINIAN STANDARD BEARER, 216BC**
There was a core of native Carthaginian troops, of which this is one. He is well-armoured and equipped with greaves, an excellent helmet, and a flexible cuirass, probably of leather.

they learned also to employ elephants themselves. Only one elephant survived the crossing of the Alps, and legend has it the elephant was Hannibal's favourite.

Mercenaries

Carthage was careful to ally itself to powers that were hostile to Rome, or fearful of Roman influence. With these alliances, the Carthaginians gained foreign troops that allowed them to make use of particular skills and assets. They employed Numidian light cavalry,

▲ *A 15th-century depiction of Hannibal's epic journey through the Alps and into Italy.*

Spanish cavalry and infantry, as well as various troops of Celtic origin to fight their wars for them. The Spanish troops can almost be classed as Carthaginian, as much of Iberia was now in Carthaginian possession, but on the whole the army led by Hannibal into Italy via the Alps was a polyglot force.

The employment of mercenary troops was always something of a chancy proposition, especially if pay fell into arrears. However, under a commander such as Hannibal, leading by force of personal example and usually winning on the battlefield, mercenary troops would become loyal to their commander, trusting in his skill to overcome all odds.

Unfortunately, much of what we know about the Carthaginian troops has come to us by second-hand source material or from information gleaned from monuments. As the city of Carthage and all its records was effectively wiped off the map by the Romans at the end of the 3rd Punic War, much information on the Carthaginian army has been lost.

▶ CARTHAGINIAN WAR ELEPHANT WITH TROOPS, 220BC *Elephants were employed by many ancient armies, the Carthaginian army being but one, and to those who had not seen them before they were a terrifying sight. Cavalry horses in particular had to be specially trained to stand their ground. Troops fought from a fighting platform on top of the elephant, protected by a chest-high casket.*

The Celts

Warlike Celtic mercenaries that fought for the Carthaginians were armed and armoured with their indigenous weapons and armour. Mail was sometimes worn, as were metal helmets with hinged cheek pieces. Celts wore plaid clothing, trousers and shirts, and wore cloaks. Some fought with no armour or even shirts in combat, but all foot soldiers carried the Celtic long swords, shields similar to the Romans and Iberians, and carried long spears. The mail differed in design from the Romans and others, but generally afforded the same protection.

The Numidians

One of the most effective forces that Hannibal commanded was the Numidian light cavalry. They were undoubtedly the most effective and expert light cavalry of the period and the Romans would later lure them away from the Carthaginians and use them to their own advantage. They used neither saddle nor reins, and controlled their horses with their knees, sometimes holding the rope around their horses' necks. They wore only a tunic that came down to mid-thigh and their only personal protection was a hide shield. Numidians carried three or four light spears that could be either thrown or used in a melee, and they were expert in its use. The Numidians could not be used for shock action, but were

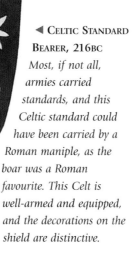

◀ CELTIC STANDARD
BEARER, 216BC
*Most, if not all,
armies carried
standards, and this
Celtic standard could
have been carried by a
Roman maniple, as the
boar was a Roman
favourite. This Celt is
well-armed and equipped,
and the decorations on the
shield are distinctive.*

▲ CELTIC SWORDSMAN, 216BC *The Celts
ranged from Britain to northern Greece and
Thrace, and were actively recruited by the
Carthaginians. They would usually serve
under their own chieftains. Tattoos, torque
jewellery, and stiff hair were hallmarks of
Celtic warriors, as were the long swords that
the Roman called spathae and with which
they would later equip their cavalry.*

excellent troops to employ in the pursuit of a broken enemy and were expert mounted skirmishers.

Because the Numidian horse was committed for action in a battle's opening stages and then after the enemy army broke, these troops were relatively fresh when sent into action, which was undoubtedly one of the factors which made them formidable opponents. The Roman historian Livy wrote that the Numidians were by far the best cavalrymen in Africa.

One of the reasons for the superiority of the Numidian light horse was their mounts. These animals were generally smaller than those of the Roman cavalry and were the ancestors of what would become the excellent Arabian breed, favoured by Napoleon for his own mounts. Numidian cavalry was expert at harassing an enemy, forming up to charge and then scattering before shock, sometimes causing opposing cavalry to attempt to pursue and

thus ruining their own formations. In this manner the Numidian horse resembled the later Cossack irregular light cavalry of the mid-18th and early 19th centuries which were considered by some as the best light cavalry of their era. These tactics were instrumental in springing the trap Hannibal set up for the Roman army at the Battle of the Trebia in 218BC. When the Numidians later turned on

Hannibal and the Carthaginians after the Romans invaded North Africa under Scipio in 202BC it was said that the Numidian light horse were instrumental in the defeat of the Carthaginian Army at the decisive Battle of Zama.

Later, the excellent Numidian light cavalry would fight for Rome, their king being interested in survival and allying himself with Rome. The Romans prized the Numidians highly, and appreciated their inate riding skills. The Romans would never have a native cavalry arm that was as capable or expert as those of her enemies, who eventually became either allies or subject peoples and part of the empire.

◀ NUMIDIAN LIGHT CAVALRYMAN. 3RD CENTURY BC *The Numidian light cavalry were some of the best in the ancient world and were superb horsemen and spearsmen, able to fight at speed, with neither armour, saddle or bridle. Their horse harness was very simple, as shown here. Due to their expert horsemanship and agility, they were most suitable for charging and then dispersing, an effective tactic for harassing the enemy and breaking up their formations. They would later be employed, and hugely valued, by the Romans.*

Italian Allies

As Hannibal ranged along the Italian peninsula, Italian allies of the Romans, such as the Campanians, Lucanians and Samnites, apparently abandoned Rome to its fate and Hannibal's mercy, and sided with the Carthaginians at least while Hannibal kept winning. They were armed and armoured as they had been in earlier wars and provided reliable, tough troops for the Carthaginians for as long as they remained loyal. Roman vengeance was not something that was taken lightly. However, they undoubtedly held ancient grudges against the Romans for the loss of independence they once enjoyed before being absorbed by Rome, and went willingly to fight for Hannibal and his victorious army.

Campanians

The people of Capua, the Campanians, were not fully assimilated into the Roman state and held what could be described as a 'limited' type of citizenship, so they were ripe to attempt to break away from Rome. With that decision was the hope that with a Roman defeat by Hannibal, Capua would become the premier city in Italy. Since Capua had access to the sea, reinforcements could easily and quickly be sent there from North Africa or Spain to keep Hannibal's troops up to strength and the veteran units intact. Hannibal's alliances, or 'agreements of friendship' in southern Italy gave him a base from which he could operate, receive reinforcements, and resupply his field army. The only problem with his new Italian allies is that they changed sides not only because of animosity between themselves and Rome, but because Hannibal was winning. A protracted war, which was eventually what Hannibal faced, was not to Hannibal's or his allies' advantage. The Italians who went over to support the Carthaginians faced Roman vengeance (a frightening prospect) if Hannibal either lost or could not force a decisive result. In the end that is what happened.

Campanian heavy cavalry fought in Hannibal's ranks after his repeated successes against the Romans. The horse furniture is quite simple and it appears that these horsemen were armed with a spear or lance, but no shield or sword. They

◀ IBERIAN CAVALRYMAN, 216BC
Hannibal's 'Spanish' troops should properly be called Iberians as there was a definite mixture of groups in the Iberian peninsula, a good portion of them being of Celtic origin. These were excellent troops, well-armed and trained, and were responsible for much of Hannibal's success. This cavalryman is armed and equipped comparable to the Roman equus.

▶ AFRICAN INFANTRYMAN, 216BC *The North African infantrymen who fought for Hannibal were most probably native Carthaginians, at least the leadership and cadres. They were well-armed and armoured as shown and in that respect they were no different to the Roman legionaries.*

might have worn a muscled cuirass and an elaborate Phrygian-type helmet with both a horsehair crest and feathers. The helmet also appears to have had small ornamental 'wings' on each side at the temple.

Samnites

The Samnite heavy infantry came to Hannibal's support and appear to have been armed and armoured as they always had been. They wore a tunic, together with a three-ring breastplate held in place by straps covered with metal plates, and probably a similar plate on their back. A sword, and sword belt were around the waist, was used and they also carried a spear or javelin. A small round shield, with appropriate decoration on the front, was carried and greaves were worn on the legs.

▼ IBERIAN CAVALRYMAN, **216**BC *These horsemen fought with the Spanish falcata, a short, one-edged blade that was concave on the lower part of the sword, but convex on top. This distributed the weight in such a way that it was capable of delivering a blow with the momentum of an axe and the cutting edge of a sword. It is said to have been much feared by the Romans.*

Lucanians

The heavy infantry of the Lucanians was armed and armoured much as the Samnites were. Red tunics might have been the norm here, but a similar cuirass was worn, along with sword, belt, shield and greaves. The helmet had cheek plates, but these were part of the helmet and did not move. Coloured feathers and horsehair crest finished off the infantryman's accoutrements.

The Lucanians were absorbed by the expanding Roman republic after allying themselves with King Pyrrhus of Epirus when he landed in southern Italy in 281BC. After Pyrrhus left Italy nine years later, the Lucanians felt the full wrath of the Romans against them. The Lucanians had settled in southern Italy and had been allied with Rome for some time before declaring for Pyrrhus against Rome. The subsequent Roman subjugation was brutal and when the opportunity to again ally themselves with an enemy of Rome came, they took it.

The Situation in Iberia, 218–13BC

In the beginning Hannibal's Iberian army was huge by contemporary standards, around 100,000 troops, but not all of it went into Italy. When Hannibal left Spain, the army remaining behind was considerably reduced. Apparently some of the native Iberians were reluctant to leave their homeland and some 10,000 were left in Spain when Hannibal moved into Gaul. While in Gaul, Hannibal recruited or allied himself with Gallic chieftains to make up the loss of troops left behind.

The Iberians that served Hannibal were excellent troops; even though Carthaginian rule in the Iberian peninsula was not popular, it would seem that Hannibal's reputation won their loyalty. Whatever the case, the bulk of his Spanish contingent that did accompany the army into Italy fought well, continuously.

The Romans did not stay idle as Hannibal organized his army in Iberia. An invasion force was dispatched from Italy to Spain in 218BC in an attempt to force the issue in the Iberian peninsula. Commanded jointly by the brothers Gnaeus Cornelius Scipio Calvus and Publius Cornelius Scipio, the army landed in Spain hoping to catch the Carthaginians before they were properly organized. The two commanders were somewhat surprised when they learned that Hannibal had evaded them and entered Gaul.

With the army, Gnaeus Cornelius Scipio Calvus continued with the mission of defeating the Carthaginian army in Spain, while his brother went back to Rome (he would return to Iberia in 217BC). The two armies manoeuvered against each other in the Iberian interior, but no decisive result was obtained by either side, even though the Romans repeatedly won battles both on land and at sea. Iberia was not the decisive theatre, though the Roman presence did prevent reinforcements from reaching Hannibal. The decisive operations would be conducted in North Africa, ending with the conclusive Battle of Zama, 202BC.

Iberians

Carthage's possessions in Spain provided both infantry and cavalry for the Carthaginian armies and they were reliable troops. The Iberians were partly of Celtic origin and their weapons and armour were

◀ IBERIAN INFANTRYMAN, 216BC *Iberian infantry in the employ of Carthage are sometimes misidentified as 'Spanish'. This is a well-equipped Iberian infantryman, though his cuirass by now was a relatively obsolete model, and he might quickly have availed himself of captured Roman armour, especially the mail cuirass, taken from the battlefields at Trebbia, Lake Trasimene or Cannae.*

▲ IBERIAN LIGHT INFANTRYMAN, 216BC
Lightly armed and accoutred, the light infantryman's job was to skirmish in front of the main Carthaginian line, and perhaps, by feigned retreat, lure the aggressive Romans into a trap, such as at Cannae.

a combination of the native Iberian material and that of the Celts who settled in Iberia for one reason or another, as the Celts were far-ranging peoples who raided and settled as they pleased. Their influence on weapon development was immense.

The Iberians generally wore a white tunic that came down to mid-thigh and both infantry and cavalry seem to have worn a leather belt around their waist that held both sword and dagger, their sword having a particularly uneven design as to the width of the blade and a particular type of hand grip. Helmets could be of a pot design, but could also be of the more elaborate Celtic preference, being pointed at the centre top. Some would have cheek pieces and others not, but the overall protection seems to have been adequate.

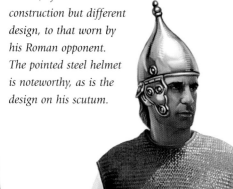

▼ CELTIC-IBERIAN HEAVY INFANTRYMAN, 216BC *The Carthaginians fielded well-equipped infantry, well-armed and armoured. This heavy infantryman, the equivalent of a Roman legionary, is armoured in a mail cuirass, of the same construction but different design, to that worn by his Roman opponent. The pointed steel helmet is noteworthy, as is the design on his scutum.*

The cavalry and light infantry carried small round shields and neither appears to have been armoured. Iberian heavy infantry were armoured in mail like their Roman heavy infantry counterparts and their multi-coloured shields were generally similar to the Roman equivalent. Spears were carried along with long broadswords, the sword being suspended from a broad leather belt at the waist. It appears that the Iberian heavy infantry also wore greaves.

The Iberians also wore a very interesting type of head covering, not quite helmet and not quite hat. They appear to have been an off-white colour and were made of sinew. They were worn by infantry and cavalry, the cavalry model being the more simple form of the head covering. The infantry version was somewhat hood-like and could be decorated with a short horsehair plume running front to rear, probably red in colour.

Generally speaking the Spanish/Iberian infantry that were in Hannibal's army were armed three different ways. There were swordsmen, those armed with the javelin, and slingers. Why the Spanish infantry came in these three categories is not known, but they were well-trained and efficient and can take a large part of the credit for Hannibal's successes.

The use of the sling was quite widespread in the ancient world, and it is the weapon that the Israelite King David, years before he was king, used to slay the Philistine giant, Goliath. The sling was a missile weapon and

▲ BALEARIC SLINGER, 3RD CENTURY BC
The sling was used as a weapon as far back as 1325BC by the Egyptians, and by the Assyrians in the 7th century BC. Small, smooth stones were launched as missile weapons by slingers in the skirmish line, and the slingers from the Balearic Islands in the Mediterranean were skilled in the use of the sling and were much sought after.

slingers were light infantrymen and were usually not armoured. The sling was made of leather and the stone ammunition was carefully picked out by the slingers so that the projectile would fly properly and hit what the slinger aimed at. Considerable skill was needed to be proficient, and the slingers were deadly at close range.

THE MACEDONIAN WARS
214–148BC

The series of conflicts fought between Rome and Macedonia are known as the First Macedonian War, the Second Macedonian War, the Selucid War, the Third Macedonian War, and the Fourth Macedonian War.

Two Fronts

The first Macedonian War was a minor distraction for Rome, for a life and death struggle was taking place with Carthage, and Italy had been invaded by Hannibal. Rome did dispatch troops across the Adriatic Sea, but the war was a small-scale affair compared to the titanic struggle in Italy and the western Mediterranean, and was inconclusive. A treaty between Rome and Macedonia ended the war.

This first war brought Macedonia, Greece, and the eastern Mediterranean to Rome's attention, and the wars that followed brought them into Rome's sphere of influence. All these territories would later become part of the empire.

Philip V of Macedon (r.221–179BC) spent his reign in a struggle with Rome to reassert Macedonian influence in the eastern Mediterranean. He fought two wars with Rome, losing both, but by his death in 179BC he had maintained the independence of Macedonia and passed the throne to his son Perseus. Perseus has the distinction of being the last king of an independent Macedonia until he was defeated during the Third Macedonian War at the Battle of Pydna in 168BC. He died two years later and Macedonia became part of the Roman Empire.

While the Romans were engaged in fighting during the 2nd Punic War, the Macedonians came into the war on the Carthaginian side and forced Rome to fight a two-front war.

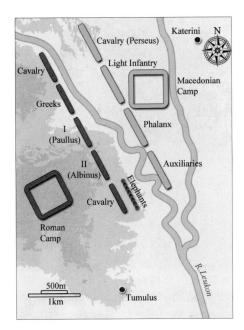

▲ *The Battle of Pydna, 168BC, sealed the fate of the Macedonian dynasty and marked Roman hegemony over the Greek world.*

The Macedonians were armed and armoured much the same as Alexander the Great's victorious armies had been one hundred or so years earlier.

Thracian Light Infantry

The Macedonians fielded Thracian light infantry, which were lightly armed and usually wore no armour.

▼ *Silver tetradrachma, showing a portrait of King Perseus of Macedonia (r.179–68BC) beaten at Pydna by the Romans, and later captured and executed.*

◀ THRACIAN INFANTRYMAN, C.200BC
Thracian light infantry usually fought without armour. This lightly accoutred infantryman is noteworthy for two things: the face mask, which would be part of his helmet, and the helmet itself. Known as the Phrygian helmet, it was worn by the heavy infantry of Alexander the Great.

Roman javelin, or in close combat. It was a versatile weapon and had become common in Macedonia, Thrace and Greece.

Macedonian Heavy Infantry

The Macedonian heavy infantry, a kind of soldier that would eventually become known in a later age as line infantry, made use of weapons and equipment which had undoubtedly served the late-age Greek hoplite as well as the phalangists of Alexander the Great (a phalangist was the Macedonian equivalent of the Greek hoplite – a heavy infantryman who fought in the phalanx). The Macedonian infantry still fought in the phalanx, which the Roman army had abandoned long before when they had to fight in the mountains and foothills of central Italy and found that the phalanx was not flexible enough to manoeuvre successfully. Uneven or rough terrain broke up the phalanx, rendering it susceptible to being taken on the flanks and causing heavy losses. This would happen in the later wars with the Macedonians and the Roman legion would prove itself the superior of the Macedonian phalanx in whatever terrain they met.

Greek hoplites and Macedonian phalangists were armed similarly with a helmet of either Greek or Macedonian origin (the Macedonian helmet was a form of the Phrygian cap), though other models of helmet were also used, as there was considerable Celtic influence in Greece and Macedonia.

Shields were round, coated in bronze or copper over a wooden frame; the infantry would also be armed with a sword, though that was not their principal weapon. The hoplite's or phalangist's main weapon was his thrusting spear, and the deadly hedge of spear points protruding from behind grim locked shields was the phalanx's main strength. During this period greaves may or may not have been worn, and while the phalangists may have been of a somewhat uniform appearance, along with arms, armour, and helmets, there was undoubtedly differences in shape and style, as well as in the designs on shields.

▲ THRACIAN INFANTRYMAN, C.200BC *Thracian troops were allied with the Macedonians, both being ethnic Greeks, against the Romans. This is a typical 'medium' infantryman armed reasonably well but with little armour. The long, curved sword is both unusual and noteworthy. It appears to be similar to the Japanese samurai sword.*

Thracian slingers were excellent shots and were highly prized, first by the Macedonians and later by the Romans, who would employ them after absorbing Greece and Macedonia into the Roman Empire. The spears carried and used by the Thracian infantry could be used for throwing, like the

▶ THRACIAN SLINGER, C.200BC *Along with other peoples, the Macedonians employed slingers as missile troops, and the Thracians had made a name for themselves with this weapon. Though relatively short-ranged, and unable to outshoot the bow at a distance, it was still a dangerous weapon.*

Greek and Macedonian Infantry

Macedonians were ethnic Greeks, and had ruled Greece since the time that Alexander the Great overran and conquered the region. Thrace, north of Macedonia, was a different matter. The Thracians were also an aggressive people, tribal in outlook and action, and were ruled by Macedonia with difficulty. After the Macedonian wars, Thrace was ruled by Rome. The Thracians were excellent warriors with outstanding fighting skills and were greatly prized as light infantry.

At the time of the Macedonian wars with Rome, the Greek and Macedonian infantry were probably at the end of their development as heavy infantry. In actuality their time had passed and they were going to be surpassed into obsolescence, along with the phalanx, by the Roman heavy infantry, organized in centuries, maniples and legions. The Battle of Pydna in 168BC clearly demonstrated the superiority of the Roman manipular legion over the Greek phalanx.

The heavy infantry, or hoplites and phalangists, were equipped and trained as they had been in Alexander's time and their main weapon was still the long thrusting spear. Their Roman opponents' main weapon was the scutum and gladius, which would allow the more flexible and better trained Romans to turn aside the shield and spear of their Macedonian and Greek opponents, get inside the thrusting range of the spear and finish off their opponents with the thrust of the gladius.

Cavalry

The Macedonian cavalry had a tradition of excellence since the days of Alexander. They were an elite force under the direct command of the Macedonian king on the battlefield and they followed him everywhere to fight at his side.

Macedonian cavalry could be of two types, light and heavy. The light cavalrymen wore no armour and might not have worn a helmet, but were probably dressed more or less in civilian wear and armed with spear and sword.

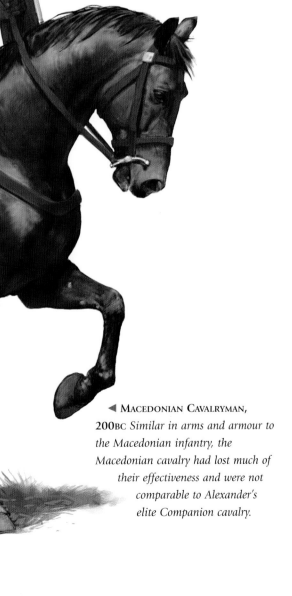

◀ MACEDONIAN CAVALRYMAN, 200BC *Similar in arms and armour to the Macedonian infantry, the Macedonian cavalry had lost much of their effectiveness and were not comparable to Alexander's elite Companion cavalry.*

Other types of horsemen, neither light nor heavy, might have worn chain mail, be armed similarly to the light cavalry, and wear a helmet of either iron or leather. The heavy cavalry may have looked more or less like a mounted phalangist. They would wear the phalangist helmet, similar in

▼ GREEK HOPLITE, 5TH–4TH CENTURIES BC
The Greek hoplite was the antecedent of Macedonian and Roman infantry. The helmet, flexible (leather) cuirass, shield and arms of this Greek infantryman are what made the phalanx. By this time, however, the phalanx was outmoded, and about to be replaced by the legion.

outline to a Phrygian cap, and a muscle cuirass. The cavalrymen were armed with sword, shield, and two or three short throwing spears or javelins, and most would probably wear a military cloak, though not in combat.

◄ MACEDONIAN JAVELINS AND ARMOUR, C.200BC *The spear and pike points (top row) were all employed by the Macedonians, as were the corresponding spear butts (bottom row). Polearms may not have been uniform by units. The bronze muscle cuirass (1) is of the type used by Macedonian heavy infantry, as is the traditional Phrygian-style helmet (2), used in the time of Alexander.*

1   2

► MACEDONIAN INFANTRYMAN, C.200BC
The Macedonian infantry facing the Romans during this conflict were the descendants of Alexander the Great's invincible army that 100 years before had never known defeat. The dress, armour, weapons, and especially the Phrygian helmet, are reminiscent of the period when no one could stand against the Macedonian phalanx. Details of the Phrygian helmet, with cheek guards, and the muscle cuirass are shown. Also shown are spear heads and butts, both of steel or iron.

ARMS AND ARMOUR

The development of weapons in the ancient world, especially those made of some type of metal, began with the Bronze Age around 3000BC. The impact of forging a metal alloy first developed in what is now the Middle East when the forging of a strong alloy of copper and tin, bronze (now called brass and made up of approximately 90 per cent copper and 10 per cent tin) allowed ancient armies to be armed and equipped in a more uniformed manner.

Weapons Technology

Bronze led to iron, and from about 1200BC, to the Iron Age, beginning in Anatolia in Asia Minor. Progress

▼ HELMETS, 5TH–2ND CENTURIES BC
1 to 8 show the different types and development of the Celtic helmet over 300 years. The helmet becomes less decorative and more functional, with the deletion of high pointed tops, and the practical addition of cheek-protection pieces. 5 and 6 are c.400BC; 1, 7 and 8 c.300BC; 2 c.200BC; and 3, 4 are 100BC. The Celtic influence on Roman legionary helmets in the later republic and empire period are clearly visible. In 9 and 10 Samnite helmets and 11 and 12 Etruscan helmets, Greek influence is overwhelming.

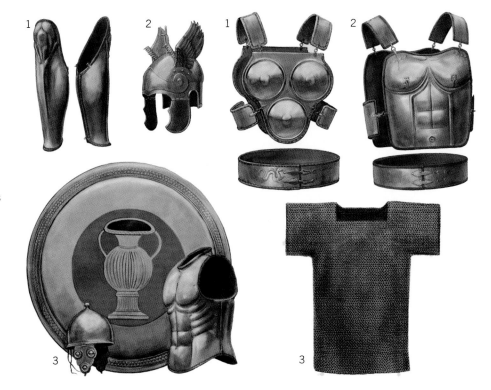

▲ BODY ARMOUR, 6TH–3RD CENTURIES BC
1 Campanian greaves. 2 Campanian winged helmet. The Samnites wore a similar helmet. 3 An Etruscan 'muscled' cuirass, an 'argive' shield and a Montefortino-model helmet.

allowed armourers to combine iron with carbon to make a primitive form of steel which, as the science of metallurgy developed, made the

▲ ARMOUR, 6TH–3RD CENTURIES BC
1 An Etruscan triple-disc cuirass. 2 A Campanian semi-muscle-cuirass. The belts with these cuirasses were very important to the warriors of central Italy and a sign of their manhood. They would not be seen without one. 3 A typical chain mail shirt worn by Roman legionaries, simple but effective and relatively easy to move while wearing it.

forging of more modern and sturdy weapons possible, ones that had a longer life span and were more deadly. The Iron Age did not reach all peoples at the same time; the technology moved westwards from Asia Minor, reaching central Europe – and, interestingly, Britain – in the 8th century BC, although northern Europe adopted the new technology about 200 years later.

Rome was developing into what would become a power in central Italy about the time that the Iron Age was coming to Europe, and first her warriors, and then her soldiers (as the state developed), benefited greatly from the ability to forge iron and steel weapons and armour.

As the technology moved westwards, arms and armour developed along similar lines for most warlike peoples, and the Greek influence was strong, especially around the Greek colonies. The first Roman soldiers, along with the Etruscans and other Italian peoples, armed and armoured themselves in the Greek style. The Hellenic helmet that could cover the head and face, and was crested with a horsehair 'mane', was common on the Italian peninsula, but that was not the only influence from outside Italy.

Celtic tribes were constantly migrating and raiding across Europe. They invaded Greece at an early date, and populated not only the British Isles, but also the Iberian peninsula. As they moved and raided, so their styles of helmet, shield, and edged weapons were seen, fought against, captured, and employed by the 'armies' on the Italian peninsula. All of these outside influences were seen and used by the Romans, and these provided an excellent cross-fertilization of ideas in the development of distinctive Roman arms, armour and equipment.

Helmets
Protective headgear could be of many designs, some of them quite bizarre, but the two types that tended to dominate during this early period of

▲ SHIELDS, 6TH–3RD CENTURIES BC
This selection of shields are Celtic (1–4) and Germanic (5–6) in design. Dacian shields would also have designs of the type illustrated in 4. 5 A typical round shield used by numerous barbarian peoples, both infantry and mounted troops. 6 Another example of a Germanic shield.

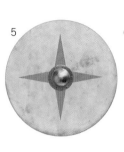

the Roman army were the full-faced Greek type, with a tall, long, coloured horsehair crest, and the pot-type helmet, either fitted with cheek scales to protect the face or with them moulded in when the helmet was cast. The first type were movable or adjustable, the second type were not. The full-face Greek type helmet would gradually evolve or merge into the pot-type helmet, the latter being both more comfortable and practical.

Decorations on top of the helmet could be a falling horsehair plume or a crest that either ran from front to rear of the helmet or was parallel with the wearer's shoulders. The latter became popular with Roman centurions and made them distinctive in appearance in the ranks of the legion.

Shields
Most shields were constructed out of wood, either glued together in strips, or nailed or bolted. The boss, which would protrude from the centre, had a cross bar in the back where the soldier or warrior would grasp his shield for use in combat. Often the face of the shield would be covered in metal or bound in metal to give it extra strength. The general shapes were round, oval or rectangular. Shields could be constructed flat, as round shields usually were or, like the Roman scutum, would be curved from right to left (viewed straight up and down). This led to a better protection for the bearer, as well as influencing the tactical employment of the Roman legion, enabling soldiers to lock shields in combat, forming a virtual wall against any enemy.

◀ SHIELDS, 6TH–3RD CENTURIES BC
1 Both sides of a Villanovan embossed bronze shield. 2 A type of hoplon, the circular Greek-inspired shield for heavy infantry. 3 The almost universal design of round shield. 4 A shield very clearly modelled on a Roman scutum. Roman shields, while having a decorative design on them, were more uniform than barbarian shields and would often be covered with a protective cloth.

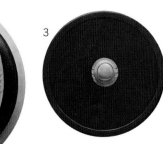

Swords

The experience of the Punic wars had a lasting impact on Roman military culture. One of the most significant steps during the conflict was the development of the shorter Spanish sword, the gladius Hispaniensis. It was a slender weapon, with a two-edged blade, and a tapering point. Handles seem to have been predominantly wooden, as were the scabbards, and an example found at Delos shows that the handle was made of three wooden parts, riveted together. The sword was

▼ LEGION STANDARDS, 1ST CENTURY BC
The Roman legion carried a variety of standards, all of which were important to the the unit. 1 The eagle standard, introduced by Marius, initially silver and later gold, there was one per legion. 2 and 3 The maniple was carried by the century and there were various designs, two of which are shown. The wreath surrounding the hand on 2 is an award for exceptional combat service.

often suspended from the waist belt, and in a scabbard with a ring on either side. It could be worn on the left or the right. It was this means of wearing the sword, and a similarly shaped dagger, that, to contemporaries, looked Spanish, although the swords the Romans produced were less ornate than those manufactured in Spain.

What the sword lacked in ornamentation it made up for in strength. The blade was extremely strong, and the point sharp and robust. The sword was subsequently shortened (producing the so-called Mainz type and its successor, the Pompeii type) but with a tendency to be broader, and more decorative. Some had wrist chains to prevent them from being lost in combat.

While it could be used for stabbing or slashing, the gladius was designed for thrusting and the Roman infantryman, using his shield together with his blade, was a dangerous proposition. Roman cavalry used a longer sword, generally of the

▲ EDGED WEAPONS AND JAVELINS, 3RD–1ST CENTURIES BC *1 The gladius, or Roman short sword, in its scabbard, on a typical belt harness with the Roman dagger. The leather strips, studded with metal, that hung from the front of the belt harness protected the legionary's groin. 2 The spatha was employed as a cavalry weapon as it had a longer reach for mounted combat, especially against infantry. It was copied from the long sword used by the Celts and Germans. 3–6 A variety of Roman javelins with wooden shafts and lead shanks at the top. The shank was made from lead, designed so that on impact the spear point would penetrate an opponent's shield, with the soft metal bending under the weight of the shaft so it could not be pulled out. The opponent would then be forced to drop his shield, to his great disadvantage.*

◀ LEGION STANDARDS, 1ST CENTURY BC *Vexila (4 and 5) carried the name and number of the legion, usually in gold, and when a detachment was sent on an independent mission, this type of standard would be carried by the cohort or cohorts so detached. They would be called vexillations.*

▶ HELMETS, 2ND–1ST CENTURIES BC *A variety of Roman helmets, demonstrating the progression in helmet design and the Celtic influence. The development of cheek and neck protection is noteworthy. 1 and 2 are from the 1st century BC. 3, 4, and 5 are from the 1st century AD and are the epitome of Roman legionary helmet development.*

▶ SHIELDS, 2ND–1ST CENTURIES BC *1 A typical round shield carried by barbarian cavalry and sometimes by Roman auxiliary cavalrymen. 2, 3, and 4 Roman infantry scutums, typically rounded rectangles for the republican period. Note the boss in the centre of the shield, which was used as a weapon in close combat. 5 A shield more often carried by Roman auxiliary cavalrymen.*

broadsword type, called a spatha. It was also an efficient weapon and had the longer reach that the cavalryman needed when mounted. Some auxiliary infantry seem to have preferred the longer swords, perhaps as a nod to local tradition.

The spatha was probably adapted from the Celtic broadsword. An excellent weapon, the broadsword was apparently made from Noric steel, made in Noricum, an area th t is now in Austria. The Romans made abundant use of this steel and weapons made from it were highly prized.

Armour

There was a variety of armour in this period, from crude metal plates covering parts of the body and held on with straps, to the elegantly worked metal cuirasses that covered both the chest and back of the wearer. Shaped leather armour was also used, as well as leather or cloth armour into which were sewn metal plates. The best type of body armour used, however, was chain mail.

▶ CAVALRY HORSE AND EQUIPMENT, 2ND CENTURY BC *The Roman cavalry horse showing the excellent Roman-style saddle and harness. On the left are two types of bit used by Roman horsemen.*

Roman mail was not as dense as later medieval types, but this made it lighter and more comfortable to wear and it still required some 20,000 rings to produce one shirt. Some of the weight of the armour could be alleviated by wearing a belt, or by extra padding at the shoulder. A thick tunic, worn under the mail shirt, improved comfort still further, and did much to add to the protection. Early styles of the shirt were longer but, during the imperial period, they became shorter and reached down only as far as the waist. Mail was effective protection against the slashing and cutting of sword arms, but afforded poorer levels of protection against flying arrows.

Horses

The stirrup had not been developed by this period in history, so the skill of a rider was paramount in keeping in the saddle. Not every cavalryman was as capable a rider as a Numidian light horseman. Saddles were moulded to help keep a man in place, and horses were controlled by the bridle, reins and knees. Sometimes armour was provided for heavy cavalry horses, which enhanced their survival. For light cavalry it would have done nothing but slow them down.

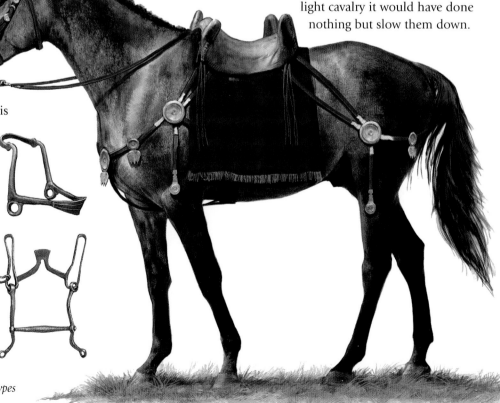

ROME AT THE HEIGHT OF POWER
146BC–235AD

After the Carthaginian threat was destroyed, Rome began to expand her overseas empire by conquest and colonization. In addition to controlling the entire Italian peninsula and much of Iberia (Spain), and because Rome was now a de facto naval power, the Mediterranean was very swiftly becoming a Roman lake. Roman expansion continued into Gaul, what is now modern France, as well as along the Rhine and Danubian frontiers. Expeditions to, and final occupation of, much of Britain made it the northernmost frontier of the Roman Empire. Everywhere that Rome's armies went, Roman civilization followed and left an impact that is still seen and felt today.

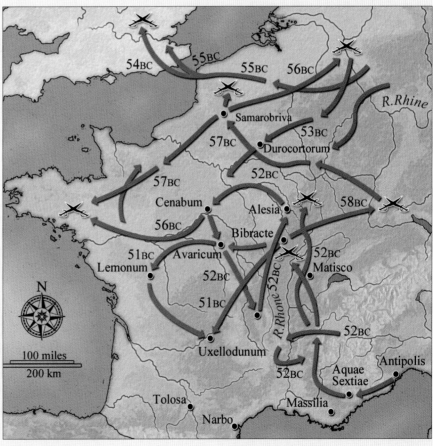

▲ *The progress of Caesar's Gallic campaigns, showing his movement through the region.*

◀ *Roman forts followed a set layout, and with baths, cookhouses, blacksmith, armourer and all other necessary support, were self-sufficient. This is an impression of the fort in London, possibly constructed around the time of the visit of Hadrian. Parts of it are still visible today.*

THE ROMAN CIVIL WARS

Rome, unlike most great powers before or since, was a dominating land and sea power. Its leaders had also clearly demonstrated an ability to fight more than one war at any one time. With the developing military organization of the legion, Rome had the best army of the period, a position that would last for centuries. The Roman infantryman was tough, ruthless, well-trained and almost unstoppable in combat.

The deadliest fighting faced by the Roman legionary in this period was probably during the three almost continuous civil wars, when legions were loyal first to their commander, who if well respected would be followed almost anywhere by his men. The usual legion motto, 'Senatus Populus que Romanus' or SPQR (For the Senate and the People of Rome), so prominent on the legions' standards and in their histories, could have been replaced by a favoured commander's name and title during this period.

On land, Rome faced both east and north, and Roman armies were loosed against the 'barbarians' (a term used for anyone who was not Roman). During this period, strong men emerged in command of Rome's

▼ Pompey the Great (Gnaeus Pompeius Magnus), one of the powerful military and political leaders of the late Roman Republic.

▲ The legend SPQR is the acronym for the Latin phrase 'For the Senate and People of Rome' (Senatus Populus que Romanus).

legions and while they compiled an impressive record of conquests for the glory of Rome they were also very aware of their own prestige, power, and glory. Personal ambition began to run amok. The most severe test the Roman republic suffered came during this period, and it was a test that it failed. In the end the republic, born out of disgust of monarchical rule, would develop into a political entity ruled by a hereditary emperor. The Senate survived, as would other outward trappings of the old republic, but Rome's future trajectory was set as an imperial power, in which the people had no official representation or voice in government.

The First Civil War

There were three civil wars during this period of Roman history. The first was a struggle for dominance in Rome between Lucius Cornelius Sulla and Gaius Marius. Sulla was the army commander who actually led an army in a march on Rome, and Marius was a soldier and general who reformed the Roman army, changing it from a citizen's militia to a professional fighting force.

The struggle between these two titans began during the Social War of 91–88BC, when Rome's Italian allies revolted and were finally suppressed and brought under Rome's rule. In 88BC Sulla marched on Rome and took the city by force, resulting in proscription lists and the slaughter of those who opposed him. Marius finally died in 86BC and Sulla handed power back to the Senate and retired.

The Second Civil War

Rome's next civil war evolved from the formation of the first Triumvirate, a power-sharing arrangement from the three then most powerful men in Rome: Julius Caesar; Pompey, soon to add 'Magnus' (the Great) to his name; and Marcus Licinius Crassus, who was later to defeat the Spartacus slave revolt. Eventually the Triumvirate was down to two, after Crassus was killed

▼ The Battle of Pharsalus in 48BC was Julius Caesar's great victory, fighting outnumbered, over Pompey the Great.

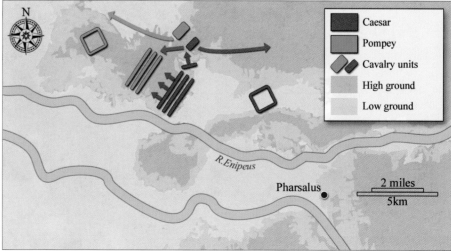

Caesar
Pompey
Cavalry units
High ground
Low ground

R.Enipeus

Pharsalus

2 miles
5km

▲ *A tetradrachma showing Mithradates VI, sometimes styled 'the Great' king of Pontus. Mithradates, of mixed Persian and Greek ancestry, fought three wars against Rome.*

fighting against the Parthians in the east at the Battle of Carrhae in 53BC. The rivalry for influence between Caesar and Pompey would be such that civil war would break out in Rome between the two and their rival armies, and this was a turning point in Roman history that would lead to the eventual establishment of the Roman Empire ruled by a succession of emperors. It meant the death of the old republic.

After Caesar's successful Gallic campaigns from 58–1BC, and Pompey's successful conclusion of the war with Mithradates of Pontus in 66BC, the struggle for power between the two men came to a head. Caesar crossed

▼ *Presented with Pompey's head, it was to Caesar's credit that both the gift and the act that preceded it disgusted him.*

▲ *Antony is brought, dying, to Cleopatra. She also committed suicide soon afterwards, bringing their war with Rome to a close.*

the River Rubicon with one legion and began open civil war with Pompey. Lasting from 49–5BC, the conflict ended with Pompey being defeated by Caesar at the Battle of Pharsalus in 48BC, the decisive battle of the war. Other operations followed in Egypt and northern Africa, with Pompey, much to Caesar's chagrin, being murdered after fleeing to Egypt after the Battle of Pharsalus. The final battle of the civil war was won by Caesar at Munda, Spain, in 45BC. On his return to Rome, Caesar was assassinated by conspirators in the Senate afraid of his increasing power.

The Third Civil War

This bloody event provoked a second Triumvirate made up of Octavian, Caesar's nephew, as well as his adopted son and heir, Mark Antony, and Aemilius Lepidus. After initial problems between them, Octavian and

Mark Antony worked out their political differences and essentially divided the Roman Empire between them, edging Lepidus out by giving him a province in Africa to rule.

Brutus and Cassius, the two main conspirators in Caesar's assassination, were hunted down by Mark Antony and Octavian and were defeated and killed at the Battle of Philippi in 42BC. However, the two most powerful men in Rome then themselves had a permanent rift, which led to civil war once again. Mark Antony was ultimately defeated by Octavian at the Battle of Actium in 31BC and later committed suicide. Octavian was now the sole ruler of Rome and after assuming the title Augustus, he eventually became emperor.

THE PROFESSIONALISM OF THE ROMAN ARMY

After the successful conclusion of the Punic wars the Roman army began to undergo a notable conversion. Instead of relying on the native population of Italy as free Romans who owed the state military service for a specific time or emergency, the Roman army became a professional army with legionaries who enlisted for long periods. These salaried fighting men were thoroughly trained and very well equipped, and were led by a professional officer corps, the same centurions of the earlier militia army of the republic, but now appointed rather than elected.

Marian Reforms

Significant changes came with the reforms of Gaius Marius, who began his career as a soldier and rose to the position of consul. As commander, he defeated the Germans of the Cimbri and the Teutones when they invaded southern Europe, and before that he defeated the Numidians after a long and drawn out war. Solid leadership and careful generalship were Marius's strong points

▼ GAIUS MARIUS, C.110BC *The Consul Marius is shown in the full armour of a legionary or a centurion (because of the greaves on his legs). Some Roman generals, including Marius, would stand in line of battle with their legionaries when they thought it necessary.*

▲ LEGIONARY'S KIT C.110BC *This assemblage shows the selection, aside from personal items and weapons, that a legionary would carry on the march following Marius' reforms. 1 and 2 The pot and cooking ladle were part of his unit's mess equipment. 3 The basket was used to carry other items. The tools included; 4 a scythe, 5 a pickaxe, and 6 a peat cutter. 7 The spike-like piece is part of the palisade the legion would build in their fortified camp at the end of a day's march.*

◄ MARIUS'S MULE C.110BC *This is a professional Roman legionary following the reforms of Marius. He wears the chain mail lorica (lorica hamata) common by this time to all legionaries, and is armed with gladius, scutum and pilum, and a pot helmet, carried on a strap on his back. All of his personal belongings and necessary kit are carried on his back with the help of his baggage pole. With this rather simple, but effective, innovation, Marius increased the overall mobility of the legion by drastically cutting the baggage train.*

▲ *A relief depicting the victorius Marcus Aurelius being presented with Germanic prisoners by his victorious legionaries.*

and these strengths brought him to the conclusion that the best army for Rome would be one of long-service professionals, not the militia-type legions that Rome had relied upon.

When an emergency or war happened, legions had traditionally been raised from Roman citizens and they were armed and equipped at their own expense. These Roman citizens had to be landed people who could afford the armour, weapons and equipment necessary to take their place in the legions' ranks. After the war was over, the legionaries were discharged from their service and they went home, not assembling again until the next time they were needed.

The catalyst for Marius' reforms was the problems he faced when he fought against the Numidians. For the Numidian campaigns, a theatre of war that was inhospitable and unpopular with the legions, not enough citizens could be mustered to meet the emergency, so Marius came up with the solution of enlisting,

▶ LEGION AND CENTURION 1ST CENTURY AD *A centurion with vine stick and in full armour, with his century. The standard bearers carry a vexillum in the centre, a wreathed maniple to its right, and a standard bearing the image of the emperor to the left.*

regardless of wealth or station. Less wealthy Roman citizens were given the opportunity to serve Rome and win a means of livelihood at the same time, albeit through a somewhat dangerous means.

These new legionaries had little or no desire to return to their previous social station after the war was over, and Rome now developed a professional fighting force that would not only defend and police the empire, but would be ready for any emergency that might arise. They were trained, armed, and equipped at the state's expense, and they evolved into the best army of the ancient period.

The Cohort Legion

During this period Roman legions changed from the manipular legion to the cohort legion. Instead of the old maniple, made up of three centuries, the legion was now formed of cohorts made up of six centuries, which gave it greater tactical flexibility on the battlefield. It also gave the cohort limited independent action ability, as there were enough troops in the cohort to stand on its own for a limited time until help could arrive from the other cohorts in the legion. The old maniples did not have enough strength

to do this independently. They had enough troops to get themselves into trouble, but not to get out of it before help arrived.

Marius also reduced the large baggage trains of the militia legions. The legionary now carried what he needed in both equipment and supplies on his back, which led to the soldiers being given the nickname of 'Marius' Mules'. This burden gave the legion much more flexibility on the march, however, and troops were now able to fight and survive for a time without their baggage train.

The number of tribunes with the legion remained the same at six. Legates (general officers, usually a senator) were the main subordinates to the army commander, but the professional officers, the centurions, were still a vital part of the army. There were 60 centurions per legion and they earned their rank by experience and competence.

ROMAN EXPANSION

The greatest extent of Roman expansion occurred from the final defeat of Carthage in 146BC until the end of the rein of the fifth 'good emperor' Marcus Aurelius in 180AD. Branching out from Italy and into Spain and North Africa, Roman civilization was spread by military conquest. Displaying the great engineering skills that allowed the Romans not only to conquer vast lands, but to occupy and administer them, the Romans built hundreds of miles of roads, public buildings, aqueducts, and other structures that gave even the reluctant new subjects something to identify with, and perhaps start to believe that they too were Roman.

Imperial Expansion

The method of Roman expansion was to incorporate as much territory into the empire as possible. Roman expansion was ruthless, and not only was resistance not tolerated, but rebellion was answered with merciless vengeance. From their viewpoint they faced a hostile world and they were at war for most of the empire's existence. Rome frequently conducted more than one war at a time, even during the great wars against Carthage Rome was also taking on the Macedonians. They faced enemies who had the same mindset, but were not as expert as the Romans in raising large armies, equipping them, and sending them

▼ *The city of Rome and its major public buildings at the time of Constantine, Roman Emperor from 306 to 337AD.*

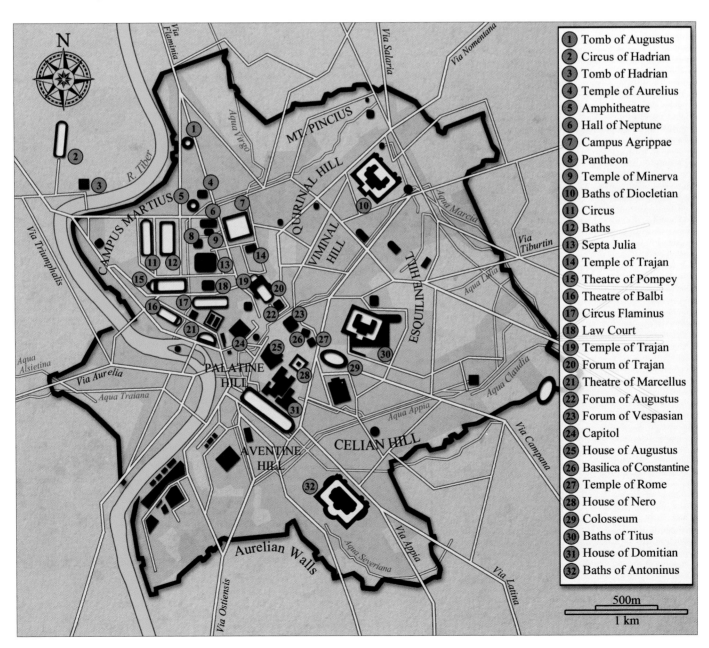

1	Tomb of Augustus
2	Circus of Hadrian
3	Tomb of Hadrian
4	Temple of Aurelius
5	Amphitheatre
6	Hall of Neptune
7	Campus Agrippae
8	Pantheon
9	Temple of Minerva
10	Baths of Diocletian
11	Circus
12	Baths
13	Septa Julia
14	Temple of Trajan
15	Theatre of Pompey
16	Theatre of Balbi
17	Circus Flaminus
18	Law Court
19	Temple of Trajan
20	Forum of Trajan
21	Theatre of Marcellus
22	Forum of Augustus
23	Forum of Vespasian
24	Capitol
25	House of Augustus
26	Basilica of Constantine
27	Temple of Rome
28	House of Nero
29	Colosseum
30	Baths of Titus
31	House of Domitian
32	Baths of Antoninus

The Wars of Rome 143BC–476AD

143–33BC Numantine War in Spain
112–6BC War against the Numidians in Africa (Jugurthine War).
105–1BC Campaigns against the German tribes. Both the Teutones and Cimbri are defeated.
91–88BC Rome's Italian allies rebel and are finally defeated in the Social War.
88–2BC Civil war in Rome caused by Sulla marching on Rome.
88–2BC 1st and 2nd Mithridatic Wars.
74–66BC 3rd Mithridatic War.
73–1BC The Spartacus Slave revolt,
58–1BC Caesar campaigns in Gaul.
55–4BC Caesar invades Britain twice.
54–3BC Rebellion in Gaul.
53BC The Battle of Carrhae, Crassus is defeated by the Parthians and killed.
52BC Vercingetorix rebels against Rome and is defeated by Caesar after the famous Siege of Alesia.
49–31BC Roman civil war between Caesar and Pompey for power in Rome. Concluded by Octavian against Mark Antony at the Battle of Actium.
16–7BC The Alpine tribes are conquered as is Pannonia and much of Germany.

15BC Germans raid Roman provinces.
12–9BC Tiberius conquers Pannonia.
9–7BC Campaigns of Tiberius in Germany.
4–5AD Tiberius's conquests in Germany extend the empire to the Elbe River.
6–9AD Revolts in Germany, Dalmatia and Pannonia. Arminius traps and annihilates three Roman legions (17th, 18th and 19th) in the Teutoborg Forest.
10–11AD Rhine frontier is pacified and secured by Tiberius and Germanicus.
14–16AD Rome continues war against Arminius, Germanicus wins victory.
43AD Britain is successfully invaded and made a Roman colony.
55–64AD The Parthian War is waged over who will rule in Armenia.
60–1AD Queen Boudicca rebels against Roman rule in Britain but is defeated.
66–74AD The Jewish people revolt against Roman rule and are defeated at Masada.
68–9AD Civil war again in Rome – the 'year of the four emperors'.
85–9AD War with Dacia along the Danubian frontier.
101–2AD Trajan wages war with Dacia.
105–6AD Hadrian wages war with Dacia.

113–17AD Trajan wages war on Parthia.
131–5AD Revolt again in Palestine by the Jews led by Bar Kochba.
162–6AD War with the Parthians once more-successfully concluded.
167–180AD Marcus Aurelius' wars against the Germans along the Danube.
193–7AD Civil war in Rome once again.
217–22AD Civil war in Rome.
251–3AD Civil war returns to Rome.
275AD Queen Zenobia of Palmyra revolts.
312AD The Battle of the Milvian Bridge. Constantine defeats Maxentius.
337–60AD The Persian War.
357AD At the Battle of Strasbourg Julian the Apostate defeats the Alamanni.
363AD Julian the Apostate campaigns against the Persians.
394AD Theodosius wins Battle of Frigidus.
410AD Alaric and the Goths sack Rome.
429AD Africa overrun by the Vandals.
451AD Attila and the Huns are defeated by Aetius at the Battle of Chalons.
469–78AD The Visigoths take Spain.
476AD The last western Roman emperor, Romulus Augustus, is deposed by the Ostrogoth Odoacer.

---

into battle one after the other, no matter how many defeats were endured. New legions were continually raised to replace those defeated or fallen, and in many of their wars, the Romans eventually simply exhausted their enemies.

Pax Romana

Where Roman rule extended, so did Roman civilization. Roman architecture and engineering were put in place to 'civilize' those regions that were conquered and pacified, the most familiar to the modern eye being amphitheatres, roads, bridges, and aqueducts. Permanent fortifications were also put in place and these were also built to last. Conquered peoples became Roman in outlook and manner as well as in customs and dress, and legions were raised or stationed in the new territories and provinces from the native population. This became commonplace after the Marian reforms when any Roman citizen, regardless of wealth, land, or social standing, could enlist in the army. Many landless men found a home in the legion, and, often never having set eyes on the city of Rome, their immediate loyalty was to their legion, centurion and commander.

▶ An artist's impression of what the great Colosseum, commissioned by Emperor Vespasian, looked like when completed.

ROMAN COMMANDERS

In the 1st century AD the writer Onasander published a work entitled *The General*, in which he discussed what the duties of a general in combat should be. The Roman general, he remarked, did not necessarily have to be brilliant, but he did have to be competent, able to rise to the occasion (especially in a crisis), able to encourage his men, by both praise and

▼ LUCIUS CORNELIUS SULLA, 138–78BC *A young Sulla, long before his political clash with Marius, is shown in leather armour, which was undoubtedly more comfortable than the more ornate and expensive muscled cuirass.*

threats as well as encouragement, and able to manoeuvre his legions to meet the enemy properly.

Command and Control

By modern standards the Roman command system was an awkward one. Sometimes dual command and responsibility between two men of equal rank led to a military disaster; such as that at Cannae in 216BC at the hands of the Carthaginians under Hannibal. However, there were capable Roman commanders who were excellent generals and leaders of men. Gaius Julius Caesar is undoubtedly the most famous. Three other Roman commanders of note, who could be studied and mentioned as 'world class' in performance and leadership are Lucius Cornelius Sulla, Scipio Africanus, and Gnaeus Pompeius Magnus, or Pompey the Great.

Some of the lesser-known Roman commanders who also deserve to be remembered are Aemilius Paulus and Quintus Sertorius. Aemilius is recalled by Livy as almost broaching a contract with the men he led: in which he promised to see that he himself carried out his duties as their commander while the legionaries, when the fighting began, did theirs. Sertorius was noted by Plutarch as being a bold commander, ready to seize the initiative at the opportune moment, and an expert at feints and at speed of execution. Other talented Roman

▶ SCIPIO AFRICANUS, 236–183BC *Each military campaign was assigned one general (dux). Generals were always aristocrats of the senatorial class, usually consuls or ex-consuls, since they had to hold at least praetorian rank in order to be granted the right to command an army by the Senate. Generals in this period usually wore a leather muscled cuirrass with fringed strips of leather over the thighs and shoulders, over a tunic.*

commanders who had their careers cut short through intrigue, ambition, or general bad luck include Mark Antony and Marcus Licinius Crassus.

Even mediocre Roman commanders had a distinct advantage over all of their opponents. They could depend on the solidarity and professionalism of the legionaries, which could make even a lesser commander a famous conqueror. The overriding concern of all Roman generals, and what was expected of them by 'the Senate and People of Rome', was complete confidence in final Roman victory in whatever military endeavour assigned to them.

▶ **GAIUS JULIUS CAESAR, 100-44BC** *Caesar was an outstanding show-off, and vain with it. He referred to his red cloak in his* Commentaries, *admitting he wore it in order to be recognized on and off the battlefield. Here, he is depicted in a simple muscle cuirass and the standard soldier's cloak.*

Dress

Roman commanders were generally conspicuous on the battlefield, not only by their actions, but also by their armour. Roman generals and senior officers, such as tribunes, could generally wear what they wished, and they would take the field in finely made armour, complete with gilded cuirass, helmet and greaves.

Their tunics would reflect their exalted position and most, if not all, would have a thin sash of rank tied around the

bottom of their cuirass, knotted in the front. For arms they would either have that of the legionary; the gladius and pugio, or they would wear the spatha, the cavalryman's long sword, depending on their taste.

The cuirass could be plain, depending on personal taste, and could also be made out of hard leather instead of gilded iron. Some metal cuirasses were quite ornate, especially if the commander was also an emperor, but some commanders would also wear mail, which would undoubtedly be more comfortable and easy to maintain and wear.

The helmet worn by Roman commanders could be of the infantry or cavalry type, depending on individual preferences, or where the commander was during the fighting or on campaign.

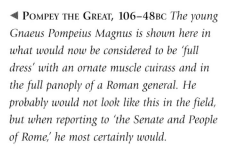

◀ **POMPEY THE GREAT, 106–48BC** *The young Gnaeus Pompeius Magnus is shown here in what would now be considered to be 'full dress' with an ornate muscle cuirass and in the full panoply of a Roman general. He probably would not look like this in the field, but when reporting to 'the Senate and People of Rome,' he most certainly would.*

▶ **MARK ANTONY, 83–30BC** *Mark Antony has been called 'the noblest Roman of them all' and he is pictured here in his best 'uniform' as a Roman general. A more-than-able commander, and loyal to Caesar, whom he bloodily avenged, he let his ego and Cleopatra get the best of him and ended up on the wrong end of his own gladius after defeat at Actium.*

ROMAN EMPERORS

The road from republic to empire was rough and bloody, and during the journey something of the essence of what Rome had been, was lost. When the dust had settled, and Octavian actually became emperor after his victory over Antony and Cleopatra in 31BC, Rome had become, for all intents and purposes, an imperial entity. Had the Roman imperium been headed and led consistently by men of character and innate leadership ability, Rome's destiny might have been different. But leaders of sense and quality were not the norm in the long line of Roman emperors.

Roman emperors taken as a group are a very mixed lot. Some were truly outstanding, but the rule of the 'five good emperors' (Nerva, Trajan, Hadrian, Antoninus Pius and Marcus Aurelius, who ruled collectively from 96–180AD) was more than counter-balanced by poor rulers such as Caligula (37–41AD), Nero (54–68AD), and the three incompetent emperors of the year 69AD: Galba, Otho and Vitellius. Poor or disastrous rulers, however, until at least 180AD, were usually succeeded by competent men who ruled well. The Flavian Dynasty (Vespasian, Titus and Domitian, 69–96AD) was a particular high point.

Octavian

The first Roman emperor was Octavian (31BC–14AD), ruling under the title Caesar Augustus. The gigantic work of reorganization that he carried out in every field of Roman life and throughout the entire empire not only transformed the decaying republic into a new, monarchic regime with many centuries of life ahead of it but also created a durable Roman peace, based on easy communications and flourishing trade.

Vespasian and Titus

The Flavian dynasty; Vespasian (69–79AD), and his sons Titus (79–81AD) and Domitian (81–96AD),

ruled Rome for 30 years. Vespasian and Titus had both commanded in Palestine during the Jewish revolt, and proved themselves with the army, which was becoming the 'king maker'. Their fiscal reforms and consolidation of the empire generated political stability and a vast building program.

Trajan

Ruling from 98 to 117AD, Trajan's civil accomplishments were impressive; his column gives us an excellent picture of the Roman army at the height of its efficiency, but it is as the conqueror of Dacia in eastern Europe, the last big

◀ OCTAVIAN, 63BC–14AD *Octavian is pictured as he might have looked at his victory over Antony at Actium in 31BC. Purple cloaks were worn, but some soldier-emperors would wear the red military cloak in the field. Sidearms, such as the pommel of his gladius, could be decorated with the eagle head.*

▶ VESPASIAN, 9–79AD *Vespasian was an experienced soldier and a commander of talent. He is depicted here as an army general with a simple muscle cuirass over a white leather fringed tunic. The unusual embellished helmet denotes his status.*

◀ **TITUS, 39–81AD** *The talented son of the emperor Vespasian. Titus is pictured in full dress as a general and commander. Titus was noted for going on reconnaissance in the field without armour, to the consternation of his escort. Even if surprised by the enemy in such a situation, Titus did not hesitate to fight.*

Hadrian

Emperor Hadrian (117–38AD) succeeded Trajan, and is famous for the wall in Britain, the travels he made through the empire, and the magnificent edifices he had built.

Marcus Aurelius

Known as the 'philosopher emperor' he fought a series of wars along the German frontier. After the expansion of the empire in the 2nd century AD, the new borders had to be guarded and maintained, and this took up most of Marcus Aurelius' reign (161–80AD). He was capable and a just ruler, caught up in wars generally not of his making.

Diocletian

An outstanding emperor, Diocletian (284-305AD) not only instituted social and economic reforms, but also reformed the army and brought order out of chaos. He also instituted the reforms that divided the empire into an eastern and a western empire, setting the stage for Constantine the Great and the development of the eastern Roman Empire that lasted one thousand years.

▼ **MARCUS AURELIUS, 121–80AD** *The 'philosopher emperor' spent most of his reign away from Rome either fighting the northern Germanic enemies or ensuring the northern frontiers of the empire remained secure.*

conquest of the Roman Empire, that he is most remembered. A conquest which added a large area to the empire's jurisdiction. Cassius Dio remarked that Trajan usually, if not always, led from the front, marching with his troops on foot instead of the usual horseback. He shared his men's hardships and was an excellent commander; understanding how to use intelligence work, and employing ruses and false rumours to thwart the enemy.

▶ **TRAJAN, 53–117AD** *Trajan is pictured as the successful general that he was, the conqueror of Dacia. He led by example and is pictured with a beard, an affectation that some of the emperors had after Titus. While the metal muscle cuirass was typical for generals, the lighter and more comfortable leather cuirass was also worn.*

THE ROMAN ARMY OF THE CIVIL WARS 91–31BC

There were several civil wars in the late Roman republic, but the most famous was the one that was provoked by Julius Caesar boldly crossing the River Rubicon with only one legion. Before this, and after, came less remembered but often no less destructive internal power struggles. They are as follows.

The Social War (91–88BC) was an internecine conflict between Rome and its Italian allies. Rome was victorious.

Sulla's 1st Civil War (88–7BC) was a struggle for power in Rome between Lucius Cornelius Sulla and Gaius Marius, the great reformer of the Roman army. Sulla was victorius.

In the Sertorian War (83–72BC): Quintus Sertorius, who had supported Marius against Sulla, revolted in Spain. Sulla was victorious.

In Sulla's Second Civil War (82–1BC) supporters of Marius again revolted but were defeated, and Sulla's position in Rome was consolidated.

The Lepisus' Rebellion (77BC) saw Marcus Aemilius Lepidus attempt a revolt against the followers of the now dead Sulla, and marched on Rome with an army. He was defeated outside Rome by Quintus Lutatius Catulus and fled.

In the Catiline Conspiracy (63–2BC) Lucius Sergius Catilina attempted to overthrow the Senate. He was defeated by a Roman army led by Quintus Caecilius Metellus Celer. Catiline's entire army was killed, all, including Catiline, dying from wounds inflicted to the front of their bodies.

In Caesar's Civil War (49–5BC) Julius Caesar led his army across the River Rubicon in a bid to become dictator of Rome. He finally defeated his great rival Pompey at Pharsalus. On Caesar's death civil war broke out again in the Post-Caesarian Civil War (44BC). This conflict was between the army of the Senate, led by Octavian, and the forces of Mark Antony and Lepidus. The two sides

▲ LEGIONARY, 10TH LEGION, C.58BC
Caesar's famous 10th Legion was recruited and formed in Spain from among the Roman population there. In this period Roman legionaries wore the gladius on their right side, so as not to interfere with the use of the shield in combat.

◀ CENTURION, C.58BC *The distinctive centurion horsehair crest, not stiffened here, is now making its appearance in the 2nd and 1st centuries BC. A flexible cuirass is worn along with greaves. Centurions were permitted to wear the gladius on their left, as a mark of their rank and status.*

reached a truce and united their armies to form the Second Triumvirate. who prosecuted the Civil War of the Liberators (44–2BC) in which the murderers of Caesar were hunted down and killed. In the Sicilian Revolt

THE ROMAN ARMY OF THE CIVIL WARS **107**

◀ LEGIONARY, POMPEY'S LEGIONS, *c.*58BC
Though fate put Caesar and Pompey on opposite sides, the legions that fought for them were identical in arms and equipment. The lorica (cuirass) here is made out of chain mail; the more familiar lorica segmentata had not yet made its appearance. Helmet plumes and ornaments could differ between legions or centuries and cohorts.

pushed towards near-chaos because of the quest for ultimate power that eventually came down to a confrontation between Caesar and Pompey the Great. Each had their own Roman army attached to them as successful generals, and civil war between them became inevitable.

Caesar was eventually triumphant and when he returned to Rome he was appointed dictator in perpetuity, and assumed the title of imperator, and pater patriae ('father of his country'). He ruled from 49 to 44BC, but after reducing the power of the Senate and granting citizenship to colonials, he made many enemies in the ruling patrician elite, some of whom believed he was planning to make himself king, and was assassinated by them on 15 March in 44BC.

The 10th Legion
The soldiers who fought in Caesar's civil war included his own 10th Legion, famous as Caesar's most faithful unit in his wars and in his quest for power. The very name of the legion has stood ever since as a model for military duty, steadfastness, obedience, loyalty and ultimate combat effectiveness.

The legion was raised by Caesar in Spain for his Gallic campaigns and it fought hard and well throughout his campaigns. It was organized, uniformed, and equipped as any

▶ LEGIONARY, LEGIONS IN GAUL, *c.*58BC
This is a depiction of Caesar's legionaries who fought in Gaul before the civil war. The cover on the scutum is made from leather and depicts legion designations. It would have been used on the march to protect the design on the shield from sun and rain.

other legion, but made a name for itself by its consistent performance and loyalty. The centurion was armed and armoured as his legionaries, but was distinguished by a horsehair plume placed on his helmet parallel to his shoulders. During this period he would generally wear a mail shirt, and be armed with pugio and gladius.

Loyalty
Professionalized by the Consul Marius, the legions would become attached to a famous or successful commander, and despite the old Roman 'designation' of SPQR (for the Senate and the People of Rome), the legions had more direct loyalty to their commanders than to the Senate.

(44–36BC) The Second Triumvirate defeated the revolt of Sextus Pompeius, son of Pompey the Great.

During the Perusine War (41–4BC) Octavian defeated the army of Lucius Antonius, the younger brother of Mark Antony, and Antony's wife, Fulvia. In the Last War of the Republic Octavian and Agrippa defeated Mark Antony and Cleopatra, ending the civil wars and uniting the empire under Octavian as Emperor Augustus.

Julius Caesar's Civil War
This was an act of defiance and personal ambition that would see the destruction of the republic. The Roman state, despite almost continuous expansion during this period, was

ROMAN ARMY REFORMS

Gaius Marius, who was often consul in Rome, was instrumental in developing the Roman army from a militia army, composed of Roman citizens capable of equipping themselves with the necessary arms and armour for campaign, to a professional fighting force armed, equipped, and paid by the state. The Marian reforms revolutionized the Roman army and transformed it into a fully professional army that would dominate the ancient world for 500 years.

Armour

Marius' reforms, while indeed introducing many new things and changing the Roman army from a militia into a professional military force, sometimes merely made some 'reforms' official, capitalizing on what was actually changing anyway. A good example of that would be standardizing chain mail armour for the entire army. The

▼ LEGIONARY IN FULL MARCHING KIT, 1ST CENTURY AD *One of the famous Marius' mules, though of a later date than Marius' times, named for Gaius Marius who reformed the Roman army in the late 2nd/early 1st century BC. This is a fully equipped legionary in marching order. He is wearing a lorica segmentata.*

▲ LEGIONARY, 1ST–2ND CENTURIES AD *This battle-ready legionary carries the pilum, designed to be thrown as a missile. Legionaries would carry more than one on the battlefield and on the approach of an enemy they would loose their pila in volleys.*

◄ LEGIONARY, 1ST CENTURY BC *This legionary is kitted out for battle. His helmet is of a different and uncommon pattern, and he is carrying, in addition to his gladius, the deadly curved Iberian falcata.*

ongoing trend was in place already, and although the armoured 'shirts' were expensive, it was excellent armour to have for the army. The chain mail shirt was constructed of interlocked iron

Roman Legion Deployments in the 1st and 2nd Centuries AD

Legion		Locations		Locations	
1st	I Adiutrix	Germany, Pannonia (Serbia)	9th	IX Hispana	Britain, Pannonia
1st	I Italica	Moesia (Bulgaria)	10th	X Gemina	Germany, Spain, Pannonia
1st	I Germana	Germany	11th	X Fretensis	Palestine, Syria
1st	I Minerva	Germany	11th	XI	Dalmatia
2nd	II Augusta	Africa, Britain, Germany	11th	XI Claudia Pia Fidelis	Germany, Moesia
2nd	II Adiutrix	Britain, Pannonia	12th	XII Gemina	Germany
2nd	II Traiana Fortis	Egypt	12th	XII Fulminata	Cappadocia (Turkey), Syria
3rd	III Augusta	Africa	13th	XIII Gemina	Pannonia
3rd	III Cyrenica	Arabia, Egypt	14th	XIV Gemina	Germany, Pannonia
3rd	III Gallica	Syria			
4th	IV Flavia Felix	Moesia	15th	XV Apollinaris	Cappadocia, Pannonia
4th	IV Macedonica	Spain			
4th	IV Sythica	Moesia, Syria	16th	XVI Gallica	Germany
5th	V Alaudae	Germany, Moesia	16th	XVI Flavia	Cappadocia
5th	V Macedonica	Moesia	16th	XVI Flavia Firma	Syria
6th	VI Ferrata	Palestine, Syria	20th	XX Valeria Victrix	Britain, Germany
6th	VI Victrix	Britain, Germany, Spain	21st	XXI Rapax	Germany
7th	VII	Dalmatia	22nd	XXII Deiotariana	Egypt
7th	VII Claudia Pia Fidelis	Moesia	22nd	XXII Primigenia	Germany
7th	VII Gemina	Spain	30th	XXX Ulpia	Germany
8th	VIII Augusta	Germany			

rings, riveted together, and while heavy, it was a supple and effective piece of armour, probably adopted from the Celts. Later this would be supplemented, but not completely replaced by, the lorica segmentata until this was finally phased out, and only chain mail remained. Greaves were also done away with, except for centurions, and the military sandal, or caliga, became standard issue footwear.

Equipment

Marius did much to increase the mobility of the army by doing away with a large part of the baggage trains that accompanied the army on campaign. The legionary would now wear or carry his armour, helmet, weapons, shield, engineer tools, three days' rations, extra clothing, as well as ancillary equipment. The legionaries 'pack' was a sturdy pole upon which was strapped his ancillary equipment, which would include cooking implements. This pack-pole was carried over his shoulder, and sometimes had a crossbar, and his helmet and shield would be strapped or hung on his body. Straps on the shield allowed this item of equipment to be carried on the legionary's back. From this extra burden for foot soldiers the term 'Marius' Mules' developed.

Many legionaries also carried a loculus, a satchel or bag made from linen or goat or cow leather. This was often waxed to make it waterproof – important given that Roman soldiers carried spare items of clothing

▶ LEGIONARY, 1ST–2ND CENTURIES AD *There were three common colours in Roman military clothing: blue, white, and red. Red and white seem to be the most common, but blue was used from time to time.*

or dry kindling for starting camp fires within the bag. It might also contain a wooden bowl, and a spoon or knife or penknife, and a sewing kit. Linen bags were also often attached to the legionary's burden and these would be used for foodstuffs, such as the ubiquitous flatbreads or hardtack, lentils, wheat, pulses and cured meat. Blankets, cloak bags and a cooking pot and pan were also commonly carried. A bladder or waxed animal skin container was also sometimes used to hold a mix of vinegar and water, should the legionaries not be able to find a secure source of drinking water. Purses, containing money or tokens used to pay for billets, were often hung from the soldier's belts.

Heavier equipment, including pickaxes, mattocks, sickles, scythes, saws and turf cutters might also be carried.

THE COHORT LEGION

The early republican legion was organized in centuries, with two centuries forming a maniple. While this organization was superior to the phalanx and other enemy formations, it lacked flexibility for more complicated manoeuvres, and the maniple was too weak for independent missions. What evolved was a reorganization of the legion into cohorts, which consisted of six centuries or three maniples. This reorganization allowed greater tactical flexibility to the legion commander, as well as to the army commander, and the cohort was strong enough for independent missions. The cohort could now accomplish missions detached from its parent legion on and off the main battlefield.

Centurions

The military role of the ever-present centurion with vine stick, distinctive helmet crest, and – like the legionaries he commanded and led – gladius and scutum, was unchanged. The centurion was expected to lead in line of battle with his century and cohort, or from the front, either rallying a broken cohort, urging his men forward in a counterattack, or fighting on alone protecting his retreating men until they were able to take up a better defensive position.

Centurions who had been awarded phalera (gold, silver, or bronze sculpted discs) for valour and service would wear them over their armour, attached to a harness. These discs were usually arranged in rows of two or three, depending on how many he had. While the phalerae were supposed to be worn for parades, many long-serving centurions would also wear them in combat. Centurions, legionaries, and auxiliaries might also be awarded a variety of other decorations such as torcs – or neck rings – armilla, a golden armband, and cups or horse trappings which were awarded to infantrymen and cavalrymen, respectively, for killing an enemy in action and then stripping them of their arms and weapons.

The two centurions pictured here are both wearing cingulums, the military belt, but they are each of a different

◄ CENTURION, C.58BC *The centurion's arms and armour have now developed to the point where he really stands out as the commander of his legionaries. This centurion has a stiffened crest on his helmet and wears full parade armour, including phalera on a leather harness across his chest. He has been heavily decorated for long and gallant service, and wears his gladius on his left.*

▶ CENTURION, 1ST–2ND CENTURIES AD *This centurion is also depicted in full dress or parade dress, this time holding his vine stick. Not only was this a symbol of rank, comparable to the modern swagger stick, but it was also the centurion's instrument of corporal punishment.*

Cornifer

Armies from antiquity before the written word were undoubtedly accompanied by musicians of some sort with either percussion instruments, or horns of some type, even if it was only a sheep's horn made for use in battle. Music can lift spirits on the march, stir men to stand fast in an emergency, and inspire them in a vicious counterattack, or to stand firmly in hopeless situations fighting to the last man.

Standards

Roman standards in the century, cohort, and legion also became standardized at this time, and each legion was issued with an eagle. While standards had always been carried in the Roman army, the new emphasis on the eagle standard was important to the professionalism and esprit de corps of the legion. Introduced by Marius, the eagle became not only the venerated image of each legion, to be defended to the death, but would also come to symbolize imperial Rome.

Both legionaries and auxiliary units carried standards, and all of the various standard bearers were 'uniformed' with animal skins so as to be visible to the ranks in order to rally in case formations were broken. These were the visible representatives of the legion in formation and combat.

Standard bearers were known as vexillarius (plural – vexillarii) and these usually held a cloth standard, hung by a cross pole under the spear point, on the terminus of the pole. Signifers carried the manipular standard, which was topped by an open palm and underneath carried

images of the emperor as well as the unit's awards. The aquilfer was the eagle bearer. Sometimes the standard bearer, especially in the auxiliary ranks would carry a standard topped with the legion's symbol, such as a boar or a bull. The draco (dragon) became a popular symbol in the Roman army, undoubtedly adopted from the Celts and Germans. It consisted of a metal dragon head on a pole, with a 'tail' made of fabric.

▲ MUSICIAN, 1ST–2ND CENTURIES AD
Cornifers, or trumpeters, for lack of a better term, were a normal part of the century, cohort, and legion. Military music was as important for the soldier then as it is now. The music of the corni went well with drums and helped on long marches for legions guarding the empire. This figure wears braccae, the Roman military trousers that were adopted by legions stationed on the northern frontier.

design. One is of plain leather, while the other is richly decorated with metal fittings and is definitely a parade belt. But whether on parade or in the heat of battle, the centurion was marked with his distinctive helmet crest.

▶ STANDARD BEARER, C.58BC *The standards of the legion could also be decorated with unit awards for valour and were awarded for the conduct of the legion, or cohort or century, that had distinguished itself in combat. These were usually placed on the maniples of the century, or on the eagle of the legion. A common one awarded would be a laurel wreath, other symbols included discs, or phalerae, and crescent moons.*

ROMAN ARMY AUXILIARIES

While the legion was the main formation in any Roman army, the Romans had always augmented the army's overall strength with auxiliary troops, which would enhance the capabilities of the army and give the legions themselves more flexibility on and off the battlefield.

Allies and Subjects

Auxiliaries were recruited from both allied and subject peoples, and, generally speaking, auxiliary units served with loyalty

Deployment of Roman Auxiliary Troops c.130AD			
Location	Alae	Cohort	Total
Britannia	11	45	56
Rhine Frontier	9	39	48
Danube Frontier	36	95	131
Eastern Frontier	16	58	74
Egypt	4	11	15
North Africa	12	45	57
Central Provinces	2	15	17
Total	**90**	**308**	**398**

and reliability, deployed for the particular martial qualities of the region or province from which they came.

As the Roman army turned professional, the overall strength of the legion was approximately 6,000 men, all ranks. Of those, approximately 5,000 were heavy infantry, the remaining 1,000 being auxiliaries, mainly cavalry and archers.

Some sources state that the auxiliary troops were not Roman citizens. This was not an inhibitor for Roman military service. As the Roman Empire expanded, the

different peoples encountered or conquered were recruited as auxiliary troops. Allied tribes or peoples were also employed as auxiliary troops.

Auxiliary 'uniforms' were varied and usually took the form of the dress from the region where they had been recruited. Archers from the east, for example, wore a long, sometimes ankle-length tunic with scale armour and a pointed helmet.

Auxiliary cavalrymen would wear a combination of their native clothing and armour, but carry Roman arms and equipment that gave them an overall 'Roman' appearance.

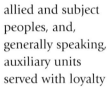

◀ AUXILIARY ARCHER, 1ST–2ND CENTURIES AD *Auxiliaries were as much a part of the post-Marian Roman army as the legions were. They were recruited from conquered or allied peoples and were usually recruited for their specialty, such as bowmen. This eastern bowman uses the powerful composite bow of his homeland, which out-performed the simpler, less powerful bow of the west.*

▶ AUXILIARY LIGHT INFANTRYMAN, 1ST–2ND CENTURIES AD *Auxiliary infantry were organized in cohorts, but not into auxiliary legions. They were intended to support the legions in line of battle, and were armed and equipped as Romans, though the shields were again flat and not usually curved.*

Archers

Bowmen were recruited from all parts of the empire from those indigenous peoples who would furnish trained archers. Some fought dismounted but horse archers were also used as the empire came under the influence of the east. The short bow was definitely used, as was a type of longbow, but the strongest one employed was the composite bow constructed of both wood and horn. The Roman auxiliary archers were formed in 32 units and supported the legions and other auxiliaries throughout the empire. The original Roman auxiliary archers were probably from Crete, dressed in red tunics with traditional headbands and, later, helmets, but eventually others were employed who were known for their expertise with the composite bow.

Infantry

Auxiliary infantry came to be much more Roman in appearance and at a glance would closely resemble legionaries. Other types of auxiliary infantry were also employed, such as slingers, who were light infantry and were generally either very lightly armoured or wore none at all. The slingers from the Balearic Islands in the Mediterranean off the Iberian coast, although deadly with their weapon, wore only their native clothing and no armour or protection.

Cavalry

In the early republican period, cavalry was supplied by Roman citizens who could afford to mount, arm and equip themselves. Reliance was later placed on cavalry auxiliaries from Iberia, Gaul, and other peoples skilled in the use and care of the horse. The Cohors IX Batavorum are a famous auxiliary cavalry unit that served in Britain on Hadrian's Wall, becoming known as individuals when some of their written tablets were discovered in Vindolanda. Auxiliary cavalry were organized in alae, mounted units about 500-men strong, and further subdivided into either 16 or 24 turmae of 32 officers and men each. The turmae were commanded by a decurion. These were the regular cavalry of the Roman army of the later republic and empire and replaced the native Roman equus. Sometimes they were formed into cohorts equitates, a combined arms cohort of infantry and cavalry.

The Romans also employed small units of mounted scouts, especially useful in Britain and in northern Europe among the Germans and Batavi. They were known as exploratores.

◄ AUXILIARY CAVALRYMAN, 1ST–2ND CENTURIES AD *Roman auxiliary cavalrymen were recruited from those people proficient as horsemen, Gauls and Germans being especially prized. They wore Roman armour and used Roman arms and equipment, the spatha for a sword and shields that were usually oval or hexagonal, though flat and not curved as the infantry scutum. They were a great improvement over the older equus of the republican legions.*

CAESAR'S CAMPAIGNS IN GAUL

Julius Caesar's most famous campaigns were against the Gauls, a Celtic people who proved to be formidable opponents especially when fighting on their own ground. Caesar made his military reputation in his Gallic campaigns. proving himself an able commander, and inspiring his troops to great feats on the battlefield. According to Seutonius, Caesar planned his operations carefully, but was able to improvise in impossible situations when needed. He was an aggressive and alert commander, and once his enemy was broken and routed, he would immediately pursue, giving his opponent no chance to rally and fight again.

Julius Caesar became proconsul of Rome in 59BC and the next year began his famous and well-chronicled campaigns in the province of Gaul, ostensibly to extend Rome's northern frontier to the River Rhine. In fact, both Gallic and German tribes were moving southward and the Romans were determined to avoid a repeat of the last time the Gauls had invaded and devastated Italy.

Caesar wrote about his Gallic campaigns in his *Commentaries* and although he extols the virtues of his troops along with his own generalship, it is one of the best historic narratives available from the Roman period.

▶ GALLIC INFANTRYMAN, C.58BC
The traditional Celtic way of fighting was on foot and the spatha was a favourite weapon. This shield is more Roman than Celtic, but there was considerable cross-fertilization of weapons and equipment and no doubt often in the fury of combat there were mistakes in identification.

The Helvetti and Sequani
Caesar's first campaign in 58BC was against the Helvetii, who originated in what is now Switzerland, but ended up crossing swords with Caesar when they attempted to migrate from their native tribal lands. When the Helvetii attempted to move south and westwards, Caesar refused them permission to do so. Ignoring him, the Helvetii moved on their own accord and Caesar promptly attacked, driving the tribe back to their starting point. At the same time tribal allies of the Romans, the Aedui, were being bullied by a rival tribe, the Sequani. Caesar turned on them and attacked. The Sequani were quickly defeated and the area pacified.

The Belgae
Another main group of Celtic peoples described by Julius Caesar were the Belgae. They were located in what is now northern France and Belgium. Caesar began his campaign against the Belgae in 57BC. The Belgae had a reputation as aggressive and dangerous warriors and initially Caesar proceeded cautiously. However, as the campaign continued the Belgae suffered progressively heavier losses, and although the campaign was hard and the fighting ferocious (and Caesar having great respect for his adversaries, praised them in his *Commentaries*) the Belgae were finally subjugated with very heavy losses, including thousands sold into slavery. There were also Belgae in southern Britain, and these would be encountered during both invasions of Britain – the temporary incursions by Caesar and permanent invasion and occupation under the emperor Claudius.

For the next eight years Caesar campaigned aggressively, and usually successfully, to gain Gaul as a Roman province. During that time the Belgae people were defeated, the Germans were strategically separated from the Gauls, and Caesar's troops were successfully employed in suppressing various revolts among Gallic tribes in the supposedly pacified regions.

the Arverni, he led it in rebellion against the Romans. Leading an organized uprising of united Gallic tribes, Vercingetorix posed a serious threat not only to Caesar and all he had accomplished, but to the future of Roman interests in Gaul. Aggressive and active campaigning by Caesar and his legions finally caught Vercingetorix in his stronghold of Alesia.

Other Gallic tribes massed and marched to Vercingetorix's support, the numbers in the field adding up to a huge army. Fully engaged in besieging Alesia, Caesar also had to deal with the added threat of the other Gallic army marching to the relief of the town. Building siege walls and outward facing defences, Caesar and his veteran legions not only finally took Alesia, and Vercingetorix, but also decisively defeated the relieving force. For the next two years, with effective organized resistance in Gaul defeated and broken, Caesar's army was engaged in pacifying the new Roman province and securing it for settlement and incorporation into the empire.

Roman Incursion into Britain

During his Gallic campaigns, in 55BC, Caesar marched to the north-western coast of Gaul and in a daring, unexpected move, crossed

what is now known as the English Channel in ships containing an invasion force of two legions. The landing, while initially successful, could not be maintained and Caesar withdrew. The next year Caesar again crossed the Channel, this time with five legions, and advanced as far inland as the River Thames. In the second invasion a Celtic leader, Mandubracius, was put in place as a Roman ally and his opponent, Cassivellaunus, was deposed.

▲ VERCINGETORIX, C.55BC This figure of the famous leader of the Gauls is based on the statue of him, erected by Napoleon III at the presumed site of Alesia. A brave and resourceful leader, he was overcome by the relentless efforts of the Romans, and since has personified gallant resistance to, and ultimate failure against, a formidable enemy.

Vercingetorix

The centre of renewed Gallic resistance revolved around, Vercingetorix of the Arverni, one of the most powerful of the tribes, living in south-central Gaul; what is now the Auvergne region of France. They had attempted to stay out of the long struggle with the Romans, but when Vercingetorix took control of

▶ GALLIC CAVALRYMAN, C.58BC The Gauls were Celts, with all that implied in ferocity and battle fury. What they lacked in overall discipline and organization, they made up for in their wild attacks and their long fight against Roman domination. They did 'adopt' Roman weapons and armour when they could get it, but they also were capable of considerable skill in metal-working themselves.

Tribute was exacted from the tribes in southern Britain, but no Roman troops remained on the island. Caesar probably could not spare any from his Gallic operations on a permanent basis, as trouble would soon again come to Roman Gaul in the form of a revolt of the Belgae.

One of the causes of Caesar's incursions into Britain was his trouble in Armorica, modern-day Brittany. The Celts there had strong ties to the Celts in Britain and may have been helping them fight against the Romans. By establishing a friendly tribal leader in Britain and exacting tribute from other tribes in southern England Caesar eradicated this problem.

Gallic Dress

The leaders of the Gallic troops would be much more richly clothed and armoured than their followers. Mail shirts, helmets and well-made weapons would be normal for them, something that the large mass of their followers could not afford. Interestingly, nobles were obviously unable to arm and equip their followers either because of the expense or because of the hard-to-come-by material.

Gallic cavalrymen were excellent and were employed by the Romans as auxiliaries. Sometimes, horses were only used to get to a battlefield and the riders would then dismount to fight on foot, so there was probably little difference in arms and equipment between mounted and dismounted Gallic warriors. The Gauls demonstrated a strong Celtic heritage in their dress, weapons, armour (if they

▼ GALLIC WARRIOR, 1ST CENTURY BC
Well-equipped tartan-clad Celtic warriors would wear chain mail shirts of interesting design. It definitely is not Roman in origin and probably was made by Gallic armourers. The shield design is particularly interesting.

▼ GALLIC LEADER, C.50BC *Gallic and Celtic leaders were frequently much better equipped than the men they took into combat. This tribal prince would be easily recognized on the battlefield by friend and foe alike. Celtic swords went through the standard development of edged weapons; they were generally single-edged, slashing weapons and did not have a thrusting ability as they had no useful, sharp point. Sometimes the sword hilts were intricately made and well-designed.*

had it) and inherited culture. They had much in common with the Celtic raiders of ancient Greece and their Celtic kinsmen in Iberia. Generally speaking many fought without protection, some also fought naked and may have painted themselves as the Celts of Britain did during the same period. Plaid trousers were worn, often without shirts, though with a helmet, shield, sword and spear. The 'mad Celtic rush' is commented upon from time to time throughout history from the initial Celtic successes of Boudicca's revolt right up to the Jacobite rebellion of 1745 in Scotland. It is also mentioned in 1793 in the insurrections and revolts in the Vendée during and after the French Revolution, where the inhabitants were the

▶ GALLIC WARRIOR, C.50BC
Gallic mounted warriors would probably be no match for the disciplined auxiliary cavalry that Caesar brought into Gaul for his campaigns. Quite often, too, the Celts used horses for transportation and then fought on foot.

descendants of the Celts of the Roman period. If an enemy were caught unawares or in disarray, that headlong rush could have a devastating result.

Gallic Arms

The Celtic tribes of Gaul were clothed as usual for the Celts of the ancient world, in tartan-style trousers, boots, and long tunics.

They were usually armed with long broadswords. Celtic-style helmets and chain mail would be worn, and long shields in the Roman style were also used. The chain mail, while essentially the same as that of a Roman legionary, was constructed differently around the shoulders, having a cape-like construction that added extra protection across the shoulders and upper back. Captured Roman arms, armour and equipment would always be used by the Celts, and was prized not only as useful protection but as visible proof of martial success against a much-loathed enemy.

SCIPIO'S CAMPAIGNS IN NUMANTIA

The Numantines were a Celtic people, correctly Celtic-Iberians, who inhabited what is now central Spain. Their main city and fortress was Numantia and they waged an effective war of ambushes and raids against the Romans in the 2nd century AD. Roman troops in the area were apparently not well led or properly disciplined, and since much of the Iberian peninsula had either been part of Carthage, or not dominated by any

one power before the Punic wars, they were hostile to the encroaching influence of Rome.

The campaign in Numantia by the Romans came at the end of the Punic wars when Carthage had been eliminated both as a Mediterranean power and as a threat to Rome. The situation in Spain had become intolerable for Rome and they sent the general who had been so successful in finally defeating Carthage, Scipio Aemilianus, named Africanus for his successes in North Africa.

The Siege of Numantia

Scipio undertook the Siege of Numantia, a city that while not overly large, was difficult to besiege and attack. The city was on the Durius (now the River Duoro) and this gave the defenders a lifeline to outside support. In order to cut off any active aid, Scipio placed defences at either end of the river and from these wooden obstacles, edged with spikes and other edged weapons, effectively barred the river from any assistance coming to the city. He also built an encircling wall, at least seven camps and other siege works around the city.

While the Romans waited, the Numantines ate through their remaining supplies and began to starve. When they finally surrendered to the Romans, after about eight months, there were only 4,000 survivors of the original city population and garrison. The Numantian revolt was effectively over.

◀ CELTIC-IBERIAN WARRIOR, 1ST CENTURY BC
Celtic-Iberian warriors were clad in their native clothing as shown and armed well, but were generally without any kind of armour, and therefore no match for the Romans in the open battlefield. The helmet is a typical Celtic type, as are the arms and equipment.

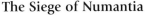

▲ CELTIC-IBERIAN WARRIOR, 1ST CENTURY BC
Another view of the Celtic-Iberian forces that opposed the Romans. This warrior is less well equipped than the figure to the right, which was a normal variation for this period. His arms and equipment are standard.

Celtic-Iberian Warriors

The Celtic-Iberians were a typical Celtic people and were armed and dressed accordingly. They may also have had weapons, armour, and equipment developed during Carthaginian rule. Their battle tactics were the same as other Celtic peoples, and in the open field they were no match for a disciplined and well-led Roman army.

Iberian auxiliaries, like the Roman soldiers of this period and campaign, were armed and equipped the same as the Roman armies of the Carthaginian wars. Chain mail was coming into widespread use and the army was

▼ IBERIAN AUXILIARY, 1ST CENTURY BC–1ST CENTURY AD *Another view of a Roman auxiliary in Spain generally along the same lines as his comrade, right. His arms and equipment are more Celt than Roman. These troops were also employed mounted.*

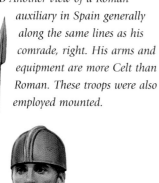

▶ IBERIAN AUXILIARY, 1ST CENTURY BC–1ST CENTURY AD *The Celtic-Iberians were good troops with excellent fighting spirit and the Romans recruited them enthusiastically as auxiliaries. Their arms in this instance were their own and not Roman and the armour worn, while chain mail, is longer than the usual Roman type.*

gradually becoming more professional, a situation which would be codified with the advent of Gaius Marius.

Roman auxiliary troops were often taken from the areas outside Rome that had been conquered, or from allied peoples that had a common enemy with those who fought against Rome. They would be armed and equipped with Roman equipment and arms and auxiliary cavalry was usually recruited from tribes and peoples who were natural cavalrymen. While armoured and armed as Romans, auxiliary units did retain certain cultural aspects of their native tribes. For instance, native Celts retained their age-old habit of cutting off a slain enemy's head and carrying it off as a war trophy, often tying it to their horse or saddle for martial display.

▼ *The Siege of Numantia in 133BC by Scipio Africanus marked the end of the Celtic-Iberian wars. This is an excellent depiction of the thoroughness of Roman siege operations with the city completely isolated and cut off from all outside assistance.*

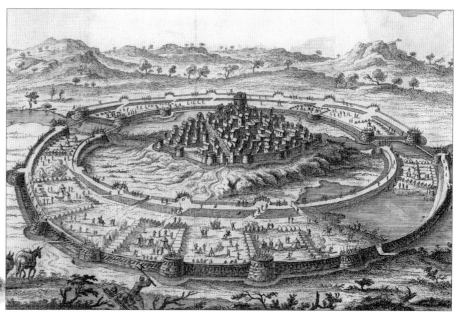

THE SPARTACUS REVOLT

One of the most serious revolts Rome faced during this period was the slave rebellion led by the remarkable figure of Spartacus.

Gladiators

Spartacus was a Thracian from northern Greece, a slave who was sent to the arena as a gladiator. Although it was possible for men to volunteer as gladiators, those sentenced to the arena to be trained for combat were often slaves, criminals, and sometimes prisoners of war. Some, if not all, gladiatorial combat was 'war to the knife' in that if you lost you could expect little or no mercy from either the powers that be or the mob. However, defeat would not always mean death, as the gladiatorial schools were reluctant to lose good fighters.

Gladiators were trained in a gladiatorial school where they were kept under guard and to all intents and purposes were slaves. One of the things that all slave-holding societies greatly feared was a slave revolt. Revolts by gladiators, especially veteran and highly trained ones, were especially feared by the Romans.

Revolution

Prior to the famous Spartacus revolt of 73–1BC there were at least two major slave revolts, in 135–2BC and 104–100BC. Both occurred in Sicily and were the result of brutal treatment of the slaves by the Romans. Legions had to be called in to quell both uprisings and Roman treatment of rebellion was brutal and final. The Spartacus uprising was one of gladiators rebelling against their situation and their treatment. The scale of the revolt seems to have taken the Romans by surprise and this allowed the rebellion to grow and prosper. The rebels were highly motivated and were all too aware that if they lost, Rome would have no mercy on them. Their success against the scattered Romans meant that the rebel armies could range the length of Italy, adding to their numbers as they marched. The slave army broke into two groups in 73BC and one, under Crixus, a subordinate of Spartacus, was defeated by an army under Lucius Gellius Publicola at Mount Garganus. Finally, an army under Marcus Licinius

◀ SPARTACUS, C.70BC *The gladiators who formed the nucleus of Spartacus' revolt were undoubtedly armed and armoured with what they took from the Romans. Chain mail armour was a favourite at this time – it was simple and afforded enough protection in close-order fighting. He carries a gladius and scutum.*

▶ MARCUS LICINIUS CRASSUS 115–53BC *The third member of the first Triumvirate (which also included Pompey and Caesar) was Crassus and he ruthlessly and efficiently defeated the slave revolt headed by Spartacus the Thracian. Crassus is seen here in the armour of a Roman army commander of the late republic. He would later be killed in action at the Battle of Carrhae.*

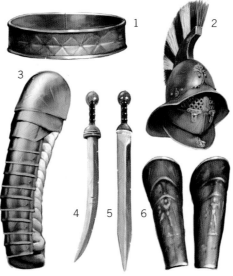

The Army of Spartacus

The gladiator army of Spartacus was no doubt armed with whatever weapons they could get their hands on. As they achieved success over Roman units they increasingly used captured arms and equipment recovered from the field of battle. Spartacus himself was probably armed as a Roman infantryman with gladius and possibly a scutum, and undoubtedly would have been wearing the mail shirt of a legionary. His followers would be similarly armed and armoured, if there was enough equipment and arms to go round. Both armies, of Spartacus and Crixus, must have presented a rather motley appearance on the battlefield compared to the uniformly armed and accoutred Roman legions.

▲ GLADIATOR PROTECTION AND WEAPONS, 1ST CENTURY BC–1ST CENTURY AD *1 The thick metal belt worn by the secutor. 2 A Thracian helmet with stiff multi-coloured horsehair crest. 3 The manica arm defence; metal armour over padding, originally this was leather but had been improved to either flexible metal armour or a type of scale armour. 4 The curved sica. 5 The straight gladius. 6 A pair of greaves.*

◀ SECUTOR GLADIATOR *Gladiators were armed and armoured differently, depending on their fighting 'specialty'. This gladiator is a secutor, wearing a type of Thracian helmet, in this case with no horsehair crest, armed with a gladius and a Roman army scutum. His legs are wrapped in padding, covered by greaves. All gladiators apparently fought barefoot.*

Crassus cornered Spartacus's force on the Silarus River in south-western Italy and annihilated it. Plutarch chronicled Spartacus' death on the field of battle, along with 60,000 of his followers.

Arms and Armour of the Arena

The weapons, armour and dress of a gladiator was not usually the same as those of the legion. Helmets had face masks for additional protection, and shields may have been legionary design, cut down to a smaller size. Nets, weighted down around the edges, were also used by gladiators who were armed with a trident. Padding, with armoured pieces on top of it, was worn on calves and arms, and daggers were employed to finish off an opponent

once he was disarmed. The gladius, the famous short sword of the legion may actually have originated in the arena, but gladiators also used curved swords.

As befitted the spectacle of the arena, the large helmets worn by some gladiators were sometimes decorated with feathers and horsehair crests, and at times both. Highly ornamented greaves were also worn in the arena, again backed by thick padding.

▶ GLADIATOR IN THE ARENA, 1ST CENTURY BC–1ST CENTURY AD *Helmets, as with other armour, came in different 'styles'. This gladiator is wearing one version of the myrmillo helmet and is armed with a gladius and small round shield. He is wearing only one small greave over linen.*

THE JEWISH REVOLT

Fighting against great odds to take, occupy and keep the land of Canaan after their long trek from Egypt, thought to be around 1200BC, the ancient Israelites had become a highly effective fighting force and one of the fiercest armies in the ancient Middle East. Beset on all sides by enemies, as well as hostile tribes inside what became the nation of Israel, the Jews of Judea were used to hardship and armed conflict. Although they finally became a subject nation, the inherent toughness of the Jewish resistance fighters, known as zealots, led them from time to time into bloody revolts against the conqueror of the moment.

The Sack of Jerusalem

Rome was never kind to those who revolted against her rule, and the Jewish revolt of 70AD was no exception. The two most memorable actions in the campaign were both sieges, the first of Jerusalem, the capital city, and the second of Masada, Herod's old mountain-top fortress in the desert.

Roman general Vespasian was the first Roman commander to manage the revolt, but during the campaign he was proclaimed emperor and had to return to Rome. Command of Judea was taken up by his son, Titus, who successfully suppressed the revolt. Jerusalem was finally taken after a lengthy siege, which had degenerated into a stalemate until the Romans breached the walls and entered the city.

The Jewish resistance had been fierce, and men, women and children had joined the zealots in the defence of the city. The Romans were savage in their response and the population was either slaughtered on the spot, crucified, sent into Roman slavery, or scattered. The walls of Jerusalem were razed to the ground, as was the Temple, with its sacred treasures looted and sent back to Rome. Titus' victory arch in Rome clearly shows the plunder carried from the Temple.

◄ JEWISH ZEALOT, 70AD *The Jewish rebels fighting Rome had to quickly develop tactics that would give them some kind of an advantage against the Roman legion. This Jewish fighting man is one of the many 'guerrilla' types that fought against Roman occupation. He is dressed as he would have been in his native village, armed with whatever he could get his hands on. Fighting on his own ground, he was a determined enemy, either in ambush in the countryside or fighting inside a fortification such as Jerusalem.*

▲ JEWISH WARRIOR, MASADA, 70AD *The Jewish fighters were barely protected and poorly armed compared to the Roman armies that came against them.*

The Siege of Masada

Surviving Jewish zealots and their families fled to the ancient Herodian fortress of Masada, on top of an isolated rocky plateau on the eastern edge of the Judean Desert. The fortress was invested, and finally taken, by the Romans after another lengthy siege as

The Jewish Insurgents

Herod (usually referred to as Herod the Great) was the Roman's client king of Judea (37–04BC), 70 years before the Jewish revolt, and as such he had an army of native Jews and foreign mercenaries. After his death, his army gradually withered away, but some remnants of its descendants, at least in theory, could have either survived to serve in the Jewish Revolt or at least to furnish arms and armour to the insurgents. Militarily poor, the Jewish insurgents armed themselves with whatever was available, from any source. Some undoubtedly wore Roman armour and carried Roman weapons, but most were probably poorly equipped and not capable of fighting the Romans in the open. Instead they relied on ambush and the use of fortifications in order to resist.

◄ HERODIAN HORSE ARCHER, 1ST CENTURY AD *While from a slightly earlier time, some of the Jewish troops who fought the Romans c.70AD could have been armed and accoutred as this cavalryman was. Jewish resistance to the Romans was savage, and they undoubtedly procured weapons and equipment where they could.*

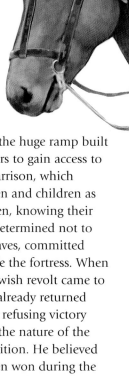

▲ *The remains of Herod's Palace in the fortress of Masada, where the zealots made their last stand against the might of Rome.*

well as ingenious engineering feats by the Roman army. Remains of the legion camps at Masada are still quite visible, as is the huge ramp built by Roman engineers to gain access to the fortress. The garrison, which consisted of women and children as well as fighting men, knowing their time was up and determined not to become Roman slaves, committed ritual suicide inside the fortress. When Masada fell, the Jewish revolt came to an end. Titus had already returned to Rome, allegedly refusing victory laurels because of the nature of the war and the opposition. He believed little glory had been won during the suppression of the revolt. Interestingly, the construction of the Colosseum in Rome was done by Jewish prisoners taken during the revolt.

ROMAN BRITAIN

The native resistance that met Julius Caesar on his incursions into Britain in 55 and 54BC was typical of the tribal foes that the Romans had encountered in Gaul and Spain; they were warriors, good ones, but they were not soldiers. Still, they managed to prevent Caesar

▼ CELTIC WAR CHARIOT, DRIVER AND WARRIOR C.60AD *The Celts of Britain sometimes fought in their native chariots, probably the most effective shock tactic in attack that the Celts in Britain possessed. The Celtic chariot needed two men, a driver and a combatant. Sometimes the driver was seated, or kneeling, but others stood; he would probably be armed with a short sword. The 'fighter' would be armed as Celtic infantry and may or may not have worn armour.*

from carrying out his conquest of Britain, and the empire had to wait another 11 years for a successful invasion of its most western territory.

The various tribes of Britons that lived in the southern parts of the country were armed and armoured much like their brethren on the continent. Sometimes they would be clothed in battle and sometimes not. They would fight on foot, mounted or from chariots.

▲ *An aerial view of the wooden Roman fort of Bremetennacum Veteranorum (Ribchester, Lancashire, England) around 60–70AD. The fort is thought to have been occupied by a garrison of up to 500 cavalrymen; the first contingent were Asturians from northern Spain. There was also a vicus – civilian settlement – established outside the fort. Use of Veterancrum in the name denotes that retired Roman veterans were settled here, quite possibly some of which were survivors from Boudicca's uprising.*

▲ BOUDICCA OF THE ICENI, C.60AD *Boudicca led the famous revolt that bears her name after she and her two daughters were mistreated by the Romans. Initially successful against the Romans and causing much destruction, Boudicca and her family perished in the Roman resurgence under Suetonius.*

Chariots

The British-Celtic chariot was a two-man vehicle, carrying a driver and an armed warrior, and was powered by two horses harnessed side by side. The driver would stand between the horses of the team holding the reins, freeing the warrior to fight. The warrior would stand on the platform of the chariot between the two rather small wheels, and he would be armed with spear, javelin, and sword. The chariot was

well-built, sturdily constructed and could stand up to the punishment of travelling over rough terrain. Compared to Middle Eastern chariots of an earlier period it was built of heavier materials but was still fast and manoeuvrable on the battlefield. While the chariot could be employed against enemy cavalry, the primary object was to get the warrior close to the enemy so he could dismount and fight on foot with his comrades.

Clothing and Weapons

The Celts wore woollen clothing, suitable for inhabiting a temperate island in northern Europe. Clothing could be plain, but could also be woven in patterns, either stripes or a checked pattern similar to tartan, although this bore no relation to any kind of clan identification as it would in Scotland centuries later. If the Celts went into battle naked, their bodies would be painted in patterns with woad and their hair was usually done up in top knots, unless wearing a helmet.

The Celtic charge was a tactic to be feared by the Romans, especially if they were caught in an ambush, but if the Celts failed to break the Romans in their first rush, the ensuing slaughter of a Roman counterattack could be devastating. As time went on, therefore, Celtic tribesmen wore more armour, especially helmets, and while some of these would be of a Celtic or Gallic pattern, equipment picked up from the Romans would also be used. When facing the enemy the Celts employed the long sword, javelins, slings and spears, shields of various sizes and patterns – usually painted in some type of tribal or ethnic design – and carried small shields.

▶ CELTIC WARRIOR, C.60AD *The Celtic influence in ancient Europe was immense. This Briton is a typical Celtic warrior, armed with a spatha and a small shield and ready for combat.*

▲ *Britain still remembers Boudicca as a national hero and resistance fighter. This statue of her was set up in London in 1902.*

ARMY DEVELOPMENTS UNDER AUGUSTUS

After winning his throne the emperor Augustus, Julius Caesar's nephew – previously known as Octavian – not only instituted a new period in Roman history but engaged in serious reforms of the Roman army, and other institutions. This period, of relative peace, eventually became known as the Pax Romana or Pax Augusta. It was a period of success, and also saw important developments in Roman army equipment.

◀ A surviving fragment of copper scale-armour from Trimontium, Scotland.

Romans themselves used remains unknown. So too is the origin of this complex system of segments and plates used to cover the soldiers' upper body. Early examples are linked to archaeological finds at Corbridge, near Hadrian's Wall, but the armour soon evolved, and was, to an extent, simplified, a process which led to the

The Lorica Segmentata

Roman infantry began to wear the kind of armour that is now largely associated with the height of Roman greatness. It is known as the lorica segmentata, but this name was coined in the 16th century; the term the

◀ ROMAN INFANTRYMAN, 1ST–2ND CENTURIES AD Roman heavy infantry adopted the new lorica segmentata and in many respects this gave better protection than the mail lorica. This Roman legionary is in full equipment ready to be placed in line of battle by his centurion. The crest on his helmet is interesting and may not have been worn in combat, though it certainly could have been. The legion number is prominent on his shield, an affectation of some legionaries.

▶ ROMAN CAVALRYMAN, 1ST–2ND CENTURIES AD This auxiliary cavalryman wears a longer-than-normal mail shirt similar to a medieval mail hauberk. Arms and equipment are typical of cavalrymen of the period, with the addition of feathers in the helmet, a throwback to an earlier period. The inside of the oval shield shows the bar for the grip – the actual purpose of the shield boss. Well-clothed for marching and fighting in cold weather he wears trousers, or braccae, a type of military boot, and stockings.

The Legions

Legions after the Marian reforms generally would recruit where they were formed, for example the famous 10th Legion was formed in Iberia by Julius Caesar for his Gallic campaigns. Other legions would recruit to fill their ranks in the area where they were stationed, and legion traditions might not always be 'Roman' in origin. For example, at the Second Battle of Cremona, or Bedriacum, in 69AD, Vespasian's 3rd Legion, was brought to Italy from Syria to restore order and suppress the civil war. It had adopted a Syrian custom of 'hailing the rising sun' – turning in its direction before engaging the enemy.

During this period the Roman army continued in the professional growth begun by Marius. The army was put on a permanent footing by Augustus, and the strength of the army was set at 28 legions of around 5,000 men each. This did not take into consideration auxiliary cohorts and cavalry attached to the legions on campaign.

Post-Augustan Legions

Of the original 28 permanent legions established by Augustus, at least three were destroyed in combat and were

◀ ROMAN CENTURION, 1ST–2ND CENTURIES AD *Roman off-duty wear could be merely civilian clothing for comfort, or a modified form of uniform, as seen here. This uniform could classify as the centurion's 'walking out dress' that he might wear for a night on the town or on leave where he might still be required to be armed. He is wearing his military cloak and caligas, and carries the ever-present vine stick of rank. He wears pteruges, the fringed 'skirt' and shoulder coverings, of cloth or leather, together with his ornately decorated military belt.*

▶ ROMAN STANDARD BEARER, 1ST–2ND CENTURIES AD *This is probably the most important man in the legion, as he carries the eagle standard, which symbolized the honour of the legion. This standard bearer is wearing a lorica squamata, or scale armour, worn in the republican army as well as in the later imperial army, and common among musicians, standard bearers, and cavalry.*

replaced by new legions with different numeric designations, even though the lost eagles of these legions were later recovered. Reorganizations, renaming, renumbering, and the addition of honorific titles to the legions tends to add confusion to any detailed study of the legions lineage, but the information that has survived has allowed researchers and historians to make definite conclusions as to which legions were in existence during certain periods, up to the end of the western empire.

so-called Newstead type. Early examples of the Corbridge armour have the different segments of armour connected through an intricate system of straps and buckles. Modified types saw the increased use of hooks and eyes, as well as straps. It seems that the buckles were weak, and tended to break, and so, later in the first century, and by the time of the Newstead-type, more robust fastenings were adopted. The number of segments decreased over time, making the lorica easier to produce but less comfortable to wear. This was probably one of the reasons why this famous piece of equipment was phased out and the troops returned to wearing chain mail.

A neck cloth (focale) protected the neck from rubbing of the armour.

GUARDS

Roman emperors and senior commanders developed a number of units of hand-picked soldiers to form bodyguards. Some of these were ad hoc, but, eventually, distinct units of bodyguards, with considerable power and influence, emerged to guard the imperial elites as well as general officers on campaign.

Praetorian Guard

The Praetorian Guard developed from cohorts of guard troops that were formed by Roman generals during the late republican era. The term 'praetorian' eventually

evolved to denote troops selected to become the bodyguard of a Roman general. They did not have to be native Romans. Caesar had a personally selected force of German cavalry for his bodyguard, and these could also be considered elite troops.

Octavian and Mark Antony both had units of praetorians for their bodyguards and after Octavian's rise to power as emperor he definitely formed and kept praetorian units for his personal protection.

Praetorian Guard formations were centred on the city of Rome itself and were garrisoned in permanent barracks. They were charged with the security of the emperor, his family and the imperial household, and of the palaces in which they lived and worked. They received enhanced pay; three times as much as normal legionaries during the reign of Tiberius.

The praetorians carried oval shields, adorned with a stars and moon device, but wore a uniform that very much resembled that of the legionaries. On escort duty they sometimes removed helmet and armour, but wore tunics, neck scarves and cloaks, and carried a

▶ PRAETORIAN CENTURION, 1ST–2ND CENTURIES AD *This centurion is not wearing armour, but is wearing an ornate helmet that the praetorians were depicted in on various Roman monuments. The scutum is also particularly ornate. The praetorians were not admired by the regular Roman army, and were finally disbanded by Constantine, who then formed his own unit of guard troops.*

◀ PRAETORIAN GUARDSMAN, 1ST–2ND CENTURIES AD *The Praetorian Guard was formed to provide a bodyguard for the emperors of Rome and although they were sometimes to be found on campaign, they remained in Rome more often than not and gained a reputation for political interference. This individual is in full duty or field dress.*

pilum and shield. Aside from these household troops, a unit of bearded German guardsmen protected the emperors from the time of Augustus until Vespasian disbanded them.

Guard Cavalry

There were also guard cavalrymen, equipped and armoured like any auxiliary cavalry belonging to the legions. Arms and armour were similar, and they were undoubtedly armed with the spatha and some form of

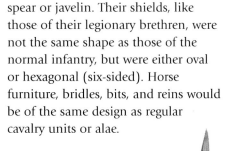

▼ Vexilla Bearer, 1st–2nd centuries ad
This is another view of a unit's vexilla or unit standard, this one belonging to the Praetorian Guard stationed in Rome. The bearer is not wearing armour but is armed with his gladius. All Roman standards had a steel or iron pointed butt that could be jammed into the ground if necessary and hold the standard upright. The bearer is a well-decorated veteran, wearing torcs and phalarie on his parade harness. This praetorian wears a high cut boot rather than caliga.

spear or javelin. Their shields, like those of their legionary brethren, were not the same shape as those of the normal infantry, but were either oval or hexagonal (six-sided). Horse furniture, bridles, bits, and reins would be of the same design as regular cavalry units or alae.

Equites Singulares
This was an elite German cavalry unit distinguishable by the scorpion design on their hexagonal shields, one scorpion in each corner. The 'Singularian Horse' was the personal cavalry of the emperor, and would escort him whenever he left Rome. It was founded in the late 1st century AD and initially contained 720 horse, divided into 24 squadrons of 30 men each. Numbers rose to around 1,000 under Hadrian. The regiment's original core component were elite Batavian horsemen, and the unit was the only regiment of the Guard that admitted imperial subjects who were not Roman citizens. On Trajan's column, and therefore by 113AD, the

▶ Germanic Auxiliary Cavalryman, 1st–2nd centuries ad
German auxiliary cavalry were greatly prized by many Roman senior commanders and were frequently employed by them as escorts and bodyguards. Julius Caesar was guarded by German auxiliary cavalry during his campaigns in Gaul. They were generally equipped and armed in the normal fashion for auxiliary mounted troops.

standards of the unit are depicted as bearing the same lightening and thunderbolt motif as the legions.

Auxiliary Guardsmen
On campaign, Roman commanders might also hand-pick troops for their escort on and off the battlefield to ensure their personal security. Cavalry, even auxiliary cavalry, would probably be selected for this duty and charged with the general's safety. They would be commanded by a known and chosen officer who was familiar with the general personally.

THE GERMANIC ENEMY

The Romans fought an incredible number of enemies over the long period of the western empire. Two of the most formidable were the Germanic tribes and the Dacians. The German tribesmen took to the field as both infantry and cavalry. While well-supplied in arms and armour, they were not uniform in appearance.

The Romans respected the German tribesmen as an effective enemy, but the Germans could not manoeuvre in the open as the legion could and their usual tactic was fighting in line and attacking headlong against the deployed Roman infantry.

▶ GERMANIC CAVALRYMAN, 1ST–2ND CENTURIES AD *Rome's northern frontier could be bitterly cold along the Rhine or in the deep, thick German forests. This well-clad but unarmoured Germanic warrior is typical of what would be found on the northern frontier along the Rhine or the Danube. A round wooden shield and javelins complete this horseman's equipment. He would also carry a spatha.*

Clothing and Weapons

German clothing might consist of long trousers and tunic, they wore their hair long and were usually, if not always, bearded. They frequently wore their long hair in a topknot, sometimes known as a Swabian topknot. Germans and Dacians both painted decorations on their shields and also carried standards, sometimes the dragon standard later carried by Roman cavalry units. Helmets, if worn, were of varied designs, and it is probably fair to say that no two Germans or Dacians looked alike on the battlefield. Early German warriors probably fought naked with either only a long sword or a sword and shield.

As the Germans became more sophisticated and learned from defeat, more body armour was employed by them, both mail and the scale type, as were helmets taken from many sources. The German armies' fighting skills also improved, and they began to win from time to time against the Romans. German auxiliaries, especially cavalry, were highly prized by the Romans and it was German tribes from Saxony that invaded Britain after the Romans had to pull out, leaving the Romano-Celts to their own devices and defence. The Dacians were related ethnically to the Thracians and were an independent people until conquered by the Romans in the 2nd century AD under Trajan. This was the last major conquest of the Romans and is represented in sculpture on Trajan's column. Like other barbarian peoples, such as the Illyrians and the Britannic Celts, the Dacians decorated their bodies with tattoos. Their leaders wore distinctive caps.

Weapons and Tactics

The Germans generally fought in a similar way to the Gauls and the Celts, and carried much the same kind of arms and equipment, so what the Romans would encounter in Germany or

▶ GERMANIC WARRIOR, 1ST–2ND CENTURIES AD *Axe, spatha, spear and shield mark this warrior as ready for combat. His cloak is a more blanket than cloak, and his shield is typical of the Germanic tribes that fought for and against Rome.*

north of the River Danube, they could expect to find in Gaul, Spain, and in Britain. The Germanic tribes' method of fighting was to get close to their enemy quickly and engage him individually in hand-to-hand combat. Fighting the Roman legion this way could be disastrous as they would first meet one to three volleys of the Roman javelin at about 15 metres, and then be advanced upon with Roman shield and short sword. With their shields weighted down by a javelin and basically useless, the German infantryman would be at a great disadvantage against trained Roman infantry using both shield and sword as a weapon.

There were a number of influences which exerted themselves on how the Germans dressed and fought. The Celtic warrior influence was strongest on Germans' fighting methods and tactics, and with the weapons and equipment that the Germans employed. Swords, shields, long bows, long swords, were all used by the Germans against the Romans. Some sources state that the Roman cavalry spathae – their long sword – was developed from the Celtic and German examples that the Romans came across.

◀ GERMANIC WARRIOR, 1ST–2ND CENTURIES AD *The Germans were no different to the Romans when it came to carrying standards. This German, while well-armed with spatha, short axe (also good as a missile weapon) and shield, is a standard bearer for his tribe or people. The draco (dragon) was a common emblem used by myriad peoples who fought for and against Rome. It was later adopted by the Romans themselves on occasion and became one of the familiar emblems of the eastern Romans.*

The Dacians

Dacian warriors were well-armed and equipped and wore scale armour and pointed, almost eastern-type, helmets. They also possessed an interesting and very deadly weapon called the falx. This was a curved edged weapon that came in two versions: a short falx that was used like a sword and the long-handled falx that was a pole arm. The falx was a very effective weapon and the Romans initially had problems dealing with it, as it was used to disarm the legionaries and lop off their arms. The long falx, however, was a two-handed weapon so the bearer could not use a shield with it, and this could put him at a disadvantage in a close-quarter fight.

ARMS AND ARMOUR

This era fields the Roman legionary most familiar through the ages: the steel helmet with a red horsehair crest, segmented body armour, rectangular shield, dagger and sword, a red or a white tunic, and hob-nailed sandals.

Helmets

The Imperial Gallic-type helmet is the best known Roman helmet, but many variations were in use and older models continued to be worn until they wore out. The helmet had come a long way from the simple, rounded Montefortino type worn by the republican soldiers. The earlier Gallic and Italic styles had also given way to something more complex, and more protective. For example, the Weisenau type helmet, which seems to have been worn in the Augustan period, had iron or brass bowls, decorated or engraved cheek pieces, cut-outs to keep the ears uncovered, and a generous neck guard. Some examples show additional decoration, perhaps added according to taste. For instance, 'eyebrows' on the front of the helmet were a popular adornment. Chin straps were fitted to rings, but often tied under the throat.

Legion armourers might produce helmets or they could be produced in Roman armouries in fortresses or major cities. The helmets could also be constructed of more than one type of metal, such as iron and bronze and some legionaries would engrave their helmets with their name and unit.

For comfort, the interior of the helmet was often padded with cloth, or a cloth cap was worn under the helmet. Helmets developed according to tactics adopted – for example lower neck guards as the Romans moved away from crouching and thrusting. They also became more effective, with reinforcing strips, sometimes in a cruciform pattern, added to deflect blows and reinforce the crown.

Armour

The Roman body armour did indeed consist of the lorica segmentata – steel segmented armour – but leather armour was also still worn, as was chain mail. The lorica segmentata was an all-plate metal cuirass that was constructed of separate steel plates buckled or tied together to afford normal movement to the wearer in order to be able to use his weapons properly. During the period of transition from the manipular to the cohort legion, the centurions and senior officers might still wear the muscle cuirass, though centurions would usually opt for either the mail shirt or the lorica segmentata.

Chain mail was constructed of iron rings riveted together forming a 'shirt' that would be of one piece, put on over the head, and sometimes laced up at the back. It was supple and allowed the wearer improved movement, and it also offered good protection.

Scale armour (lorica squamata) was also worn during this period and it would not be uncommon to see all

◀ LEGIONARY 1ST–2ND CENTURIES AD
This legionary wears his lorica segmentata, carries his gladius on a baldric and his pugio (dagger) on his belt. He is also equipped with the usual scutum and javelin.

▼ HELMETS, 1ST–5TH CENTURIES AD
This selection of helmets are those worn by the enemies of Rome and are generally either Celtic or Germanic in origin. Helmets of this type would be worn by later generations of Roman troops in the 4th and 5th centuries AD. 1 A Celtic-type helmet with nasal protection and a chain mail aventail to protect the neck. 2 A Celtic-type helmet with both a nasal guard and neck protection as part of the helmet. 3 and 4 Front and back views of a late period Germanic helmet.

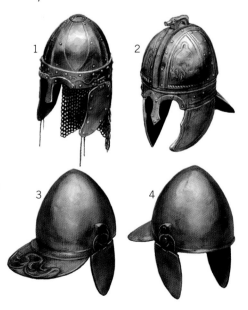

▲ ROMAN HELMETS, 1ST–5TH CENTURIES AD
1 and 2 Bronze Montefortino infantry helmets, early 1st century. 3 Imperial Italic infantry helmet, early 2nd century. 4 Imperial Gallic infantry helmet, 1st century. 5 Imperial Italic infantry helmet, 2nd century. 6 Iron and bronze imperial Italic infantry helmet from the late 1st century. 7 Bronze imperial Italic infantry helmet from either late 1st or early 2nd century. 8 Roman cavalry iron helmet, 2nd century. 9 Roman cavalry helmet, 1st century. 10 Roman cavalry helmet, 2nd century.

three types of armour being worn in the same legion. Greaves generally disappeared from use in the Roman army during this period.

It seems that some legionaries took to wearing a manica, or arm protection, around the time of the Dacian wars. This segmented armour did not cover the elbow but was worn on the upper side of the arm. Such a development might have been introduced to protect legionaries from the Dacian falx, a curved sickle, which came in two verions: a one-handed weapon wielded like a sword and a much larger two-handed weapon.

Belts

The gladius – for the infantry, and the spatha – for the cavalry were designed to be attached to either belts, worn at the waist, or baldrics, which were worn over the shoulder. Belts could be simple leather, at first somewhat thin, later much wider. They were often highly decorated with studs, plates and plaques, all according to the taste of the individual wearer.

The pugio, or dagger, often in a heavily decorated scabbard, was also attached to a belt and accessed on the left-side of the body, and one early sword and dagger harness design was made up of two thin leather belts, worn simultaneously, one holding the pugio, the other the gladius, which would form an 'X' at the wearer's waist. Later, wider belts held both weapons.

Leather 'aprons' or sporrans, covered in discs or small plaques, would hang from the front of the waist belt. It was once thought that they might have been to protect the legionary's groin, but it seems they were used more to keep the hem of the tunic down and preserve the soldier's modesty.

Footwear

The military sandal (caliga) was a stoutly constructed open-toed sandal which extended to just above the

▶ EDGED WEAPONS, 1ST–2ND CENTURIES AD
1 and 2 Germanic Spatha and scabbard. 3 Celtic or Germanic sword scabbard. 4 Roman gladius. 5 Roman cavalry spatha. 6 Roman cavalry spatha. 7 Roman gladius and scabbard with a baldric instead of a belt to attach it to the body. 8 Roman belt with dagger attached. 9 A Roman spatha and belt.

ankle. The sole of the caliga was built up of layers of leather, it was held together with stitching and reinforced with iron nails or studs on the sole. The leather was waxed or oiled for waterproofing.

Weapons

The gladius, or short sword, was worn and used by all ranks. It was a relatively short, thrusting sword, and deadly in the hands of a well-trained

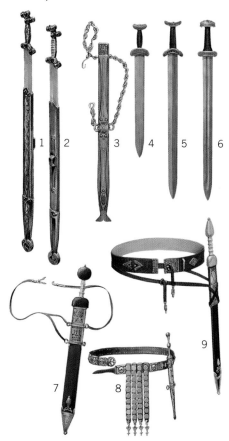

legionary. It was combined in combat with the rather large, heavy scutum or shield, with a central iron boss, behind which was the handle to hold and control the scutum.

Roman gladii were not uniform in manufacture and could be of different designs. As already mentioned, the early gladius was both a stabbing and a slashing weapon, but the latter models were designed for stabbing with a relatively long point and sharpened on both edges. The rather simple design led to ease of manufacture with wooden hilts or grips. There was no sword guard. Models for centurions and senior officers might have more elaborately designed hilts, ivory was not unknown for senior officers and could be

▲ SHIELDS, 1ST–3RD CENTURIES AD
A selection of Germanic shields in use in the 1st through 3rd centuries. The intricate designs are tribal or clan markings and sometimes would also identify the bearer. 1 to 4 A selection of Celtic/Germanic shields. 5 and 6 Round cavalry shields, the one on the left, smaller than usual, coming into use with heavily armed and armoured cavalry.

▲ SHIELDS, 1ST–2ND CENTURIES AD
1 A Roman cavalry 'dress' shield used for parades and unit games, not usually used in combat. 2 A bronze shield boss from the Legio VIII Augusta, stationed in Britain during the 2nd century. 3 The construction of a Roman legionaries' scutum. The upper left corner shows the layers of laminated wood used in the main construction. This was then covered with hide, and lastly with a linen cover attached by the boss, and decorated with the typical Roman designs.

◄ GERMANIC WARRIOR, 1ST–5TH CENTURIES AD This warrior demonstrates how the various types of weapons would be carried. The various Germans that fought against the Romans wore captured Roman armour, especially helmets and mail loricas.

elaborately carved. Sword hilts could also be made of decorated metal.

Scabbards could be constructed of metal, leather, or wood, or combinations of two or three of the materials. Leather or wooden scabbards might be decorated with metal, either simply to reinforce the main material or also for decoration. Wooden gladii were used in training.

The pilum, or javelin, was for throwing, and the legionary would be armed with two or more. It was constructed with a wooden lower shaft, a steel or iron tip (later a flat head), and a metal shaft between the head and the wooden part of the pilum, which was made of lead. Once the pilum was thrown and the head struck an enemy's shield, the heavy wooden part of the shaft would bend the lead shaft, making it difficult to remove from the shield, thereby rendering it worthless. The pilum could be retrieved and the head straightened. Some pila had spherical weights added to increase momentum and impact.

Shields

The shield was made of wood, with a steel or iron boss, and could be used as a weapon itself on the battlefield. The legionaries' scuta were generally rectangular, sometimes oval in shape, curved from the centre to the sides and outlined in iron for strength. The wooden base was covered front and back in leather and the front also had a linen cloth covering. Some shields had decorative metallic rims and most seem to have been coloured in red.

▼ HORSE EQUIPMENT, 1ST–4TH CENTURIES AD
This horse is fully loaded for campaign, carrying equipment needed for the cavalryman as well as forage for the horse in the netted bag on the side. Canteen and cooking utensils are shown, as is a weapon cover. 1 The chafron, head and face armour for the horse. 2 The Roman saddle. 3 Another form of Roman chafron for the protection of the horse's eyes and head. 4 Horse body armour, which was coming into use by the 5th century.

Cavalry

Roman cavalry would usually be armed and equipped similarly to a legionary, with the following exceptions. Shields would be oval or hexagonal in shape, and would be flat instead of curved in the case of the legion infantry. The gladius was not carried by Roman mounted troops; they used the spatha, a longer broadsword-type weapon copied and developed from German tribesmen. It was an excellent weapon and would eventually replace the gladius in the later empire and in the eastern Roman Empire.

Various helmets were worn, similar to that worn by the legion infantry with two exceptions. Firstly, the neck guard was shorter in case the cavalryman was unhorsed; the wearing of an infantry helmet would endanger the horseman and might break his neck in a fall. Secondly, the ears were covered by some cavalry helmets, which could be a disadvantage in a melee as, for example, the sounds for recall might not be heard.

Parade helmets were used for formal occasions, especially by standard bearers. These helmets fully enclosed the head, front and back.

In addition to the spatha, a lance or spear was carried for either mounted engagements or for use against infantry, which gave the cavalryman a length advantage. Daggers were undoubtedly carried by many or most of the Roman horsemen.

Horse Furniture

The Roman cavalry saddle was of the usual type, still without the stirrup, which would not be developed into general use in Europe until the late 6th or early 7th century. The cavalryman would grip the horse with his knees and thighs, his feet pointed downward at anything faster than a walk. The saddle was fastened to the horse with a girth across the horse's belly, and with breast and rump straps to steady the balance of the saddle on the horse.

The reins were attached to the bridle by an iron bit, the entire ensemble looking quite modern. Decorations would not be used in combat, but horses were combed and curried for parades, and some type of parade harness and armour might be used for formal occasions. Cavalry standards were carried; one of the most common being the draco, or dragon standard.

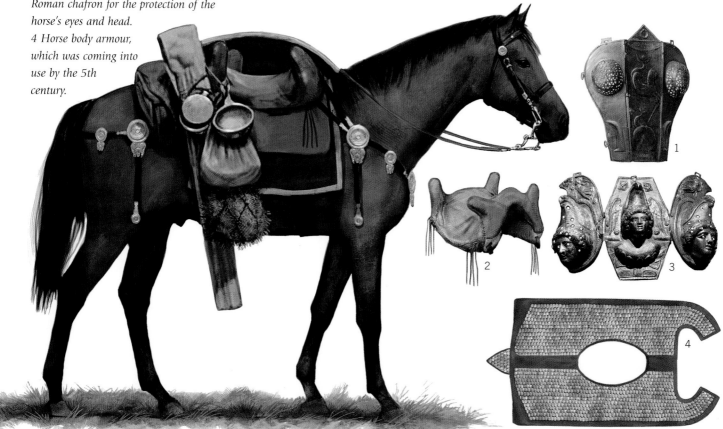

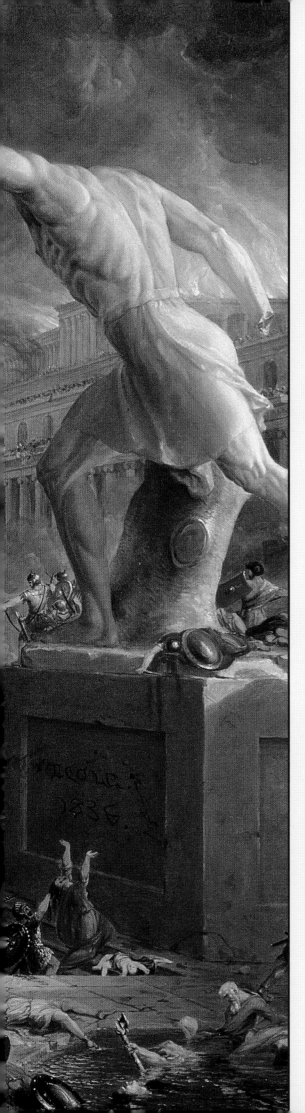

DECLINE AND FALL OF THE WEST 235–476

There was not one reason for Rome's fall, or a definite date for the beginning of the long decline, and it might not have been as cataclysmic as was believed for quite some time. Many and varied reasons have been given by historians for the fall of the western Roman Empire. Corruption and instability in central government certainly had a major part to play, but so had the reliance on foreign mercenaries instead of native soldiery in the later Roman armies, and once the institution of the Roman army began to disintegrate, so did the Roman Empire. The invading barbarians arrived in successive waves, over generations, not in one overwhelming tsunami. Most importantly, many Roman institutions were kept intact by the new rulers, and the following era referred to as the Dark Ages may not have been as benighted as was previously believed. For Rome's military, this was a period of flux, when more and more barbarian peoples served as auxiliaries.

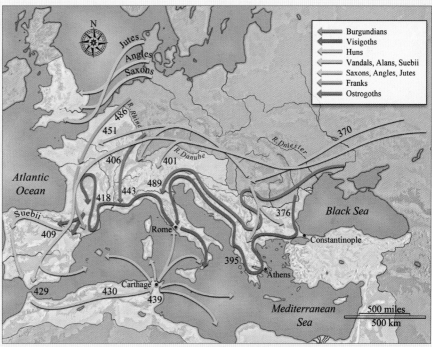

▲ *The distribution of the barbarians coming into western Europe between 370 and 489.*

◄ *The fall of Rome to barbarians was dramatic, but the decline of the western empire took centuries, by which time the eastern half of the empire was strong enough to stand alone.*

THE ROMAN EMPIRE IN DECLINE

'We had been told, on leaving our native soil, that we were going to defend the sacred rights conferred on us by so many of our citizens settled overseas, so many years of our presence, so many benefits brought by us to populations in need of our assistance and our civilization. We were able to verify that all this was true, and, because it was true, we did not hesitate to shed our quota of blood, to sacrifice our youth and our hopes. We regretted nothing, but whereas we over here are inspired by this frame of mind, I am told that in Rome factions and conspiracies are rife, that treachery flourishes, and that many people in their uncertainty and confusion lend a ready ear to the dire temptations of relinquishment and vilify our action. I cannot believe that all this is true and yet recent wars have shown how pernicious such a state of mind could be and to where it could lead. Make haste to reassure me, I beg you, and tell me that our fellow-citizens understand us, support us and

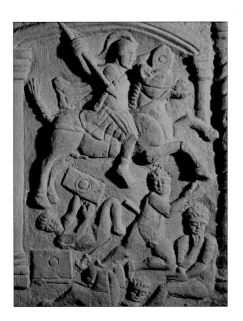

▼ *A sandstone milestone bears a carving symbolizing the Roman conquest. From Bridgeness, West Lothian in Scotland, and dated to c.142AD, it marks the northern extent of the Roman Empire.*

▲ *The Temple at Garni, Armenia, in the easternmost part of the empire. It was constructed in the 1st century AD by King Tiridates I of Armenia, probably funded with money the king received from Nero during his visit to Rome, and possibly constructed as a declaration of Armenia as a Roman province.*

protect us as we ourselves are protecting the glory of the empire. If it should be otherwise, if we should have to leave our bleached bones on these desert sands in vain, then beware of the anger of the Legions.'
*Centurion Marcus Flavinius,
2nd Cohort, Legion Augusta, c.20BC.*

The above quotation by a veteran Roman centurion stationed outside Italy neatly sums up what was probably the feelings and beliefs of Roman legionaries who fought and died far from their homeland. It also outlines some of the problems faced by both the Roman army and the Imperial Roman government in the 2nd to 5th centuries AD. Weak emperors, mutinies by some of the legions, the replacement of unpopular emperors by either the army or the praetorians, and more frequent defeats by the encroaching 'barbarians', led to frustration within the empire, the government, and most importantly in the ranks of the army. This dissatisfaction with the Imperial government was one of the ways by which the Roman Empire in the west would eventually fall in 476AD.

In the long decline there were bright spots of the old Roman solidity and a refusal to be defeated. However, the old empire was dying on its feet and not enough Roman citizens stepped forward to take up arms in her defence. The old Roman army faded away, transforming into something else entirely, while a new army arose in the east to serve as Europe's bulwark for centuries to come.

An Overextended Power

Rome had been invaded before. The Celts had crossed the Alps into Italy early in Rome's history and had taken and sacked Rome, but the city and its people had survived and prospered again. Romans were again invaded, and three of her armies disastrously defeated by the Carthaginians under Hannibal. The city of Rome was not taken that time, and she recovered

▲ Barbarian 'settlements', after the migrations from Asia and the east, in the 4th century. The overwhelming impact of these invasions was too much for the western Roman Empire to endure.

sufficiently to drive the enemy from Italy as well as invade his homeland and take his capital, finally defeating the Carthaginians. So why did the barbarian incursions this time bring Rome down, never to rise again as the western empire?

One of the main reasons, if not the main reason, was that the old Roman army, that of the legions of solid infantry, were no longer there to defend her. In name the legions still existed, but the old solidity of the native Roman soldiery was gone. In its place stood mercenaries and people of many nations that fought for different causes than the defence of the empire.

Uniform Changes

The overall appearance of the Roman army changed in the second half of the third century. The lorica segmentata disappeared to be replaced by a chain mail shirt. The long-serving gladius was abandoned in favour of the longer spatha and the old, reliable curved scutum gave way to a round shield, still decorated on its face with many representations, some of which can be seen in the Notitia Dignitatum, a Roman document listing the units of the Roman army, and its different aspects and equipment.

Roman clothing also changed to a more Germanic appearance. Longer tunics, trousers, longer hair and sometimes beards became common in the late Roman army and gave the army the appearance more of a barbarian force than a traditional Roman one.

▼ Roman departure from Britain was sudden and abrupt. Most troops, recalled to defend the homeland, had left by 400AD, but many veterans, as well as established Romano-Britons, remained to stand against the Saxons.

BARBARIAN MIGRATIONS TO THE WEST

Just as it took centuries for the Roman Empire to be built through conquest, sweat, and blood (both Roman and that of many other peoples), the decline of the western empire did not happen overnight. One of the reasons, however, was the continued migrations of peoples, originally tribal peoples, from the east in search of new lands and eventually new opportunities.

Throughout the ancient period, migrations came out of Asia and moved to the west. Some peoples, such as the Huns and later the Mongols, came westwards in search of conquest, booty, and riches. Other tribes or peoples, moved westwards because they were being pushed by forces stronger than they were. Some of these barbarian tribes and peoples made peace with Rome, and many served Rome as mercenaries or subject peoples. This could be a double-edged sword, however, because if maltreated by Rome, these peoples, now trained in the Roman way of war, could turn on their former benefactors and cause trouble inside the empire and not merely on the frontiers, such as along the Rhine or the Danube.

▼ *Thorismond the Visigoth was an ally of Aetius and aided him decisively in defeating Attila at Chalons in 451.*

▲ *The frontier along the River Danube, with its amazing bridges – seen in the background here – commemorated on Trajan's column, was one of the first under threat from Germanic tribes. Note the standards top left.*

The Germanic peoples who lived on the Rhine and Danube were made up of different tribes and groups who became more distinct as peoples as the migrations continued and conflict with Rome became more common.

Huns
The Huns were an Asiatic nomadic people that were, if not the cause, then a catalyst of the westward migrations of barbarian tribes. They were similar to the Mongols in their methods, although on a much smaller scale, and they were neither as disciplined nor as well led as Genghis Khan's armies of the 13th century would be.

The Huns originated east of the River Volga and they appeared in Europe around 370AD. United under their outstanding leader and chieftain, Attila, the Huns were eventually successful in establishing an empire

after numerous, almost overwhelming victories over the Romans, but were finally halted at the Battle of Chalons in 451 in Gaul, by the Roman General Flavius Aetius. Just two years later, however, in 453AD, Attila died, and in the space of a year his empire had withered away.

▼ *The Romano-Celts beg unsuccessfully with Roman general Aetius for support against the barbarian incursions in Britain.*

Goths

The Goths were an eastern German people who later split into two different groups and became known as the Ostrogoths and the Visigoths. The Ostrogoths had fought for the Huns and were controlled by them; the Visigoths crossed into Roman territory in 376AD in order to get away from the Huns. The Ostrogoths would later o upy and settle in Italy and the Visigoths would move into Spain and southern France. Two of the clans or family groups that comprised the Visigoths were the Greuthungi and the Tervinvi. It was the Visigoths, under the leadership of Alaric, who took and sacked Rome in 410AD. Interestingly, they fought each other at the Battle of Campus Maruiacus in 451AD, the battle being between the Roman army of Aetius and the Huns under Attila (the Visigoths fought for Aetius and the Ostrogoths with Attila).

The Visigoths fought in ranks on foot, and the Ostrogoths were mounted as the Huns were and they do seem to have met and fought on that field against each other.

Lombards, Vandals and Gepids

The Lombards were a Germanic tribe from the western part of Germany that would eventually make their way into Italy in the 6th century. They were late

▲ Alaric, the Visigoth chieftain who famously sacked the city of Rome in 410AD, quickly moved on from the city to invade Africa, where he died of fever in the same year.

arrivals and the carnage and confusion that remained in Italy after the wars with the Goths helped them establish their kingdom in northern Italy.

The Vandals were another Germanic tribe that had crossed the Rhine in 406AD and went westwards and south. They crossed France, as well as Spain, and eventually crossed into North Africa, establishing a kingdom there.

Another eastern Germanic people were the Gepids, who were enemies of the Goths. Curiously, this tribe did not

participate in the migration, quite possibly because the Goths, who were later absorbed by the Huns, did. However, Gepids did not assimilate into the Hunnish tribes and they were involved in, and could quite possible have been the instigators, of the revolt of the united German tribes against the Huns. In the 6th century, both the Avars and the Lombards conquered and absorbed Gepid territories.

The Asian Threat: Sarmatians and Alans

Two migrant groups from the steppes of Asia who were not Germanic in origin, probably being either Persian or Turkic, were the Alans and the Sarmatians. The latter group lived along the Danube during the period and generally stayed independent from the Germanic tribes, but the Alans on the most part allied themselves with the Germans and accompanied them on their migrations and conquests. Some, however, did not enter the Roman Empire and were absorbed by the Huns in their travels and wars against the Romans.

▼ Some barbarian nations allied themselves with Rome for protection against other tribes who were stronger than they. Other barbarian nations banded together to fight against Rome. The Alans and the Huns, shown in combat here c.374, were two such barbarian groups who later joined together bent on conquest, loot, and pillage. Neither would survive the invasion of Italy as a force of note.

THE COLLAPSE OF ROME IN THE WEST

It is difficult to pinpoint when Rome went into decline, but it was a process speeded not only by the almost constant pressure of the seemingly endless westward migrations of barbarians, but also by a combination of weak leadership on the part of the Roman government, a fatal weakening of the army, and the ponderous administration of the empire itself, which was why Diocletian split the empire into two parts in *c.*284AD, each with its own emperor.

The combination of internal and external pressures applied to the weakened empire proved fatal. Pressures from without came from barbarian tribes, who while not necessarily hostile to Rome, per se, but through either necessity, hostility on the part of the Romans themselves, or because of inspiration from a dynamic leader, such as Attila or Alaric, wanted to carve out kingdoms of their own. Neither Attila nor Alaric were

▼ *When Rome finally fell in 476AD, the city was no longer the capital of the western empire, but was still its spiritual heart. Its fall was a shock to the western world.*

▲ *Flavius Honorius Augustus was the western Roman emperor from 395–423AD. Son of Theodosius I, he was a weak emperor and did little to stop the long decline of the empire.*

successful themselves, but their peoples and the other migrating tribes, with their successive assaults against the western Roman Empire, eventually weakened Roman rule to a point where it finally did collapse.

The Dark Ages

In western Europe the period following the fall of Rome is generally referred to as the Dark Ages. However, this period may not have been so 'dark' as has been described. It appears that some of the new overlords retained Roman law and customs, even to the point of adopting them themselves. Large Roman landholders, for example, might have been left their lands and estates, if they pledged loyalty to the new rulers and paid them, instead of Rome, the required taxes. By accepting the new social order, and pledging to support and fight for it if necessary, the process might have been somewhat painless. Roman civilization was not all destroyed; much of it was maintained and later absorbed as the old Roman citizenry and aristocracy served the new order and eventually intermarried.

Roman Britain and the Romano-Celts

A good example of this is Roman Britain. After the last of the Roman troops were withdrawn (and the emperor in Rome, Honorius, belatedly and cynically sent the Romano-Celts in

▲ An engagement between Theodoric the Great and Odoacer is depicted on this relief, at the Church of Saint Zenon in Verona.

Britain a message that they now had to defend themselves), the remaining Romano-Celts assumed leadership of Britain and for years held off the barbarian invasions of Britain by the Saxons. Too much of the source material for this period is unreliable, but it seems likely that the Romano-British 'Dux Bellorum' (Duke of Battles), Ambrosius, was fighting Visigoths in Gaul c.468AD, eight years before Rome finally fell in the west. His successor may have been Arturus, the Romano-Celt warlord who inspired the later legends of King Arthur. It is possible that Arturus successfully held off the Anglo-Saxon invasions, routing them completely at Mount Badon in 516AD. After a period of peace Arthur was mortally wounded fighting Saxons again at Battle of Camlann in 537AD. If so, the Romano-Celts held onto their Roman and Celtic heritage for over 60 years after the fall of Rome. After that period, the now Christianized Saxons overwhelmed Britain, but perhaps absorbing the native Britons rather than eliminating them, and finally becoming Anglo-Saxon.

What happened in Britain, though a special case in that it was an island and partially insulated from the European continent, also happened on a much larger scale in Germany, Gaul,

North Africa and Italy. The Roman civilization that had been spread for centuries was not destroyed, but modified and absorbed by their new overlords, be they Visigoths, Ostrogoths, or Vandals. Italy is a case in point, with Roman influence remaining strong, and Ravenna emerging as Theodoric's elegant capital after the defeat of Odoacer. Some

▼ Out of the last-ditch defence of Britain arose the legend of Arthur and his warriors, shown here as medieval Christian knights, though the reality was less royal, the task grimmer, and the culture Romano-Celtic.

barbarians, however, chose not to remain, as with the Huns, and, leaving nothing but destruction and fear in their wake, retreated into Asia.

Now the new lords of the lands formerly belonging to Rome built new kingdoms, based on a Roman civilization that was too firmly planted to be uprooted by invasion and conquest. Governmental systems and Roman law were adopted by the new kings and princes, and from these seemingly chaotic beginnings a new Europe was forming, initially violently, but then by gradual settlement and assimilation.

THE LATER EMPIRE

After Marcus Aurelius' death in 180AD the ability and leadership of the Roman emperors gradually declined. There were notable exceptions, one of them being Diocletian who ruled from 284–305AD. He reorganized and revamped the Roman army, a badly needed reform, as the empire was no longer expanding, but had to defend what it controlled. Diocletian reformed the army into field and border units. This was done in order to have troops on the borders of the empire to defend against barbarian incursions or invasions, while the field units were to be employed as a mobile reserve to be sent where needed, especially if the border units could not contain the enemy.

Centurions

The centurions who commanded centuries and cohorts, and who formed the officer corps of the legions were still very much in evidence. Sometimes leather armour would be worn, lighter and more comfortable than either the lorica segmentata or the mail shirt. This could be worn on duty, but generally in battle the greater protection offered by plate armour or mail was preferred. Centurions would wear the same helmets as the men, with or without crest. If a crest was worn, it would be the traditional centurion crest, worn parallel with the shoulders so that the legionaries could readily identify their leaders and commanders, who fought alongside them with gladius (or spatha) and shield in formation. Many centurions would wear their decorations in battle in order to stand out to both friend and foe. These would be worn on the chest in a square pattern much like that of a chessboard. As with their predecessors of the earlier empire and republic, the centurions still carried the venerable vine stick as their symbol of

◀ LEGIONARY, 3RD CENTURY AD *While still in typical helmet and armed with the standard scutum, this legionary is changing to a more general and less 'rigid' form of wear. The lorica segmentata has disappeared and a return to the chain mail lorica was becoming the usual body armour.*

▶ TRIBUNE, 3RD CENTURY AD *Off-duty wear for senior officers would be as comfortable as conditions allowed, though they would rarely set down their sidearms. The warm full trousers, gathered at the boot level, and fringed cloak, are noteworthy.*

rank. Even without their unique form of horsehair crest, the centurion could be identified by the legionary by his vine stick, which was still a centurion's symbol of rank, and by being allowed to wear their sword on the left hand side of their body.

Tribunes

As they had been since the Marian reforms, in this period legions were assigned six tribunes, but their duties and responsibilities had changed; becoming more of a political position than a military rank. The second in command to the

◀ LEGATE, 3RD CENTURY AD *Legion commanders during the later empire period would probably be armed and accoutred as usual, but by their own preference. A muscle cuirass after 300AD was unusual, but the general's white 'sash' is one of the traditional symbols of rank.*

▶ CENTURION, 4TH CENTURY AD *The colour of the armour and the muscle cuirass is unusual, at least for this period, and the absence of the traditional vine stick is either a mistake on the part of the centurion or it is being 'phased out'. The absence of a helmet plume is also noteworthy.*

army, including the senior officers, and cloaks would be worn. Military cloaks were usually red, but off-duty civilian cloaks, of similar design and construction, and of various colours might be worn. The military cloak, used by all ranks, was generous and warm, and would frequently be the legionary's bed and blanket, as well as protecting him from the elements.

Field Command

The Roman officer who held overall command of a legion, was the legate. Of senatorial rank, often a former tribune, a legate would generally be appointed by the emperor and would outrank all tribunes. In a province with only one legion assigned to it, the legate would also serve as provincial governor. Senior Roman commanders from the early days of the republic were too many times politicians first and soldiers second. Tribunes assigned to the legions sometimes matured into excellent soldiers and competent commanders, but the Roman arrangement of political appointees sent out to the legions, gave the Roman army an unprofessional senior officer class, which sometimes resulted in military catastrophe. Competent, and sometimes excellent senior commanders, however, such as Julius Caesar, Pompey, Marius, Sulla, and Scipio did lead armies to legendary feats of martial prowess and established the reputation of a combat force that has come down in history as

legate would be of senatorial rank, the other five were from the equestrian class with military experience. They would generally be armed and equipped as a senior officer and undoubtedly ornate muscle cuirasses would be much in favour. Helmets, more ornate than usual, would also be worn. It is questionable whether tribunes were popular or respected by the rank and file legionaries.

Tribunes in 'off duty' wear would probably wear a combination of military and civilian dress and would also be armed, usually with a spatha, as they were mounted on the march and in combat. As the empire progressed, comfortable tunics and trousers were adopted by most of the

one of the great armies of all time. Some senior commanders ignored the tribunes assigned to them and instead listened to, and trusted, the opinions, experience and advice of officers who had proved themselves on the battlefield, such as the veteran, hard-bitten centurions.

Commanders wore ornate muscle cuirasses and a white belt at the high waist position as their symbol of rank. Arms would be more expensive than the usual, but would be of the same model, either gladius or spatha, or both, depending on preference. Ornate helmets with stiffened horsehair crests or plumes were generally worn by officers needing to be seen by their men on the field.

Uniform Development

Roman uniforms and equipment at the beginning of this period were essentially the same as in the great days of empire building and conquest.

While cracks could be seen in the edifice of the empire, the legions still seemed to be triumphant and dominating. The army, however, was beginning a slow decline that would see the legion changed completely by the time of Diocletian's reforms. More auxiliary troops were being employed from among the barbarian peoples that were beginning to encroach the borders, and an overall change in armour, equipment, and weaponry was taking place.

The lorica segmentata was still being worn in the 3rd century AD, but as before the adoption of this type of plate armour, mail shirts were again becoming more common among the rank and file. The lobster-tailed helmet was still being worn, but more use was being made of mail hoods that covered the entire head.

Tunics usually came in three main colours, white, red, and blue, the blue being a medium or deep sky blue and quite striking in appearance. The rectangular, curved scutum was still in use in the legions, and this could also be found in the usual red with gold ornamentation or in deep sky blue with gold ornamentation.

Legion Standards

Unit standards were a visual representation of the unit, what it had done, what it was trusted to do, and the traditions and esprit de corps that the unit represented. Further, while the personnel in the legion would change, the traditions and reputation of the legion did not, and the standards represented those intangibles to new recruits and veterans alike.

◀ STANDARD BEARER, 2ND–3RD CENTURIES AD *One of the standard bearers would carry the imago, bearing an image of the emperor, hopefully the current one, though that would be difficult to maintain during a period of civil war or when change of heads of state was frequent.*

▶ STANDARD BEARER, 3RD CENTURY AD *The maniple standard was a tradition from the republican legions and the wearing of animal skins made the bearer easily identified in the noise and mess of combat. Awards for valour were often placed on the maniples of a century. The open hand on the top, called the manus, symbolized the Roman soldier's oath of loyalty.*

When the disaster of the Teutoborg Forest destroyed three legions and their eagles, and other standards were lost, those legions were never reconstituted, even when Germanicus later recovered the three standards where they fell. Disgrace was permanent, and those three legions not only died deep in a German forest, but as units were dead forever in the eyes of the empire and the army. The Roman's own term for the Battle of the Teutoborg Forest was the Varian Disaster, after the commander who led the army, Publius Quinctilius Varus.

The standards of a legion would not be entrusted to just any legionary, but to veterans who had

◀ Legionary, c.3rd century ad *The chain mail head covering is an interesting variation for wear without the helmet. The lorica and chain mail combination definitely is demonstrating a change in body armour for the Roman legionary.*

Arms and Equipment

The gladius was still in wide use by the legionaries and the dagger was still worn. However, the spatha, usually used only by Roman cavalry and Germanic barbarians, was coming into use by the Roman infantry. This being a slashing rather than a stabbing sword as the gladius was, it meant changing one of the essential fighting traits of the legion.

As with arms and armour, the shield, or scutum, was changing in the ranks. The old rectangular, rounded scutum was going out of favour and round or oval shields, once used only by auxiliary infantrymen and cavalrymen, were now becoming the norm in the ranks of the legions.

Late Roman Infantry

As the empire progressed and the army changed, especially after the reforms of Diocletian in the late 3rd century AD, the older, tougher legions began to disappear from the Roman army. The general appearance of the legionary gradually changed in almost every aspect. Armour became almost completely different with the disappearance of the lorica segmenta and the old imperial-style helmets. Some of this was the result of barbarian influence in the army as the proportion of mercenaries grew and that of native Roman soldiery from inside the empire diminished. This change was gradual, but unrelenting and a legionary from the 1st century AD would not have recognized his counterpart 300 years later.

distinguished themselves in combat and could be trusted to die in the defence of the unit standards, especially the legion's eagle.

The standard bearers of the legions, the eagle bearers (aquilfers) and other standard bearers (imagnifers) were still the visible symbols of the legion and its individual cohorts, and the usual dress and armour of the ordinary legionary was still being worn, though sometimes tunics would be worn over the armour. The lion and bear skins were still worn by the standard bearers, bearskins for the imagnifers and lion skins for the aquilfers, and this was worn over helmet and armour.

▶ Legionary, 3rd–4th centuries ad *The Germanic influence on uniform is easily identified. The armour has changed to scale, as has the shape of the shield, which is no longer the traditional rectangular curved shape of the older scutum. A single spear has replaced the javelins. The legion has now changed from the older, steady Roman infantry to a lesser organization that would contribute to the decline of the empire in the west.*

Auxiliary Infantry

German infantrymen in the Roman army were wearing their native linen tunics embroidered with their tribal designs. Leggings or trousers were worn under the tunics, and the tunics would usually come to mid-thigh. Roman-type helmets would be worn, and body armour that was normally used was either iron chain mail shirts that would come to the top of the thighs or scale armour of the same length. Sometimes, the armoured shirts, either mail or scale armour, would come down almost to mid-thigh and cover the tunic completely.

Cloaks were also worn by the barbarian soldiers, either from their own traditional clothing styles or borrowed from the Roman practice.

Auxiliary Cavalry

Roman auxiliary cavalrymen were usually recruited from allied or conquered peoples and while some, if not many, of these horse soldiers wore Roman dress and armour, including helmets, many did not. Native arms

▼ AUXILIARY INFANTRYMAN, 4TH CENTURY AD *The influence here in clothing, arms, equipment, and lack of body armour, reflects the almost overwhelming Germanic appearance of the later western empire armies. Even the haircut reflects a Germanic/barbarian influence.*

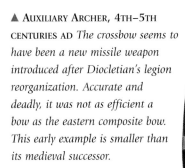

▲ AUXILIARY ARCHER, 4TH–5TH CENTURIES AD *The crossbow seems to have been a new missile weapon introduced after Diocletian's legion reorganization. Accurate and deadly, it was not as efficient a bow as the eastern composite bow. This early example is smaller than its medieval successor.*

◄ AUXILIARY INFANTRYMAN, 4TH–5TH CENTURIES AD *Little remained at this point of traditional arms. The helmet is definitely of Roman influence, and the spatha, though adapted for Roman use years before, is now being used as a standard weapon by infantry, both legionary and auxiliary.*

and armour were often used by auxiliary cavalrymen, such as the conical helmets, or Phrygian-style helmets worn by the variety of barbarians that usually constituted a Roman army's mounted arm. Frequently, the standard carried by these cavalry units was the draco, definitely derived from the east and one that became common in Roman armies of the late Roman period in the west. It is possible that the draco has also passed into legend as the standard that inspired the pendragon device, carried by the British troops of Arturus, or King Arthur, in his campaigns against the Saxon invaders.

Auxiliary cavalrymen carried a round or oval shield, and sometimes one that was hexagonal in shape. The spatha and spear were the usual weapons. The mail shirt or scale armour was preferred by the Roman mounted arm, the same types as in the infantry, though they might be a little longer to provide some protection for the thighs. Roman cavalrymen, especially the draco standard bearers, had parade armour as well, highlighted by a helmet with a complete face mask in the form of a human face. The helmet entirely covered the head. This was not, for practical purposes, worn in combat.

As previously mentioned, there was a 'light' and a 'heavy' form of dress on campaign, the 'light' being without armour, with the exception that helmets might be carried and worn. If not, a small round furred cap was worn for fatigue and everyday wear, as well as on the march. 'Light' dress would also be worn for drill, archery practice, as well as on recruiting duty.

Both the short bow and the crossbow were employed, but it should be noted that the short bow was a western European bow, not the more complicated and powerful composite bow that the Romans encountered in the east.

◀ AUXILIARY CAVALRYMAN, 4TH–5TH CENTURIES AD
Roman cavalrymen were developing into more of a heavy cavalry based on Roman experience against the Parthians and Sassanians in the east. The helmet is unusual and reflects northern European practice from the later Vikings. The draco (dragon) standard was favoured by many units, both Roman and eastern.

Diocletian Reforms

When Diocletian took the throne in 284 he realized the army was seriously in need of reform. Primarily, he felt, the empire's borders needed strengthening, and he established border units, or limitanei, composed of professionals but with limited training. More mobile field units, or comitatenses, were also commissioned. These were more highly trained, and could assume both defensive and offensive missions, as the situation required. Some of these units were newly organized and formed by Diocletian, but others were formed from the older legions which were

The New Legions

Old Legion Number	Number of Subunits
1st	13 (1)
2nd	7 (2)
3rd	5 (3)
4th	3 (4)
5th	2 (5)
6th	5 (6)
12th	1 (7)

New Legion Subunit Names and Numbers:

(1) 1st Flavia Constantia, 1st Flavia Gallicana Constantia, 1st Flavia Martis, 1st Flavia Pacis, 1st Flavia Theodosiana, 1st Illyricorum, 1st Iovia, 1st Isaura Sagittaria, 1st Iulia Alpina, 1st Martia, 1st Maximiana Thaebanorum, 1st Noricorum, 1st Pontica
(2) 2nd Britannica, 2nd Flavia Constantia, 2nd Flavia Virtutis, 2nd Herculia, 2nd Isaura, 2nd Iulia Alpina, 2nd Felix Valentis Thebaeorum
(3) 3rd Diocletiana, 3rd Flavia Salutis, 3rd Herculea, 3rd Isaura, 3rd Iulia Alpina
(4) 4th Italica, 4th Martia, 4th Parthica
(5) 5th Iovia, 5th Parthica
(6) 6th Gemella, 6th Gallicana, 6th Herculia, 6th Hispana, 6th Parthica
(7) 12th Victrix

◄ INFANTRYMAN, 4TH–5TH CENTURIES AD *The long tunic, trousers and boots, along with a Germanic-type helmet and shield identify this later western empire legionary. The shield is the Germanic round type and he would usually be armed with spatha and spear.*

disbanded or absorbed into the newly organized army. These units were held in reserve, behind border fortifications far enough to be out of striking distance of any foreign threat, but close enough so as to be able to react to any adverse situation on the border. They were formed into seven legions, numbered 1 to 6, and 12.

Diocletian also formed a third type of unit, a cross between the limitanei

▲ INFANTRYMAN, 4TH–5TH CENTURIES AD *The western Roman decline was long and slow, and, depending on your point of view, the change in the Roman army was the same. The leggings on this infantryman, with protective strips of leather wound round the lower leg, are interesting and have a distinct Germanic look to them. The arms and accoutrements have the same origin. The round shield is not the norm for Roman infantry, but the helmet still has Roman elements. The horsehair helmet plume may have been a unit identifier.*

and the comitatenses, dubbed the pseudocomitatenses. Formed from the old legionary army, these units, neither border or line troops, were frequently sent to the field army in support of their operations. Sometimes this transfer of units and functions was permanent, depending on the situation. These new units were made up from both comitatenses and pseudocomitatenses troops and were stationed throughout the empire. The biggest difference was in the strength of the new legions. They usually ranged from 500 to 2,000 legionaries depending on the units' mission and probably to confuse the enemy as to the actual strength of the new legions.

Diocletain's reforms were confirmed and extended by Constantine, who disbanded the Praetorian Guard and replaced its function as the bodyguard of the Roman emperors by the scholae.

Behind these bodyguards were the more formidable palatinae, or palace troops, which held the primary place of seniority and honour in the

▼ CAVALRYMAN, 4TH–5TH CENTURIES AD
Typical Roman cavalry accoutrements and saddle, along with a variation of the Roman helmet, distinguish this Roman cavalryman. The mail shirt is longer now and the shield is a typical Roman auxiliary cavalry shield.

reformed Roman army. While formed mainly from the old Praetorian Guard, these troops were originally carefully screened for loyalty to Rome and the emperor, to ensure that no internal palace revolt took place.

Constantine's emphasis on the eastern part of the empire, symbolized by the empire's capital being established in the new city of Constantinople, began the change in the eastern army from an infantry force to a mounted army.

The change wasn't immediate, but the enemies the Romans faced in the east were constituted in large measure with cavalry, both heavy and light, and the advent of the horse archer would make a definite impact on the future of the Roman army. Along with the horse archer would come the biggest revolution in mounted warfare up to that time: heavily armed and armoured heavy cavalryman, and the eastern empire's future in warfare – the dazzling and powerful tanks of their day – the cataphract.

DEATH OF THE OLD ROMAN ARMY

The beginning of the death of Rome arguably began with the catastrophic defeat of a Roman army at the hands of the Goths and Alans at the Battle of Adrianople in 378AD (see page 188). Although this battle occurred close to Constantinople, and hence in what was actually the eastern Roman empire, it was a harbinger of the downfall of Rome in the west.

Western Woes

The western army adapted to the defeat by over-recruiting foreign troops, and this influx of 'recruits' into the army, usually taken as whole units, diluted the quality of the Roman army. Weapons were now diverse and were generally now not provided by the state, as they had been since Marius' sweeping reforms that put the Roman army on a professional footing in the 1st century BC. Training and cohesion, those all-important military attributes that lead to esprit de corps and was the moral strength of the old legions, was either too weak or lacking altogether, and this undermined the army down to its very core. Foreign troops followed their own leaders in the ranks, leaders who may or may not be loyal to the state, and perhaps not even to the Roman commanders appointed to lead them.

The army took on the character of a collection of bands of mercenaries and auxiliaries, rather than the disciplined and homogenous legions of old.

Eastern Tactics

The eastern army, however, learned its lesson from Adrianople and adapted to new methods of warfare. Cavalry became the main striking force of the eastern empire, and while infantry would still be important, it was now a secondary arm, used to garrison fortresses, stabilize the frontier, protect the older provinces, and form a line on the battlefield from behind which the cavalry could emerge or rally for a new charge

The equipment used by the individual Roman soldier, be he infantryman, cavalryman, or archer, bore little or no resemblance to the Roman soldier of antiquity, be he a republican legionary or one of the stalwart legionaries of a Caesar, Vespasian or

◀ ROMAN INFANTRYMAN, AT THE END OF THE WESTERN EMPIRE, 476AD *Legionary uniforms and equipment were simplified over those of this infantryman's predecessors of two centuries before. Gone also was the older, more formidable legion organization that had conquered and held the empire together.*

▶ ROMAN ARCHERY INSTRUCTOR, AT THE END OF THE WESTERN EMPIRE, 476AD *Very little, if anything, remained of the older, steadier infantry by the fall of Rome. Interestingly, this instructor from the archery section is armed with a gladius, a throw back to a time when the legions marched when and where they chose within the empire and beyond.*

Marcus Aurelius. Armour had changed, and was most likely to be a long chain mail shirt. The shape of his shield had also reverted from oval to a rounder shape, and his usual sidearm was now the spatha, the traditional gladius being now a thing of the past.

Horse equipment had not changed a great deal, and the Roman cavalryman still rode a

saddle that was not equipped with stirrups. Cavalry shields were also smaller and rounder. In overall appearance, infantrymen and

▶ ROMAN CAVALRYMAN, AT THE END OF THE WESTERN EMPIRE, 476AD *This horseman does have reminders of the legions in their prime. The parade helmet with parade mask is a definite holdover from the glory days of the legion. The horse harness and saddle are definitely Roman, as is the typical cavalry shield. This is another iteration of the draco standard.*

cavalrymen were equipped in a similar way and were almost identical in clothing and equipment when dismounted. Archers wore the same clothing and equipment as their infantry and cavalry brethren, and

infantrymen might double as archers, with the addition of bows, quivers, and arrows to their regular equipment.

While the old, venerable legions had gone from the world stage, and the old Roman army was in its death throes, the new cavalry army, which was being formed by trial and error in the east, was on its way to becoming one of the most formidable armies ever fielded by Rome, east or west. The cataphracts, horse archers, and well-trained heavy infantry organized in well-defined units and led by able, aggressive commanders would establish themselves as the bulwark of Europe and allow the newly formed nations and kingdoms of western Europe to grow and mature without interference from enemies in the east.

THE GERMANIC TRIBES

The Germanic tribes that migrated to the west and came into conflict with the Roman Empire were much more sophisticated than those the Romans had faced a few centuries before. They were better clothed, armed and armoured, and had much improved weaponry, though the axe was still much-favoured both as a missile weapon and in hand-to-hand combat.

German Arms and Armour

The Germans, at least their leaders, in the 4th century AD were sometimes well-armoured, but that was expensive, and the Germanic 'rank and file' probably did not have much protection, not even helmets. They were armed with spears for throwing or hand-to-hand combat, the long sword which the Romans called a spatha and with which the Romans armed their auxiliary cavalry, as well as simple short bows, in contrast to the composite bow which came

▶ WARRIOR, 4TH–5TH CENTURIES AD *The Goths, later 'separated' or further distinguished as either Ostrogoths or Visigoths, were among the nomadic peoples who either attacked Rome outright or settled on the empire's borders in search of refuge or allies against other nomadic peoples who were pushing them westward. This well-equipped and well-armoured cavalryman would either be a formidable enemy or a helpful ally, depending on whose interests, Roman or Gothic, coincided with their goals of the moment. He is using stirrups, an innovation that made it much easier to fight from the saddle.*

out of the eastern steppes. Shields were round or oval in shape, with a central iron boss, sometimes coming to a point which allowed the shield to be used as a weapon, but prohibited its use in formed ranks as it could cripple or kill the man in front of the bearer. Shields were also decorated with animal renderings or star-shaped decoration, or other device depending on the tribe and the bearer's family or clan.

Clothing

Germanic clothing was made of both wool and linen, and was often embroidered or dyed, or both. Some type of leggings and/or long boots were usually worn, and some Germans wore vests of wool or sheepskin, usually with an undergarment that went to mid-thigh.

The Introduction of the Stirrup

One of the most important innovations for mounted combat was imported to Europe during the period of the fall of the Roman west: the stirrup. In order to be able to fight from a steady platform mounted, a good saddle is necessary, though there have been notable exceptions to this rule, such as the Numidians of the Punic wars who rode bareback. However, as practical as the Roman saddle was for mounted combat, and as good a horseman as the Huns, Goths, and others were, the necessary evolution for mounted combat was the stirrup. Traditionally thought to have been developed in either India or China around the 4th century AD, it probably was not in widespread use in Europe until the 6th century AD. Some modern illustrations of Goths and other barbarians show them with it during the 4th or 5th centuries, and though this is possible, it is

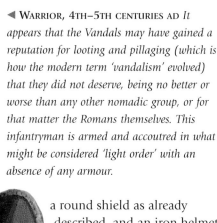

◄ **WARRIOR, 4TH–5TH CENTURIES AD** *It appears that the Vandals may have gained a reputation for looting and pillaging (which is how the modern term 'vandalism' evolved) that they did not deserve, being no better or worse than any other nomadic group, or for that matter the Romans themselves. This infantryman is armed and accoutred in what might be considered 'light order' with an absence of any armour.*

a round shield as already described, and an iron helmet that might be decorated with feathers – as Roman helmets were during the republic – as well as animal fur. Leggings of some type, either long or knee-length might also be worn. Sometimes the trousers were gathered at the ankles.

Vandals

Other Germanic tribes, such as the Vandals, would be armed and armoured (if they wore it) similarly to the Goths. As the barbarian incursions went further into the territory of the Roman Empire, and the Germans fought more frequently against the Roman troops, Roman arms and armour would be picked up and used by the Germanic tribesmen. Undoubtedly the two sides fighting each other might sometimes be indistinguishable, and mistakes must have been frequent. Scouts from one side or the other may come across what they believe to be a friendly unit, and report back as such to their commander. Proceeding on incorrect information, that commander might approach the opposing unit and unhappily find out too late that his scouts were mistaken.

▶ **WARRIOR, 4TH–5TH CENTURIES AD** *It is often difficult to distinguish exactly what nomadic group or people is being studied. There was considerable cross-fertilization of weapons, armour, and equipment among the nomadic peoples depending on who they fought. Further, the Gothic tribes fielded both cavalry and infantry, making further positive identification hazy at best.*

The Vandals were another tribal group (actually two tribes, the Hasdingi and the Silingi) from the eastern portion of what is now Germany and later were generally allied with the Persian Alans. They originally came into contact and conflict with the Romans in the late 2nd century AD and finally settled in Dacia. They wandered into Roman territory at the beginning of the 5th century, quite possibly under pressure from the westward-moving Huns, and again came into conflict with the Romans. They also moved into both Gaul and Spain and they eventually established a kingdom in North Africa. They are most remembered for sacking Rome in 455AD.

probably premature. Whatever the case, the introduction of the simple stirrup revolutionized mounted combat and helped to make the cataphract and horse archer so formidable in battle.

The Alamanni

A league or confederation of German tribes, the Alamanni emerged in the 4th century AD. Their warriors wore a dyed linen tunic coming to mid-thigh, as well as a cape or cloak that would fasten with a clasp at the shoulder. A waist belt might hold a small haversack, as well as knife or dagger, long broadsword, with possibly a short throwing axe tucked into the belt. Shield and spear or javelin would complete the warrior's outfit as well as

The wanderings of the Vandals is an interesting footnote to the barbarian invasions of the Roman Empire. They moved into Gaul in 406AD, and after much fighting finally defeated the Franks before crossing the Rhine. As they moved through Gaul, the amount of devastation they caused was impressive, but this was undoubtedly in revenge for the loss of life they incurred in fighting the Franks, and the Vandals were no worse than Rome's other barbarian enemies. Interestingly, although the term vandal has come down through history as denoting a savage, wilful destructiveness, the Vandals were only as bad in terms of rape, pillage and destruction as the other barbarian tribal groups that attacked the Roman empire. The term 'vandalism' was in fact coined in 1794 during the French Revolution by a French bishop. It has to be said that the Vandal kingdom in North Africa was noted as being one of the new kingdoms that continued Roman culture beyond the fall of Rome rather than destroying it.

In late 409AD the Vandals crossed into Spain, and from there they moved across the strait of Gibraltar into North Africa where they finally established their permanent kingdom in 429AD. While in Spain, the Vandals came into conflict with the Visigoths, who had defeated the Alans, the allies of the Vandals.

The surviving Alans accompanied the Vandals into North Africa, basically being absorbed into the Vandal culture. The Vandal kings were at this point known as 'King of the Vandals and Alans'.

The Vandals remained in conflict with Rome, but peace was reached in 435AD. The capital of the new Vandal

▶ WARRIOR, 4TH–5TH CENTURIES AD
Ostrogoth cavalrymen would undoubtedly be armed and accoutred with some type of helmet, a spatha-type sword and round shield. They may or may not have worn body armour unless they looted it from a battlefield.

kingdom was established at Carthage, and the Vandals continued to raid Roman possessions from time to time, and built a navy which engaged in raids along the coasts of both the western and eastern Roman empires. In 460AD both the western and eastern Romans sent their navies to deal with Vandal ships, but the Vandals were victorious against both. It would remain for the eastern Romans to deal

with the Vandals once and for all, during the reign of Justinian I in the 6th century AD.

Goths

The Germanic Goths, either Ostrogoths or Visigoths, would be dressed and accoutred similarly, and the tunics might be embroidered at the hem of the garment, at the end of the sleeves, and around the collar. Swords were particularly well-made, the Goths being quite advanced in metallurgy and in the art and science of sword-forging. Scabbards would also be decorated and the helmets were becoming much more advanced.

Generally speaking the German helmets were of the 'pot' kind, constructed in two halves and bolted together along a ridge that ran from front to back, and cheek pieces were common. The more wealthy warriors and the leaders might have gold on their helmets, and centre plumes might also be worn on occasion. A well-armed Goth might also have a shirt of chain mail, and well-to-do German nobles might have their band of warriors all in sufficient armour and very well-armed.

Goths fought both mounted and on foot, as at the Battle of Campus Mauriciacus when they fought each other under different commanders. Germanic tribes in general would also mix mounted warriors with lightly armed and armoured infantry in reconnaissance missions or when skirmishing before the heavy fighting would commence.

The Goths, and many other Germanic tribes, also used lamellar armour, metal plates fixed to an underlying garment of leather or other durable material, which was developed in the east and brought westward during the barbarian migrations. This was a tough, durable type of armour, which the late Roman armies would also at least partially adopt.

Those Germans who were employed by, and fought for, the Romans as auxiliaries were either 'uniformed' and equipped as regular Romans in Roman armour and with Roman weapons, or they would combine their native dress with Roman armour, arms and equipment.

Personal Combat

The Germans had a preference for individual combat before an action taken, and brave or overconfident warriors, some of them senior in rank, would ride between the two forces preparing to fight to issue a challenge to any opposing warrior hardy enough to come out and be killed in front of his own army. Usually the challenge would be taken up, especially when both armies might be made up of Gothic units. Personal or blood feuds could be settled in this way, as well as the prestige a warrior might gain for personally killing an opponent on the field of battle.

One such occurrence was recorded by Procopius, a soldier-chronicler who lived in the 6th century AD. The fight was between Alaris, a Goth, and Artabazes, an Armenian serving with the Romans, and it occurred during the Gothic War in Italy. Procopius tells us that both men were mounted, and armed with spears and shields. They charged each other, and Artabazes hit first, thrusting his spear into Alaris side, killing him

▶ WARRIOR, 4TH–5TH CENTURIES AD
The helmet with cheek protectors and some type of light body armour is worn by this cavalryman. Armed and accoutred similarly to his comrade, left, he might still be considered a 'light' cavalryman and may have at times dismounted to fight on foot.

instantly. However, as he fell, the butt end of Alaris spear hit a large rock, forcing the point through Artabazes neck, killing him as well. According to Procopius, single combats of this type also took place among most of the armies of the period, especially the Romans, Persians, Germans and Huns.

▲ *Belisarius, general of the eastern Roman Empire retook the city of Rome from the Ostrogothic army in 535AD, then held it under renewed attack two years later. The Goths offered to surrender if Belisarius became their emperor. He refused.*

Barbarian Advances

After victory in the west and overrunning the remains of what Rome had built over centuries, some of the 'barbarian hordes' then turned eastward to try their luck with the eastern Romans. Most, however, settled in the west, some spilling across the Pillars of Hercules (Strait of Gibraltar) to carve out a kingdom in North Africa and once again raise the old site of ancient Carthage as a thriving seaport.

Those who did turn eastward found they had overreached themselves. Ready and eager to repel all comers to their capital of Constantinople, the eastern Romans were realizing they were now alone to face the barbarian threat and they built up their army with native soldiery as well as barbarian mercenaries eager to fight other barbarians under able eastern Roman commanders like Belisarius under the emperor Justinian. However, it would not be wars of conquest against the barbarians overrunning too much of Rome's old territory, but holding what was left in the east. It would be at least another 50 years and the advent of one of the greatest of eastern Roman generals before any type of reconquest in the west could take place.

THE HUNS

The Huns were a nomadic, horse-dependent people from the steppes of Asia. They not only travelled, hunted, and fought on horseback, they almost lived on horseback.

Horsemen

It has been said that the Huns, like the Mongols who followed almost 800 years later, learned to ride before they could walk. Fierce warriors, the Huns came out of the east in a whirlwind to sweep across Europe, and under their talented leader Attila – dubbed the 'Scourge of God' by some terrified churchman – they swept nearly all before them.

But the Huns were not always as all-conquering as has sometimes been portrayed. Finding the eastern Romans too hard to overcome, they moved westwards for an easier foe. While the Huns usually are thought to have been successful over what was left of the western Roman Empire, one Roman general stands out as having stopped their advance in Gaul at the Battle of Chalons in 451AD.

Aetius

As a youth, Flavius Aetius, son of a magister equitum (master of cavalry) spent some time as a hostage with the Visigothic leader Alaric, and later with the Huns, acquiring valuable knowledge of both tribes. Sometimes referred to as 'the last Roman', he had been appointed or elected consul three times in his career and for a time was in fact, as well as

◀ HUN MOUNTED ARCHER, C.450AD *The lightly accoutred and armoured Hunnish horse archer was a mainstay of the Hun nomadic armies that burst on the western empire from Asia. Hard to catch and harder to defeat, Huns would later arm and equip themselves with a variety of armour and weapons taken from those they defeated.*

▲ GENERAL AETIUS (396–454), VICTOR OF THE BATTLE OF CHALONS, 451AD *Aetius is dressed here in the typical fashion of a senior Roman commander in the late empire. One of the best of the Roman commanders from any period, the manner of his death was a disgrace to the empire and an illustration of administrative decay in the western empire.*

in deed, the Roman head of state. A popular general with both Roman and barbarian troops, in the end he incurred the wrath of the emperor Valentinian III, who had Aetius murdered in 454AD. In revenge for this deed, two Roman soldiers, both of them Hun auxiliaries, approached Valentinian, at archery practice on the Field of Mars in Rome, and together they stabbed him to death, then turned on his advisor Heraclius, believed to have persuaded Valentinian to have Aetius assassinated, and killed him too. Although there were Roman troops on the field at the time, none moved to protect Valentinian or Heraclius, suggesting they too believed that justice had been done.

Aetius might very well have been the glue that was holding the western empire together. It has been said that by assassinating Aetius, Valentinian had 'cut off his right hand with his left' and the empire suffered as a result.

Attila

Ruler of the Huns from 434AD until his death in 453AD, while Attila was not the invincible commander of nomadic horseman that single-handedly

brought down the Roman Empire, he was certainly a commander of high ability who was able to exploit a situation to his own benefit, and gain notoriety on the fear he spread among the Roman civilians.

Attila was undoubtedly Asian in appearance and was probably short, lean, and bearded with a moustache. There is evidence that from time to time the Huns bound the heads of their young so as to develop an elongated skull, and there is archaeological evidence to support

this, but how widespread the practice was is unknown. There is also evidence that the Huns practised scarification, at least on the face, but again it is unknown how widespread that was.

Dress

The Huns were not uniformed, though their clothing was usually made to the same basic pattern. Their tunic was made in one piece of either goat hair or wool, gathered at the waist by a belt, probably made of leather. Their footwear was tall, to the knee, and also of leather, probably of oxhide. The soles and heels were soft and were moccasin-type in appearance with no elevated heel and no attached sole. Stockings made of felt were also probably worn underneath the boot. Clothing could be sewn together, and hats with ear flaps made of either goatskin or fox fur. Thick coats, or kaftan-like overgarments, and headgear were worn in winter and fur was used to line and edge them. Loose pantaloons were worn, gathered at the ankle; all in all it was an outfit highly suitable for mounted warfare.

▶ ATTILA THE HUN C.450AD
Attila is pictured as he probably would have been when armed and equipped for war; similar to the 'rank and file' Huns, but probably more complete and in better clothing as befitted his station as leader and commander.

Cavalry

The Huns were originally nomadic herders, tending herds of cattle as well as flocks of sheep, and goats. Their primary domestic animal, however, as well as the strength of their livelihood, was the horse. Hunnish armies therefore naturally developed into cavalry armies and they fought mounted with bow, javelin, and sword. Their dress and manner of fighting was described as savage and frightening. They were short, agile fighting men; expert horsemen who were compared to 'wild beasts' and described as being 'cruel'. The onslaught of a Hunnish cavalry army would sweep all resistance before it and it required a general of character and skill to stop, let alone defeat, a Hunnish army.

Horses

Similar to the Mongols, also herders and nomads out of central Asia, the Huns could live off little while on campaign. If necessary they would use their mounts for sustenance, sometimes drinking some of their horses's blood, or eating horsemeat if necessary, a practice the Romans found to be 'barbaric'.

The Huns rode the tough small breed of the steppes. Procopius gives a good

◄ HUN
CAVALRYMAN, C.450AD
The Huns were excellent horsemen, with or without stirrups, and this representation of a Hunnish horse archer is undoubtedly what the Romans encountered when the Huns made their first appearance from the east. The lightly armed and equipped horse archer was very difficult to fight and the Romans had to vary their tactics to meet them on anything like an equal footing.

description of the horses, starting with their unkempt appearance, and bluntly referring to them as 'ugly'. He also states, however, that they were excellent mounts, ideal for the type of warfare practised by the Huns, and he particularly commended their endurance. Undoubtedly, remounts would be hard to come by in central and western Europe, and when the Huns captured Roman mounts they would have had to adapt to a quite different kind of horse, larger, less tough, and needing very different care and command in comparison to those of the steppes.

The saddles used by the Huns differed from those of the Romans. While the stirrup was not used by the Huns, the saddle itself was much more modern in appearance, with a high cantle much like the later medieval European saddle. It was still a basic wooden frame, but the design was innovative and quite modern, and gave a good seat to a horse archer for both stability and staying power.

Arms and Equipment

The Hun was essentially a mounted archer. His main weapon was the powerful composite bow made of horn, wood, sinew and bone. The bow was asymmetrical in appearance, the upper half being longer than the lower half when the bow was strung. The Romans were very impressed with the performance of this composite bow and apparently as soon as the Romans worked out how to construct and use it, they adopted it for their own use. It was a large bow, not easily employed mounted, and requiring considerable skill on the part of the bowman to use it properly. As the main weapon of the Huns, it was impressive and its use accounted in large part for the initial success of Hunnish armies against the Romans.

The Huns were also armed with a type of broadsword, probably of Sassanid origin, and quite suitable for mounted action. It was both long-bladed and long-hilted and was a cutting rather than a thrusting weapon. The Huns were also equipped with a dagger and a spear, and, curiously, a lasso-type rope, which probably came from their origins as herders, and which they used to catch and drag a man from the saddle.

A small shield was also carried, along with the quiver for arrows that was strapped on the left side along the thigh. If body armour was worn, it was undoubtedly of the lamellar type. As with other barbarian tribes, the more the Huns campaigned in Europe the more they captured and used western weapons and armour, and Roman and Gothic helmets were probably seen among the Huns.

The Huns also used a type of javelin that could be thrown while mounted. This would be similar to how the Numidian light cavalry who had served both Hannibal and later the Romans fought, but it was not their primary weapon. The Huns were responsible for introducing the composite bow into Europe. Although they apparently had weapons made of iron, the tips of their arrows and javelins were still made from bone.

▼ HUN CAVALRYMAN, c.450AD *The horse archer could also be armed with lance and shield. The Hunnish armies would take on a very different appearance after campaigning in central and western Europe, undoubtedly making use of western Roman and Germanic weapons and armour after plundering the battlefields.*

▲ HUN CAVALRYMAN, c.450AD *The Huns wore no uniform, but the clothing was that of central Asian herders and horsemen. They would be comfortably clad for winter, coming from territory where winters were harsh and long. Sometimes in fair weather no upper garments would be worn. Whether or not the Huns used stirrups in 450AD is debatable, as use wasn't widespread in Europe until the 7th century. But as the stirrup came out of Asia it is entirely possible that individual Hunish cavalrymen used them this early. Hun warriors like this would later fight under Belisarius.*

THE PERSIAN EMPIRE 205–498

The Persian Empire was vast, largely centred in what is now Iran, and was an ancient empire that had been through many iterations and shapes. It was an aggressive and, for much of the time, a dangerous neighbour for Rome, bent on conquest of its rivals.

The ancient Persian Empire under its king, Darius, had attempted the first incursion into Europe against the Greeks, and would meet defeat at the Battle of Marathon in 490BC. His son, Xerxes, tried again 10 years later only to meet grief at the Pass of Thermopylae, then defeat and disaster at the naval Battle of Salamis, and the land defeat at the Battle of Plataea 479BC. Then, in 331BC another Darius was defeated by Alexander III of Macedonia, known as the Great. This victory for all intents and purposes placed Persia under the rule of Alexander until, after his death, his empire fragmented.

While the Romans conquered many peoples, they never actually conquered the Persians, meeting some of their worst defeats at their hands. Crassus had been killed fighting the Parthians, who were Persian, at the Battle of Carrhae in 53BC, and he was not the first Roman who would meet with disaster in the east. Peoples emerging from that empire would pose a considerable challenge to the Roman Empire in later years.

The Parthians

Parthians, known for fielding heavy armoured cavalry, or cataphracts, were a formidable Scythian foe to the Romans. Their empire was established in 246BC and lasted until overthrown by the Sassanians in 224AD. Ethnically they were Scythians, they had developed a feudal system and were well-known as a warrior people. They fielded a mounted army and were excellent horsemen. Their armies appear to have been task-organized but they may just have fielded the troops that were available. Sometimes their armies were horse archer-heavy, sometimes not.

The Parthian horse archer was famous for the 'Parthian shot', which was later copied by other armies in the east, including the eastern Romans. The Parthian shot was quite simply when the mounted archer, while his horse was on the move, usually at a fast trot or gallop, would turn in his saddle and fire to the rear. While appearing relatively simple, this required an excellent horseman (stirrups were not yet introduced) as well as an accomplished bowman if he expected to hit anything.

Parthian horse archers were lightly accoutred and were without armour. In contrast, the Parthian cataphract was heavily armed and armoured and his mount was also heavily armoured. The Parthians also used the draco (dragon) as a standard. Some historians believe that its first use was as a wind sock to judge the direction of the wind for the use of the horse archers.

The Romans never conquered the Parthians, and their general Crassus, who had defeated the Spartacus Revolt,

◀ PARTHIAN ARCHER, 2ND–3RD CENTURY AD
The Parthians preceded the Sassanians in Persia and were famous for their lightly armed and accoutred horse archers. They perfected what was known as the 'Parthian shot' with the archer turning to his rear, aiming and shooting his bow with precision while the horse was in motion, even at full gallop.

was killed campaigning against them. The Parthians were finally defeated and overthrown by the Sassanid Persians, who defeated them early in the 3rd century AD. By this time the Parthians had ruled in Persia for almost 400 years and had held their lands against the strongest empire in the western world for all of that time.

War Elephants

The Sassanians also trained elephants for the battlefield. Sometimes the elephants would be armed in a type of scale armour, but they often wore less protection. They were used in conjunction with the heavy cavalry when fighting the Romans. The employment of elephants could be terrifying for an enemy, but if met

properly, with innovative tactics, elephants could be brought down; a hugely successful morale boost against the elephant-equipped army.

Sarmatians

Another threat against Rome from Persia consisted of incursions from the Sarmatians, a nomadic people that the Romans first came into serious

contact with during the Dacian Wars of 85–8AD and 101–5AD where they allied themselves with Dacia against Rome. Troubles with the Sarmatian peoples continued through Diocletian's reign, but later the Romans allowed the Sarmatians to settle inside the empire to balance problems with the Goths. The Sarmatians settled along the Danube during the period and generally stayed independent from the Germanic tribes.

▶ SASSANID WAR ELEPHANT, AND TROOPS 3RD CENTURY AD *The Sassanids, or Sassanid dynasty, was yet another iteration of the Persians, and the empire they formed was one of the two most powerful in the east. Along with horse archers and armoured heavy cavalrymen, the Sassanids also employed war elephants, manned in the howdah set on top of the elephant's back.*

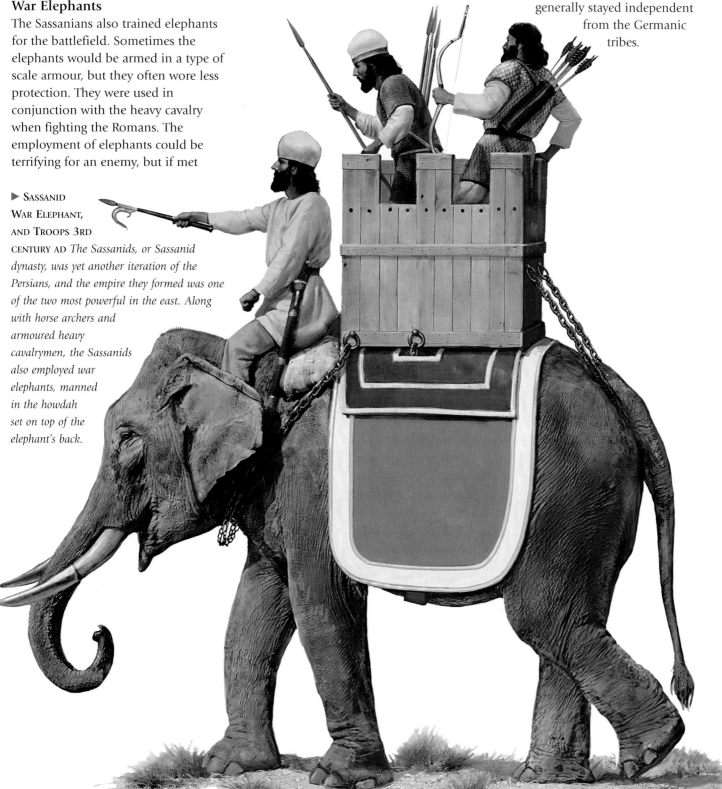

Sarmatian heavy cavalry was armoured in scale or lamellar armour with a conical helmet. Expert horsemen, they were armed with a long lance that they handled in combat with both hands, guiding their horses at speed with their knees. Their mounts were also armoured. The

▼ SASSANID CATAPHRACT, 4TH CENTURY AD

The Sassanid heavy cavalryman in full armour, with his horse in various stages of armour, greatly impressed the Romans and in the 5th century was copied by them, though it took years for the Roman cataphract to become as efficient as his Sassanian adversary. Initially riding in full armour without the stirrup, which required a horsemen of great skill, the cataphract became very effective and deadly after the introduction of the stirrup in the 6th century AD.

Sarmatian horse archers were armoured, but their horses were not. They were expert archers and horsemen, particularly adept at the 'Parthian shot'; turning in their saddle while moving and firing to the rear over the horse's haunches.

Alans

The Alans, another Sarmatian people, first encountered the Romans in 73AD. By early in the 2nd century the Alans dominated the Pontic steppe, but that ended with the Goths sweeping across the territory in force, around 215–50AD. Alans ended up fighting with the Goths against Rome, as well as with the Huns. Some Alans fought with the Romans against their enemies, but later allied

themselves with the Vandals, who turned on the Alans in about 416AD, slaughtering them in large numbers. Some Alans, however, had not entered the Roman empire and these were later absorbed by the Huns in their travels and wars against the Romans.

The Parthians, meanwhile, had been overthrown by the Sassanid Persians. The Sassanian dynasty was founded in 224AD and the monarch styled himself the 'King of Kings'. The Sassanid army was highly organized, well-trained, and usually well-led, with a high level of skill on the battlefield as well as experience in siege warfare. They only met their match on the battlefield with the emergence of the eastern Romans and their development of a mounted army as well, if not better, organized than that of the Sassanians.

The Sassanians also mastered the art of metallurgy and were considered to be the best armourers in the Middle East and Asia Minor, forging excellent weapons that were generally superior to those of their opponents.

Cataphracts

The Sassanian cataphracts (sometimes the term 'clibanarius' is used as a synonym for cataphract, but the two terms are not the same) developed over time and became very

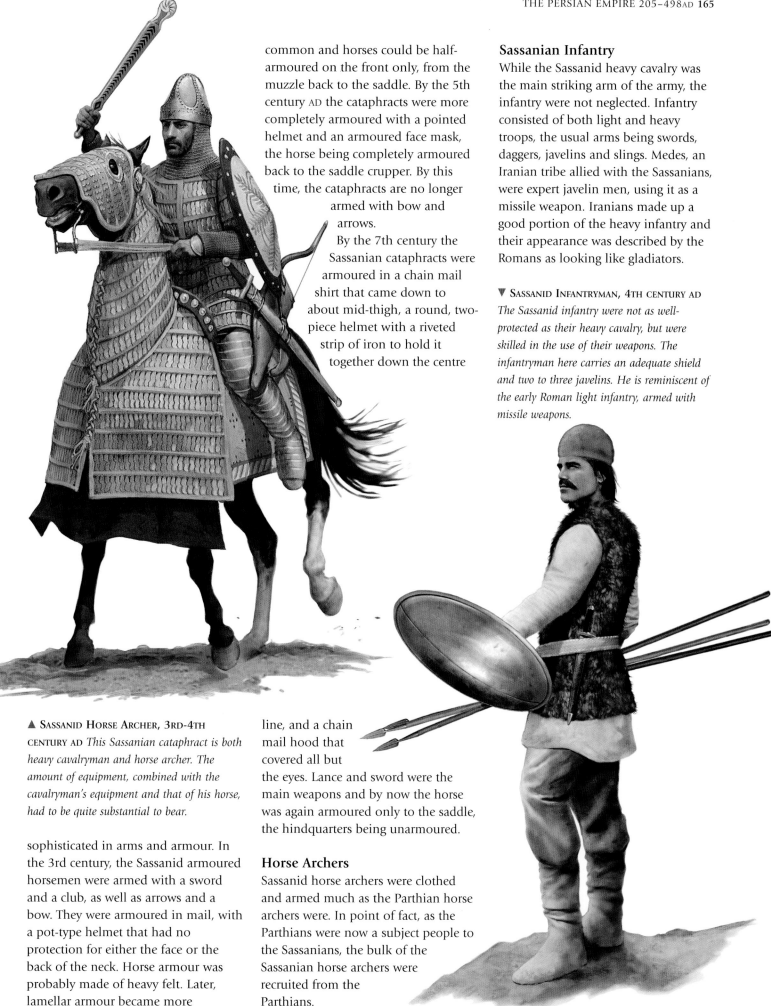

common and horses could be half-armoured on the front only, from the muzzle back to the saddle. By the 5th century AD the cataphracts were more completely armoured with a pointed helmet and an armoured face mask, the horse being completely armoured back to the saddle crupper. By this time, the cataphracts are no longer armed with bow and arrows.

By the 7th century the Sassanian cataphracts were armoured in a chain mail shirt that came down to about mid-thigh, a round, two-piece helmet with a riveted strip of iron to hold it together down the centre

Sassanian Infantry

While the Sassanid heavy cavalry was the main striking arm of the army, the infantry were not neglected. Infantry consisted of both light and heavy troops, the usual arms being swords, daggers, javelins and slings. Medes, an Iranian tribe allied with the Sassanians, were expert javelin men, using it as a missile weapon. Iranians made up a good portion of the heavy infantry and their appearance was described by the Romans as looking like gladiators.

▼ SASSANID INFANTRYMAN, 4TH CENTURY AD *The Sassanid infantry were not as well-protected as their heavy cavalry, but were skilled in the use of their weapons. The infantryman here carries an adequate shield and two to three javelins. He is reminiscent of the early Roman light infantry, armed with missile weapons.*

▲ SASSANID HORSE ARCHER, 3RD-4TH CENTURY AD *This Sassanian cataphract is both heavy cavalryman and horse archer. The amount of equipment, combined with the cavalryman's equipment and that of his horse, had to be quite substantial to bear.*

sophisticated in arms and armour. In the 3rd century, the Sassanid armoured horsemen were armed with a sword and a club, as well as arrows and a bow. They were armoured in mail, with a pot-type helmet that had no protection for either the face or the back of the neck. Horse armour was probably made of heavy felt. Later, lamellar armour became more

line, and a chain mail hood that covered all but the eyes. Lance and sword were the main weapons and by now the horse was again armoured only to the saddle, the hindquarters being unarmoured.

Horse Archers

Sassanid horse archers were clothed and armed much as the Parthian horse archers were. In point of fact, as the Parthians were now a subject people to the Sassanians, the bulk of the Sassanian horse archers were recruited from the Parthians.

◀ SASSANIAN CATAPHRACT, 4TH CENTURY AD
The horse armour on this cataphract is noteworthy in that only the front of the horse is protected. This would be a disadvantage in a retreat being pursued by enemy cavalry, though the horse would be able to move faster and for longer. The armour and helmet are both more modern in design and the similarities here and with the eastern Roman cataphracts is evident.

▼ SASSANID INFANTRYMAN, 4TH CENTURY AD
Apparently, this is a 'heavier' infantry, armed and equipped with spear and shield and is undoubtedly meant for the line of battle, based on his shield shape. The Sassanids though were a cavalry army and their main striking arm was the cataphracts supported by horse archers.

was defeated at Edessa, captured, imprisoned and eventually killed. The details of his treatment in captivity are not known for certain. Valerian enjoys the dubious distinction of being the only Roman emperor to be captured alive, an insult which the Romans felt deeply. Shapur II eventually defeated the Roman emperor Julian the Apostate, who was killed in action at the Battle of Samarra.

Middle Eastern Empire

The period of the Sassanian dynasty, which would last until 621AD, was the last great flowering of the ancient Persian civilization before falling to the Muslim conquest under the Arabs.

Rome, both east and west, was greatly influenced militarily by the Sassanians and suffered humiliating defeats at their hands. The empire ruled by the Sassanians was huge and encompassed what is now Iraq, Iran, Afghanistan, Syria and the Caucasus as well as extending into what is now Turkey in Asia Minor, the area of the Persian Gulf and the Arabian Peninsula

as well as part of Pakistan and India. The proper terms to be used are the Sassanid Empire and the Sassanians when referring to the people themselves.

The Sassanian King Shapur I made a habit of defeating Roman emperors who took the field against him. In 244AD Gordian III was defeated and killed by Shapur's army at the Battle of Misiche. His successor, Philip the Arab, was also defeated by Shapur I, the Roman army sent to fight the Sassanians being largely destroyed at the Battle of Barbalissos. Finally, Emperor Valerian

Clash of Empires

The Sassanians were an aggressive people intent on expanding their empire and for some time they were successful against the Romans, defeating Roman armies and taking and occupying Roman territory. The first hostile contact between the Romans and the Sassanians occurred in 230AD with raids into the territory controlled by Rome. The Romans almost immediately reacted to the raids, but the fighting was not decisive for either side, though the Romans attempted to put the best face on it.

Thirty years later, the resurgent Romans decisively defeated the Sassanians in Anatolia in 260BC, winning back all of the lost territories. The Roman emperor Diocletian continued Rome's offensive against the Sassanians, sacking the Persian capital at Ctesiphon and conquering territory in Armenia that had been ruled by the Persians for over 50 years.

Tactics

Warfare continued between the two empires in 293AD, the Roman emperor Galerius winning decisive successes against the Sassanians in Armenia in 298AD, where the Roman legionaries defeated the Persian cataphracts and horse

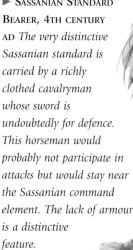

▶ SASSANIAN STANDARD BEARER, 4TH CENTURY AD *The very distinctive Sassanian standard is carried by a richly clothed cavalryman whose sword is undoubtedly for defence. This horseman would probably not participate in attacks but would stay near the Sassanian command element. The lack of armour is a distinctive feature.*

archers through skilful use of terrain. Persian territorial losses to Rome were heavy in the treaty that followed. However, although the Sassanid Empire outlasted the western Roman Empire it continued a long struggle with the eastern Roman Empire.

The Persian army had an excellent reputation, and was the mainstay of the Sassanian Empire. Infantry was composed of both light and heavy infantry. The light infantry were well-trained javelin men who also had skilled slingers in the ranks. The heavy infantry were well-armed and armoured, as well as being a well-trained and well-disciplined force.

The Sassanian cavalry was composed of both cataphracts and clibanarii. Both of these of mounted warriors were heavy cavalry and their employment, if done properly, could really 'sweep the field'. Once in motion they were hard to stop or deflect, but it could be done – as seen at their defeat in Armenia in 298AD by Emperor Galerius and his legionaries. Light cavalry, usually horse archers, were also employed by the Sassanians.

DESERT ENEMIES

The Roman legions fought many wars in the deserts of North Africa, the Middle East, and Persia, the first of them being during the Punic wars when the Romans invaded Carthage and fought at Zama in the 2nd Punic War. The desert was familiar to the Roman legions, who had marched and fought over some of the worst terrain in the world, not least of which was the Judean Desert during the Jewish revolts.

Rome's desert opponents were many and varied, and it speaks volumes for the toughness, versatility, and endurance of the legions that they fought, usually successfully, against enemies in Asian and African wastes who were fighting on their home terrain. The Romans did not always win, but they were victorious more often than not, and the provinces they created from their Asian and African conquests became some of the richest provinces in the empire.

▶ Arab Dromedary Rider, 2nd–5th centuries ad
Camel-mounted troops were common among the eastern desert peoples and it does not seem that the Romans copied them, though the Romans undoubtedly used the camel for their baggage trains. Camel-mounted troops could move swiftly across most terrain and were ideal in the arid eastern deserts, from which they could raid or attack unsuspecting enemies. The use of the bow mounted on the camel is noteworthy. Camels might have been a more stable firing platform than a horse in motion.

Some of the peoples the Romans encountered in North Africa and the Middle East were mere nuisances, such as the Berbers and some Arab tribes. Others were more serious threats, such as the inhabitants of ancient Palmyra, the ancient Jews, and further east the Parthians and their more deadly descendants the Sassanians, who have already been covered on previous pages. One way or another, the greater majority of the desert peoples eventually accepted the suzerainty of Rome and became Romans by default.

African Warriors

Many of the desert peoples were unsophisticated in military terms. They wore their native clothing and were considered primitive peoples by Roman standards. These included, but were not limited to, the Berbers, the Garamante, the inhabitants of the Sudan, the Tanukhids, and the Nabateans. Clothing and weapons were simple, but the Nabateans were excellent dromedary soldiers (the dromedary is a camel with one hump, the bactrian has two) and the Sudanese were warlike desert fighters. Spears and primitive shields were common, and the Nabateans used a type of short bow.

Three of the more advanced peoples were the Palmyrans, other Syrians, and the Numidians. The Arab peoples were not yet united (this would not happen until the 7th century AD under Mohammed, and then they would be a very formidable enemy and cause the eastern Romans considerable difficulty). The Palmyrans, Syrians and Numidians were known to have worn mail shirts, and carried oval shields and well-worked broadswords. They also had well-armed and well-equipped heavy

troops. Besides lances and shields for the heavy cavalry, the Palmyrans were also armed with long cavalry swords and daggers. Under Queen Zenobia (240 to 274AD) Palmyra continued its advance into Roman-held land, and conquered Roman Egypt, the grain from which was crucial to Rome.

The Romans retaliated and launched an offensive against the Palmyrenes that not only defeated Zenobia and her cavalry army, but also took Palmyra itself, ending any continued threat from Palmyra. Queen Zenobia was captured and sent to Rome as a prisoner, but was not mistreated and lived out her life there in relative comfort.

Blemmyes

The Blemmyes were a nomadic tribe, probably similar to the Nubians who, after the 3rd century AD, were in almost constant conflict with the Roman Empire. The Blemmyes were probably from territory to the south of Egypt. They fought, and were defeated by, the Romans in 253AD and 265AD when they were brought under the control of the empire. The Blemmyes rebelled against Rome in 273AD in support of Queen Zenobia of Palmyra. Defeated once again, the Blemmye army was almost totally destroyed.

The Blemmyes were a persistent enemy to the Romans and had to be suppressed once again during the reign of Diocletian in 298AD. Enthusiastic raiders, the Blemmyes were capable of self-sustaining military action and even though repeatedly defeated, usually were ready to fight or raid shortly afterwards.

The Blemmyes were known to have used elephants in small numbers from time to time and their mounted troops would use horses as well as donkeys. Apparently camels were not used by the Blemmyes, possibly until after 200AD, but served as transport rather than as a

fighting platform. Blemmyes wore scale armour and white robes sometimes decorated in blue patterns, and were armed with knives, maces, and javelins (similar to the Numidians of the Punic wars period). Blemmye infantry were usually bowmen.

▼ **PALMYRAN INFANTRYMAN, 3RD CENTURY AD** *Palmyra was a rich Syrian city with a competent government and that is reflected in the arms and armour of this infantryman. The torso is well-armoured in a lamellar-type material and he carries both sword and spear with an adequate, well-made and designed shield. His helmet is distinctively eastern in design.*

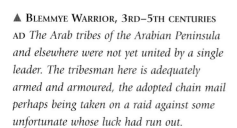

▲ **BLEMMYE WARRIOR, 3RD–5TH CENTURIES AD** *The Arab tribes of the Arabian Peninsula and elsewhere were not yet united by a single leader. The tribesman here is adequately armed and armoured, the adopted chain mail perhaps being taken on a raid against some unfortunate whose luck had run out.*

cavalry from Hatrene. The Yemenis and Ethiopians had arms and equipment as good as that of the Romans.

Palmyrans

A wealthy trade city in north-eastern Syria, Palmyra conquered Roman Syria in the 3rd century AD and had a formidable army of 1,000 heavy cavalry and about 9,000 horse archers, who were considered to be excellent

Arab Enemies

Yemen and Oman were small Arab enclaves in the desert made up of Semitic tribesmen who, with little or no centralized control until the coming of the Islamic armies in the 7th century, survived as nomads, with raiding each other or outsiders as a somewhat lucrative sideline.

Ancient Yemen was supposedly ruled by a class of religious priests who doubled as kings. These were called mukarribs, but after a time, their priestly duties and position were abolished and the Yemeni monarchy became secular. This form of government gradually degenerated into rule by qayls, or dukedoms, although they were probably more akin to warlords than the honorific title of dukes. However, ancient Yemen produced quality arms and armour made of 'hardened leather' probably akin to jacked leather, which was boiled into hardness, but this is conjecture. The tough, native Yemeni soldiery were thought to have been skilled in the javelin, which was their main armament. They were also armed with swords.

Both Yemen and Oman would eventually become part of the Sassanian Empire, and sailors from Oman would be especially prized by the Sassanian navy.

Lakhmids

The kingdom of the Lakhmids was probably founded in the 2nd century AD from one of the Arab tribes that had emigrated from Yemeni territory. It was initially an independent kingdom which, after forming a formidable army and even becoming a naval presence in the region, raided as far as Persia. Irritated by the continuing raiding the Sassanians attacked the Lakhmids and other Arab states in the region in 325AD with a large army. The Lakhmids were decisively defeated by the Persians and became a client state. By the 4th century the Lakhmid kingdom was situated around the Christian city of Hira, in what is now southern Iraq, and had developed essentially as a semi-independent client state of the Sassanian Empire. Much later, in the early 7th century, the Lakhmid kingdom was abolished and annexed outright by the Sassanians.

◀ YEMENI INFANTRYMAN, 4TH CENTURY AD *Yemen was Arab in origin and the settlements there were ancient, but the infantryman shown has primitive weapons and equipment and virtually no armour except for the badly designed helmet that affords little protection against better-armed and armoured opponents. This infantryman is holding a tribal banner.*

▲ OMANI INFANTRYMAN, 3RD–5TH CENTURIES AD *While he was contemporary with the Romans and Sassanians, this infantryman's arms and equipment have not progressed beyond that of ancient Israel at the time of the Exodus from Egypt. Yet another Arab nomadic tribe that attempted to settle permanently in what is now Oman, they would have to wait for the coming of the Islamic tide to gain better arms and equipment as well as a national identity.*

The Lakhmids were better organized, armed and equipped than the Arabs of the region. Lakhmid armies copied Sassanian military organization, oftening relying on exiles and mercenaries and young hostages from subject tribes. This did not prevent them becoming a formidable military force, described by Procopius as 'the most difficult and dangerous enemy of the Romans.' Their splendid leather tents were also commented on by contemporaries, which, unlike the woollen Arab tents, were a mark of wealth and prestige.

Arab clothing

Both the Omanis and Yemenis were greatly influenced in dress and weapons by the Sassanians. The clothing worn by all the desert peoples was designed to be cool in the unforgiving terrain in which they lived. Each tribe would have their own form of identification shown in their flags. For weapons the Arabs generally used

▶ LAKHMID HORSE ARCHER, 4TH CENTURY AD
Horse archers were not particular to Asia or Asia Minor, and this example of an Arab horse archer is one that is well-equipped and armed and is mounted on an excellent example of what might later become the Arab horse breed in more modern times.

swords and spears, the swords being of the short-sword variety and the spears or lances being noted as being quite long. Bows were not unknown. These were, however, bows constructed out of one piece of wood and were definitely not the composite bows of others who were noted as archers, especially horse archers such as the eastern Romans, the Parthians, and others.

The Arabs usually fought on foot or with camels, and the few horses they

posessed were used as transportation. There was a reluctance to use any type of mounted troops when faced with archers, as the Arabs did not want to lose their horses or camels. The Arabs used captured arms and military equipment, such as armour and helmets, when they could get hold of it or capture it in raids and excursions into foreign territory.

Arab 'armies' appear to have been quite disciplined and organized in 'divisions' of the tribes, which were marked by tribal flags. Arabs in the field did not follow Greek traditions at all, although much Arab territory had been conquered by Alexander the Great. Their military tradition appears to have been influenced by much older Semitic traditions.

THE END OF ROMAN BRITAIN

Rome's successful invasion of Britain occurred in 43BC, and by 122AD they had subdued most of Britain, but delineated a northern frontier by building Hadrian's Wall. It was built during the reign of Emperor Hadrian, being started in 122AD and finished by 128AD. It was 119km/74 miles (80 Roman miles) long, extended across the width of the entire island, and, with one exception, was continually garrisoned for over 300 years. To the south was Britannia, to the north the unconquered territory of the Picts and Scots. For many years it was the furthest northern extent of the Roman empire. Britons north of the wall would remain hostile to Rome throughout the legions' stay in Britain.

Picts

North of the wall were the barbarians known as the Picts. Raiders, warriors and tribesmen, these barbarians never succumbed to Rome and would fight the Romans at each and every chance. They were Celts, as were the Britons south of the wall, but they chose not to be Roman.

The Pictish warriors fought as did their Celtic ancestors, painted or tattooed in woad or blue dye and often naked. Clothing might be in a plaid pattern and long tunics or trousers might be worn. As with other barbarian tribesmen, the short axe for throwing or hand-to-hand combat was a favourite weapon. Long broadswords were also used, and sometimes bits and pieces of armour, especially helmets, were worn. Small round shields, as well as longer hexagonal shields, were used. Sometimes shields were not used at all, particularly in the Celtic charge, so characteristic of this warlike people, which was also experienced by the Romans and the Romano-Celts during and after the Roman occupation.

Roman-British Troops

The Roman infantry remained the main strength of the legions in Britain, and Roman cavalry retained its traditional role of support, reconnaissance, and mounted incursions north of the wall. By the end of the Roman era in Britain troops

◀ PICTISH WARRIOR, 4TH CENTURY AD *The Picts of northern Britain generally maintained their traditional weapons and clothing throughout the Roman period, including from time to time, painting their bodies in woad and other colours.*

▶ PICTISH WARRIOR, 4TH CENTURY AD *The Picts were armed as other Celtic tribes in Britain and were fierce and determined warriors. Roman units that were slackly commanded were susceptible to sudden Pictish onslaughts.*

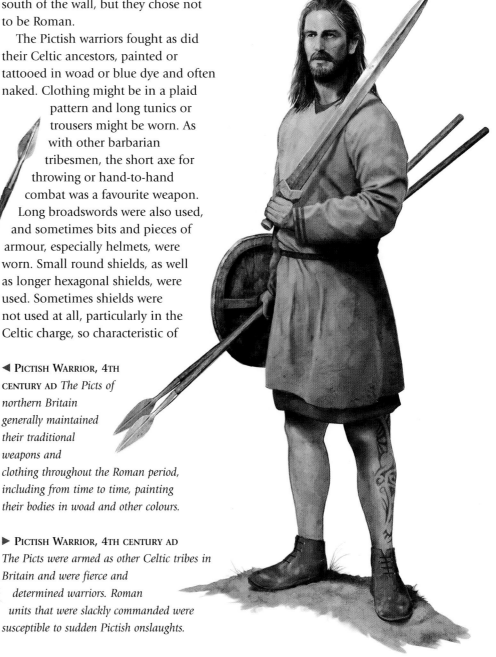

▶ *After the Romans left, substantial buildings such as these granaries of Birdoswald's Fort on Hadrian's Wall, were used by local chieftains.*

had probably adopted the mail shirt as the main form of body armour. Many and varied types of helmets were worn, some with horsehair crests, some without. Tunics extended to mid-thigh and trousers were also worn, either gathered and tied at the ankle or wrapped into some type of legging or lower leg covering. Tunics were of linen or wool, depending on the season and the weather, and the military cloak was worn by all ranks. Different types of shoes or footwear were also worn, the traditional caliga eventually being replaced by shoes more suitable to the northern temperatures in Britain.

Both infantry and cavalry were armed with the spatha, the cavalry broadsword, and javelins or spears of a variety of types. Shields were round or oval with varied designs on them, some of them originally Roman, others of more native design. The now common draco standard was undoubtedly carried by the cavalry units.

◀ **ROMANO-CELT CAVALRYMAN, 5TH CENTURY AD** *The Romano-Celts left behind by the departing legions were the basis of the Arthurian legend; Arthur, or Arturus, being possibly the last Romanized war duke of Britain and leader of the Romano-Celts. These troops were based on the Roman tradition, but the mounted arm became more important.*

▶ **ROMANO-CELT INFANTRYMAN, 5TH CENTURY AD** *The part of Britain that benefitted from the Roman occupation became Romanized in language, dress, and culture. They were recruited as auxiliaries to the legions stationed in Britain and gave good service. When the legions left, these warriors turned their skills to resisting the Saxon invaders.*

The legions were eventually made up of Romano-Celts, children of Romans and native Britons, to whom the defence of the island would be given when the legions, were called home to defend Rome.

ARMS AND ARMOUR

In the latter years of the western Roman Empire, the Roman army underwent major changes in organization and fighting style. Cavalry became more important and the dominance of the sturdy Roman infantryman, fighting in disciplined cohorts, rank upon terrible rank, began to decline in both quality and fighting ability. There too Roman arms and armour definitely changed.

Just as the barbarians were influenced by Roman arms and armour, and used it either when it became available to them or they took it as spoils on the battlefield, the Romans were influenced by the developments in their enemies' arms and armour.

Arms, armour, and military equipment went through a distinctive change from the mid-3rd century to the end of the western empire near the end of the 5th century. A 3rd century legionary would probably not have recognized one at the end of the western empire, let alone those tough 5,000-man legions that conquered an empire and set the standard for a professional military force that had not been matched up to that time. The army that emerged in the east from the collapse of Rome in the west and the debris of the western army was quite different from what had come before it. However, this army would maintain the eastern Roman empire for the next 1,000 years and would always consider itself Roman.

Helmets

The older, traditional Roman helmet would finally give way to simpler designs that were more conical in shape and may or may not have cheek guards. These newer helmet designs were the forerunners of the medieval conical helmet, and sometimes were decorated with coloured horsehair plumes suspended from a short central pike at the top of the helmet. These

helmets were simpler than the earlier legionary helmet, and they gave good protection as their conical shape helped to deflect blows from weapons.

Standards

Roman standards of the later empire were adapted from their enemies or were brought into the army by the foreign elements that signed up to fight for Rome. The draco, or dragon, standard was in use for centuries before being adopted by the Romans, and it would live on after Rome fell, used by different peoples.

The horsehair standard was also adopted from Asian nomadic peoples. It was a simple standard, easy to spot on the battlefield, and in use generally with mounted troops. It would be a mainstay as standards went in the east, and would be finally brought westward again out of Egypt by the very early 19th century by Napoleon after his campaign in the east, when it was used by his Mamelukes on the battlefields of the Grande Armée.

Shields

The old Roman rectangular or oval-shaped scutum was giving way to either a round shield or a less severe

▲ HELMETS 3TH–4TH CENTURIES *1 The berkasovo helmet, a version of the ridged helmet with Roman cheek and neck guards. 2 A version of the spangenhelm, not as elaborate as 6. The cheek pieces and neck guard were Roman additions to the basic helmet. The spangenhelm generally replaced the Gallic helmet. 3 One of the last models of the Imperial-Gallic type a Roman legionary helmet made of bronze. These were phased out in the second half of the 3rd century AD. 4 Ridge helmets began to be used in the 4th century AD and might have been mass produced by the state in factories. It was a simple, effective and easily produced design that did not neglect either cheek or neck pieces. 5 The Leiden helmet is also from the 3rd century AD and has a chain mail neck guard. 6. This elaborate Gothic helmet is a spangenhelm and is probably of Sarmatian origin. The helmet was constructed in segments and held together by the bronze decorated pieces. 7 This steel pot-type simple helmet is Visigoth and is modelled on a basic Roman helmet. 8 A later, more elaborate version of the Leiden helmet with a horsehair plume, which may have been a unit identifier.*

oval shield. Unit or tribal designs were painted on the front, and sometimes the designs were religious in nature.

There is a Roman official document, the Notitia Dignitatum, which dates

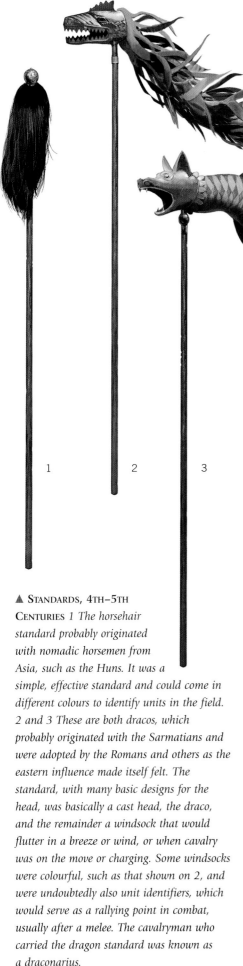

from the late 4th and early 5th century AD that shows Roman governmental organization for both the eastern and western empires. The document also has considerable information on the Roman army of the period. One very valuable section shows the shield patterns of the different Roman units, in colour, and gives excellent insight into the organization of the Roman army after the smaller legions, post-Diocletian, were formed and organized.

Missile Weapons

Two types of javelins were in use at this time, a long one for the line of battle and a shorter one, with a longer throwing range, for use in raids, ambushes, and reconnaissance. Throwing darts were becoming standard equipment and were stored on the reverse of the shield in specifically constructed 'shelves'. These were handy, granting the legionary ready access to a weapon that was in itself a miniature javelin.

A very formidable opponent for the Romans, and which the Romans, especially the eastern Romans would later employ, was the horse archer. This was a light cavalryman that would not become decisively engaged but would stand off and fire at their opponents

▼ SHIELDS, 4TH–7TH CENTURIES *The Roman Notitia Dignitatum has colour representations of shield decoration and design from the 4th century AD. Most of those shown here, with three exceptions (5, 6 and 9), are from that significant and enlightening document. These are the insignia of the Magistri Peditum and identify the designs of Roman shields on the senior western Roman infantry units of the period: 1 Pannoniciani. 2 Thebai. 3 Armigeri Junio. 4 Celti Senio. 5 Numerus Felicium Theodosiacus. 6 The back of a Roman infantry shield showing the method of stowing plumbatae (throwing darts). 7 Ascari Junio. Both infantry and cavalry at times employed throwing darts, the cavalry 'model' being longer, and the Sarmatians were noted for this weapon. 8 Herculiani. 9 An elaborate Germanic shield used as late as the 6th–7th centuries AD. 10 The device called Joumiani in the Notitia Dignitatum.*

▲ STANDARDS, 4TH–5TH CENTURIES *1 The horsehair standard probably originated with nomadic horsemen from Asia, such as the Huns. It was a simple, effective standard and could come in different colours to identify units in the field. 2 and 3 These are both dracos, which probably originated with the Sarmatians and were adopted by the Romans and others as the eastern influence made itself felt. The standard, with many basic designs for the head, was basically a cast head, the draco, and the remainder a windsock that would flutter in a breeze or wind, or when cavalry was on the move or charging. Some windsocks were colourful, such as that shown on 2, and were undoubtedly also unit identifiers, which would serve as a rallying point in combat, usually after a melee. The cavalryman who carried the dragon standard was known as a draconarius.*

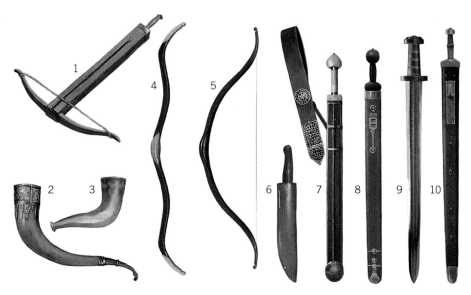

1 An early, crude crossbow. 2 Two views of a composite bow, unstrung and strung. 2 and 3 Two signalling horns made from animal horn such as cattle. 6 A large knife or dagger. 7, 8, 9 and 10 Different versions of a spatha and scabbard, first used by the Germans and other barbarians, then by the Roman cavalry arm, then finally replacing the infantry gladius. This type of long sword was also used by the eastern Romans both infantry and cavalry. All of these weapons, bows and edged weapons are non-Roman.

while mounted. They were capable of firing and hitting a target while their horses were moving. They used a short, powerful composite bow and they were usually not armoured. The composite bow was not constructed from a single

▼ **CATAPHRACT MOUNT, 4TH CENTURY AD**
This eastern Roman cataphract mount is in full armour and accoutrements. 1 The helmet detail shows how the rider's chain mail 'mask' was attached to the conical helmet. 2 The double-sword arrangement is for an eastern Roman cataphract. One is for 'heavy' work, the other, slightly curved sword, for light work. The harness was so arranged in order to allow the cavalryman to draw whichever sword he wished with ease.

piece of wood, but different layers of wood and, often, bone that would be glued together, this gave it immense strength for its size. Horse archers used a shorter bow than dismounted bowmen. Nevertheless, it was still a powerful weapon in the hands of an experienced archer.

The Mongolian draw, sometimes called the Mongolian release, was a type of draw on the bow string that used only the thumb, and not multiple fingers. This enabled a single draw by the strongest digit of the hand to enable a controlled

release of the arrow. This was especially useful for horse archers. The two- or three-fingered draw and release, sometimes called the Mediterranean draw, could sometimes affect accuracy as all the fingers employed might not let go at precisely the same time.

Edged Weapons

Roman arms developed (or declined, to take an opposing view) to the point where the arms used on a battlefield by a Roman army were hardly any different from those used by their opponents. The gladius, the mainstay of the legion in its prime, gave way to the spatha, or long broadsword, which was originally a cavalry weapon.

Shields became round or oval for both cavalry and infantry, and while a Roman-style helmet was still in use during the later empire period, other types of helmet were being adopted for use, or were in use by barbarians, especially cavalrymen, employed by the Romans as auxiliaries. The spatha could be worn suspended from a leather waistbelt, but it appears that a baldric was much more common.

Armour

As the cavalry came to be the dominant arm on the battlefield, the fully armoured cavalryman, or cataphract, was adopted by the Romans. The cataphract had been used for years by the Parthians, Persians, Sassanians, and Armenians, and a

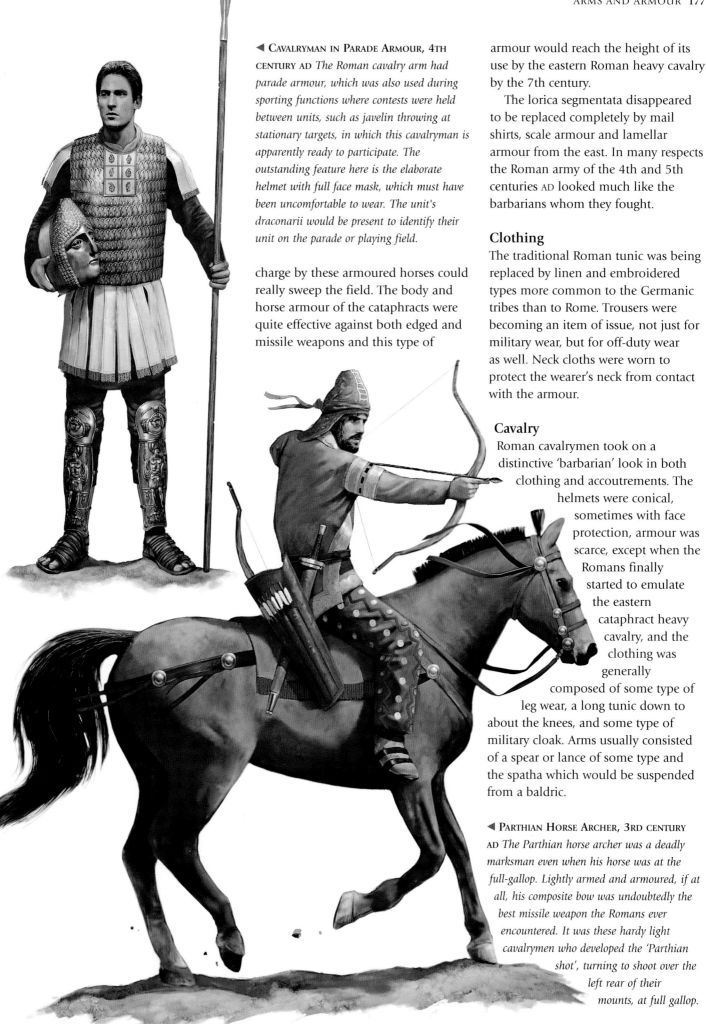

◀ CAVALRYMAN IN PARADE ARMOUR, 4TH CENTURY AD *The Roman cavalry arm had parade armour, which was also used during sporting functions where contests were held between units, such as javelin throwing at stationary targets, in which this cavalryman is apparently ready to participate. The outstanding feature here is the elaborate helmet with full face mask, which must have been uncomfortable to wear. The unit's draconarii would be present to identify their unit on the parade or playing field.*

charge by these armoured horses could really sweep the field. The body and horse armour of the cataphracts were quite effective against both edged and missile weapons and this type of

armour would reach the height of its use by the eastern Roman heavy cavalry by the 7th century.

The lorica segmentata disappeared to be replaced completely by mail shirts, scale armour and lamellar armour from the east. In many respects the Roman army of the 4th and 5th centuries AD looked much like the barbarians whom they fought.

Clothing

The traditional Roman tunic was being replaced by linen and embroidered types more common to the Germanic tribes than to Rome. Trousers were becoming an item of issue, not just for military wear, but for off-duty wear as well. Neck cloths were worn to protect the wearer's neck from contact with the armour.

Cavalry

Roman cavalrymen took on a distinctive 'barbarian' look in both clothing and accoutrements. The helmets were conical, sometimes with face protection, armour was scarce, except when the Romans finally started to emulate the eastern cataphract heavy cavalry, and the clothing was generally composed of some type of leg wear, a long tunic down to about the knees, and some type of military cloak. Arms usually consisted of a spear or lance of some type and the spatha which would be suspended from a baldric.

◀ PARTHIAN HORSE ARCHER, 3RD CENTURY AD *The Parthian horse archer was a deadly marksman even when his horse was at the full-gallop. Lightly armed and armoured, if at all, his composite bow was undoubtedly the best missile weapon the Romans ever encountered. It was these hardy light cavalrymen who developed the 'Parthian shot', turning to shoot over the left rear of their mounts, at full gallop.*

MA

THE EASTERN ROMANS 476–1453

Rome had fallen in the west. Even though the old imperial capital had been moved by the Romans themselves, first to Milan in northern Italy and then to Ravenna, the heart and soul of the empire had been lost. In the east, however, the territory ruled from Constantinople remained for another thousand years. Although the eastern Roman Empire is referred to as the Byzantine Empire, that is not the correct term. It was given to the eastern Roman empire in the 16th century by a German author, Hieronymus Wolf. The eastern Romans referred to themselves, in thought, speech, and the written word, as Romans. In fact and name, the eastern Roman Empire was the true successor to the empire of ancient Rome.

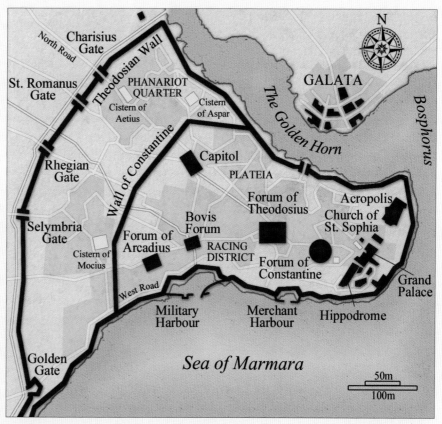

▲ *A map of Constantinople, 600AD, showing its defences, especially the Theodosian Wall facing the land side of the city, and the three bodies of water that surrounded it.*

◄ *Justinian I and his general, Belisarius, are both pictured in this period mosaic. Justinian is the central figure and Belisarius is to his right. Both are shown in court dress.*

THE EASTERN ROMAN EMPIRE

The reforms of Emperor Diocletian at the end of the 3rd century began a process that would make a division between an eastern and western empire inevitable. The emperor Constantine went further, making Constantinople his new seat of empire.

Diocletian and Constantine

Around 286 Diocletian had divided the empire into four distinct administrative entities. The two western regions, with capitals at Milan and Trier, included western Europe and North Africa as far as Egypt. The eastern region had Sremska Mitrovica in Serbia and Izmit in Turkey as capitals. It included Egypt, the Balkans and the Middle East. This fragmentation would lead to civil war after Diocletian's death, and a period of reunification, but the principle of a split between east and west was established and a new and different empire would emerge in the east.

Constantinople

That eastern empire's capital was Constantinople. The city was designed in a triangular shape with two sides on bodies of water, and the third side, the land side, which would have to be fortified. Later, under Theodosius and then finally under Justinian I, all three sides of the city would be formidably fortified, and the great walls of Constantinople withstood multiple sieges from many enemies and were only successfully stormed twice; first in 1204 when the crusaders from western Europe of the 4th Crusade took the city, and then secondly in 1453 when the Turks finally breached the walls of the city with their artillery and infantry assaults.

Early Eastern Roman Emperors

The emperors of the two halves of the empire were equal in both power and prestige, and this division of the empire actually set the stage for the survival of the eastern empire when Rome fell to the barbarian, Odoacer, who took the throne of the Caesars for himself in 476AD.

The Emperor Zeno was ruler of the eastern empire when Rome fell, and became the surviving Roman Emperor during his reign from 474–91, with a

▲ *Justinian I. The figurative 'halo' shown in this and other renderings of Justinian are particular to the eastern Romans.*

▼ *The Palace of the Porphyrogenitus, known later as the Tekfor Palace, is the last intact example of late eastern Roman architecture in Constantinople (now Istanbul). Named for a son of the emperor Michael VIII, Constantine Palaiologos, it suffered damage in 1453.*

brief interlude from 475–6 while the incompetent Basiliscus the Usurper occupied the throne. The eastern Roman throne was as subject to plots, usurpations, and civil wars as was its western Roman counterpart, but eventually the eastern Roman government settled down into a more or less stable monarchy supported by a large and competent bureaucracy.

Justinian I (527–65)

The first great eastern Roman Emperor was Justinian I, in the 6th century. He presided over a great reconquest of much of the western Roman lands in Italy, North Africa, and Spain and was a true lawgiver as well as emperor.

Justinian ruled long and well, and is famous not only for his statecraft, but also for having married a former actress and prostitute, Theodora, and made her empress. This was a position to which she proved well-suited. On at least one occasion, she saved Justinian's reign and although childless they were a well-matched pair.

▲ *A medieval view of the city of Constantinople. While this might be seen as a naive depiction of the city, it does, in some detail, show the strength of the walls and other fortifications.*

The Justinian code of laws, the Corpus Juris Civilis (or Body of Civil Law) was developed from 529–34 and imposed some sense into the confusing and contradictory laws inherited from Rome. It was one of the great leaps forward in the legal world. Justinian did not write the new code himself, but appointed a lawyer, Tribonian, to draw it up. He formed a group to write the new code, and the process was successful.

Emperors, Good and Bad

The long list of eastern Roman emperors following the rule of Justinian includes the good and bad, competent and incompetent, along with a few usurpers thrown in for good measure. Some of the eastern Roman emperors were also successful generals, or began their careers in the army, becoming effective officers, rising in the ranks, and then finding themselves wearing the purple. Both Maurice and Heraclius were such soldier-emperors who deserve mention.

Maurice (582–602), a descendant of Justinian, ruled well for 20 years and left a valuable military treatise that gives insight into the eastern Roman

army tactics and organization. He was deposed by a usurper, Phocas (602–10), who was in turn deposed by Heraclius (610–41), another successful soldier. He was the emperor who finally defeated the Persian Empire. Heraclius was emperor during the time of the Islamic threat, and lost territory to the Arabs threatening the empire.

Another great soldier-emperor was Basil II (976–1025) who probably ruled the resurgent eastern empire at its strongest. Basil's distant successor,

▼ *John II Comnenus, of the last effective ruling house in eastern Rome, is shown with Empress Irene and the Madonna and Child between them. Christianity was definitely a dominating factor in the empire.*

Romanus IV, however, lost the pivotal Battle of Manzikert in 1071 which began the long eastern Roman decline and set in train a destructive 10-year civil war.

Alexius I founded the Comnenian dynasty, and assumed the purple in 1081. He ended the civil war and began an eastern Roman resurgence that was continued by his son John II. John's son, Manuel I, also sometimes called 'the Great', was the last emperor to rule over an empire that was still powerful and continued to reclaim lost lands, but the dynasty died out five years after Manuel's death, to be succeeded by the incompetent Angelus dynasty in 1185, and the long road to defeat and destruction.

WARS OF THE EASTERN EMPIRE
TIMELINE 502–1453

502–6 The eastern Romans, with their capital at Constantinople, go to war with Persia, the other major power in the east.

526–32 The 2nd Persian War.

533–54 The eastern Roman emperor, Justinian, launches attempts to reconquer Italy, North Africa and other former western Roman lands around the Mediterranean. His armies, led by generals Belisarius and Narses, are largely successful. The eastern empire reaches its largest size.

628 The Avars fail in their attempt to take Constantinople.

634–8 The Arab conquest of Syria.

637 The fall of Jerusalem to the Arabs.

638–9 Mesopotamia and Armenia are lost to the Muslim onslaught

653 Cyprus and Crete fall to the Muslims.

668–77 Arabs repeatedly attack and besiege the city of Constantinople and fail each time.

860 The Rus (Russians) fail in their attack on Constantinople.

867 An eastern Roman revival begins with the accession of the Macedonian dynasty in Constantinople. Emperor Basil I begins a period of expansion marking a resurgence of eastern Roman military and civil fortunes.

902 Successful Roman naval expedition against the Muslim forces on Crete.

907 The Rus again fail in an attack on Constantinople.

941 Another Rus attack against Constantinople fails for the third time. The eastern Roman fleet destroy the Rus fleet using Greek fire.

994 Basil II campaigns successfully in Syria against the Muslims.

999 Basil II campaigns successfully again in Syria against the Muslims.

1000–18 Basil II successfully campaigns against the Bulgarians, and in Georgia and Armenia. The eastern Roman Empire is at its strongest since the reign of Justinian I.

1071 The eastern Romans are disastrously defeated by the Seljuk Turks at Manzikert. Much of Anatolia

▲ *The Emperor Basil II, the Bulgar Slayer (Bulgaroctonus) pictured on a gold coin. Sometimes the only likeness of a Roman emperor available are on coins of the period.*

falls to the Turks. The eastern Roman army is badly damaged.

1071–81 Civil war in the empire. The army again is badly mauled in this internecine warfare and never recovers its efficiency. This is the turning point in the fortunes of the empire.

1087–91 Campaigns against the Pechenegs.

1122 The defeat of the Patzinaks at the Battle of Eski Zagra.

1122–6 Venetian War

1128 Hungarian invasion of imperial lands defeated.

▼ *The Ponte Solario, the old Roman bridge across the River Aniene, a tributary of the River Tiber, was rebuilt by the eastern Roman general Narses in 565 during the reconquest of much of the old western Roman Empire.*

▼ *During 1096 to 1254, seven crusades were waged against the Muslims of the Middle East by armies dispatched from western Europe. It was eastern Roman emperor, Alexis I, whose plea for help launched the First Crusade.*

▲ *The crusaders of the Fourth Crusade, led by Venice, turned on their fellow Christians of the eastern Roman Empire and laid siege to Constantinople in 1204.*

1136–9 Eastern Romans reconquer Cilician Armenia and northern Syria. This solidifies the recovery of a large portion of Anatolia from the Turks.
1146 Indecisive war waged with the Seljuk Turks.
1149–52 Serbian rebellion and war with Hungary ends in Roman victory.
1155–6 Hungarians again defeated.
1155–8 Victory over the Normans at the Battle of Andria. However, the eastern Romans finally withdraw from Italian possessions in 1158.
1158–61 Successful expeditions against the Seljuk Turks.
1165–7 Successful war against Hungary. Provinces in the Balkans are recovered by Romans.
1171–7 Successful war with Venice, the operations of the eastern Roman fleet being decisive to the outcome of the war. Treaty not signed until 1183.
1176–80 Disastrous defeat at the hands of the Seljuk Turks at the Battle of Myriokephalon. Large portions of Anatolia are again lost to the Turks.
1185 Incursions by the Normans

defeated, though the cities of Dyrachion and Thessalonika are taken and sacked.
1204 The empire is largely conquered by the western Europeans of the 4th Crusade, Constantinople falling to them by direct assault. A Latin empire is formed by the crusaders.
1204–1302 The Latin empire is eventually ousted by resurgent eastern Romans. However, the eastern Roman Empire is fractured into different components by constant civil war,

revolts, and incursions by its enemies. The result is the shrinking of the empire into a relatively small enclave in and around Constantinople.
1302 The final and most deadly enemy of the empire, the Ottoman Turks, defeats the eastern Romans at the Battle of Bapheus.
1329 Ottomans defeat the eastern Romans at the battles of Pelekanon and Philokrene.
1354–64 Constant encroachment by the Ottomans reduces the empire to the city of Constantinople, the Morea, Thessalonika, and small islands in the area.
1366 Adrianople becomes the Ottoman capital.
1371 Ottomans conquer Serbia.
1372 Bulgaria becomes an Ottoman vassal state.
1373–85 Civil war in the eastern empire.
1384–7 Ottomans besiege and capture Thessalonika.
1395 Ottomans defeat eastern Romans in the Morea.
1453 Constantinople finally falls to the Ottomans in the Turks' fourth siege of the city.

▼ *Another view of the fall of Constantinople in 1453. The last eastern Roman emperor, Constantine XI, died in the defence of his city. Mehmet II declared himself the new Roman emperor, but the title meant nothing as the empire died with Constantine.*

THE EASTERN ROMAN ARMY

When the western empire fell, the troops who were left in the east simply became the eastern Roman army. They were no different, initially, in organization, weapons, equipment, and leadership than the army that had been in existence in the west.

Organizational Developments

It was not long, however, before differences in unit organization and a change in emphasis from an infantry dominated force to a cavalry dominated force began to develop. Some of that would be due to the defeat at the hands of the Gothic cavalry at

Adrianople in 378AD, but most of it would be because of the types of armies that the eastern Romans faced as the empire expanded eastwards. The employment of horse archers would become key in the development of the eastern Roman army, and the main striking force of almost every eastern Roman army after the fall of Rome would be the heavy armoured cavalryman, the cataphract.

Military Writings

Several military treatises of note have survived down the centuries and can now be studied to find out how the eastern Roman army was organized and trained. Here there was an emphasis placed on military intelligence as well as studying the enemies of the empire, in order to

'know your enemy' and hence how to fight them. They also placed immense faith in God in fighting their enemies in nearly every treatise.

The Emperor Maurice (who ruled from 582–602) was a soldier who became an excellent emperor and who left the eminent military treatise *Strategikon*, which not only put down all the known information on the enemies of the empire, but established 'classifications' of their strengths and weaknesses. For example, that mountain tribes should be campaigned

◀ ROMAN HEAVY INFANTRYMAN, 4TH CENTURY AD *After Diocletian's reforms the old Roman legion fundamentally changed. So did the appearance, equipment, arms and armour of the legionaries. The old lorica segmentata was abolished, along with the gladius. The latter was replaced by the spatha – this continued with the new eastern Roman army, the spatha being the 'regulation' sword for both infantry and cavalry.*

▶ ROMAN LIGHT INFANTRYMAN, 4TH CENTURY AD *The eastern Romans fielded light as well as heavy infantry. Generally speaking light infantry were intended to skirmish and were less well-equipped than their heavier, better armed and armoured comrades. The distinctive hat is authentic, but the origin of the style is unknown.*

Eastern Roman Army Strength 300–1453

These strengths are approximate only and reflect the best estimate of the troop strength that could have been fielded by the eastern Roman army at the date shown.

Year	Line Strength
300	310,000
450	300,000
520	270,000
540	340,000
570	150,000
640	100,000
670	100,000
770	80,000
800	90,000
840	120,000
960	140,000
1020	250,000
1050	200,000
1080	20,000
1120	20,000
1140	50,000
1180	40,000
1200	30,000
1280	20,000
1320	3,000
1453	8,000

There are also three anonymous treatises in existence, translated and published in English with the original text on the facing pages: *The Anonymous Byzantine Treatise on Strategy; Skirmishing; and Campaign Organization and Tactics*. All of the eastern Roman treatises on warfare give an insight on how the eastern Romans fought, and are worth careful study today to discover the reasons for eastern Roman military success over the centuries, at least until the crushing defeat at Manzikert in 1071, where the eastern Roman army was virtually shattered and much of it destroyed.

A New and Different Army

The old legions, armed with gladius and a long shield and wearing a metal cuirass, steel helmet and red tunic, were gone. Now Roman troops went into combat wearing mail, carrying a spatha, a round shield, and wearing long tunics, trousers or long leggings. The helmet was now developing a more standard appearance among Romans of east and west, as well as among the barbarian armies they faced.

Weapons

Foremost of the weapons used by the eastern Romans was the spatha, once the cavalry sword of the Roman auxiliary cavalryman, but now the main sidearm of both the eastern Roman cavalry and infantry. Heavy two-handed swords as well as one- and two-handed axes were also used by eastern Roman infantrymen, the large two-handed axe later being the favoured weapon of the famous Varangian guardsmen.

The bow adopted by the eastern Romans was the composite bow that originated in Asia among the nomadic peoples. Stronger and more powerful than the simple bow used in the west, it was made of both wood and bone,

◄ HORSE ARCHER, 4TH CENTURY AD
The legions found great difficulty fighting against the mounted armies in the east, especially those fielded by the Persian Empire. The horse archer became a mainstay of the mounted arm of the eastern Roman Empire. The unusual chain mail 'vest' worn by this figure afforded some protection but allowed vital freedom of movement for his arms.

against in the winter when they were the weakest and easiest to locate; nomadic peoples should be attacked in the late winter months when their usually hardy horses would be short of usable forage and not in the best of shape; Slavs who lived in marshes should be hunted when the rivers and marshes are frozen over so the enemy could not use them to their advantage.

Leo VI ('the Wise', 886–912) penned his military treatise, *Tactica*, specifically to recommend how to campaign against the Muslim threat. His emphasis was on the type of cavalry tactics to be used to fight against and defeat the redoubtable Muslim horsemen. The tactics and techniques illustrated by Leo in his excellent work served the eastern Roman armies well and led to further successes in the field against this most deadly of enemies.

and was constructed in such a way as to give its projectiles more power and penetration, even when the smaller version was used by mounted bowmen. It became a main weapon of the eastern Romans.

The eastern Romans were influenced by the weapons of either the indigenous peoples of the empire and/or the weapons of their enemies. The cavalry mace, basically a more complex club, and very effective in close-quarter fighting, was used by the cataphracts (armoured horsemen), as were the curved swords first employed by either the enemies of the empire or their own mercenary light cavalry. Swords and maces were usually either slung from a belt or baldric or sometimes attached to the

▶ IRREGULAR INFANTRYMAN, 5TH CENTURY AD
Light infantrymen always had a place in Roman warfare both for the Romans and against the Roman army. Irregulars would take their place on the battlefield when regular troops were deployed elsewhere, or when ranks had been depleted. Usually, however, irregulars would engage in what would later be known as partisan warfare and be at their best in raids, ambushes, and other aspects of the 'little war'.

saddle. Slings were also used with great skill by eastern Roman light infantry.

Both the infantry and cavalry used spears, the eastern Roman infantry also using javelins, which might also be employed by the Roman light cavalry, in the same way as the ancient Numidians had made use of the weapon. Infantry polearms were long, pike-like weapons for use in a massed infantry formation, sometimes very phalanx-like, with the troops in a rectangular-shaped formation six or eight men deep. This presented a formidable appearance to an enemy, especially as the pikes would look like a well-ordered forest in mass formations.

Initially, the Roman armies in the east continued in the tradition of the Roman army that had been in existence for a millennia, but based on experience fighting eastern enemies, as well as those of western Europe that had overrun the western empire, the army began to change.

Dress and Equipment

While the old Roman army still existed in the eastern empire in the 4th and 5th centuries AD, based on the old

◀ ARMOURED INFANTRYMAN, 5TH CENTURY AD
The eastern Romans employed well-trained infantry, even though they were not the main striking arm of the army. The motif on the shield is 'chi ro', the symbol of Constantine's victory at the Battle of Milvian Bridge, after the vision that converted him to Christianity. It is still a Catholic symbol today.

Roman legion, there were significant changes. The lorica segmentata, the steel cuirass made of plates of articulated armour used by the Roman legionaries, was being discarded and a reliance on chain mail for body armour was more the norm, as it was in the old republic. The rectangular, curved scutum was now gone in favour of flat, round shields; these were still decorated with emblems of the empire, but not the older design of lightning bolts and eagle wings.

The old legionary helmet, with or without crest or plumes, had given way to a more modern design that had less neck protection than the older helmet, and was sometimes crested with stiffened horse hair in various colours, usually of red and blue. The older, more colourful and distinctive centurion crest set parallel to the shoulders was either going out of use or was not used at all.

Infantry

Roman infantry during this period had both a heavy and light role, the same troops usually being used for both. Heavy infantry in combat in line would wear full armour and be armed with sword, spear or javelin, and often throw-darts, which were stowed on the back side of the shield. In light dress, armour would not be worn, although the helmet might be used by some of the troops and officers.

The shield, sword, and light javelins, which were shorter than the usual javelins used in line of battle, were carried and this order of dress would be used for reconnaissance in heavily wooded or rough terrain, and in raids, ambushes, and other irregular types of warfare. A conical felt or fur cap would be worn if the helmet was not, and this headgear would also be worn on the march. In period mosaics, this light mode of dress is also depicted being worn for leisure and for hunting.

Roman troops in the east came more regularly into contact with the horse archer. Lightly armed and equipped, on smaller, agile horses, the horse archer who came from the east in the almost never-ending migrations, became a formidable and mobile enemy, especially if there was no means to confront them and their elusive tactics. The horse archer would become a mainstay of the eastern Roman armies, armed later with the powerful composite bow.

Cataphracts

Heavily armoured horsemen, or cataphracts, had been encountered by the western Romans in their campaigns in the east. These

▼ CATAPHRACT, 5TH CENTURY AD *The cataphract first appeared in the ranks of Rome's eastern enemies. It was adopted by the western empire, inherited by the eastern empire, and then adapted by them as an effective counterattack to their enemies in the east, in particular the Persians. The eastern Roman cataphract would develop to such an extent, especially after the introduction of the stirrup, that it became the main striking arm of the eastern Roman army. Combined with the lightly accoutred and very mobile horse archer, it made a very deadly and complementary force on the battlefield.*

cavalrymen were very effective. As the eastern Roman army came into its own, the cataphract became more developed and the eastern Romans set their own tactics for the employment of their heavy cavalry supported by more lightly equipped horse archers.

Cavalry

For the heavy cavalry, the horses were usually heavily armoured as well as the cavalryman himself, and, especially with the introduction of the stirrup, mounted combat became viable as the horseman could now fight from his horse as a steady combat platform.

While both cavalry and infantry were usually armoured, the armour followed more of an eastern influence than a western one. Lamellar armour became more in use than the flexible plate of the lorica segmentata, but chain mail armour, especially for the torso, was also popular and quite effective. Helmets gradually became more conical in shape, replacing the usual round pots of the legionary, and chain mail face and neck covering became common.

THE BATTLE OF ADRIANOPLE

The question remains, however, why did the Roman army change from a mainly infantry force, based on the legion, to a mainly cavalry army, or an army whose main strength and striking power was the cavalryman?

▼ CONSTANTINE THE GREAT, C.312AD *The magnificent statue of Constantine in York, England, inspired this figure. His choice of a leather muscle cuirass is understandable as it would be lighter and more comfortable than a metallic cuirass, especially if he was not in combat but wanted to be seen in military dress. The decorations at the top of his boots denote his status as an army commander and emperor.*

In order to understand how the eastern Roman army developed and went its own way after the fall of the western empire, it is necessary to look at a catastrophic defeat of a Roman army under the emperor Valens at the Battle of Adrianople. This took place in the east near Constantinople, and was fought by a Roman army generally made up in the old way, namely as an infantry army supported by cavalry.

The Opponents

The Romans were commanded by Emperor Valens, the barbarians by Fritigern the Goth. To some historians this battle clearly demonstrated the superiority of cavalry over infantry and ended the long period of the ascendancy of the Roman legion. Initially, the battle was a fight between two infantry forces, the Gothic cavalry being absent on a foraging expedition. At that point, the Romans were winning, but the return of the Gothic cavalry, and the routing of the Roman cavalry, turned the battle decisively. The Roman infantry was herded into a central point by the Goths and slaughtered almost to a man.

The Battle

Adrianople (sometimes called Hadrianopolis, now Edirne in Turkey) is a town located on the western side of the Bosporus in Thrace. The Goths, with some attached Alans, had been pushed towards the coast by incoming migrations from central Asia and had moved along the Danube frontier, asking permission from the Romans to establish themselves in Roman territory for safety against the oncoming nomads. The Romans gave permission, but tension between the two soon turned belligerent. Emperor Valens

made the decision to move against the Goths without waiting for any support from the west, ostensibly because he did not want to share any of the glory

▼ EMPEROR VALENS AT THE BATTLE OF ADRIANOPLE, 378AD *Valens was the eastern Roman emperor at this time and this is an excellent example of a Roman commander in the field, whether eastern or western. The Roman army at this time was, though divided between different emperors, generally armed and equipped similarly. Of note is the old-style muscle cuirass, which was certainly normal dress for a Roman emperor in the field.*

◄ ROMAN INFANTRY, BATTLE OF ADRIANOPLE, 378AD *One of Valens' legionaries in a typically late-empire combat attire. Shields were now round, with unit designations still displayed. The late-style Roman helmet is typical of the mid-4th century and the simplified combat harness of plain leather still carried the older style gladius. The chain mail 'shirt' comes down to mid-thigh, almost covering the normal tunic. During this period the mail cuirass or shirt became longer than its predecessor to offer more protection.*

► ROMAN CAVALRY, BATTLE OF ADRIANOPLE, 378AD *This late-empire cavalryman is beginning to take on the distinctive eastern look that would continue to develop in the eastern Roman Empire. The lamellar-armoured cuirass is definitely eastern and the trousers and boots are a departure from the old classical 'Roman' look. The helmet, on the other hand, is quite Germanic in appearance and was adopted by the Roman army of the 4th–5th centuries from both Germanic and Celtic influences.*

Goths who had been defending the camp were counterattacking to Valens' front when the Gothic cavalry struck the Roman left flank units.

Surrounded, and by some accounts pressed so closely together by the combined pressure of the Gothic infantry and cavalry that they could not use their weapons effectively, the Romans were systematically slaughtered, Valens falling among his men.

The Aftermath

While taking place within the writ of the eastern half of the Roman Empire, Adrianople was the harbinger of the fall of Rome in the west and the eventual dissolution of the western Roman empire. Adrianople was a defeat from which the eastern Roman empire eventually recovered, but left the western half in disarray and an isolated new target for the repeated Barbarian incursions that would eventually force its collapse.

Initially, the eastern Roman army was composed of native troops recruited from the eastern lands and

of defeating the Goths. When Valens finally attacked, his infantry were successful in driving back their opponents. Valens had just succeeded in overrunning the Goths' encampment when the Gothic horsemen returned.

The Goth cavalry immediately attacked the Roman cavalry on Valens' left flank, routing them. Seeing half the Roman cavalry flee the battlefield, the remaining Roman cavalry on the Roman right flank decided to go with them, leaving the Roman infantry in the centre, with Valens at their head, alone to fight outnumbered against the encircling Gothic horsemen.

The Roman infantry were pressed closed together from all sides, the

mercenary troops. After Adrianople it began to become an army that would rely mainly on its developing cavalry arm to carry the fortunes of the empire into battle. The change from an infantry force to a cavalry army was greatly influenced by the peoples and armies that the Romans had fought in the east for years. The development of two types of cavalrymen, the mounted archer and the cataphract, or heavily armoured heavy cavalryman, were the result of having to fight on equal terms the mounted armoured troops that were employed by many enemies, including the Parthians, Armenians, Sassanians and the Persians.

ENEMIES OF EASTERN ROME

The eastern Roman Empire and its army steadfastly held the eastern borders of Europe against myriad enemies for one thousand years after the fall of the west to the Barbarian incursions. The eastern Roman emperors, and their field commanders, realized that they could not fight every one of their enemies at the same time, and they knew they could expect no outside help. The western empire was gone, conquered, broken up, and now ruled as individual barbarian kingdoms by barbarian chieftains who were self-made kings.

The enemies of the eastern Romans were numerous and diverse, both culturally and in the ways in which they fought. Whether Avar, Bulgar, Slavs, the Rus (Russians), Normans, Persians, Franks or Arabs, the eastern Romans had to be able to fight each successfully, and this necessitated studying not only the art of war, but their enemies' strengths and weaknesses, how they fought, when they preferred to fight, and their habits, good and bad.

To aid their study they wrote what today would be their military doctrine, which

would not only put in writing how to fight, command, and win wars, but how to fight on two fronts if necessary, or, conversely, how not to fight at a particular time and to come back later

▼ BULGAR CAVALRYMAN, 8TH–9TH CENTURIES AD *This horse soldier wears a mail shirt that extends to his upper thighs. For added protection in the front he wears scale armour over the mail. His helmet is designed to deflect sword blows over the head, and the face is protected by a nasal piece and chain mail that covers his neck and face. He is armed with a curved sword, a short axe and a lance.*

◀ AVAR CAVALRYMAN, 5TH–6TH CENTURIES AD *Another nomadic horse archer migrating out of Asia, this Avar wears no armour, except for knee guards, or helmet. He wears full trousers, knee-high boots, and a tunic that would come to mid-thigh or the knee. His horse harness is quite modern, and the circular stirrups were typical of nomads from central Asia. His bow, made of wood and bone, and short enough to be able to be used on horseback at speed, would be carried on the left, attached to the saddle.*

to confront the initial problem. Different methods were taught to campaign against and fight different enemies in different terrain, be it desert, mountains, or swamps. This is relevant to armies today, who might engage in conventional warfare against one enemy, and then fight an unconventional war against another, sometimes as the eastern Romans did.

▼ BULGAR WARRIOR, 6TH CENTURY AD
The Bulgars were a warlike people, tough, able opponents under capable leadership, they were well-armed and equipped. This infantryman wears scale armour that reaches the top of his thighs and carries a curved sword similar to a Turkish scimitar. His helmet is well-designed and made. His lance or spear is designed for infantry combat.

Unfortunately, the warfare, combat organization, and flexible combat doctrine of the eastern Romans is almost entirely overlooked today and their military treatises, though still available, are often ignored.

Avars

The Avars were nomads who originated in Asia, possibly India, and developed into a Eurasian league that migrated westward, undoubtedly being pushed by other tribes or tribal alliances, which were larger and stronger. They eventually allied themselves with the Persian Empire and with them helped to besiege Constantinople in 626. That siege ended in failure and defeat and with it went the Avars' prestige and strength. After that period they no longer posed a threat to the eastern Romans and were eventually absorbed by other, more permanent peoples in eastern Europe.

The Avars fielded excellent horse archers as well as armoured cavalrymen. Their native clothing usually consisted of trousers and tunics, which extended to mid-thigh. This could be embroidered according to their custom and the clothing was undoubtedly comfortable and made to fit their role as cavalrymen. Horse archers were not armoured and may not have worn any type of head protection at all. The heavier cavalrymen were armoured in mail or scale armour and wore a steel or iron helmet that was either slightly pointed or more likely rounded at the top. Swords and daggers were probably worn by all mounted men, and the mailed horsemen carried a long lance.

Bulgars

The Bulgars were another people who probably originated in Asia and migrated to the west. They settled in eastern Europe and allied themselves with the eastern Romans initially, during Zeno's reign. They later established their own kingdom in

▲ SLAVIC WARRIOR, 6TH CENTURY AD
The Slavic peoples would eventually populate most of eastern Europe as well as parts of Russia, but during this period they were nomadic. This light infantryman wears no protective armour except for a well-designed and made helmet, which might be a trophy from the battlefield. He is armed with throwing spears, a round shield and a short axe for close combat. He has no footwear, which could be remedied on the next battlefield or plundering expedition.

eastern and south-eastern Europe and fought the eastern Romans. They were finally defeated by Basil II, of which more will be discussed later.

The Bulgars were armed and clothed similarly to the Avars, to whom they were probably either related or initially allied. Steel or iron helmets, lance, sword, and dagger, as well as round shields, were the usual armament of the Bulgarian armies and they were formidable enemies to the eastern Romans until the late 10th or early 11th centuries.

Later Bulgars

The Bulgar men at arms adopted more sophisticated weapons and armour, which is one of the reasons that they became a more formidable foe to the eastern Romans as time went on. Long suits of chain mail or other types of armour became common, and

Bulgar cavalrymen also began to be deployed in large numbers. While they may not have been as organized and sophisticated as their eastern Roman enemies, they certainly became more effective, but were decisively defeated, and their army destroyed, by Emperor Basil II.

Slavs

The Slavs were yet another Indo-European ethnic groups that migrated westwards and eventually settled in eastern, south-eastern, and central Europe. Not all of them, however, moved into

◀ TURKISH ARMOURED ARCHER, 8TH CENTURY AD *Turkish horse archers appear to have been well-armoured and this bowman is almost Chinese-like in arms and equipment. He is by no means a light cavalryman, but almost a cataphract in appearance and armed with the powerful composite bow of eastern origin. He is armoured heavily for a horse archer, in both mail and scale armor. He has mail 'trousers' extending to his ankles, which cover the tops of his boots and armour on his forearms to his wrists. His helmet has no nasal protection and the feathers on top of his helmet are both for decoration and unit identification.*

▶ MUSLIM MERCENARY, 8TH CENTURY AD *The Muslims encountered by the eastern Romans after the 7th century AD were not a monolith, though in the main, be they Arab or Turk, they shared common weapons and equipment. They often warred on each other, being part of different caliphates and dynasties, which had no time for the other. In that jockeying for power, many would end up fighting for the eastern Romans. This figure is clad in scale and mail armour and his upper body and head are well protected. The combination of helmet, and chain mail all-round protection for the head and neck, was a common element in eastern armour. His trousers are decorative and perhaps embroidered. They are gathered at the ankle and lower calves with a type of legging that comes to the top of the shoes. A lance completes his attire.*

eastern Europe and settled both in Siberia and central Asia. Apparently, the Slavs were motivated to move into eastern and central Europe by the German migrations of the 5th and 6th centuries AD, along with the Huns, Bulgars, and Avars.

The strength of the Slavic tribes was very great, as witnessed by the eastern Roman written account of territory picked clean where they had passed, and what had been rich grasslands devastated after the Slavs army had departed.

The Slavs moved and fought as any other nomadic people and they undoubtedly relied on their inherent mobility when fighting. They were armed and equipped similarly to the Bulgars and Avars.

Mercenaries

Not all of the Islamic warriors stayed within the Muslim Arab armies, or later in either the Saracen or Ottoman armies that finally conquered Constantinople. Muslim troops were also hired out to other overlords Christian or Muslim, and many would also fight for the eastern Romans from time to time.

Generally speaking, the Muslim troops of the 7th–8th centuries were 'uniformed' and accoutred alike. Mail, lamellar, and scale armour were used, leg armour – such as the eastern Romans wore – was wrapped around their calves below the mail hauberk, and a steel or iron helmet was worn. Arms would include lance, sword (usually the curved scimitar and not the straight long broad sword or spatha of the Europeans or eastern Romans) and a dagger.

Clothing worn under the armour would usually be comfortable and probably decorated in some type of coloured embroidery. Mail hoods could be found worn under the helmet, as was becoming common with well-armoured cavalrymen.

Turks

The Turkic peoples originated in central Asia as well as in Siberia. They were very warlike and migrated west and southwards to establish two great empires, one of which eventually developed into the Ottoman empire in Europe, Asia Minor, and the Middle East, and the other which developed into the Moghul Empire of India and surrounding territories. The latter empire, which had little or no effect on the eastern Romans, was founded by Timur the Lame, later known as Tamerlane, and would last for about seven centuries. The civilization would flourish and was rich in culture with a ruling administration usually known for its efficiency. Both Tamerlane and his descendant Babur were also excellent soldiers and they extended the Moghul Empire outside the Indian subcontinent.

The Turks who migrated to and settled in the Middle East were the Islamic adversaries of the European crusaders as well as the eastern Romans, and it was they who would eventually conquer Constantinople and make it their capital. This was the second Muslim wave of attack, overcoming their predecessors, the Arabs.

▶ TURKISH ARMOURED CAVALRYMAN, 8TH CENTURY AD *The Turks, especially the Seljuk Turks, were originally warlike nomads who raided Persian and eastern Roman lands without distinction. This Turkish cavalryman is very cataphract-like, and it was troops such as these who would defeat the Arab Muslim caliphates and become the dominant Islamic power in the east. These cavalrymen would wear either lamellar or scale armour, both being equally efficient, and his armour covers him from shoulder to mid-calf. His helmet is typical for the period, the two feathers harking back to the Roman Republic. His mount is armoured fully in lamellar, with a steel chafron to protect the head.*

The armour of the Turkic cavalry consisted of long, coat-like suits of lamellar or scale armour, sometimes with mail underneath and also wearing mail hoods under their helmets. Their arms were standard for the eastern nomads, curved sword or scimitar, dagger, shield, and lance.

Interestingly, some of their horse archers were armoured and armed

▲ *October 10, 732, marked the conclusion of the Battle of Tours between the Franks, led by Charles Martel, known as The Hammer, and the Moors of North Africa, arguably one of the most decisive battles in all of history.*

like their heavy cavalry, except for the lance. Decorations on the steel or iron helmets consisted of some type of feathers, as in the old Roman legions of the republic.

Persians

The Persians, of whatever dynasty, still fielded lightly armed horse archers, and sometimes in addition to their archery equipment, they carried a lance of some type for close combat and probably self-protection. How they kept a grip on their lance and fired arrows accurately while mounted is something of mystery, especially before the introduction of the stirrup in the 6th–7th century. Some of the horsemen who came

◀ PERSIAN HORSE ARCHER, C.500AD *Like the Romans, the Persians eventually made their heavy cavalry their main striking arm, unlike the Parthians whose horse archers were their main emphasis. However, horse archers, lightly armed and equipped, were still part of the Persian armies and remained effective against the enemies of their empire until it was overwhelmed by the Islamic Arabs in the 7th century.*

out of Asia wore a type of long coat over their armour, similar to the surcoat that would be developed by the European knights. This coat would be colourful and heavily embroidered, but it is not known if motifs and designs were markings for individuals or tribes.

The Persian Empire was exhausted by the continuous wars with the eastern Romans and were finally and decisively defeated by the emperor Heraclius. Unknown to both empires, this was just before the dam broke on the first series of Muslim conquests, a deluge that would not be survived by the Persian Empire. Most of the territory of the Persian Empire was taken and occupied by the new caliphate that was established by the Arab Muslims.

Franks

The Franks developed out of the barbarian conquests in the Roman west and they carved a homeland out of parts of the old western Roman Empire. They were not a mounted warrior people, but usually rode their horses to battle and dismounted to fight. It was troops such as these that followed Charles Martel, the Frankish leader under the Merovingian dynasty, in 732 to defeat a Moorish incursion into France at the Battle of Tours.

The Muslim conquest beginning in the 7th century swept northward and westward from the Arabian peninsula. The eastern Roman Empire was not only caught off-guard by the sudden unsuspected offensive of a new power in the east, but the emperor Heraclius, just victorious over the Persian Empire could not muster enough strength to stop it. This contest would continue against Arab, Seljuk Turk, and the Ottomans until 1453 and the fall of the empire.

The Muslim juggernaut sweeping westward across North Africa gobbled up the eastern Roman Empire's North African possessions until it finally reached the Strait of Gibraltar. From there, the now-named Moors of North Africa swept across the Pillars of Hercules and into Spain, conquering most of the peninsula and establishing its kingdoms and civilization and culture there. In 732 a large Moorish raiding party slipped across the Pyrenees and into the Frankish territory up to the town of Poitiers, near Tours in southern France.

The warlike Franks, like their Christian brethren of the eastern empire, mustered to meet the new threat, and led by the Mayor of the Palace, and the real power behind the Frankish throne, Charles Martel, met and defeated the Moors at the Battle of Tours. The Moors retreated back across the mountains into Spain, never to cross the Pyrenees in strength again. There, in Spain, they would continue to fight the Christian Spanish until finally defeated and expelled in 1492.

The Franks were armed, equipped and clothed as western European warriors of the period, their favourite weapon being the long

◀ FRANKISH WARRIOR, C.700AD *Franks under Charles Martel defeated the Moorish incursion into France in 732AD. They were armoured infantry, though they did use horses for mobility and then dismounted to fight on foot. The eastern Romans who encountered these tough western warriors, were at this stage were much more sophisticated in the art of war than the Franks. It would not always be so. This infantryman wears a standard mail shirt and is heavily armed in the western fashion of the 8th century. The helmet is an older type of Celtic or German design. Noteworthy is the smaller knife carried on the outside of the scabbard of the larger knife. This was probably used for preparing food, though could be a weapon. The leg wrappings cover the calf from knee to ankle.*

▲ ASIAN CAVALRYMAN, 8TH CENTURY AD *Islamic in appearance with a colourful overcoat or surcoat over this armour, this cavalryman is very similar in arms and equipment of the eastern Roman 'medium' cavalry. Noteworthy here is the steel mace he carries, and the long, handsomely embroidered tunic that covers his armour.*

handled, two-handed axe, the broadsword and a round wooden shield. Chain mail and a steel or iron helmet completed the arms and equipment, though many also carried a dagger for close fighting (or eating). There was no armour on the legs at all, foot and leg coverings being the normal clothing of the period.

EASTERN ROMAN RECONQUEST

During the 6th century the eastern Romans launched an attempt to win back the territories of the old western empire. The drive began in earnest under Emperor Justinian, and his two most famous generals, Belisarius and Narses. Justinian was paranoid about the loyalty of those closest to him, and this often clouded his judgement, although well advised by his strong-willed and able empress, Theodora.

The Campaigns of Belisarius

One of the eastern empire's most effective generals was Belisarius. He is sometimes called the 'last of the Roman generals' but that is not only inaccurate, but demonstrates a lack of understanding of the eastern Romans. Belisarius may well have been the most able general to serve eastern Rome, but all of the generals that served through the centuries were Romans and considered themselves as such. Belisarius served loyally and ably, although at times he was unjustly accused by Justinian of pursuing personal advancement.

In 533, after five years of successful campaigns against the Sassanids and in quelling an uprising against Justinian, Belisarius was sent on campaign against the Vandal Kingdom. His success in regaining Carthage for Rome earned him a triumph, the last ever granted, when he returned to Constantinople. Belisarius was then sent to attack the Ostrogothic Kingdom in Italy, where he succeeded in capturing Naples in 536, and then Rome. A year later he defended Rome against an attack from the Goths, then moved north to take Mediolanum (Milan) and the Ostrogoth capital of Ravenna. Shortly before this, the Ostrogoths offered to make Belisarius the western emperor. Belisarius feigned acceptance and entered Ravenna accompanied by his personal regiment, and once within the

◀ FLAVIUS BELISARIUS (500-565AD) *This rendition of the great Belisarius, dressed in court clothing, is taken from a contemporary mosaic. Belisarius is sometimes referred to as 'the last of the Roman generals' but there were more to come of similar stature and military prowess. There is no image of Belisarius in armour, but it can be assumed that he wore period armour embellished as befitting his rank as a general and army commander. He would chose to dress in the field to be easily recognizable to his men in combat. The heavy broadsword is similar to that carried by the Emperor Constantine.*

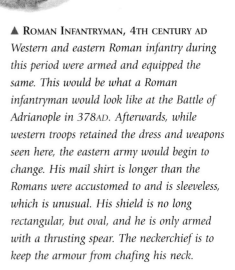

▲ ROMAN INFANTRYMAN, 4TH CENTURY AD *Western and eastern Roman infantry during this period were armed and equipped the same. This would be what a Roman infantryman would look like at the Battle of Adrianople in 378AD. Afterwards, while western troops retained the dress and weapons seen here, the eastern army would begin to change. His mail shirt is longer than the Romans were accustomed to and is sleeveless, which is unusual. His shield is no long rectangular, but oval, and he is only armed with a thrusting spear. The neckerchief is to keep the armour from chafing his neck.*

city walls proclaimed its capture in the name of Justinian. Unfortunately this subterfuge raised the suspicions of Justinian and Belisarius was recalled to Syria where he waged a brief, inconclusive campaign ending in a truce. Belisarius returned to Italy where the Ostrogoths had recaptured Rome and much of northern Italy. Starved of supplies and reinforcements by a jealous emperor, Belisarius's second Italian campaign was unsuccessful. Justinian relieved him in favour of Narses, who thanks to both military competence and cooperation from the emperor, was able to bring the campaign to a successful conclusion. Belisarius retired, although he was briefly recalled in 559. In this last campaign Belisarius defeated the Kutrigur Bulgars.

In the study of Belisarius and his campaigns it is fortunate that he was usually accompanied by his own chronicler, the eastern Roman historian Procopius, who was his secretary. It is not clear whether or not Procopius 'approved' of Belisarius, or even liked him, but he wrote about the period for an extended time, in clear language, as a contemporary of Belisarius. He was also valuable as a writer who witnessed the events that he writes about. This greatly assists any study of the period and the operations of the eastern Roman army.

The Eastern Army's Military Appearance

While Belisarius and Narses and other eastern Roman commanders were reconquering a large part of the old western empire, what would become the professional eastern Roman army, composed of native eastern Romans who would generally fight at any odds and win was still in its infancy. Mercenaries still made up a large part of the army, and these tended be loyal to the commanders who paid them, and not to the emperor and the central government. This was probably why Justinian was so ready to be suspicious of his generals, although he does seem to have been particularly sensitive about Belisarius.

The eastern Roman infantry of the reconquest period looked very similar to the infantry at the end of the western empire. They were not now, however, the main striking arm of the army, the cavalry was. The cataphract had been adopted by the western Romans after facing them in the east. That adoption was carried to its natural conclusion by the eastern Romans in the change from an infantry to a cavalry army. The other practical adoption by the eastern army was the horse archer. The cataphract and the horse archer would work together on the battlefield, one a heavy cavalryman, the other a light horseman, and they were the tip of the spear, so to speak, of the eastern Roman reconquest in the west.

► CATAPHRACT, 5TH CENTURY AD
The Romans adopted the idea of armoured heavy cavalry from the Persians early, before the fall of Rome. It would take some time for them to become the dominating battlefield weapon that they would under the eastern empire – still, it was a beginning. This early cataphract wears a mail coat that extends to his knees and a mail head covering, but no helmet. His horse is fully armoured, including his eyes, while the rider is armed with a spatha and a long lance, designed for shock action. The stirrup was not yet introduced into western Europe and balance was dependent on leg muscle and dexterity.

Eastern Roman Cavalry

By the 4th century the cataphract had begun to be introduced in the western empire. More heavily armoured than any previous Roman cavalry, this was not quite yet the battle-winning, heavy cavalry that would develop in the east, but it was the beginning of the transition of the Roman army from an infantry army to a cavalry army.

The cataphract at this time was not only more developed as a type of cavalryman for the eastern armies, his appearance was becoming more eastern than western. The almost full-length armoured 'coat' was either mail or scale armour, though as already discussed, lamellar was becoming more common as copied from the eastern enemies of the empire. Arms were developing with the newer armour, and two swords, both worn on the left side, one long and one shorter and slightly curved, would eventually be worn. Maces were becoming more common with the cataphracts, and the long lance, the primary offensive weapon of the heavy cavalry, was used

▶ THRACIAN CAVALRYMAN, 6TH–7TH CENTURIES AD *This is a local cavalryman, a 'medium' type. The three types of eastern Roman cavalrymen were not only distinguished as such by their arms and armour (or lack of it) but by the size of their horses. Medium cavalry, an all-purpose type of horseman, would ride a horse between the small, nimble mounts of the mounted archers, and the large, strong horses of the cataphracts. This man is similar to what would later be termed a dragoon, though this eastern Roman cavalryman would not fight on foot unless he had to.*

to arm most of that cavalry type. There are some authorities that state that the cataphract was armed with both the lance and the bow, as were Turkic heavy cavalry, or, alternatively, some were lance-armed and some with the bow, but that seems to be an inaccurate assessment as specific bow-armed horse archers were definitely in existence as cavalry units. Still, it is an interesting hypothesis to be pursued and investigated.

There appears to have been a 'medium' cavalryman that developed in the eastern armies, neither archer nor cataphract. He would be capable

of closing with other cavalry and fighting hand-to-hand, but also capable of the type of missions for which the cataphract would not be suitable, and would work in conjunction with the horse archers.

A New Structure

The troops with which Belisarius and the other eastern Roman generals of the period reconquered a large part of the old western empire (which would include Italy, North Africa, and parts of Spain) was not the eastern Roman army that would later develop with the 'theme' system. There were still large numbers of mercenaries employed, though native troops within the empire's borders were recruited, trained, and employed in ever-growing numbers.

The organization of the army was very different from the old western Roman army. The infantry were organized in units called a tagma, and the cavalry were now formed in units called a numera. A tagma was a battalion-sized unit of between 300 and 400 men.

Roman legions were still in use. Comitatenses were the eastern Roman regulars, recruited from the native provinces of the empire. Under Belisarius these were called stratiotai.

The limitanei were still employed as garrison troops, as in Dioceltian's day. They were stationed on the empire's marches (frontiers). A new type of soldier, organized and employed by the eastern Romans was the foederati, these were the cavalry arm of the army and were recruited among the various barbarian horsemen that either lived in the empire or around its fringes. The officers were Romans, and the troops were all volunteers.

◀ GUARD INFANTRYMAN, 6TH–7TH CENTURIES AD *The eastern Romans' attitude towards troops designated as 'Guards' was odd. The main strength of the eastern army at the height of the empire was the locally recruited native soldiery from Asia Minor and the European themes in the Balkans and beyond. Guard units were often recruited from 'foreigners' or mercenary units, but this system seems to have worked well for the eastern Romans. This soldier's armour is worn under the shirt and over the tunic, the latter extending to the knees. It is a lamellar-type of armour, light but strong. The figure carries his shield over his back, a comfortable and utilitarian way of keeping it out of the way when not in action, but having it ready for use. His greave-type calf armour, with padding underneath, completely encases the lower legs for the best protection.*

Allied units were also employed by the eastern Romans of the period, just as they had been for quite some time. Recruited among the warlike barbarians, and probably mostly mounted, they were in turn awarded land for good service.

Finally, the bucellarii were the personal troops belonging to, and paid by, eastern Roman generals, recruited from peoples who would be loyal to the general personally. Generally speaking, they were cavalrymen, and would be used by eastern Roman generals not only to guard their person and baggage, but to be committed to combat in emergencies as a ready reserve.

Two or more tagmata would be organized into what would now be called a brigade, called a moira. The moira would be further grouped in units of two or more and form a meros, what would today be called a division. Two or more meros would be formed into an army.

The eastern Roman army had six types of troops; guards, comitatenses, limitanei, foederati and bucellarii. Guard units were formed for duty in Constantinople for both internal security and as a central reserve for emergencies. The old terms from Diocletian's reorganization of the

▶ CATAPHRACT, 6TH CENTURY AD *Eastern Roman cataphracts now began to take on a definite 'Roman' look, starting the evolution of the heavy horsemen whose charge could quite literally 'sweep the field'. The long armoured mail 'coat', split up the centre for ease of riding, seems to be a Roman development in the east, as is the coloured plume on the helmet, which would identify this cavalryman's unit. This cataphract is armed both as a heavy cavalryman and a mounted archer. While sometimes the bow was carried on the waist belt in its protective cover or sheath, at other times it would be carried on the saddle with only the arrows being carried on the waist belt.*

Reconquered Lands

The eastern Romans also reconquered in the east, particularly in Syria and Palestine, then known in the west as the Holy Land. Military dress could be modified for the terrain and climate, at least while on the march, and the clothing worn by the army was usually comfortable, probably of linen with wool only being worn in the winter because of the cold. Senior officers would wear armour in combat, but their dress when not on campaign could remind one of the casual dress of old Roman tribunes or senators.

Eastern Roman cavalrymen, especially the medium cavalry in the east, could campaign in light marching

▼ **EASTERN ROMAN SENIOR OFFICER, 7TH CENTURY AD** *Roman senior officers probably wore this type of clothing either in court dress, as in Belisarius' case, or for their leisure at home. The ankle-length tunic is rich enough to designate the officer's status, yet comfortable enough to be a welcome break from his armour.*

▶ **ARMENIAN NOBLEMAN, 6TH–7TH CENTURIES AD** *Armenia was one of the territories in Asia Minor that was constantly fought over until at least 1071 and the aftermath of the Battle of Manzikert. Eastern Roman 'noblemen' might lead their own troops into combat with the army or have a commission themselves during this period. This is typical 'travelling' garb for a period nobleman.*

▼ **SENIOR OFFICER KIT, 7TH CENTURY AD** *The arms and equipment of an eastern Roman senior officer would be similar to that of the troops he commanded and led, except usually of better construction and perhaps more showy in appearance. 1 The quilted padding worn under armour, with the chain mail beneath that. The method of wearing the two types of cavalry swords, as done by cataphracts, is clearly shown. 2 The outer armour. 3 Horse armour, covering head and neck. 5 The helmet of a heavy cavalryman. 4 and 6 Two helmets worn by medium cavalry or archers.*

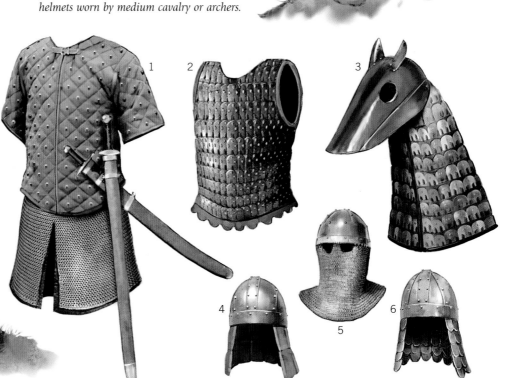

order, only donning armour of any type when battle was imminent. This could be a disadvantage in an ambush or a sudden skirmish, but the eastern Romans studied their enemies closely and intelligently, demonstrating a tactical professionalism of a very high order. Well-armed but unarmoured, or minimally armoured, troops can fight and win.

The eastern Roman infantry were well-trained, well-armed and well-equipped. They protected rallying cavalry on the battlefield and could and did provide the 'hard shoulder' of the army from which the cavalry – horse

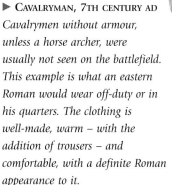

▶ CAVALRYMAN, 7TH CENTURY AD *Cavalrymen without armour, unless a horse archer, were usually not seen on the battlefield. This example is what an eastern Roman would wear off-duty or in his quarters. The clothing is well-made, warm – with the addition of trousers – and comfortable, with a definite Roman appearance to it.*

archers, cataphracts and medium horse – could manoeuvre and fight. They were well-organized and, it appears, also well-led, even though in the western campaigns the infantry might not always be the most important part of the army.

Commanders and Armies

Eastern Roman senior officers could be nobles, although officers could win their commissions through good service and favour. On campaign and off-duty the officers and nobles would attempt to both live and dress well, and their arms probably were of a better quality than the rank and file.

Eastern Roman armies of this period were generally small, usually between 15,000 to 25,000 men of all arms. The most important striking force would be the cavalry, and they usually numbered less than one half of a Roman army. With small forces of this type, Belisarius and Narses manged to reconquer a huge amount of territory and defeated larger numbers of Goths, Vandals, and Persians.

Because of Belisarius' expert employment of his army in North Africa, not only was the kingdom destroyed, but the Vandals themselves

◀ ARMOURED INFANTRYMAN, 6TH–8TH CENTURIES AD *This rear view of an eastern Roman infantryman shows how the cloak was worn, and how the sword, a variation of the much-older spatha, is ready-to-hand even though this infantryman is wearing his cloak. The inside of the shield showing the construction is noteworthy.*

were absorbed as a people by the eastern Romans and their individual identity disappeared from history.

The eastern Roman army of the reconquest was not the finely organized and highly trained military machine that it would become after the reconquest. However, it was a dynamic army of native born soldiers and hard-bitten mercenaries, under commanders that displayed outstanding military and leadership abilities. It was this army and those commanders that gave the eastern Roman Empire the ability to grow, prosper, and survive in a tumultuous period of history.

DEFENDING THE EMPIRE

Although wealthy in comparison with its enemies, the resources of the eastern empire were not endless. Often the imperial treasury was empty during a political situation that was fluid and precarious. Troops who were not paid might mutiny, be they mercenaries or native-born. Emperors, as in the old western Roman Empire, could be made and unmade through popularity with part of the army. Civil war was a real danger with rival factions supporting candidates with imperial ambitions.

Through all of these troubles it should be recognized that the eastern empire was an empire always at war or preparing for conflict. Faced with and surrounded by enemies or potential enemies, with no real allies, the empire had to fight to stay alive and might be at war simultaneously on more than one front with more than one enemy.

Imperial State Clothing

The ceremonial and day-to-day dress of an eastern Roman emperor was magnificent, with richly embroidered clothing, and gold and bejewelled crowns and accoutrements. The court and the eastern Roman governmental bureaucracy, and what they wore on a

◀ **BYZANTINE STANDARD BEARER, 6TH CENTURY AD** *Another example of the Roman use of the draco standard, this time by an infantryman. He is armed and equipped as a typical infantryman of the period. What is noteworthy here is the emblem on his shield, which is the 'sign of Constantine' and was adopted by Constantine as his standard and personal emblem after his victory at the Milvian Bridge in 312AD against his rival for the throne, Maxentius. The emblem, called the Chi Rho, represents the first two letters of 'Christ' and is still used as a Christian symbol to this day.*

▶ **BYZANTINE EMPEROR, 6TH–9TH CENTURIES AD** *This richly dressed and accoutred eastern Roman emperor could be Justinian I in his court best, richly attired to awe and inspire friend and foe alike. At this point in the history of the eastern Roman Empire, the official language was still Latin, and Latin influence would still be great in the empire; later the Greek language and culture would take precedence, but the rulers of the empire would still consider themselves Roman.*

daily basis to show their rank, could be equally expensive and this often proved a burden on state resources.

Standards

The eastern army adopted the draco as a standard, undoubtedly inherited from the western empire and from the myriad other peoples that used it. Standard bearers would be targets of the enemy in any engagement, as taking the enemy's standards was cause for reward and promotion, as

Eastern Roman themes 7th–11th century

(In order of creation, the year established in is parenthesis)

7th century	8th century	9th century	10th century	11th century
Armeniakon (668)	Sicily (700)	Macedonia (802)	Samos (c.900)	Bulgaria (1014)
		Cepohellenia (809)	Nicopolis (900)	Sirmium (c.1020)
Anatolikon (670)	Cibyrrhaeots (c.720)	Peloponnese (811)	Mesopotamia (911)	
Thrace (680)	Crete (767)	Paphlogonia (c.820)	Lykandos (916)	
Opsician (680)	Bucellaria (768)	Cappadocia (c.830)	Seleucia (934)	
			Cyprus (965)	
Tharesians (687)	Optimates (775)	Klimata (833)		
Thessalonika (c.690)		Chaldea (c. 840)	Sebasteia (911)	
Hellas (c.690)		Koloneia (863)		
		Strymon (840)		
		Dyrrhachium (842)		
		Aegean Sea (c. 840)		
		Charsiannon (863)		
		Dalmatia (899)		
		Longobardia (892)		

▲ INFANTRYMAN, 6TH CENTURY AD *A very differently dressed infantryman from the same time period as the one to the right. Arms and armour are typical of the Roman army at the fall of the west, but the tunic is now longer and is reminiscent of the surcoat western knights wore in the 11th–13th centuries.*

well as an act celebrated by your comrades as brave and resourceful. Likewise, a unit that lost a standard in combat was in disgrace, unless there was no one alive left to defend it.

The infantry of the eastern army, as their western predecessors, could be armoured and also operate in a light order, wearing only the helmet, and carrying shields and weapons. While crests were not usually worn during this period in the army's history, plumes and feathers were worn by

different units and the units might be distinguished from each other by the colours of the feathers and plumes.

The Military Themes

A significant military development occurred in the first half of the 7th century that was to have an important impact on the eastern empire's fortunes. The old Roman provinces that had been established by

▶ INFANTRYMAN, 6TH CENTURY AD
An infantryman of Belisarius' day carrying a religious standard. The eastern Romans were a very religious people and even in their military treatises there are myriad references to God and the Christian religion. The hat worn by this infantryman is similar to the Phrygian cap worn later by French revolutionaries in 1789.

Diocletian were abolished and a new system of provinces particular to the empire was established. Their actual origin was military and they were organized around the military establishment in the new provinces. The new provinces were named 'themes' and this term not only meant the territory itself, but the military organization that belonged there. Consequently, the military commander of each theme was also the governor of the province. No two themes were organized in exactly the same way, nor would their strengths be equal in order to confuse enemy intelligence efforts.

Initially six themes were organized in Asia Minor,

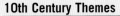

10th Century Themes

The following table illustrates the typical thematic military structure used by the eastern Romans in the 10th century. At full strength, a typical eastern Roman theme would be 9,600 strong.

Title	Strength	Subordinate Units	Commander
Theme	9,600	Four Tourmai	Stratego
Tourma	2,400	Six Droungoi	Tourmarches
Droungos	400	Two Banda	Droungarios
Bandon	200	Two Kentarchiai	Count
Kentarchia	100	Ten Kontoubernia	Kentarches
Kontoubernion	10	2	Dekarchos
Advance Guard	5	N/A	Pentarch
Rear Guard	4	N/A	Tetrarch

and six in the European half of the empire. As the empire was reorganized and new territory taken and settled, new themes were established by the central government. The original themes were Armeniakon, Anatolikon, Opsician, Thrace as well as the naval division of Carabisiani; these eventually included Cibyrrhaeots in the 8th century. In order to maintain its navy, the eastern Romans also established naval themes along the coast of Asia Minor.

Eastern Roman Commanders

Commanders in the field could wear whatever armour they chose and carry whatever weapons they preferred. Commanding armies that were essentially mounted armies would necessitate that the commander be mounted too and common sense

◄ EASTERN ROMAN OFFICER, 6TH–7TH CENTURIES AD *An infantry officer would lead his men on foot, armed and equipped as they were, though with certain aspects of his arms, such as the helmet here, being richer in detail. The interesting insignia on his shield is probably a combination of personal, unit and religious symbolism.*

► EASTERN ROMAN HORSE ARCHER, 7TH CENTURY AD *The influence of the eastern enemies of the empire is evident on this horse archer. The helmet, armour and tunic are all eastern in inspiration.*

dictates that he would wear something distinctive to make himself easily recognizable to the men he commanded. When he took the field, Emperor Alexis I dressed and equipped himself as a cataphract, for example, and engaged in combat if necessary. Like their officers at every level, the army commanders needed to have skill at arms in order to defend themselves if necessary. In addition, if they were to gain the respect of their troops, officers had to be good leaders and skilled tacticians.

Horse Archers

The eastern Roman horse archer during the 7th–9th centuries wore a padded overgarment that would afford some protection to enemy weapons, though his main defence was his mobility and training. His horse did not wear armour, and would probably be the tougher, smaller breed of horse that was bred for endurance and speed.

Medium Cavalry

The eastern Roman medium cavalry at this period was coming into its own as a battlefield force. Their horses, larger than those of the horse archers and smaller than the horses of the cataphracts, were lightly armoured for some protection against enemy missile weapons, and the cavalryman himself definitely wore a steel helmet and body armour. The troopers' weapons included sword and dagger, lance and shield. They were trained to operate in conjunction with the other arms of the service, both infantry and cavalry.

Infantry/Cavalry Cooperation

The basis for eastern Roman tactics was the cooperation between the two main arms of the army, the infantry and cavalry. Infantry was to form a bulwark in battle from which the cavalry could gain some respite and protection. This was especially critical if fighting an army whose cavalry arm

outnumbered that of the Romans. The infantry would form for battle with intervals between units through which the cavalry was sent forward to manoeuvre and fight and through which the cavalry could return to rally and reorganize. Against an army that was mostly infantry this was not necessarily the way in which the army would fight, but cooperation between the two arms was still essential for success.

▼ CLIBANARIUS, 7TH–8TH CENTURIES AD
A clibanarius was for all intents and purposes a cataphract, and the two terms are virtually synonymous, at least in reference to the eastern Roman army. This cavalryman could be considered the ultimate in the eastern Roman cataphract and he is completely armed and equipped and ready for combat. His horse is also completely armoured. The pennant on his lance matches in colour the plume on his helmet, both of which identify his unit and perhaps his commander as well. The design on his shield is Greek-inspired, demonstrating the Greek influence that was affecting the eastern Romans.

Cooperation between the three types of cavalry was also essential. The cataphracts were the battle-winning arm and could really sweep the field if launched at the proper time – few armies could withstand the full weight of a well-directed and led charge. But back up in the form of rapid support from the medium cavalry – who were lighter in arms and armour than the cataphracts, but heavy enough to be employed in massed charges if necessary – was vital. The medium cavalry could manoeuvre more swiftly than the heavy cavalry and were able to quickly react to changes and orders on the battlefield.

The Roman horse archers, as skilled in their duties as their opponents from whom they originally learned their profession, would weaken the opposing enemy lines and formations, looking for an opening into which the medium and heavy cavalry could attack. Likewise, they could cover a withdrawal or retreat of their heavier brethren, keeping a pursuing force at bay until the heavy and medium cavalry could rally, reorganize, and again go over to the attack.

Basil the Bulgar-Slayer

The late 9th and early 10th centuries saw the era of the emperor Basil II (957–1025), also known as the Bulgar-Slayer. He brought the empire back from the brink of disaster, as the Islamic threat, the most dangerous the empire would ever face, had been successful in making large inroads into eastern Roman territory. Basil began inauspiciously, but learned from defeat and disappointment and went on to

became one of the best of the eastern Roman emperors and commanders. At the end of his reign in 1025, the eastern empire stood in the best strategic position that it had attained since the reign of Justinian I.

The Bulgars had once again encroached on the empire and Basil led an army out to oppose their invasion. Not only were the Bulgars completely defeated in 1014 at the Battle of Kleidion, but most of the invading army was captured. Basil is said to have had all of the prisoners, at least 14,000 men, blinded, with the exception of one man in

◀ IMPERIAL INFANTRYMAN, 10TH CENTURY AD *Well-armed and equipped heavy infantry, the legacy from the old legions, while not the main striking arm of the eastern Roman army, was still a cornerstone of that army and the manner in which they fought. As much care was taken in their recruiting and training as with the cavalry. They were identified by the coloured tufts on their helmets. The two-handed axe was not 'native' to the eastern Romans but was adopted from what would become the Varangian Guard.*

▶ OFFICER OF THE DANUBE LEGION, 9TH CENTURY AD *The frontier on the River Danube had to be manned and guarded as carefully as that of the east. Defending a river line is sometimes easier than open plains or desert, but no less dangerous. Officers were identified by the richness of their clothing, armour, and weapons and from their military cloaks. This officer's arms and armour are typical of the period; besides his sword and spear his sidearms include a one-handed axe and a dagger in a horizontal sheath, hanging from his waist belt for easy access.*

spot, the shock being too much for him. Basil went on to subdue the Bulgars and won some temporary respite, although conflict rumbled on for the next few centuries.

Basil II usually took to the field in his imperial finery. His armour was made of the finest material, as was his clothing, and there is no doubt that in such a uniform Basil would be recognized on the field, and in combat, by his troops. Basil II was a true warrior-emperor, but the gains he made would be wasted by his successors. His reign illustrates both the strength and the weakness of the eastern Roman system of government. His indomitable and forceful personality and his shrewd statesmanship were offset by the inherent weakness of an imperial autocracy that depended so much on the character of the ruler.

The Height of the Empire

Infantrymen of Basil's army wore the same type of padded jacket as the horse archers, and instead of a helmet wore a turban wrapped around a central cap. Long calf-high boots were worn with trousers tucked into them. The long lance was more like a pike than a spear and the imperial infantry, on the defensive to support the cavalry, would mass in ranks similar to the old Greek phalanx.

Other imperial infantry would be heavily armoured in scale or lamellar and be armed with sword and dagger (as would those infantrymen armed with pikes) and would also use the battleaxe.

On the empire's eastern marches regular and irregular lightly armed and armoured cavalry would be employed both on and off the battlefield. While not professional soldiers as the regulars were, they were a valuable intelligence-gathering force as well as giving early warning of enemy incursions and raids.

The imperial tagmata was another form of cataphract or heavy cavalry and were armed and armoured as such. They were not part of the military thematic troops and were kept in central reserve in Constantinople and its environs. They were under the eye of the emperor and would accompany him on his campaigns.

▼ IMPERIAL TAGMATA, 9TH CENTURY AD
Eastern in appearance, western in outlook, this is a soldier of the eastern Roman regular army stationed in and around the capital of Constantinople. The imperial tagmata would back up the 'divisions' stationed in the themes and would also be in the front line of the defence of the city against any kind of threat.

▲ BASIL THE BULGAR-SLAYER (958–1025)
Emperor Basil II was the last great eastern Roman emperor before the disaster at Manzikert in 1071. He was a talented commander who finished the Bulgars as a threat to the empire, and gained back much territory that had been lost. His talents would not be matched again until the middle of the 12th century during the resurgence under the Comnenians. He is dressed and armed for parade, not active service.

every hundred, who were left with one eye intact so that they could lead the other 99 in each group home. When their king saw the wreckage of his army, he collapsed and died on the

THE BATTLE OF MANZIKERT

The successors to Basil II were not as capable as he had been, and the efficiency of the army began to deteriorate. Strong commanders in any era are few, but the eastern empire discovered to its chagrin that by the time of the accession of Romanus IV in 1068 the army had been riddled with interference from a growing aristocracy that permeated the eastern Roman bureaucracy. In addition, a new, more deadly threat from the east

had come into play. The Seljuk Turks, once merely a raiding nuisance on the empire's eastern marches, were now taking power in the Muslim lands and were challenging the empire for supremacy in the east. Under their sultan, Alp Arslan, they had developed into a conquering army.

The Battle of Manzikert in August 1071 was the pivotal point in the overall fortunes of the eastern Roman Empire. The Roman defeat is frequently characterized as the loss of a well-trained and organized eastern Roman army, after which the empire and the army went into a decline. However, while the army at Manzikert did suffer heavy losses, and the emperor who commanded that army, Romanos IV, was captured, many eastern Roman units remained intact and withdrew from the field unmolested by the victorious Turks. Romanos was later released, but his 'homecoming' was a disaster, and it was the internal problems that followed, added to the defeat of territory, which damaged the empire.

The Battle

Romanus marshalled the army and led it out against the Turks, the two sides facing each other at the Armenian fortress town of Manzikert on 26 August 1071. Even though Romanus had to contend with wavering support from some of his subordinates, one of whom left the field with his troops before the battle, the eastern Romans

◄ INFANTRYMAN, 11TH CENTURY *A rearview of an infantryman with a different type of headgear, which gives better protection to the head and neck. This would be the appearance of an eastern Roman heavy infantryman at the time of Basil II.*

initially enjoyed success against the Turks. That changed when some of the eastern Roman nobles betrayed their army and their emperor by treacherously abandoning the field. The bulk of the army, under Romanus, was then surrounded and

▼ INFANTRYMAN, 11TH CENTURY
Eastern Roman infantry wore various types of headgear, this one being very Turkish in appearance. This gives an excellent view of the infantryman's padded 'coat' worn during this period. The length of the spear, or pike, is not exaggerated, and the eastern Romans would make this out of a single piece of wood for its natural strength. The shield was now kite-shaped, as in western Europe, demonstrating definite western influence.

slaughtered. The emperor was captured with his survivors, and forced to bow to the victorious sultan. Roman power and prestige in Armenia was shattered, and the rot spread through Asia Minor.

Aftermath

This defeat was far-ranging in its results. Much of what is now Asia Minor consequently fell to the Turks, as the Roman losses at Manzikert were so severe that the

▼ INFANTRYMAN, 11TH CENTURY
Though this is the same time period as the figures to the left, a conical steel helmet is worn here. This is without any identifying plume or coloured horsehair tuft. Noteworthy are the infantryman's boots – solidly constructed and comfortable, the most essential piece of equipment for active service.

army was unable to recover immediately. Much of the theme system, and with it the recruiting grounds used by the eastern Romans for hundreds of years, was also destroyed, and mercenaries were to become once again dominant, or at least a significant part of the army. The native soldiery of the army was almost completely destroyed.

Romanos was humiliated by his defeat and subsequent capture, and upon his return to Constantinople he was defeated in more fighting by the powerful Doukas family. Subsequently, he was deposed, blinded, and exiled, the circumstances of the blinding eventually killing him. The loss to the Turks (against a commander who would later face, and lose to the heavy cavalry of the western Europeans of the 1st Crusade in the late 1090s) was overwhelming and completely avoidable. The sense of loss went beyond the amount of troops killed or taken, and the loss of prestige amongst the empire's enemies.

Meanwhile the empire was plunged into ten years of bloody civil war, and it was this that ruined the army, and began a period of long decline for the empire. Never again would the empire be in the condition it was at the death of Basil II earlier in the century.

In short, the eastern Roman Empire could very well have recovered from the defeat at Manzikert if it hadn't been for the disastrous civil war that followed. Only when the Comnenus dynasty came to the throne in 1081 would the decline be arrested. The Roman civil war that followed, combined with an army that was not only depleted, but in disarray, allowed the Turks to conquer and plunder almost at will.

Roman Infantry

The infantry arm of the Roman army during this period really did not change in appearance, and once the army began to recover, after the Battle of Manzikert, some of the old standards were reintroduced.

Arms and armour remained

▲ INFANTRYMAN, 12TH CENTURY *Well protected in lamellar-type armour and wearing an oddly shaped Phrygian type helmet, this infantryman is shown with sword and shield, as he would be armed in a melee, the spear being too long for close work. Noteworthy here are the high calf-length boots, which were becoming more common in the period, more usually, however, for cavalry.*

the same, however, as did the organization of the infantry. Emperor Alexis I cautiously allowed the European Crusaders to cross the empire's territory in the First Crusade, and also took this opportunity of a foreign invasion of the Turkish lands to take back some of the eastern Roman territory lost after the catastrophic defeat at Manzikert.

THE POST-MANZIKERT ARMY

After the defeat at Manzikert the eastern Romans began to come in contact with the encroaching and land-hungry Normans now present in southern Italy and Sicily, as well as those who were a part of the army of the 1st Crusade. The Normans willingly fought the eastern Romans for territory, and while the eastern Romans were finally able to hold the Normans at bay, the fighting was bitter, especially as both warring parties were Christians with a common enemy of the preeminent Muslim threat still a frightening prospect.

The Comnenian Dynasty (1081–1185)

The advent of the Comnenian Dynasty after the disaster at Manzikert, and the devastating 10-year civil war that followed, ushered in what many believed was to be an eastern Roman resurgence. Alexis I, the first of the Comnenians, was a competent emperor who ruled well and set the stage for his son, John II, dubbed 'the Beautiful' and who, luckily for the Romans, was also an excellent general and commander.

Taking the offensive against the deadly Turks, the new emperor not only took back important lands in Asia Minor that had once been Roman territory, but he also proved himself adept at siege warfare. In order to do this John II continued the work of his father in rebuilding the sagging Roman army and

reinstituting the old standards of training, leadership, and organization that once again made it a force to reckon with.

The rebuilt and regenerated Roman army successfully campaigned in Asia Minor, the Balkans and Egypt, as well as Palestine and even Hungary. Generally speaking, under the inspired leadership of John II and his son Manuel I, the Roman army grew in skill and confidence. Old provinces were reclaimed and reconquered and native troops flocked once again to the banners of the eastern empire.

◄ MEDIUM CAVALRYMAN, 10TH–11TH CENTURIES *More like a western medieval knight in appearance, this type of Roman cavalryman was able to remain in battle contact with the enemy for longer, because of the relative lightness of his arms and equipment compared to a cataphract. Their horses would not be used up or winded so quickly. They were sometimes mistaken for cataphracts and would engage the enemy in charges, supported by horse archers.*

▶ INFANTRYMAN 11TH–12TH CENTURIES *After the disastrous Battle of Manzikert there followed 10 years of civil war that damaged the empire, and the army, perhaps even more than Manzikert did. The remnant of the army that escaped the battle was largely destroyed in the civil wars and had to be rebuilt by the Comnenian dynasty. This is an infantryman at the beginning of that period. Not as well equipped as the army had been before Manzikert, and with a larger shield, he would perform the same function as his predecessors.*

◀ CATAPHRACT, COMNENIAN ARMIES, 11TH–12TH CENTURIES *The Comnenian dynasty rebuilt the eastern Roman army after the civil wars and still fielded excellent heavy cavalry which was now very much eastern in appearance. The layered armour of the cataphracts was excellent in both construction and protection, each layer made of a different material. This skilful use of padded clothing and armour made it almost impenetrable to western weapons of the period.*

▶ HORSE ARCHER, 10TH–12TH CENTURIES *The horse archer remained a mainstay of the eastern Roman army for centuries. Well-armed, mounted and equipped, and armed with the excellent Roman composite bow, he would work in concert with medium and heavy cavalry on the battlefield, providing mobile fire support. His dress at this period is more eastern than western and light enough for both mobility and protection.*

Unfortunately, eastern Roman fortunes took a turn for the worse on the death on Manuel I in 1180. His successors were not up to the task of maintaining the improved army and defending a hard-won empire.

The Normans

During the reign of Alexis I the era of the great crusades from western Europe began. The aid of the west had been summoned by Alexis, but the huge western European force that travelled through the eastern empire, albeit in stages, was alarming to the emperor. In it he met an aggressive western European power – the Normans – a formidable foe well remembered by the Anglo-Saxon Varangians from the invasion of England in 1066. Alexis

was understandably wary of them. The Normans eyed the lands of the eastern empire with envy and were determined to make gains in that part of the world, as they had in both England, Italy and Sicily. Normans under Robert Guiscard had already fought against Alexis in 1081 when Alexis took the throne, during the ten-year civil war. This continued until Guiscard's death in 1085. Subsequently, the land taken by the Normans was slowly recovered, but these gains were under threat with the coming of the crusading armies, one of them led by Robert's son, Bohemond, later known as Prince of Antioch. Alexis was at once wary and forearmed. As Bohemond kept moving eastward, the threat passed, and Alexis was able to attend to more pressing matters, fighting enemies in every quarter and attempting to rebuild the empire.

The Comnenian Army

The eastern Roman infantryman in this period wore different armour and carried different equipment than his better equipped and trained predecessors. The shield was now kite-shaped, probably because of western

influence. The infantryman generally wore less armour, and only on his upper body and torso, and the helmet was much simpler in design and function. A sword and spear or lance completed the infantryman's appearance and equipment.

The cavalry was still the mainstay of the eastern Roman army and the three types of cavalrymen were still employed by the army. None of these were changed in appearance or function since before the Battle of Manzikert, but as the native portion of the army decreased and mercenaries began to dominate the ranks, the general appearance and function of the mounted arm of the army was beginning to change for the worse, and lessen in both efficiency and function.

THE ANGELUS DYNASTY AND THE END OF THE OLD EMPIRE 1185–1204

The successor dynasty to the competent Comnenians was the Angelus Dynasty, which ruled from 1185–1204. In short, they were incompetent and not only did the army suffer neglect and defeat under their rule, but it was under Isaac II and his son Alesis IV that the empire was put under attack by the perfidy of the 4th Crusade from western Europe, in conjunction with the greed and betrayal of the Venetians.

Seeing the incompetence of the new dynasty as well as their general neglect of the eastern Roman army and navy, the enemies of the empire plotted and closed in for the kill.

The untimely attack by the Europeans of the 4th Crusade was probably a shock only for the Romans, but a boon for the empire's other enemies.

The knights and troops of the 4th Crusade assaulted Constantinople from the sea and finally got a foothold on the city's ramparts. The Varangian Guard died to a man defending the city, but the European crusaders were not to be denied. The city, and the empire fell and a Latin empire was established in its stead. This only lasted until 1261 when the eastern Romans took back their capital and surrounding territory. But the damage had been done and it was only a matter of time before the eastern Roman Empire, once the bulwark of Christendom against all the enemies from the east, would fall.

Heavy Cavalry Standards

With a few exceptions heavy cavalrymen were the epitome of the eastern Roman heavy cavalry of the middle period of the empire. What is

◀ CAVALRYMAN, 11TH CENTURY *Medium cavalrymen were probably more numerous in the eastern Roman order of battle than the more expensive cataphracts. Still, the arms and armour worn cost money that the state could ill-afford. Note the coloured horsehair plume on the helmet and shoulders, which matches his shield.*

▶ MEDIUM CAVALRYMAN, 10TH CENTURY *Too much emphasis cannot be placed on the importance of the eastern Roman cavalry arm in its effectiveness in countering the cavalry armies from the east, and on the merits of the different types (horse archer, medium cavalry and the cataphracts). Here is a medium cavalryman wearing different personal protection, but still with lance pennant and helmet plume in unit colours. Sometimes cavalry shields were as small as this figure's, as it was easy to carry and allowed better use of arms.*

noteworthy, and was an essential part of the unit organization of the eastern Roman army, was the banner standard; a fabric flag with 'tails'. Usually, cavalry standards of this type had between three and five tails, which signified the size of the designated unit and the colours defined the unit identification. The cross insignia was often used on the banner, a typical motif for eastern

Roman civil and military trappings, as religion was central to the eastern Roman administration. Christianity and the Church played a very important part in the cultural, legal and military life of the eastern Romans.

▼ INFANTRYMAN, 11TH–12TH CENTURIES *Clothing during this period was becoming more elaborate, even for infantrymen. Embroidery was common, and the army was taking on a distinctively eastern look. While this infantryman is armed and equipped in a more up-to-date manner, he is still the basic infantryman of the empire. Note the helmet and how the infantryman's neck is partially protected from sword strokes.*

Shields

The shields of this period were either round or kite-shaped, and of different sizes. The kite-shaped shields were new to the eastern Roman army and were undoubtedly introduced because of contact with western European armies, either as allies, observers, or in fighting their encroachment into empire lands.

Unit Distinctions

The coloured plumes on the helmets and the lance pennons were also an indicator of unit identification and would match the colours on the banner standards.

The armour on all of these cavalrymen is undoubtedly eastern Roman at this period, and that would only begin to change with outside influences after the disaster at

▶ CAVALRYMAN, 11TH CENTURY *In addition to helmet plume and lance pennant colours for unit identification, units also had marker flags for each unit in the chain of command, marked in the unit's identifying colour. The number of tails on the guidon denoted how many subunits were controlled by the unit indicated, and each tail was in the colour of the subordinate unit. These pennants were most helpful in rallying a defeated unit or after a melee.*

Manzikert in 1071 and the reorganization of the eastern Roman army in the 10 years of civil war and general unrest that followed this lost battle.

THE ISLAMIC THREAT

The most serious threat to the eastern Romans, and the one that would ultimately conquer Constantinople, was the one that arose out of the Arabian desert and swept across North Africa and into Spain. The new threat was both a religion and a form of conquest – the rise of Islam. And it struck just as the eastern Romans under Heraclius had finally defeated the Persian empire, which was now exhausted.

Islamic Power Rises in the East

The first onslaught came from the Arab desert tribes, such as the Umayyads, Abassids and Azarbayjanis, who united under Mohammed's banner. More than a desert nomad and founder of what would eventually be one of the world's great religions, Mohammed was also a soldier, and his 'movement' to spread the word of Allah was one of conquest. Uniting the tribes was a feat of leadership that the Arab world had not experienced before, and now, mounted on horse and camel, their armies swept all before them.

The Muslim juggernaut also moved north through the Middle East to the borders of the eastern Roman Empire and beyond; halted in 732 by Charles Martel near Tours, France, the Islamic hold on Spain was only finally terminated in 1492 by King Ferdinand and Queen Isabella.

The Muslim army was a daunting sight. The disparate tribes and peoples collected and converted to Islam would all have their own tribal, clan or family banners and this added both a colourful and daunting aspect to a Muslim army. The number of flags and banners could give the impression of more numbers than were actually in the field, giving the Muslim armies a psychological advantage even before the clash of arms.

◄ ANSARI WARRIOR, 8TH–9TH CENTURIES AD
The men who first followed Mohammed were from Medina and became known as Ansari or 'supporters'. They were infused with the fanaticism of a new-found religion and burst out of the desert to make war on anyone who had not embraced Islam. Well-armed, and with stirrups, troops such as these defeated multiple enemies and took huge areas of territory. Traditional headgear was modified for military use, usually a turban that was wrapped around the helmet when on duty.

▲ UMAYYAD INFANTRYMAN, 8TH CENTURY AD
The Umayyad house was one of the major clans of the Quraysh tribe. In many respects, this Arab infantryman is similar to his eastern Roman foes, and quite possibly superior to other enemies across North Africa.

The Arab Armies

Lamellar armour, colourful garments, some of them with intricate and colourful embroidery, and made for both comfort and utility, were the hallmark of the Arab and other Muslim peoples that combined to make an almost all-conquering army that respected no boundaries in the name of religion. Arms and armour

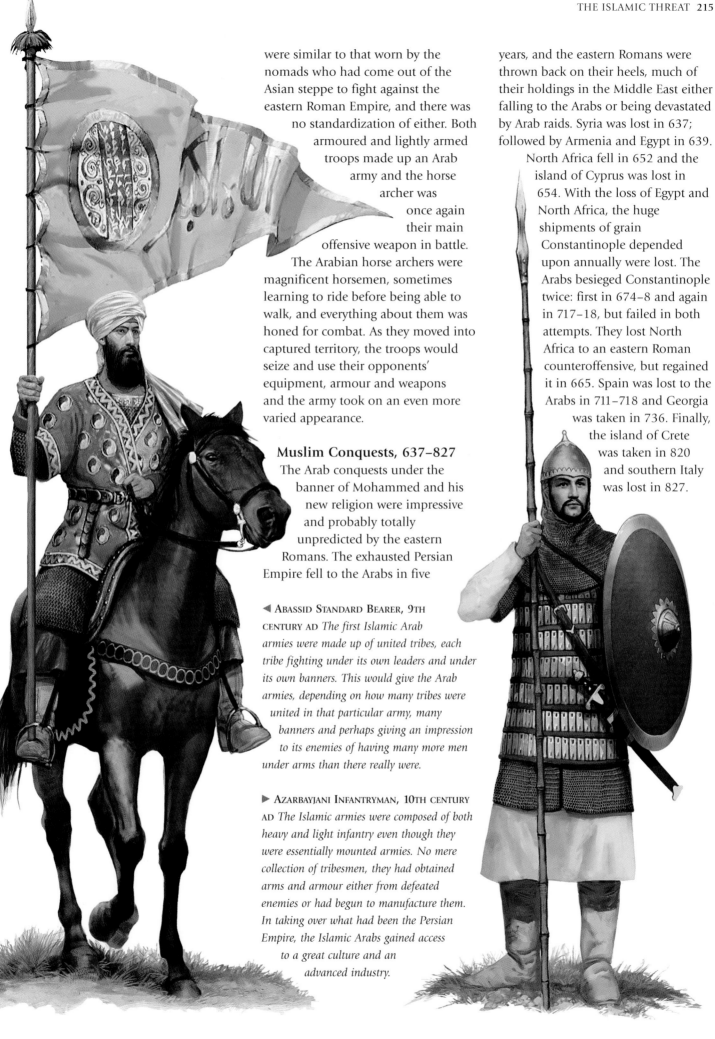

were similar to that worn by the nomads who had come out of the Asian steppe to fight against the eastern Roman Empire, and there was no standardization of either. Both armoured and lightly armed troops made up an Arab army and the horse archer was once again their main offensive weapon in battle. The Arabian horse archers were magnificent horsemen, sometimes learning to ride before being able to walk, and everything about them was honed for combat. As they moved into captured territory, the troops would seize and use their opponents' equipment, armour and weapons and the army took on an even more varied appearance.

Muslim Conquests, 637–827

The Arab conquests under the banner of Mohammed and his new religion were impressive and probably totally unpredicted by the eastern Romans. The exhausted Persian Empire fell to the Arabs in five

◄ ABASSID STANDARD BEARER, 9TH CENTURY AD *The first Islamic Arab armies were made up of united tribes, each tribe fighting under its own leaders and under its own banners. This would give the Arab armies, depending on how many tribes were united in that particular army, many banners and perhaps giving an impression to its enemies of having many more men under arms than there really were.*

▶ AZARBAYJANI INFANTRYMAN, 10TH CENTURY AD *The Islamic armies were composed of both heavy and light infantry even though they were essentially mounted armies. No mere collection of tribesmen, they had obtained arms and armour either from defeated enemies or had begun to manufacture them. In taking over what had been the Persian Empire, the Islamic Arabs gained access to a great culture and an advanced industry.*

years, and the eastern Romans were thrown back on their heels, much of their holdings in the Middle East either falling to the Arabs or being devastated by Arab raids. Syria was lost in 637; followed by Armenia and Egypt in 639. North Africa fell in 652 and the island of Cyprus was lost in 654. With the loss of Egypt and North Africa, the huge shipments of grain Constantinople depended upon annually were lost. The Arabs besieged Constantinople twice: first in 674–8 and again in 717–18, but failed in both attempts. They lost North Africa to an eastern Roman counteroffensive, but regained it in 665. Spain was lost to the Arabs in 711–718 and Georgia was taken in 736. Finally, the island of Crete was taken in 820 and southern Italy was lost in 827.

Muslim Against Muslim

As the Arabs and their allies were conquered by the newly emerging Turkish armies, who had also adopted the Muslim faith, the Islamic armies became much more efficient. The Arabs probably could never have taken Constantinople by siege, and soon the Seljuk Turks supplanted the Arabs in the Muslim lands. Caliphates rose and fell, and under the surface of a Muslim monolith, different sultans warred on each other, an opportunity that the eastern Roman emperors failed to take.

Each of the three Muslim waves of conquest, however, were deadlier than the previous one. The Seljuk Turks overran the initial Arab conquests, but it was the coming of the Ottomans and their ruthless and efficient

government and institutions that were eventually strong enough to take on the weakened eastern Romans. They also built and manned an efficient navy that was coming into its own just as the once-redoubtable eastern Roman navy was disappearing as a formidable force in the Mediterranean. The ascendancy of the Ottomans sounded the death knell of the eastern Roman Empire.

Seljuk Turks

The Seljuk Turks had been ruled by the Romans for about 1,000 years before striking out on their own after their conversion to Islam. Their infantry usually wore lamellar armour and their cavalry were well-armed with sword, lance and shield. Shields were circular, and helmets usually came to a point, often with a turban wrapped around the bottom. Sometimes cloaks or long coats were worn outside the armour, giving them the appearance of not being armoured at all, a deceptive and a deadly assumption.

The Turkish horse archers were formidable enemies and looked very

◀ TURKISH HORSE ARCHER, 12TH CENTURY *The Seljuk Turks turned from Nomadic warriors and raiders into first-class conquerors. The ankle-length kaftan-like garment worn here must have been difficult to ride in. His bow is the short composite eastern bow common to horse archers, and its carrier, or sheath, is attached to his sword belt with arrows on the opposite hip. He wears the leather wrist guards common to experienced bowmen.*

▶ TURKISH SPAHI, 14TH CENTURY *The Ottoman Turks 'replaced' the Seljuk Turks as the dominate Islamic power in the east and it would be the Ottomans who finally destroyed the remnants of the eastern Roman Empire from 1453–61. The spahis were elite Ottoman heavy cavalry, heavily armed and armoured as shown. He wears his shield slung on his back and carries a mace, a common Turkish weapon of the period. The wrist guards have a double function – to protect his wrists when firing arrows and also in close combat. He carries his sword in a bow case attached to his belt on his left hip.*

similar to the eastern Roman horse archers of the 10th century. Armed and equipped as mounted archers, they were well-led and disciplined and were an excellent striking arm on the field.

The Ottomans

By 1328 the Ottoman Turks, who inherited the Islamic empire, were bent on destroying what was left of the eastern Roman Empire. From 1328–41 the eastern Romans, under the emperor Andronicus III, attempted to establish some type of Roman hegemony in the eastern Mediterranean, and although meeting with initial success, this offensive ran out of steam against considerable Ottoman

the main differences being in the style of armour and that they were always armed with a powerful bow in addition to their other weapons. Their horses were also armoured. The Ottomans also fielded a medium cavalry as the eastern Romans once did, which had the same function and were flexible with horsemen capable of acting in different roles.

▶ FARGHANA CAVALRYMAN, 11TH CENTURY *Farghana was in a strategic location on the old Silk Road trade route and thus important to the new Islamic caliphates. Whether or not Islamic troops from Farghana came as far west as Palestine is unknown, but the appearance of these cavalrymen was close to many Islamic cavalrymen.*

Ottoman Infantry

There were a number of kinds of regular and irregular infantry and their arms and equipment reflected local traditions within the Ottoman territories. The most famous were undoubtedly the janissaries. Ottoman janissaries were an outstandingly tough, well-trained infantry arm that would lead the assaults on Constantinople that would finally succeed in 1453. Recruited from non-Turkish elements within the Ottoman empire, they would eventually become kingmakers, like the old western Roman Praetorian Guard, and in the long run weakened the Ottoman sultanate and made that empire prey to others, such as the Russians in the 18th century.

▲ OTTOMAN GHAZI, 14TH CENTURY
Ghazi in Arabic translates as to strive, aspire, or carry out. The related word ghazawan 'to carry out a military expedition' is derived from this root. Ghazi warriors depended on plunder for their livelihood and were fluid in organization, jumping between leaders and factions, depending on their prestige and success. The Ottoman ghazi differed little in arms and armour to his Roman opponents.

strength. Once again, civil war followed in eastern Rome, and left a weakened empire little more than a vassal state to the Ottomans.

Ottoman Cavalry

The Ottoman Turkish heavy cavalry, or Spahis, were similar to the eastern Roman cataphracts in their prime,

THE VARANGIAN GUARD

The Varangian Guard is arguably the most famous unit of the eastern Roman army and empire and this is unfortunate, for it gives the impression of the eastern Romans relying mainly on mercenaries to defend them. The Varangians were excellent troops, reliable and loyal, but they were mainly employed for only three centuries out of the thousand-year eastern empire, and while valuable to both study and appreciate, they were never the mainstay of the eastern Roman army.

The first Varangians are thought to have been Christianized Russians and Scandinavians who served in the time of Constantine Porphyrogenitus (*c*.930–50). Under Basil II, the troops from the land of Kievan Rus were organized into a separate unit that became known as the Varangian guard. Whether these initial troops were Scandinavian or Slavonic is still open to dispute, but from the founding of the Varangian Guard to the end of the 11th century, the major component of the unit was indeed Scandinavian, recruited from Rus' principalities, and later from Sweden, Norway, Iceland, Denmark and Anglo-Saxons refugees from Norman England.

Unusual Guards

The Varangians were atypical of the eastern Roman army, especially when they were formed by Basil II around 988. Although they were classed as guard troops, it appears they were also employed as shock troops on the battlefield. They fought stoutly, generally refusing to give up ground, and sometimes fought to the last man.

After the Saxon defeat in England in 1066 by William of Normandy (also known as William the Conqueror), Saxon troops looking for a new homeland after refusing to serve

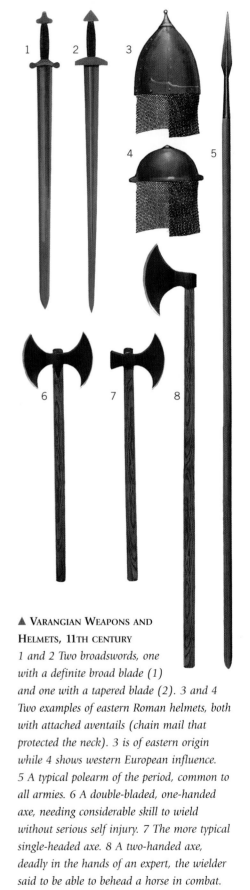

◀ VARANGIAN GUARDSMAN, 10TH CENTURY
Roman Guards were often mercenaries instead of native troops. Emperors and generals in the field benefitted from the fact that the mercenaries were loyal to them personally as long as they were paid regularly. This guardsman is armed and equipped both lavishly and expensively. The axe was a favourite weapon, usually two-handed, a fearsome weapon in the hands of an expert.

▲ VARANGIAN WEAPONS AND HELMETS, 11TH CENTURY
1 and 2 Two broadswords, one with a definite broad blade (1) and one with a tapered blade (2). 3 and 4 Two examples of eastern Roman helmets, both with attached aventails (chain mail that protected the neck). 3 is of eastern origin while 4 shows western European influence. 5 A typical polearm of the period, common to all armies. 6 A double-bladed, one-handed axe, needing considerable skill to wield without serious self injury. 7 The more typical single-headed axe. 8 A two-handed axe, deadly in the hands of an expert, the wielder said to be able to behead a horse in combat.

▲ SHIELDS, 11TH CENTURY
This selection of round and kite-shaped shields, with various markings, show the different types of shields used by eastern Roman troops from the 11th century. The kite-shaped shields are adopted from western European designs, while the round shields are typical of those used traditionally by the eastern Romans and their enemies. The markings would show either the identity of the owner, or the identity of the unit to which he was assigned.

William, took employment with the Varangians. Apparently, there were also Scandinavian Varangians in Saxon England before the Norman Conquest, and survivors undoubtedly went east with their Saxon comrades-in-arms.

The original contingent of Varangians enlisted by the eastern Romans could have numbered as high as 6,000. Apparently, they were not reformed after the resurrection of the eastern Roman empire.

Two-Handed Axe
The Varangians' favourite weapon was the long-handled or two-handed axe. While they were well-equipped with other auxiliary weapons, it was the axe that the troops favoured and they wielded it effectively.

Clothing
The Varangians eventually came to wear the colourful and embroidered overgarments of the eastern Romans. Being of Russian, Anglo-Saxon, and Nordic stock, many were blonde, and large for their time. It is also likely that as time went on, the majority of the guardsmen was made up of Saxons, or Anglo-Saxons.

▶ VARANGIAN GUARDSMAN, 11TH CENTURY
This guardsman is armed with a two-handed axe, often used without a shield, or a shield would be strapped to his back for later use if the axe was lost. His general appearance is close to the Saxon housecarls (bodyguard) of King Harold of England, with the addition of eastern Roman embroidered trousers, and armour on his forearms and calves. His helmet is Anglo-Saxon in style.

▶ VARANGIAN SHIELD, 11TH CENTURY *The typical kite-shaped shield of western European origin. The owner's own device may be displayed, or as a Varangian, it might be a unit insignia. Bird motifs were common.*

THE EMPIRE FALLS

The last emperor of the eastern Roman empire was Constantine XI, of the Paleologus dynasty. By the time the Ottomans attacked Constantinople the city was virtually all that remained of the empire's territories. Constantinople itself was underpopulated and dilapidated, and between 1346 and 1349 had lost almost half of its citizens to the plague.

Although eastern Roman emperors had recently attempted to reach an accommodation with the Turkish leaders, the Ottomans were now an expanding empire and in their view any truce with Constantinople was just a breathing space until they could muster enough strength to take the city. Mehmet II, the Ottoman sultan, and eastern Roman emperor Constantine XI did not like each other. Constantine's military operations in Greece interfered with Mehmet's desires and ideas of expansion into the Balkans, and Mehmet

▲ CATAPHRACT, 12TH CENTURY *This cavalryman is armed for close combat with sword and shield, and his shield has Greek markings, denoting the melding of the Greek and Latin cultures in the eastern empire.*

◀ HORSE ARCHER, 11TH CENTURY *At the time of Manzikert, the eastern Roman horse archers were still in their traditional and functional clothing along with their traditional weapons. The horse archer, copied from eastern opponents of the empire in the beginning of the 5th century, made himself decisive on the battlefields of the empire against varied and myriad enemies.*

decided to finally rid himself of the spent power of the eastern Romans. By the time the Ottomans appeared in front of the city to begin siege operations, the eastern Roman army was a shadow of what it had been. The eastern Roman navy was nonexistent, and although naval forces from Genoa and Venice came to help in the defence, they were no match for the navy of the Ottoman Empire.

After Constantinople fell, all that was left of the 1,000-years-old empire was a few scattered Roman outposts that held out against the Ottomans before being overwhelmed in 1460–1.

Western Military Influence

By the end of the eastern Roman Empire, the army had taken on a distinctive western European look. The heavily armoured horsemen, no longer cataphracts, looked more like western heavy cavalry and plate armour was in evidence among both the infantry and cavalry.

▶ CAVALRYMAN, 14TH CENTURY *Late eastern Roman cavalrymen could easily have been mistaken for a western European man-at-arms from the helmet, armour and weapons. Uniquely, however, the surcoat, or long undergarment is worn under the armour, instead of over, so was not used for identification. When mounted, this horseman would also wear a sword and belt, and a shield that could be attached to his saddle to give him more freedom of movement on foot.*

The earlier cataphract had clearly shown the elaborate armour and dress of an eastern Roman heavy cavalryman with his panoply of personal weapons. This eventually changed into more western-looking armour and accoutrements, and the ubiquitous presence of the western-inspired kite-shaped shield was probably universal by the end of the 12th century. Mail became the preferred choice in body armour,

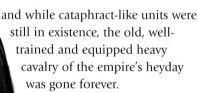

and while cataphract-like units were still in existence, the old, well-trained and equipped heavy cavalry of the empire's heyday was gone forever.

In many ways, however, the eastern Roman army, while also shrinking to under 10,000 regular troops, was becoming militarily bankrupt, and the native population base had decreased to the point of the army being almost entirely composed of mercenaries. These troops, however, fought well in defence of the city and the rump of an empire that remained.

▶ CAVALRYMAN, 12TH–13TH CENTURIES *This tunic is more colourful than was usually found in western Europe, though the Europeans that remained in the Holy Land did adopt eastern clothing and armour. The absence of leg and arm protection is unusual, and the use of scale armour is sparse.*

ROMAN ARTILLERY, FORTIFICATIONS, AND NAVY 753BC–1453

Whether it was building fortifications, from the camps at the end of a day's march, to permanent fortifications such as Hadrian's Wall or the Black Gate at Trier, the Roman army excelled at military architecture and were preeminent in the art of siege works. The Romans also created a powerful and useful navy, first to fight the Carthaginians, and later to control the Mediterranean, the Roman's Mare Nostrum. In a variety of roles – sweeping pirates away from preying on Roman merchant ships, raiding towns along a Roman coastline, manning a river flotilla in central Europe, or fighting an enemy fleet – the Romans learned the lessons of being a naval power.

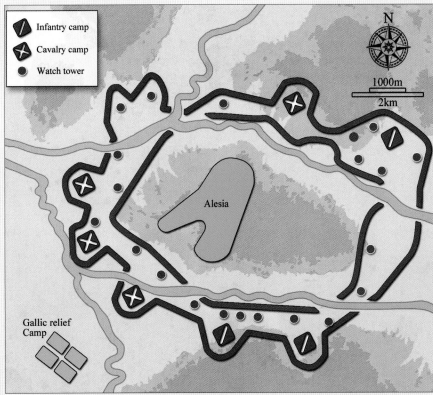

▲ *The siege works erected at Alesia, in 52BC, by Julius Caesar. Interior walls were surrounded by another series of works, facing outwards to protect the siege from attack.*

◄ *Diocletian was one of the few Roman emperors that retired. He built this palace/fortress at the port of Split in Croatia, where from May 305AD he spent a comfortable retirement.*

ROMAN ENGINEERING
AND PROWESS AT SEA

The power of the Roman Empire is usually symbolized by its legions, but it was not by its infantry-heavy troops alone that Rome built the sprawling empire that encompassed not only the Mediterranean world from Gibraltar to Palestine and Egypt, but also northwards into Germany and finally to Britain.

The legions brought along with them their artillery – the catapults of various designs and sizes that supplemented the legion when on defensive campaigns and during sieges. And out of strategic necessity, the Romans were also forced to develop and build a navy – awkward at first, but one that progressively improved. This naval tradition would be taken up by the eastern Romans and their navy eventually dominated the Mediterranean against all comers.

Roman Artillery

Artillery is neither a modern invention nor merely a product of the development of gunpowder. Artillery's origins are ancient but Roman launchers of projectiles, of whatever type, were revolutionary, designed to

▲ *A Roman siege, showing a battering ram being used to break in a gate, three testudos being used against the wall, and a ballista and an early trebuchet in the front.*

do their enemies as much harm as possible in order to support the infantry of their legion. The Romans were great exponents of their artillery arm and as the legion developed into a permanent military force, artillery became an integral part of the legion on campaign.

Roman period artillery pieces were usually referred to as catapults, and

they launched different types of projectiles in both field operations and sieges. Eventually the Roman legions would all be equipped with these field pieces. At one point, the usual allotment of artillery per legion was 64 pieces of varying size and purpose, and these could be broken down into component parts for transport with the legion, not as an auxiliary to the legion.

▼ *A relief of a Roman naval galley. This vessel is foreshortened by the artist; in reality galleys were long, graceful vessels.*

▼ *Roman legionaries construct the standard 'marching camp' on campaign, depicted on a portion of Trajan's column.*

Siege Warfare and Fortifications

The Romans army's persistence and genius for siege operations allowed the reduction of large fortresses in such disparate regions as Gaul and Palestine, and on the civilian side (which inevitably assisted military and naval operations) constructing a long-lasting road and bridge network, many of which are not only still standing, but are still in use in Germany and Spain. The Romans built to last.

The Roman Navy

What the Romans achieved on land was made possible by the development of a formidable navy that eventually triumphed over Rome's enemies at sea, initially against the excellent and expert Carthaginian navy, but also in eliminating pirate fleets and in supporting the legions on Europe's navigable rivers such as the Rhine and the Danube. The Roman navy also supported the Roman invasions of Britain, enabling Rome to incorporate over half of Britain into the empire.

Rome began its long list of conquests on the Italian mainland until it was forced by circumstances to develop into a sea power too. Following the example of her more sea-going neighbours, Rome quickly adapted, establishing an awkward navy

▼ An artist's view of a Roman bridge from the 2nd century BC. Roman military bridge-building techniques were quite modern, and their construction was both strong and simple.

▲ An excellent artist's view of the siege works at Alesia. The seige tower is armed with an onager, named 'wild ass' by the Roman legionaries because it jumped when fired.

to face the almost overwhelming threat of the great Mediterranean seapower, Carthage. Willing to learn and determined to win, the Romans became skilled enough to build their own galleys to challenge 'mighty Carthage' at sea. Recognizing that they were new to the sea, and especially to warfare at sea, the Romans adapted their galleys to reflect their expertise in fighting on land.

As Roman naval skill increased over time, they eventually developed considerable skill as ship builders and seamen. By the time of the fall of the western empire, the Romans were very formidable in naval warfare indeed, as well as having developed considerable amphibious capability, and mastered naval logistics. These skills would be passed on to the later eastern empire, where they would continue to grow.

▼ A depiction of a galley from the 14th century. Noteworthy is the fighting tower, or 'castle' on the galley's forecastle, from which archers would fire down on their opponents.

ARTILLERY AND SIEGE WARFARE

Roman artillery was of two distinct types, what would later be known as field and siege artillery. Field artillery could be easily transported by the army and used on the battlefield. Siege artillery was of larger construction, was generally immobile once constructed and was designed to damage or destroy enemy fortifications. It was more powerful than field artillery and took an extra effort to transport. Both types, however, had the same operational technique – they threw missiles designed to hurt and destroy the enemy, be they in the open in battle or behind fixed defences in a siege.

The catapults and ballistae could be taken apart for ease of transport; when the battle position was reached, the artillery was ordered into action and the various 'field pieces' were then assembled by their crews.

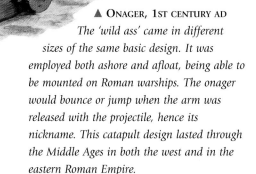

▲ ONAGER, 1ST CENTURY AD
The 'wild ass' came in different sizes of the same basic design. It was employed both ashore and afloat, being able to be mounted on Roman warships. The onager would bounce or jump when the arm was released with the projectile, hence its nickname. This catapult design lasted through the Middle Ages in both the west and in the eastern Roman Empire.

Artillery Dress and Armour

There is no evidence of any particular uniform for Roman artillerymen. They were taken from the ranks of the centuries and cohorts of the legion itself and were not distinguished from the other legionaries by any special designation of their function. Tunics would be the same colour and design as that of the legionary, as were the weapons and armour.

Onager

Roman artillery design developed from that used by the Greeks, but was adapted over the years by Roman engineers into several different types. The onager was very typical in structure and deployment. It was a catapult designed and built on a rectangular base, which could be fitted with either a sling on the end for projectiles or a type of 'spoon' on a moveable arm, which held the projectile and then 'threw' it when the lever was released. Most of the evidence points to the

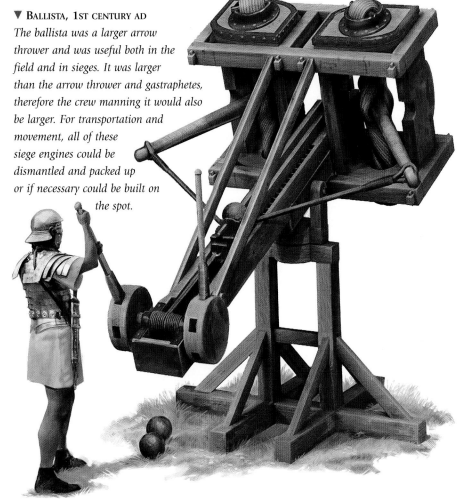

▼ BALLISTA, 1ST CENTURY AD
The ballista was a larger arrow thrower and was useful both in the field and in sieges. It was larger than the arrow thrower and gastraphetes, therefore the crew manning it would also be larger. For transportation and movement, all of these siege engines could be dismantled and packed up or if necessary could be built on the spot.

onager being without wheels on the rectangular frame, but later designs suggest they were added; though this might have been outside this period.

The onager was nicknamed the 'wild ass' as it jumped considerably when fired. Some authorities believe the onager did not come into use until the middle of the 4th century AD, but it is hard to understand why such a simple and effective catapult was not developed earlier.

The onager came in different sizes, possibly categorized by the weight of stone shot that it threw (as gunpowder artillery pieces would be rated after the 14th century and even into the 19th century), and the number of artillery crewmen would of course increase with the larger onagers. It was an effective catapult, was metal-reinforced, and would survive into the eastern

Roman army as well as the European armies of the Middle Ages.

Ballista

The ballista, or 'arrow thrower' was an engine that threw various types and sizes of large arrows depending on the size of the ballista. There were many examples of this type of engine and the size of the 'gun crew' would depend on the size of the ballista. The earlier Greek models were known as 'stone throwers' and all of them seem to have been designed as large crossbows, whether or not they threw stones of various weights or large arrows.

The most common size of ballista was that which threw a 60-pound 'round'. This was also a torsion 'powered' artillery piece and became more sophisticated as the republic and empire progressed in their warfare and siege techniques. Like the small arrow firer, it was constructed with a type of crossbow mechanism, was stationary once emplaced, and was enhanced in construction with metal parts that reinforced all the stress points. It was, as were all of these artillery pieces, both effective and deadly and was one of the reasons that the Roman army was so successful at siege warfare.

▼ **ARROW THROWER, 1ST CENTURY AD**
The arrow thrower was a simple artillery piece that would fire a single, arrow-like projectile in the manner of a large crossbow. The crew would be one or two men and this piece could be placed on the wall of a fortress or Roman encampment as well as on the deck of a Roman galley.

▲ **GASTRAPHETES, 1ST CENTURY AD**
The gastraphetes was a larger version of the arrow thrower that could fire two larger missiles. This was also a simple artillery piece that could be employed in various places to advantage. The bow could not be drawn by manpower alone and was equipped with a winch at the rear of the piece.

Arrow Thrower

A smaller torsion catapult that fired arrows was also in use, which could be put into action and manned by two crewmen. It was a simple artillery piece and quite effective at short ranges. This 'model' of arrow firer was also a new design of field piece and was an improvement over older designs, different weight arrows would be used. A legion probably employed one arrow thrower for each century. Sometimes, it was apparently positioned in a type of field or fortress 'emplacement' that would offer some protection for the crew, as the arrow firer itself provided no protection for the crews.

Gastraphetes

The gastraphetes was an early type of ballista that was powered by a composite bow. These machines were probably developed in the 4th century BC and were large and difficult to move after being emplaced. Some fired one projectile; some were constructed to fire two at once. Very little metal was used in their construction and they were winch-powered at the 'trail' of the piece, as were later models of catapults.

Cheiroballista

The wooden cheiroballista was a catapult that came into service around 100AD. Wood was the main construction material for all artillery, but metal came into use more as it was sturdier and held the catapults together much better than wood did. Catapults would eventually wear out from continued firing and artillery artificers would be employed to keep the artillery in service and in action, especially during the prolonged firing in a siege. The cheiroballista was the beneficiary of metal construction and metal-reinforced wooden construction, and was a definite step-up in technology for the legions and their inherent artillery support.

Scorpion

The small scorpion, or scorpio, was another artillery piece that 'threw' a two-foot long dart. It was in service as early as 50BC and was very similar in appearance to the cheiroballista, although probably not as efficient.

Ammunition

Artillery ammunition usually came in two general types: stones or stone balls of a certain weight, and arrows or darts of different sizes. Stones could be picked up on the battlefield and either shaped if time permitted to make them more aerodynamic so that they would travel further and faster to the intended target, or they could be loaded as needed and fired.

Arrows, bolts, or darts were generally made out of hardwood (ash was a favourite and was preferred by some) with an iron head, constructed so that the wooden shaft would fit into it. Different types of heads were used (flat or pyramidal were common shapes that were made) and 'feathers' for flight stability were made out of leather or wood. Sometimes stones were blackened by their crews so that the flight of the projectile could not be tracked by the intended targets. Field-expedient ammunition for ballistas and the smaller arrow throwers could be constructed on the spot; these would have wooden heads, shaped to a point, and if there was time could be fire-hardened for toughness, durability, and penetration power.

Field Artillery

The adaptability of the catapult-type of artillery, whether it be a stone or an arrow thrower, was twofold: first, it could be built on the spot by the legionaries and, second, it could be broken down into its component parts for

◄ CHEIROBALLISTA, 1ST CENTURY AD *The cheiroballista was another type of crossbow artillery piece that was more modern or advanced than the ballista or arrow throwers. Winch-powered, it was small enough to be emplaced on encampment walls. Noteworthy is the advance in artillery technology denoted by the brass supports on the front of the piece, the older models having wood instead.*

▲ SCORPION, 1ST CENTURY AD *The scorpion was a small catapult that 'threw' small, deadly darts, and was powered by a winch to draw back the operating device.*

ease of transport. Repairs to damaged pieces, either during transport or in action could be quite easily done by the local procurement of wood. This process, though, would definitely be hampered in desert terrain that was devoid of any type of wood, as in the siege of Masada in the middle of the Judaean Desert. Here the Roman commanders, artillerymen and engineers had to be capable of 'making bricks without straw.' That this siege was successful was a credit to Roman ingenuity, adaptability and skill.

Siege Towers

An essential asset for any besieging force was a number of siege towers. The tower was built to get troops close to the walls of the enemy fortress in order to scale the wall defences at that point. If the attempt worked, troops would enter the fortress through a small entry on the top of the wall, overwhelm the defenders and get as many attacking troops into the city as quickly as possible. The towers were constructed with a drawbridge at the top which, when dropped, would be level with the parapet of the wall. Troops waiting on the tower's top level would then charge across this ramp and onto the fortress walls. Other friendly troops would be coming up the ladders constructed at the back of the tower to keep the numbers of attacking troops coming, regardless of losses.

The towers were much more efficient than ladders placed against the walls and offered some protection to assaulting troops until they could actually get on the enemy ramparts. Animal skins would be layered on the outside three faces of the towers to protect it against enemy fire weapons and the towers were also mobile, so that they could be built or assembled out of range of enemy missile weapons and artillery, and with large wheels constructed on the bottom of the tower they were then pushed against the walls of the besieged fortress.

Battering Rams

The ram was a siege weapon from ancient times and was designed to either batter down an enemy gate (preferable) or batter a hole in the wall, causing the upper weight of the wall to collapse on the breach, allowing the attacking troops to assault the fortress from ground level. Interestingly, many ancient rams had an iron head in the form of a ram's head and this lasted through the Roman period.

Rams could be used in the open but this was not ideal as the machines vulnerable to fire, and the crews were exposed to enemy missile weapons, so a protective shed of wood covered by animal hides would be constructed to 'house' the ram and its crew until its work was done and it was withdrawn.

▼ RAM, 1ST CENTURY BC *The ram was an ancient and simple siege engine used to batter down a section of wall or a gate. While it could be used in the open, the crew would be vulnerable to missile weapons. It was best used with a shed-type structure around it that afforded some protection.*

▲ SIEGE TOWER, 1ST CENTURY BC *While the siege tower is familiar to those who study warfare of the Middle Ages it was a classic design also used in antiquity by the Greeks and other armies. The Roman siege tower bears a definite similarity to the design used by western European armies in their sieges. Its use was simple: it was pushed up to the city or fortress walls, a ramp was dropped and emplaced on top of the enemy walls, and troops attacked across the ramp to get a foothold on the enemy's walls.*

Eastern Roman Artillery

The armies raised and employed by the eastern Romans retained the expertise of the old Roman army of the west in both artillery and engineering. One new siege engine the eastern Romans developed themselves was the early trebuchet, or mangonel.

Eastern Ballista

The new ballista was adapted from the earlier Roman model and was probably developed further to be more efficient. Constructed from both wood and metal it was simplified and constructed so that it could be elevated and depressed as well as moved horizontally. It was not mobile, in that once emplaced it could not be easily moved, but it was a mainstay of the eastern Roman artillery arsenal.

Trebuchets

The trebuchet, called an 'alakation' by the eastern Romans, might have been inspired by an Arab artillery piece. Whatever the case, it was a significant development in stone-throwing siege weapons. It was not counterweighted as later trebuchets would be, but was man-powered in that men on the opposite end of the throwing arm would pull down on ropes attached to a 'T' built onto the arm itself. On the command to fire, all the men would pull at once, swinging the arm up and around, releasing the missile from the sling attached to the other end of the arm. It was simple but effective and became more so when a large counterweight

was added for the pulling ropes, which increased both the range and the deadly effect of the weapon.

The frame of the weapon could be covered in animal skins on the outer frame to flame-proof the trebuchet. As the eastern Romans were very efficient in the use of fire weapons, they were conscious of protecting themselves and their wooden structures from fire.

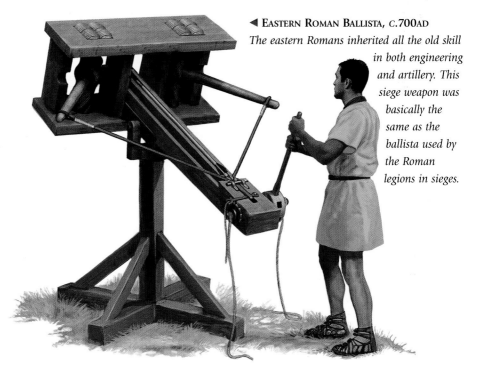

◀ EASTERN ROMAN BALLISTA, C.700AD
The eastern Romans inherited all the old skill in both engineering and artillery. This siege weapon was basically the same as the ballista used by the Roman legions in sieges.

▼ EASTERN ROMAN TREBUCHET, C.800AD
While this siege engine/catapult was 'officially' termed a mangonel, it is actually an early trebuchet. This machine, however, was not counterweighted by a weight for the firing mechanism; the power of this catapult was man-made. The ropes hanging from the arm of the catapult in the front of the siege engine were each held by the crew, and when the catapult was loaded at the rear, a signal or command was given, and the crew at the front would violently pull on the ropes, thus swinging the arm and launching the projectile in the sling. The quick, violent motion of the arm swinging forward gave great impetus for the projectile being launched. Strength and energy of the crew would be vital to the successful operation of this machine, and undoubtedly the team were replaced often by a rested crew.

◀ **EASTERN ROMAN BORER, C.700AD** *Borers were used to penetrate fortress or city walls. It was a slow process, needing time to be effective, so a protective tortoise was essential.*

Testudo

Not a weapon, per se, the testudo was a technique used to get troops through a breach in the walls of a fortress or a city without prohibitive casualties. Testudo is Latin for tortoise and there were two uses of the term in Roman military terminology. Initially, a testudo was a formation of troops that employed their shields in front, to the sides, and above their heads to make them almost impervious to incoming enemy missile weapons. This would, if used in a siege, protect the troops in the formation from rocks and other missiles being dropped on them from the walls of the fortification. On the field it would be used to absorb an enemy charge. A testudo was also a siege machine. Constructed of wood it was basically a shed on wheels. The roof, either level or sloped, was covered with animal hides to make it fire retardant. The taller end of the testudo would be towards the enemy fortification. Troops could move closer to a wall or gate under the testudo, or deploy a battering ram or other siege machine. The eastern Roman term for the testudo was a 'foulkon.'

Borers

The borer was used to undermine the walls of a fortress or a city. It was developed from the ram, but was not used to batter walls, but actually bore into them, starting a breach that relied on the inherent weight of the wall to collapse on itself. Borers would use the same protective sheds as a ram and were a significant advance in siege warfare.

▼ **EASTERN ROMAN TESTUDO, C.700AD** *The tortoise was a protective wooden 'shed' that could be wheeled up to the wall of a fortress or a city in order to undermine the walls. All wooden siege machines, such as the tortoise and siege towers, were usually covered on the sides towards the enemy with animal hides in order to protect the structure from fire launched from the fortress, usually by missile weapons. Sometimes a tortoise was actually a front-facing shield, at others it was pointed at the centre and therefore had two sides at 90 degree angles to each other.*

▲ **TESTUDO SHIELD FORMATION, 1ST CENTURY AD** *The testudo shield formation was highly effective, and was used by both the western and eastern Romans for generations.*

ROMAN ENGINEERING

The Romans, both in the west and in the eastern empire after the fall of Rome, were the great proponents and practitioners of engineering in the ancient world.

Field Fortifications

The Romans were active 'spade men'; wherever the legion camped for the night, fortifications were thrown up to protect it. Marches were planned so that there was time at the end of the day for the camp to be constructed.

Roman fortifications were built on the same design and shape, no matter where they were. The camps themselves would be 'laid out' by an advanced party on each day of movement and if the camp was going to be either occupied for a period of time or as a permanent base, gradual

improvements to the base camp would be made. This not only strengthened the camps against enemy attack and put a sense of permanence into the area to awe any potential enemies, it also kept the legionaries busy.

The camps were geometrically laid out, usually in the form of a square, with designated areas for officers, the headquarters complex, and living spaces for the men and animals. Gates into Roman camps and fortresses were usually at least one per wall, placed in the centre. Streets were laid out geometrically, and two main thoroughfares would run through the camp, connecting the four

▲ ROMAN GATE AND TOWERS, 2ND CENTURY AD *Permanent fortifications, such as the walls of Rome or the Black Gate at Trier, were usually massive. This is one of the main gates to Rome with fortifications added to it as the years passed and the threats grew. Some of these gates still stand today.*

gates. Usually, if not always, camps and forts were surrounded by a ditch, the earth from which would be used to build the walls of the encampment. The ditch might have obstacles placed in the bottom to impede any enemy assault, and caltrops would be placed in front of the ditch. Clear lines of fire for archers were always ensured. Walls were made out of soil or sod, and faced with wood if time permitted.

Permanent Fortifications

The Romans built their walls to fit the circumstances. Initially camps or fortresses could begin with a sod wall, topped by a palisade of logs sharpened at the top. Other sharpened stakes might be placed in the walls above the ditch in order to impede any assaulting enemy. Gradually, if the fortifications became more permanent, the walls might be faced with timber and after a time with stone or other masonry. A stone or masonry wall was usually filled with earth or scattered debris, and not be solid rock or brick all the way through.

Among the most impressive examples of Roman walls are the Aurelian Walls of Rome itself, built in

▼ ENGINEER'S TOOLS, 1ST–CENTURY BC–3RD CENTURY AD *The tools of a Roman engineer would be familiar today. 1 A peat or sod cutter to begin building walls in fortifications. 2 and 3 Pick-axes, used as digging tools along with shovels. 4, 5 and 6 obstacles for the defense of fortified places: 4 was used to construct a palisade, and 5 and 6 are two versions of caltrops, made of iron and either scattered across (5) or stuck in the ground (6) as obstacles against attack.*

▼ ENGINEER AND GROMA, 1ST–CENTURY BC–3RD CENTURY AD *This engineer officer is using a surveying instrument called a groma, which was accurate, even by modern standards, and was the forerunner of the aiming circle and theodolite.*

the 3rd century AD. Much of these still stand. The Aurelian Walls were massive, and studded with square or rectangular towers. Existing structures were used to fit into the fortifications, one notable one being the pyramidal tomb of Caius Cestius, which was built in the 1st century BC, and still stands complete. Triumphal arches of former emperors were also integrated into the new walls and defences.

Gates were always constructed of wood and sometimes these were faced with metal to reinforce the wooden construction. Gates could be massive in permanent fortifications, but wooden gate complexes in the semi-permanent forts along the frontiers would be flanked by wooden towers, often built in a square pattern.

Towers

Along the walls, and generally at the gates, the Romans would build towers to fortify the vulnerable gateways and

▼ TRESTLE BRIDGE, 1ST CENTURY AD *Three views of the construction of the different sections of a military trestle bridge. This would be constructed on campaign to cross large water obstacles. Bridges like this were built across both the Rhine and the Danube. If necessary, the bridge could be dismantled later to prevent an enemy force from using it.*

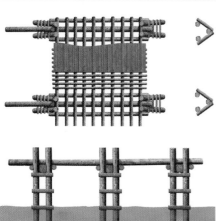

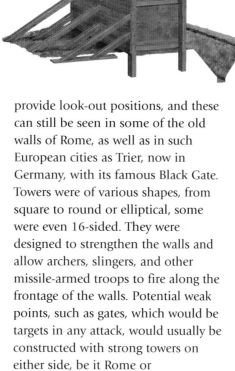

provide look-out positions, and these can still be seen in some of the old walls of Rome, as well as in such European cities as Trier, now in Germany, with its famous Black Gate. Towers were of various shapes, from square to round or elliptical, some were even 16-sided. They were designed to strengthen the walls and allow archers, slingers, and other missile-armed troops to fire along the frontage of the walls. Potential weak points, such as gates, which would be targets in any attack, would usually be constructed with strong towers on either side, be it Rome or Constantinople, or the gates of a legionary camp or fortress.

Hadrian's Wall

A series of fortifications was built across Britain to separate Roman Britain from the barbarian tribes in what is now the borders of Scotland. The fortifications, known as Hadrian's Wall, were commissioned by the emperor Hadrian in 122AD, and built in a continuous line across the island, stretching for 80 Roman miles without a break and reaching 3.6 metres (12ft) high and 2 metres (7ft) thick.

Along the wall's length, forts were built to house troops manning the wall, the forts being, like the entire fortification, built of stone. At intervals of one Roman mile, milecastles were built, square in shape, holding small

◄ ROMAN WALLS, 1ST CENTURY AD *Roman fortifications, whether permanent or temporary, were well thought out and constructed. This is a cutaway view of a semi-permanent fortification built of wood and sod, the soil from the ditch being used to construct the wall. The palisade at the top of the wall is made of wood.*

◄ *This wall follows the same concept as the one above, but is built to a different design. Soil from the ditch is used to construct the wall, but wood shoring is constructed to reinforce the wall.*

garrisons (16–20) of auxiliaries. There were gates at the north and south end of the milecastles.

Larger forts, some quite elaborate, were also built along the wall to house the permanent garrisons. There were 17 of these, built within a supporting distance of each other (about one half-day's march) and their layout was very similar, if not identical, to a legionary fort. Apparently, the wall's first construction was earthworks, later to be faced with stone. Ditches on the northern side were built for defence.

▼ *This view of the ruins of Hadrian's wall show the foundations of a connected mile fort. This was begun with a wall constructed of peat by legionaries on fatigue duty, and was gradually built up with masonry. The remains of it attest to the strength of its construction.*

THE WALLS OF THEODOSIUS

Some of the finest examples of Roman engineering were in the eastern part of the empire, and the fortified walls of Constantinople are the most famous.

Constantinople's Defences

The city of Constantinople was besieged at least ten times during the history of the empire by various enemies, but it was taken only twice in its history. The first time occurred in 1204 when the western Europeans of the 4th Crusade, ostensibly on the way to the Holy Land (Palestine) to fight

▼ SIDE VIEW OF CONSTANTINOPLE'S TRIPLE WALLS, C.1000AD *The Theodosian Walls were built in three 'layers', each succeeding wall being taller and thicker than the one that was in front of it. Towers were placed along both of the inner walls checkerboard-wise so as not to block the field of fire. The ditch would be the first obstacle faced by any enemy, and, even if dry, was still a considerable obstacle. The white line shown here from a high point in the third wall is drainage piping that runs into the ditch on one side, and back into the city on the other.*

the Saracens and claim the Christian holy places from the Muslims were convinced by Venice to assault Constantinople instead. The assaults of the crusaders were from the sea side of the city and they eventually won a breach by getting on the walls and then clearing them. As more crusaders poured into the city, the defenders were overwhelmed and the city taken and sacked. The second, and final time the city fell was in 1453, an act that marked the end of an empire. This time, there would be no restoration of the eastern Empire, Constantinople would become and remain Turkish and the old eastern Roman Empire disappeared from history after surviving the fall of Rome for one thousand years.

Impregnable Fortifications

The fortifications of Constantinople were immense, and expertly built, with a double wall, towers, and ditch surrounding the city, the defences being strongest on the land side of the city where the most dangerous threats would occur.

Constantinople was shaped roughly as a triangle, flanked on three sides by water: the Sea of Marmara on the

▲ RAMPART, C.1000AD *The inner walls of Constantinople were topped by a wide easily manned rampart. Troops moving along the walls would have easy access both to the numerous towers and succeeding sections of the ramparts.*

south, the Bosporus to the east, and a waterway known as the Golden Horn on the north. All along those sides of the city, seawalls were built for defences, but these, though effective enough, were not as elaborate as the walls facing the land side of the city to the west.

On the land side, what were known as the Theodosian walls provided a layered defence. Firstly, a moat protected the defences and was the first obstacle that had to be overcome to get into the city. On the inside 'edge' of the moat was a parapet at the level of the moat. Then the outer wall was built, covering both the moat and the aforementioned parapet. Behind this

The walls and towers of Constantinople presented an imposing picture and a difficult siege problem to any possible attacker. This is a view of the triple walls and ditch from the point of view of a potential attacker.

outer wall, and towering over it, was the huge inner wall. The walls of the city were grandly imposing and effective, undoubtedly the most impressive and practical fortifications of the ancient and medieval period.

The record of major sieges repulsed or survived is impressive. The Avars and Persians besieged the city from 626AD; the Arabs from 674–8 as well as in 714. The Bulgars besieged the city in 813 after the eastern Roman emperor, Nicephorus I, was killed in action against the Bulgars in 811. The Russians besieged the city in 860 and the western Europeans of the 1st Crusade attacked and were defeated in 1097. The success of the 4th Crusade has already been mentioned and the Ottomans besieged the city four times, the last attempt by Sultan Mehmet II being finally successful in 1453. By that time the once-mighty empire of the eastern Romans had shrunk to strips of territory in and around Constantinople and with its fall went the eastern bulwark of Europe that had protected it for a millennia.

Towers
Both the inner and outer walls were reinforced by towers, placed so as to be mutually supporting. While the towers of the outer wall were imposing enough over the moat, the towers of the inner wall, the main defensive belt, were huge. The towers in both walls were not uniform in shape. They could be square, round, or five-sided, but all of them were built so that they projected from the walls.

Gates
There were 13 gates in the outer wall, and all of them went through the inner wall as well. There were also numerous other gates around the city in the sea wall, as well as several 'harbours' and anchorages for the fleet and merchant shipping. The famous Golden Gate (Porta Aurea in Latin) was on the far left of the walls from the defenders' perspective. Begun as a Roman triumphal arch built by the emperor Theodosius I (the Great) in 390AD, there were originally no city walls to defend it. The gate was a triple arch, the main, and larger, central arch

having two smaller arches to either side. Later, as the arch was incorporated into the defences of the city, the two smaller arches were bricked up and closed. Apparently, it was genuine gold on the structure, giving the gateway its famous name.

When Theodosius II completed his huge fortifications of the city in 423AD, the arch itself was not equipped with gates; a smaller gateway constructed of marble being built in front of the arch. The gate itself was not actually part of the defences of the city, but protected by them. The gate itself was used as a triumphal entryway by a number of successful eastern Roman emperors after winning victories in the field against the empire's myriad enemies. It was a showplace of the city and could be surmounted with sculpted statues. Probably the most well known of these, *c.*850AD, consisted of two winged victories over the smaller arches and a centrepiece of four elephants.

▼ **THE GOLDEN GATE, C.900AD** *This gate was a magnificent structure on the southern tip of the Theodosian Walls. The massive scale of it can be judged by how small the people are next to the entrance.*

EARLY GALLEYS

The type of ship, and eventually warship, that would become known as the 'galley' was developed in the eastern Mediterranean. It is highly likely that the galley type known as the trireme was developed by the ancient Phoenicians, a seagoing people who lived in what is now Lebanon and Israel. They built sleek, beautiful seagoing vessels powered by both oars and sails, with a centrally located main mast with one yardarm to hold one sail. Steering was done by two oars located in the stern of the vessel. It was the Phoenicians that founded Carthage, a colony that would evolve into a powerful maritime empire, which challenged the supremacy of Rome in the Mediterranean.

The Trireme

Classical Greek city states adopted the galley as a warship and, according to Thucydides, the Corinthians were the first to build galleys, probably launching triremes around 700BC. The galley was built for war at sea. Crossing oceans was a very risky undertaking in a galley for they were not strong vessels. They were designed to be highly manoeuvrable and were built for one thing – ramming opposing vessels in combat and sinking them. They were capable of the high speeds, necessary for effective ramming, but only for

short periods of time, and a successful ramming was dependant on the training of the oarsmen and how efficiently the vessel was commanded.

For their size, early galleys were not considered to be heavy, and evidence suggests they could be manhandled out of the water. For docking purposes, the ships were usually beached in shallow waters and put in sheds to protect them from the elements.

The trireme's rowers were organized in three banks, upper, lower, and middle banks – thranatai (62 rowers), thalamioi (54 rowers), and zugioi (62 rowers), respectively. Along with 10 hoplites, or more commonly, marines, four bowmen, and 16 officers and other sailors, the complement of a galley was about 200. Sometimes, up to 40 hoplites were aboard, but that appears to be more of a war-footing than standard practice.

The ram was bronze-plated and was the main weapon of a trireme. The manner in which the ram was constructed also aided the galley in

acting as the bow of the ship as it travelled through the water. The design of the galley was simple. There was the section of the ship for the rowers, and a single deck above for the rest of the crew. This enabled enough galleys to be built in a very short period of time especially in emergencies, as in the two Persian invasions.

Galleys could fight singly, but were most effective in fleet actions, such as at Salamis, the great Greek naval victory in 480BC following the Battle of Thermopylae against the Persians.

Harbours would sometimes be circular, as in the galley sheds at Peiraieus where the galleys would be doubly protected: sheds in the winters to keep the galleys in good condition until next needed, and the harbour itself fortified for overall protection.

Greek triremes were sometimes painted, although often the wood would be kept in its natural hue. A typical feature of Greek galleys was the eyes painted on the bow of the ships as a talisman to keep the crew safe.

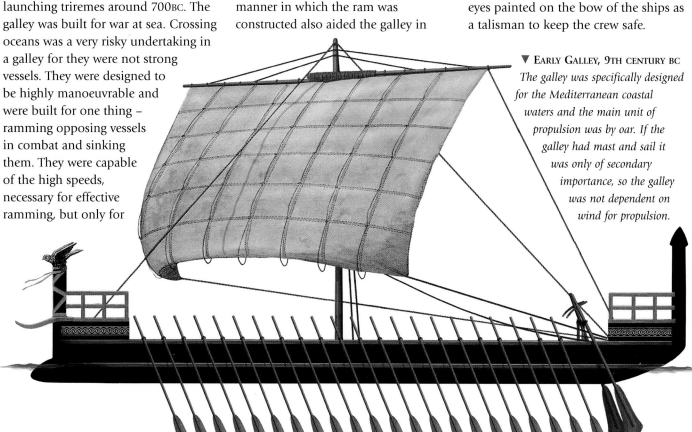

▼ EARLY GALLEY, 9TH CENTURY BC
The galley was specifically designed for the Mediterranean coastal waters and the main unit of propulsion was by oar. If the galley had mast and sail it was only of secondary importance, so the galley was not dependent on wind for propulsion.

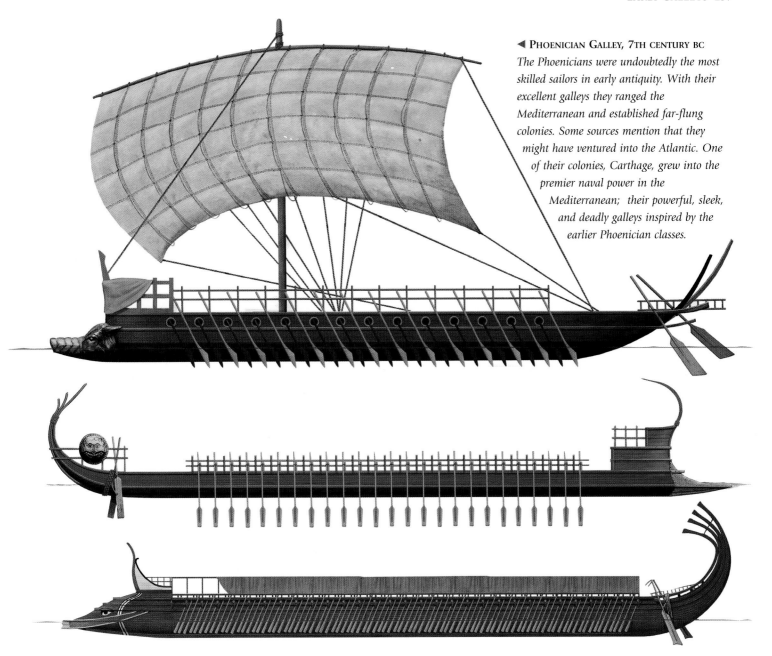

◄ PHOENICIAN GALLEY, 7TH CENTURY BC
The Phoenicians were undoubtedly the most skilled sailors in early antiquity. With their excellent galleys they ranged the Mediterranean and established far-flung colonies. Some sources mention that they might have ventured into the Atlantic. One of their colonies, Carthage, grew into the premier naval power in the Mediterranean; their powerful, sleek, and deadly galleys inspired by the earlier Phoenician classes.

▲ (MIDDLE) GREEK GALLEY, C.480BC
The Greeks were expert seamen and their galleys were perfect for the type of naval warfare they waged. The ship's ram was positioned to lie underneath the waterline to cause maximum damage. The upper deck of the galley was easily used by the naval infantry who also were part of the crew.

The galley was used effectively by the early Greeks, the Athenian navy being the dominant naval force in Greece for a considerable period. From ancient Greece, through the classical Roman period and to the end of the eastern Roman Empire and beyond, the galley was a preeminent warship in the Mediterranean until finally overcome and made obsolete by the square-rigged sailing warship that was

▲ (ABOVE) GREEK GALLEY, C.480BC *The greatest Greek naval victory was undoubtedly the Battle of Salamis in 480BC, which destroyed the naval power of the Persian King Xerxes and led to the defeat of the second Persian invasion of Greece in 10 years. Undoubtedly the galleys that fought in that sea battle were of this design.*

equipped with ship-destroying cannon fired in a broadside, whereas the later galleys only carried guns fore and aft.

Galley Development
The Greek galley was basically the same in the Roman age as it was in ancient Greece. Sleek, fast and deadly in a sea fight, the galleys of Mediterranean naval warfare all had a similar, if not identical design.

A trireme could maintain a speed of up to 7.5 knots, and the bronze battering ram weighed over 181kg (400lbs). The long, narrow ships were powered by banks of oars on each side, although all galleys were equipped with either one or two masts with one sail each. When stripped down for battle the sail could be left ashore, and the highly trained oarsmen supplied all of the propulsion and manoeuvrability that made these ships deadly. Under full oar the trireme was capable of inflicting fatal damage on its target, in some cases even shearing another ship in half. Once the enemy ship was impaled upon the ram, the attacking ship's soldiers would use planks and grappling hooks to bring the vessels alongside for hand to hand fighting.

THE CARTHAGINIAN NAVAL THREAT

The Carthaginians were a naval people, descended from the Phoenicians who founded the city as a colony. Their main focus was trade and dominance in the Mediterranean and when the Punic wars began, their ships ranged the region unchallenged.

Carthaginian Naval Base

The huge naval base at Carthage gave proof to their emphasis on naval matters and to their preeminence in naval and trade matters. In any war between major powers where one is dominant at sea and the other on land, the question is how one or the other is able to attack its enemy.

Carthage was certainly the leading naval power at the beginning of the Punic wars while Rome was the emerging land power in Italy and had brought the entire Italian peninsula under her rule. The Carthaginian solution was to invade Italy with a mercenary army. The Roman solution, at first awkward, was to create and build a navy, defeat Carthage at sea, invade the Carthaginian homeland, destroy their army and take their capital. In military history there are few empires or nations that could be dominant at sea and on land simultaneously, but the Roman Empire, and its successor the eastern Roman Empire, succeeded at that task.

The Carthaginian navy was superb in both ships and personnel, and its shipyard at Carthage was magnificent, both in design and functionality, reminiscent of the Greek naval bases, but larger and more elaborate. Everything that needed to be done in order to have a first-class navy was available in the naval base; construction, ship sheds, constant repair, formidable defences, and the skilled artificers and leadership to swiftly accomplish any mission.

Naval Tactics

Unfortunately for them, Carthaginian naval commanders were unable to come to grips with the aggression of the new Roman naval commanders

▼ CARTHAGINIAN WARSHIP, C.220BC *A sleek, powerful warship, designed and built by the Carthaginians. From a bird's-eye-view (bottom), the sleek lines of the ship are clearly visible. The power of a well-trained crew would propel this warship with its deadly ram into the side and bowels of an enemy warship with catastrophic effects. Two 'arrow throwers' are positioned on the forecastle of the galley and the soldiers' shields are positioned along the sides for stowage, as space was very limited on a galley.*

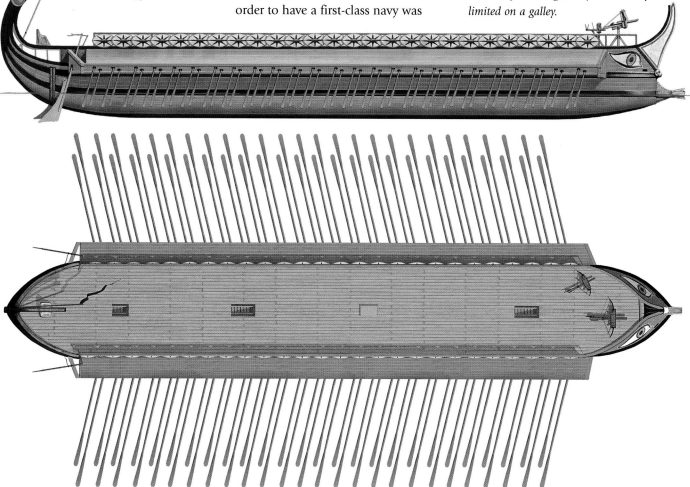

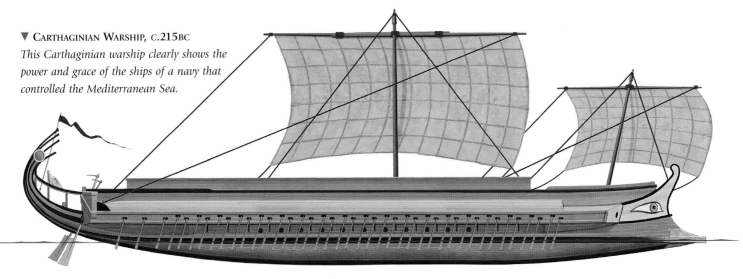

▼ CARTHAGINIAN WARSHIP, C.215BC
This Carthaginian warship clearly shows the power and grace of the ships of a navy that controlled the Mediterranean Sea.

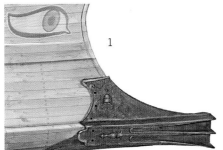

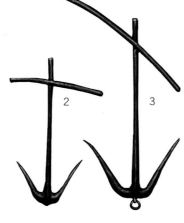

▲ *1 The iron ram was attached to the wooden bow of the galley. This design is copied from the remains of an original ram. 2 and 3 Anchors were made of iron. Both of these are copied from originals recovered from a wreck.*

with their adapted ships and use of the novel and newly designed corvus – a gangway or bridge that allowed the boarding of enemy vessels. The Romans did not manoeuvre to ram, they closed parallel to the Carthaginian vessels, locked them together with the corvus and spike, and then boarded in an overwhelming infantry assault.

Ram technology had not changed since the great days of the Athenian navy. Technological advances were generally in the size of the ships, and perhaps their seaworthiness, but during the fighting of the Punic wars the only real naval innovation was the Roman corvus.

Galley Construction

The construction of galleys had not changed very much from the introduction of the galley by the Phoenicians and its use as the primary warship by the Greeks and Persians. There were basically two ways to construct a hull of a ship during the

days of the Greeks and Romans. The first was to lay the keel, the central 'backbone' of the ship from bow to stern. The ribs of the hull were then built, these were the vertical supports attached to the keel and at right angles to it. Finally the planking would be installed to cover the ribs, either overlapping, attached end to end, or laid side to side for a smooth surface.

The second method, used for the Mediterranean galleys of the period, was to lay the keel and then construct the outline of the hull without the ribs being attached. Then the hull planks would be attached to fill out the form of the hull, these would be laid end to end so as to give the hull a smooth surface, which would increase its speed, and provide less resistance in the water. Then the ribs would be attached to the hull planking.

After the hull was built, the interior of the ship would be constructed, including the places for the rowers, and the top deck. The number of oars and oarsmen would be determined by what

type of galley was being constructed. For example, a trireme would have three banks of oars on each side of the ship. A mast would be constructed and erected on the main deck, usually with one yardarm and a large single sail.

Most of the crew would be oarsmen, and as a warship there would be infantrymen, or marines, assigned too. A Greek-style trireme would have 170 oarsmen, arranged in three rows on each side, two rows of 27 and one of 31. Total crew was 200, with 11, including the captain, to sail the ship, and 19 to fight it. Roman oarsmen were not slaves, but sailors and freedmen.

▼ NAVAL ARROW THROWER C.220BC *The Roman navy, both republican and imperial, would embark small artillery pieces like this arrow thrower, to be used aboard ship.*

THE ROMAN NAVAL RESPONSE TO CARTHAGE

The first Roman ships were awkward, as were their inexperienced crews. The Romans adapted their naval fighting techniques from the main tactics of the legions. What they invented and then implemented was the corvus.

The Corvus

Each Roman galley had a large gangway constructed on the fore part of the galley. This ramp was raised and lowered by a system of pulleys. Instead of trying to ram the Carthaginian galleys in combat, the Romans would pull their galleys alongside those of the Carthaginians, and swing the corvus – one end of which was fixed to the deck of the Roman galley – onto the opposing Carthaginian vessel, placing it onto the deck of the enemy galley. The end of the corvus had a large spike which would fix itself by the falling weight of the corvus onto the Carthaginian galley and this system would give the Roman infantry a

boarding ramp onto the Carthaginian vessel. The Romans would then count on their legion infantry to charge onto the enemy galley and take it in hand-to-hand combat as if on land.

This system was an interim solution to Rome's naval problem. While it was successful, and the Carthaginians were taken by surprise by the novel naval innovation, there were problems with it. The corvus was an awkward device and undoubtedly made normal sailing of the galleys somewhat difficult, especially in anything but a calm sea. In addition, if the corvus itself missed hitting the deck of the enemy vessel, it would put the Roman galley at a distinct, if momentary, disadvantage in a sea fight. If the large spike at the end of the corvus could not be quickly taken out of the opposing galley's deck after the ship was taken, the corvus itself might have to be let go into the sea, removing the galley's

▼ ROMAN GALLEY, C.220BC *A side view of a Roman galley shows the method of mounting and carrying the corvus. The placement of the corvus would make the galley unseaworthy in anything but a calm sea, but this naval innovation would give the Romans an advantage over the Carthaginian navy, and the corvus and its employment was something the Carthaginians were not prepared for.*

▼ ROMAN GALLEY, C.220BC (BOTTOM) *The top view of a Roman galley clearly demonstrates the inherent unwieldiness of the corvus. The galley was not only bow-heavy, but unbalanced because of the majority of the weight of the corvus being to the port (left) side of the galley. Further, there is no evidence that the Romans attempted to balance the extra weight of the bow by adding a corresponding weight to the stern.*

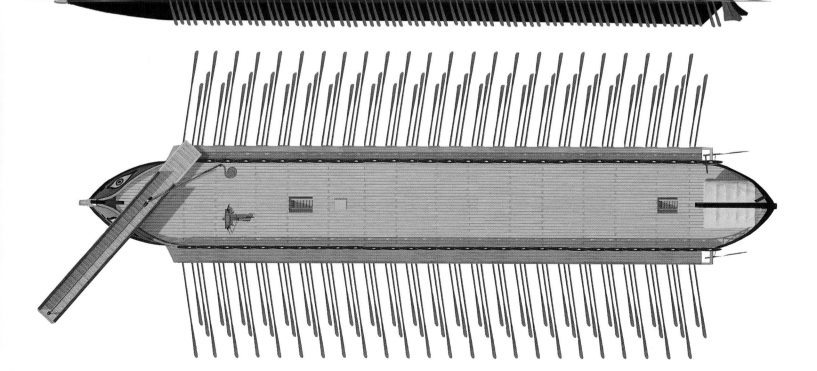

▼ ROMAN CORVUS, OR BOARDING RAMP, C.220BC *The large corvus was unwieldy and must have made the Roman galleys equipped with them quite top-heavy. This would definitely cause seaworthiness problems in anything but a calm sea. However, it was successful and was employed until the Roman naval crews learned their new profession.*

▶ ONAGAR, C.220BC *Small onagers, such as this one, could be used aboard ships at sea. Like most gunnery at sea, however, it would be much less accurate because ships moved through all axes on a naval platform, whereas on land they were much more stable. Skilled gunners with good eyes could still register multiple hits at sea with practice.*

Innovations

Roman and Carthaginian vessels were much alike, and both sides made use of the heavy quinquereme; a galley manned by five banks, the design of which, according to Polybius, the Romans copied from a beached Carthaginian vessel, although its original design was Greek.

Polybius also tells us that during the First Punic War, Rome commissioned 100 of the large galleys, and 20 triremes. Quinqueremes had 90 oars on each side, and 30-strong files of oarsmen. The Romans also added collapsible towers to the galleys' decks, which allowed projectiles to be rained down onto enemy ships from above.

The Romans initially organized their navy on what they knew and were comfortable with; army and legion terms were used to identify how the Roman fleets were organized. When a fleet was making ready for an engagement and the

commander organized his ships tactically in lines of galleys, the lines were named numerically and called 'legions.' Sometimes the early Roman fleets would name lines after the legionaries that held that place in the manipular legion of the republic, such as hastate, principles, and triarii.

As the Roman navy matured and was victorious, naval terms replaced the early usage of army terminology. For naval ranks of the senior officers, Greek naval terms were adopted. Ship captains were 'trierarchs', and squadron commanders became 'navarchs.' However, fleet commanders were given, and kept, a thoroughly Roman title, that of 'prefect.'

primary means of attack. As the Romans gained experience, both with individual ship handling and seamanship, as well as handling fleets at sea and in combat, the corvus became obsolete, and the Romans relied on the usual weapons of the galley and naval artillery, such as small onagers and ballistas that were designed specifically for warfare at sea.

▼ ROMAN QUINQUEREME, C.220BC
A quinquereme, commonly known as a 'five', was a large galley of five banks of oars. It was a formidable ship, which not only had a larger crew than the typical trireme, but also could carry more troops for boarding enemy vessels. This one has two fighting castles on board.

Crew and Marines

The first Roman infantry to get their feet wet were taken from the legions and assigned duty with the fleet. Their dress and equipment was undoubtedly identical to the Roman legionaries that remained ashore. In many modern references these troops are termed or designated 'marines' but that is an overused term both historically and realistically. Roman commanders were able to place large numbers of men onboard. Mark Anthony loaded 20,000 legionaries onto his fleet at Actium.

The number of soldiers allocated to each vessel varied, but Polybius states that quinqueremes had 300 oarsmen and a further complement of 120 soldiers at the most. A quadrireme would have around 70

▲ *This modern rendition of a galley underway gives an excellent idea of what the ships under sail and full oar power would look like. Early galleys had one mast that could be lowered and stowed aboard ship if necessary. The mainmast had one yard, which carried a large mainsail. The fighting castle on the forecastle of the ship is clearly visible as is the galley's primary weapon, the ram.*

such soldiers. These seem to have received some training from officers of the crew, no doubt quickly supplemented by experience at sea. Roman 'naval' ranks corresponded directly, if not identically, with those Roman troops stationed ashore. While they might appear to be different to their land-bound brothers-in-arms, the function and

◄ ROMAN MARINE (CENTURION), 3RD CENTURY BC *Centurions aboard ship were uniformed and equipped as on land, especially in the navy's first era. His armour is typical of the period, but he has his sword scabbard on his left side. His greaves are of an interesting pattern, and might be a personal preference. There is no insignia on his shield, which is also unusual.*

▶ ROMAN AUXILIARY NAVAL PERSONNEL, 2ND CENTURY BC *Scale armour was often used by Roman auxiliary troops. This archer is armed with a composite bow, an arrow sheath strapped to his back for easy access, and a gladius. The neck scarf stops chafing from the armour.*

◀ **ROMAN MARINE, 3RD CENTURY BC** *Arms and equipment for marines were identical to those of the land-based legions. The boar representation on his shield, a favourite motif of the legions, is a unit designation. His square breastplate would be matched by a square backplate, attached to each other by the leather harness. His gladius is attached by a leather baldric to the waist belt. He wears his gladius on his right side, so that his left hand can carry the heavy shield in formation if needed.*

The Romans had no marines as such, though the term is usually applied to the legionaries who served aboard ship as infantry. They were detailed from the army and were dressed, accoutred, and armed as legion infantry of the particular period with little or no special equipment to designate them as naval infantry. They were assigned to the fleet by centuries and were led as usual by their centurion and his second in command, the optio.

Eventually, legion infantrymen assigned to either the main classis, or fleets, or to the coastal and river flotillas might, through long and successful service, designate or identify themselves with their naval service and 'modify' their legion identification accordingly with naval or sea symbols.

Roman infantrymen who were fully equipped and armoured, and may or may not have been able to swim, were at a particular disadvantage in a sea engagement. If the legionary was unlucky enough to be forced or fall

overboard, his equipment would likely drag him under and he would disappear and drown. During a naval engagement, the usual flotsam and jetsam of the wreckage of badly damaged or sunken galleys, both friend and foe, would undoubtedly litter the sea around the ships, and if a sailor or soldier fell overboard and was able to grab hold of any type of floating debris he might survive. Then, he would have to be seen and picked up by his comrades, or perhaps his enemy, and dragged on board the rescuing vessel. A Roman sailor or legionary picked up by a surviving enemy probably had little chance of surviving that particular course of action.

purpose, as well as the organization, of the Roman naval troops would serve the same purpose when ashore. The number of contingents would be greater, and their individual strengths would be less, as the space aboard ship was limited. Centuries, cohorts, and legions would be divided up between the ships they were assigned to, and this would put much more responsibility on the lower ranking officers and legionaries, especially in the confused melee of a sea fight.

▶ **ROMAN MARINE, 3RD CENTURY BC** *New to naval service, the Roman infantry detailed to serve as 'marines' would undoubtedly be quite uneasy at sea aboard ship until they acquired their 'sea legs', assuming they survived the rigours at sea or fighting the Carthaginian fleet. During this period Roman legionaries of all three types of heavy infantry in the legion wore one greave on the left leg, the leg put forward when throwing the hasta or pilum.*

ROMAN NAVAL TROOPS

The Romans constructed their ships, and developed their naval tactics to match, and support, their military strength on land. What they wanted to do was to get their infantry aboard the enemy vessels in order to fight them hand-to-hand. The initial naval infantry of the Romans were merely land troops who had been assigned to the fleet. After that fleet was successful against the Carthaginians, the Romans developed units to stay with their various fleets and by necessity developed and trained permanent naval troops, who today would be termed 'marines'.

Uniforms and Equipment

Roman sailors did not have a uniform as we would know the term today. They might dress similarly to each other, but they dressed first and foremost as seaman. Both the seamen and naval troops were considered to be better dressed than troops serving permanently on land. Their clothing was probably water-proofed to have it last better under sea conditions, as salt and spray would have a deteriorating effect on regular clothing. Short tunics were worn, as were a variety of cloaks, both short and long. These were similar to the same clothing items worn by troops ashore but modified for sea duty. Short and long trousers of varying designs were also worn and sailors wore a type of pointed cap that had been in use for centuries. Phrygian caps were also worn. Grey, light and dark blue seem to have been favourite colours for tunics and other clothing, while red was also in use.

Arms and Armour

Body armour for commanders and naval troops in the fleet consisted of the usual kind employed by the land armies. Evidence of muscled cuirasses has been found, and chain mail could be found

◀ ROMAN OPTIO, 70BC *An optio was second in command of a century, and was elected by his comrades. A mail lorica is worn here along with the usual curved scutum. His gladius is worn on a baldric.*

▲ OCTAVIAN MARINE, 31BC *Greek influence is obvious for this naval infantryman of Octavian's fleet at the Battle of Actium. He wears a leather muscle cuirass and a Greek-style helmet. His scutum is oval and the trident symbol is undoubtedly one adopted by naval troops aboard ship.*

throughout the different Roman fleets during the period. Apparently, leather armour was popular both because its light weight was helpful in moving around the tight confines of a ship, and also because of the ever-present danger of falling overboard. Whereas the weight of metal or steel armour might pull you down, leather armour could give the wearer a fighting chance of staying afloat until rescued.

Helmets were of the normal variety in the fleet for naval troops, similar to those worn by the infantry on land. They would change in style along with the army units and depending on the unit would be decorated with feathers or horsehair crests. Shields would be smaller, and of round or oval shapes, although rectangular scuta would also be present. There is also evidence that some shields might have been made of leather. Both spears and pila were used afloat and the gladius was carried by many, if not most of the naval troops. Troops might also carry a dagger.

▶ ROMAN TRIBUNE, 2ND CENTURY AD
As senior officers, tribunes were usually uniformed and equipped more elaborately than centurions. This one is no exception. His unit served on the Danube in the Danube Riverine Flotilla and was armed and equipped for fighting on land. The hexagonal shield is curious as it was usually used by auxiliaries. The trident, again, is undoubtedly a naval symbol and probably a locally added affectation because of long sea service. This officer is wearing his awards over his armour and his excellent helmet is adorned with an elaborate feathered crest so that he will be identifiable to his men at all times afloat or ashore.

Roman naval infantry in Octavian's time might have been 'uniformed' and armed differently from the infantry of the legions on land service, but this did not seem to last long. Naval troops generally were armed the same as the legionaries on land service, though there would be differences in clothing and 'decorations'.

◀ MARINE, MISENUM FLOTILLA, 3RD CENTURY AD *During this period the Roman soldier was in transition, especially in body armour and equipment. Quite often not even a chain mail lorica would be worn, and weapons would be simple – a spear or javelin and a round shield, smaller than usual for the navy. This infantryman would be stationed around Naples where the Misenum classis was based.*

▼ *This painting portrays a Roman galley at anchor in harbour. The ship's mast is down and stowed. Of interest in the lower left of the painting is the raft-like craft, probably used to move supplies to anchored shipping.*

◄ *A model of the port of Roman London, on the River Thames, c.100AD, based on information from archaeological excavations on the river. The harbour itself is quite modern in appearance, with warehouses at the quayside, and lighters alongside the merchantman in the foreground resupplying the ship for the next voyage.*

praetorian classis, Portus Julius being deactivated and the ships, troops, and equipment being divided between the imperial dockyards at Misenum and Ravenna. After gaining naval superiority in the Mediterranean, these two praetorian classis acted more as a 'central naval reserve' under the emperor's control and did

River Operations

Besides the major flotillas on the Rhine and the Danube, the Romans also employed river flotillas, or fleets (classis) along or on other major waterways of the empire.

The Romans had three main classis in the Mediterranean. These were stationed at Portus Julius, near present-day Marseilles, Ravenna in Italy, and Misenum, on the north side of the Bay of Naples. Later, these were combined into only two

◄ ROMAN MARINE, RHINE FLOTILLA, 4TH CENTURY AD *The arms and equipment of this infantryman are simple. The round shield is usual for the period and the clothing is very much Germanic in influence. The arrow-like object in the right hand is probably not a weapon, but a symbol of rank or status.*

▶ ROMAN MARINE, RHINE FLOTILLA, 4TH CENTURY AD *The classical arms and armour of the legionary have by this time given way to those influenced by the barbarians that the Romans came into contact with and either fought or employed as auxiliaries. The sword of choice is now the spatha, shields are round, and helmets are more Germanic in appearance than traditional Roman.*

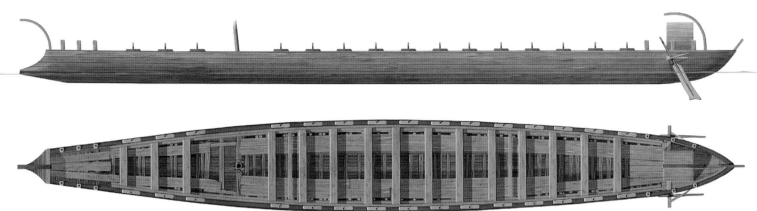

▲ RHINE RIVER PATROL BOAT *The Romans had a can-do attitude to water navigation, which translated in to using Europe's large, navigable rivers, such as the Rhine and the Danube, for military purposes. Suitable craft were built for the transport of supplies, as well as patrolling and controlling the rivers and the adjacent land. These are side and top views of a vessel of the Rhine River Flotilla. The Roman naval ships on the rivers could be either docked, if there was suitable facilities, or beached if necessary. Landing troops from these vessels appears to have been easy to do.*

not see as much active service as the smaller provincial fleets that acted in close cooperation with the army.

The operational provincial fleets were responsible for maintaining control of local coastlines and for patrolling and controlling inland waterways. They operated naval craft that was usually, but not always, composed of small, easy to handle vessels suited to their mission. The Nile River in Egypt was controlled by the classis stationed in Alexandria. In the English Channel, stationed at Boulogne, the Britannica classis maintained communication with Roman Britain and provided naval support for the army when necessary.

Along the Rhine and the Danube, there were three flotillas, the classis Germanica on the Rhine, the classis Pannonica on the Upper Danube, and the classis Moescia on the Lower Danube. Pannonica also patrolled the Black Sea and Germanica would venture from time to time into the challenging waters of the North Sea.

Some of the legions detailed for naval service (milites liburnarii –

probably named such after the excellent light galleys employed on the inland waterways and along the coasts of the empire) were then Legio XXII Primigenis, which operated on the Rhine and Main rivers in Germany, and Legio X Fretensis that operated in Palestine on the Jordan River and the Sea of Galilee.

Supplies and Transportation

The flotillas were a water-borne supply system, which would bring food, equipment, arms, armour and other supplies. They also transported troops either to reinforce other units, rescue units in trouble, or aid in routine troop movements. The establishment and employment of the river flotillas gave Roman commanders on the northern frontier excellent strategic mobility and increased Roman combat power.

The ports along the rivers would home not only vessels for the transportation of troops, but also rafts or skiffs and equipment used for the establishment of pontoons. This would allow large bodies of men to be transported across rivers, and so negate these obstacles. Sexaginta Prista, which is now Rouse in Bulgaria, and which was founded in the rule of Vespasian, was one such port, and it was well positioned where the Danube was at its widest. Its Roman name seems to be derived from the term 60 rafts, which gives a clue as to the kind of vessels kept there. Odessus (Varna), Nicopolis (Nikopol) and Novae (Svishtov) also housed fleets used in the naval flotillas.

▼ OFFICER, RHINE FLOTILLA, 4TH CENTURY AD *The muscle cuirass appears to be a throw-back to an earlier time. His helmet, though, is more eastern than Roman or Germanic, but the military cloak is in blue, probably because of his naval service. The spear has a decorated shaft, which might have been ceremonial, or an award.*

NAVAL DESIGN AND OPERATION

While naval design and construction techniques of the Roman galleys created larger vessels at times, the basic design for sea warfare was a constant during the period of the Roman republic and western empire. Larger galleys were made and employed, but they were not practical.

A problem with larger wooden warships, and one that was never completely overcome, even in the heyday of the square-rigged sailing warship, was 'hogging'; when the ship

started to sag, at bow and stern, from the middle of the ship. This was a dangerous situation and caused irreparable damage. With smaller galleys, inexpensive and easy to replace, the problem was not serious, but with the larger ships it was.

The liburnian galley was a later development of the standard galley and was usually a bireme with two rows of oars. Shorter, lighter, and of shallower draft than the standard galley, it was used by the Romans as the eyes of the fleet – much as frigates were later employed by the navies of the 18th and early 19th centuries. They were not usually employed in battle and did not originally have a ram. Lightly built, they were later 'bulked up' with a ram and more heavily built. They were increasingly used during the empire period (*c.*100AD).

Employing sailors as galley oarsmen instead of slaves was a great advantage to Roman naval commanders as the sailors were serving more or less voluntarily and were not forced to serve in the navy. Claudius would seem

to have given legal privileges to men who had served in the fleet, granting them and their families citizenship after 26 years' service.

Artificers

These troops were specialists in naval construction and undoubtedly those in charge of artificer units were also responsible for designing vessels for specialist service on the rivers. They would also be part of the crew, sailing, operating, and maintaining the ships during sea and river service.

Naval artificers were crucial. Shipwrights might design the ships and ensure construction was on schedule and ensuring the materials for construction were available, but the artificers, the carpenters, coopers, and blacksmiths were the vital, skilled personnel who ensured that the ships were ready for sea or for service on the rivers. Generally, artificers did not go afloat and stayed in the harbours and naval bases, but it is probable that good commanders carried experienced artificers on board ship to repair

◀ ROMAN NAVAL ARTIFICER, 200AD *Roman artificers were skilled civilian workmen, hired by the Roman navy. They were essential for the task of keeping Roman naval shipping afloat and at sea.*

▼ *During the siege of Syracuse by the Romans in 212BC, the Romans were outwitted by anti-siege devices designed by Archimedes. One, 'the claw of Archimedes', lifted the ships out of the sea, then dropped them back in.*

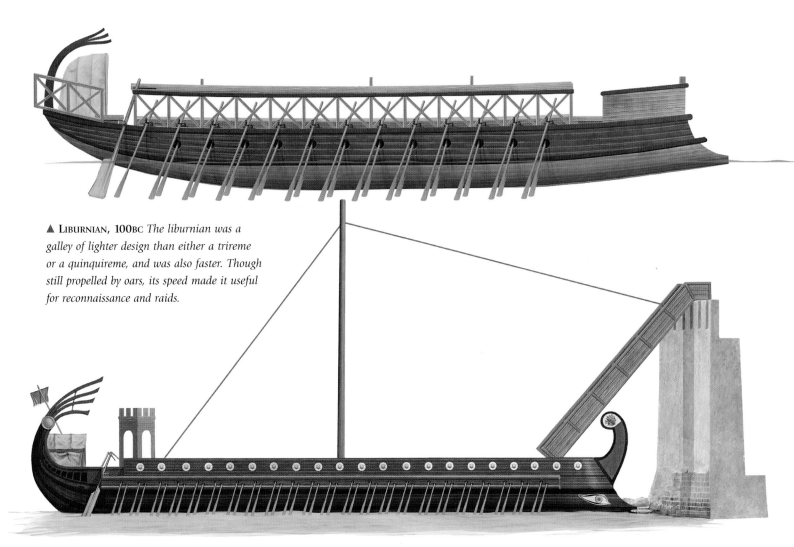

▲ LIBURNIAN, 100BC *The liburnian was a galley of lighter design than either a trireme or a quinquireme, and was also faster. Though still propelled by oars, its speed made it useful for reconnaissance and raids.*

▲ SIEGE GALLEY, 100BC *Siege galleys were built when necessary during a siege of a city or fortress with assailable walls along a seacoast. Suitable ramps were attached to a large galley, such as a quinquireme. The galley was then manoeuvred up to the city or fortress walls and the ramp was lowered to the walls to allow troops access. It was the naval equivalent of a siege tower. Sometimes ramps were employed using two galleys. As ships move through a 360 degree arc, this could be a very unstable way of using siege machines. Frequently, they did not work.*

damage from fight or weather. The naval artificers were undoubtedly armed, but their first duty was not to fight and they were too valuable to be risked in any engagement unless it was an emergency.

Galleys in Siege Operations

Specialist ships were also produced during the period. This was very true for shipping used during sieges of strategic ports, such as Syracuse. The problem with besieging a port is that the necessary naval blockade to cut off the port from outside aid could be broken for periods and the port swiftly reinforced and resupplied. The Roman navy, or any other of the period, did not have the ability to blockade an entire coastline. They could and did blockade ports, but clever and daring sea captains and commanders of flotillas and fleets could fight their way into a besieged port or stealthily approach a harbour mouth at night.

The siege of Syracuse, from 214 to 212BC, pitting the besieging Romans against the Greeks of the city, is an interesting case study in the combination of land and naval forces. Pictured above is a 'siege galley', used to assault the city from seaward. This ultimately failed, in part because of the ingenious siege engines designed by Archimedes which defeated every attempt to gain access to the city from the sea. The Romans proved innovative with their employment of siege galleys, but Archimedes and the defenders' countermeasures more than made up for those Roman innovations. One of the specialist ships developed by the Romans was a galley adapted to an assault from the sea or harbour side of a port equipped with a large boarding ramp for troops to get on top of the city's walls and effect a breach. The siege galleys would head for the target area and either sail up to the wall if the water was deep enough, or beach themselves before planting the attached assault ramp. These type of modified galleys must have been difficult to handle and vulnerable to both missile and fire weapons on the approach and while landing troops.

The amphibious nature of the Roman navy was impressive. During both invasions of Britain the Roman fleet assigned to the mission was very proficient in both transporting the army and all of its necessary equipment to the target area and then landing the army without heavy loss.

THE EASTERN ROMAN NAVY

▼ *Greek fire was the eastern Roman naval secret weapon of the period. To this day the actual formula for the combustible mixture is not exactly known. Further, the exact method of projecting the fire onto enemy vessels is at best a good guess. What is certain is that it was extremely effective, feared by the eastern Romans' enemies at sea, difficult to extinguish (it burned in water), and when fired against any enemy it was decisive.*

The navy of the eastern Roman Empire was superior to all of its opponents during most of its existence and for many centuries had virtually no opposition in the Mediterranean. This gave the eastern Romans the ability, especially in the early centuries after the fall of the western Roman Empire, to move troops from one place to another across the Mediterranean unopposed. That advantage in strategic mobility gave eastern Roman commanders, such as Belisarius and Narses, the ability to strike when and where they wished and the appearance

▲ *An 11th-century illustration showing the distinctive rows of round shields flanking the sides of an eastern Roman galley.*

of an eastern Roman army in North Africa, Spain, or Italy provided surprise against the empire's enemies.

The Dromon

Initially, the eastern Roman galleys continued with the designs of the other galley fleets in service with other powers in the Mediterranean. Gradually, though, galley design both improved and changed as the decades and

centuries went by. The dromon was a particular type of galley used by the eastern Romans and it was by all accounts an excellent ship design. It had two masts with lateen (triangular rather than square) sails, one per mast. It was a sleek, beautifully designed warship and was a match for any potential enemy. The dromon was a much-improved design over earlier galleys and it added to the combat power of the eastern Roman navy. For at least the first five to six hundred years of the eastern empire, the dromon allowed the eastern Roman navy to maintain its superiority.

Greek Fire

One of the deadliest weapons ever developed for warfare at sea was the feared and mysterious Greek fire. This terrifying weapon was used to great effect by the eastern Roman

▼ DROMON, 700–1100AD
Eastern Roman galleys were equipped with apparatus to employ the deadly Greek fire. Here, the firing apparatus is attached to the bow of the ship in the shape of a dragon's head.

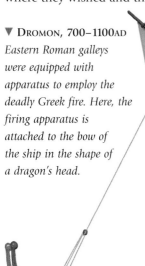

navy. The impact it had is described in ancient manuscripts of the period, but the exact composition of the liquid fire is virtually unknown, as is the method of delivering it from an eastern Roman galley to an enemy ship. There is speculation on the delivery system, which was probably a type of pump mechanism, but the results in combat are certainly known and understood.

The apparatus was emplaced on the ship near the bow and when the galley came within range of its target, the liquid fire was 'shot' through the weapon system in a stream that would hit and attach itself to the enemy vessel and personnel. It was in effect a flame thrower and the composition of the fuel could have been quite like modern napalm. Whether or not the liquid fire was 'sticky' and could not be put out by normal means of 'fire prevention' is unknown, but the amount of liquid projected from the eastern Roman vessel seems to have been enough to overwhelm any attempts by the enemy crew to extinguish the flames and save their ship.

Eastern Roman Naval Decline

Despite such advantages, the eastern Roman navy fell into a period of neglect, and was in poor shape by the 12th century. The naval themes had been lost to foreign conquest and the funds necessary to build and maintain a navy were shrinking. The emphasis was quickly becoming the

▼ **EASTERN ROMAN GALLEY, 700–1100AD**
This smaller, one-masted ship was lighter than the dromon and could be employed as a reconnaisance and messenger vessel. It was equipped and manned for fighting.

▼ **DROMON, 700–1100AD** *The eastern Roman dromon was an excellent galley that was the mainstay of the imperial fleet. It had two masts rather than one, and replaced the square sails of antiquity with triangular ones. The galley was sleek and deadly and was manned by expert crews who controlled the eastern Mediterranean for centuries.*

defence of the remaining lands and of Constantinople itself.

The crusaders of the 4th Crusade in their assault on Constantinople saw the remainder of the navy used poorly, sunk as hulks to prevent Venetian galleys from attacking the city from the sea. In the final defence of the city and empire in 1453, galleys from Genoa and Venice aided in the last-ditch defence, and it was they that took on survivors to make good their escape as the final defence collapsed.

GLOSSARY

Ala (alae): A Roman cavalry unit of approximately 30 horsemen.

Alakation: Eastern Roman trebuchet.

Antesignani: Roman soldiers who took their place in line of battle in front of the unit's standards.

Aquila: The Roman eagle, the symbol/standard of the Roman legions instituted by Marius in the 1st century BC. At first cast in silver, it was later cast in gold. The devotion afforded to the eagle by the legionaries was legendary.

Aquilfer: Eagle-bearer. The legionary who carried the eagle. In addition to his arms and armour, he also wore an animal skin, either a bear or a lion, over his head and down 5his back.

Armillae: Armbands, often gold, awarded as Roman military decorations. Centurions would wear these both for parade and in combat.

Auxiliaries (Auxilia): Troops, usually recruited from allies or conquered peoples, who were not part of the Roman legions, but employed in the support of them. These auxiliaries would usually consist of archers, slingers, infantrymen and cavalrymen.

Baldric: A shoulder belt for carrying a sword or daggar.

Barding: Horse armour.

Braccae: Roman military trousers worn in colder areas, such as in Britain and the northern frontier.

Bucinator: A military musician who played the bucina, a wind instrument that was used in forts and camps to signal change of the watch or guard.

Caliga (Caligae): The Roman military shoe or boot.

Cataphract (Cataphractoi): Heavy cavalry, armoured from almost head to foot, who

▼ *Macedonian muscled cuirass and helmet.*

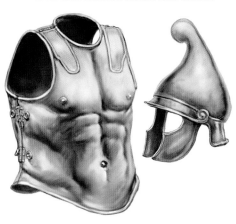

rode large armoured horses. They originated in the east and because of their experience against them, the Romans started forming their own units, which became the mainstay of the eastern Roman armies.

Centurion: Roman lower- and middle-grade officers who commanded a century.

Century: The company-sized unit in a legion that numbered 60 men in the manipular legion and 80 in a cohort.

Chamfron: Head armour for a horse covering the face, fully or partially.

Cingulum: The Roman military belt.

Civic crown: The second highest Roman military decoration. Awarded during the republic and empire up to Diocletian's time.

Clibanarius: Another term for a cataphract.

Cohort: Six centuries (*see* century).

Cohortes Equitatae: An auxiliary cohort made up of both infantry and cavalry.

Comatatenses: Later Roman military term beginning in Diocletian's reign, denoting the mobile Roman army.

Corvus: The moveable landing ramp on early Roman galleys.

Cornicen: A Roman military hornist who went into combat with his instrument, the cornu, stationed in formation with the unit's standards.

Corvus: A spiked boarding plank used on Roman ships.

Decuria: A Roman cavalry unit made up of ten troopers.

Decurion: The commander of a decuria; a Roman cavalry officer. Confusingly, a decurion would also command an ala.

Draco: A cavalry standard with the head of a stylized dragon and the tail like a windsock. Used by barbarian and Roman units alike, its origin was probably Sarmatian.

Draconarius: The senior cavalry trooper who carried the draco.

Dromon: An eastern Roman galley.

Droungos: A military unit of between 1,000–3,000 men.

Equites: Early Roman cavalrymen recruited from the equestrian class.

Eques: Roman cavalry trooper.

Explorator: A scout, usually recruited from among the mounted auxiliaries.

Falcata: A curved, early Iberian sword.

Falx: The Dacian sickle-like edged weapon. Later, the term was used by the Romans to denote a siege hook.

Focale: A neck cloth used to protect the neck from rubbing from the soldier's armour.

Foederati: Barbarian troops, usually cavalry,

▲ *Two examples of early crested Roman helmets of Greek-inspired design.*

who served under Roman officers. This type of unit served in both the western and eastern empires.

Foulkon: The eastern Roman equivalent of the old Roman testudo.

Gladius: A short sword from Iberia, used by gladiators.

Grass crown: The highest military decoration only awarded to a Roman commander who broke the blockade of a surrounded Roman army.

Greave: A leg protector for the shin.

Groma: The Roman surveying instrument; the ancient equivalent of the modern theodolite.

Hasta pura: The Roman spear carried by the hastati in the old manipular legion. This was not a missile weapon like the pilum, or javelin.

Hastati: The front line of Roman armoured infantrymen in the manipular legion.

Hoplite: The heavily armed and armoured Greek line infantry.

Hoplon: The Greek round shield from which the hoplite took his name.

Imago: Standard with the likeness of the current emperor.

Imaginifer: A standard bearer who carried the imago.

Lamellar: A type of armour made of overlapping plates attached or sewn together with heavy thread or light rope and sometimes fixed to an undergarment made of leather.

Lancea: The older Roman javelin; it could also be a light spear or lance.

Legate: A Roman general sometimes in command of a legion.

Liburnia: A light galley used for reconnaissance and other non-line-of-battle missions.

Limitanei: Roman fortress or garrison troops after the reform of the army *c.*284AD under Diocletian.

Loculus: A linen bag carried by legionaries containing personal items.

Lorica: Roman body armour; a cuirass. These could be of four main types: the muscle cuirass inherited from Greece; the leather cuirass which might resemble the 'muscle' type or not; the chain mail lorica, and the most familiar of them all, the lorica segmentata, which was made of metal plates attached together and gave some movement in action.

Lorica hamata: The accurate term for a cuirass of chain mail.

Lorica plumata: An expensive type of body armour, basically a chain mail lorica with metal scales attached to the iron rings of the mail.

Lorica squamata: Scale armour worn by musicians, cavalrymen, and centurions, among others.

Manica: Arm protection worn by gladiators, and by some legionaries.

Maniple: Two centuries; or a Roman century standard recognizable by the image of an open palm at the top of the standard.

Miles: Another term for a legionary.

Naval crown: Military decoration awarded to the first man in a naval engagement to board an enemy vessel.

Optio: The second in command to a centurion in a century.

Phalanx: Originally Greek, and later Macedonian heavy infantry formation. It was a solid rectangle of troops much wider than deep that presented a wall of shields and spears against an enemy. It was designed to fight to its front. When faced with the more flexible manipular legion, the phalanx was overwhelmed and defeated.

Phalera: Sculpted discs of gold, silver, or bronze worn over the armour for parades and sometimes in action.

Pilum: The heavy Roman javelin with a lead shank and wooden shaft.

Plumbata: Weighted, heavy, throwing dart

▲ *Celtic/Germanic shields, decorated with tribal designs, from the 3rd century.*

used by both infantry and cavalry. The throwing dart was used very effectively by the Sarmatians and was adapted by the Romans in the late empire period.

Praetorian Guard: The personal guard of a Roman emperor. These 'household' troops were often less than loyal and would 'make' or 'unmake' emperors. They were finally disbanded by Constantine the Great.

Primus Pilus: The senior centurion in a legion who commanded the first cohort. That cohort was twice the size of the other nine in the legion.

Principes: Heavy Roman infantry of the second line of a manipular legion.

Pteruges: Flexible strips of cloth or leather worn around the waist or at the shoulders, and below the armour.

Pugio: The wide-bladed Roman dagger.

Scutum: The Roman shield, specifically the rectangular curved shield of the classic legionary.

Signifer: Roman standard bearer.

Signum: Roman standard.

Spatha: The long, double-bladed Roman cavalry sword adapted from Celtic and Germanic tribes. It would finally replace the

gladius in the legions and also be used for centuries in the eastern Roman Army as well.

Speculator: An executioner attached to the army.

Tagma: The main imperial army, usually stationed around Constantinople.

Testudo: A Roman protective formation where shields were interlocked in front and above the formation used in siege and field.

Theme: The military province system developed by the eastern Romans which replaced the old Roman provinces. The military commander of the thematic units in the theme was also the governor of the province.

Tiro: A Roman recruit.

Torc: A metal neck ring of Celtic origin awarded for distinguished service

Triarii: Roman heavy infantry of the third line of the manipular legion.

Tribune: Senior field grade officers of the legion who were usually politically appointed to serve a limited number of years or campaigns.

Tourma: A military unit supposedly composed of 9,600 men. In reality its strength would range from 3,000-10,000, depending on how many men a particular theme could muster when mobilized for active service.

Umbo: Shield boss.

Velites: Unarmed light infantry of the manipular legion.

Vericulum: Light Roman spear.

Verutum: A javelin or throwing dart.

Vexillarius: A standard bearer who carried the vexillum.

Vexillarii: Detached units from the legion who carried their own vexillum.

Vexillum: A Roman cloth standard, usually red with the Legions designation and identification on the standard. It was suspended from a horizontal bar on the standard's pole.

Vigil: A nightwatchman or firefighter.

ACKNOWLEDGEMENTS

There are numerous people to thank in the creation of a new book, especially one such that was so complex. First of all, my Project Editor in this third book together, Joanne Rippin, patient with my failings, insistent at the same time to get the best done on a difficult subject, who is becoming a fine military historian in her own right. She has also become a dear friend. Jonathan North, military historian and author, a comrade of many years, gave time and expert advice, and is also a valued friend. Artists, Simon Smith, Matt Vince and Tom Croft, whose talent flows through the book, for their superb artwork. As always, I could not have accomplished this work without the support of my wife Daisy and son Michael, who are the blood of my heart. Lastly, to Ann and John Elting, both now departed who encouraged my study of military history. And, finally, to the Centurion, 'Bring Another', who personified the Roman soldier and the legions…

▶ *The legendary centurion of Rome.*

INDEX

▼ *Shields from a senior Roman infantry unit of the 4th century.*

▲ *Left, a bronze Imperial-Gallic type legionary helmet, 3rd century* AD. *Right, a ridge helmet, 4th century* AD.

▲ *The Roman testudo formation.*

▼ *The gastraphetes, a larger version of the arrow thrower.*